Mozart and Vienna

Mozart and Vienna

H. C. ROBBINS LANDON

SCHIRMER BOOKS
A Division of Macmillan, Inc.
New York

Maxwell Macmillan International
New York   Oxford   Singapore   Sydney

First American edition published in 1991 by
Schirmer Books
A Division of Macmillan, Inc.
866 Third Avenue, New York, N.Y. 10022

Macmillan, Inc. is part of the Maxwell
Communication Group of Companies

Maxwell Macmillan Canada, Inc.
1200 Eglinton Avenue East, Suite 200
Don Mills, Ontario M3C 3N1

First published in Great Britain by Thames and Hudson Ltd., London

Library of Congress Catalog Card Number: 91-7648
Printed in the United States of America
printing number
1 2 3 4 5 6 7 8 9 10

Library of Congress Cataloging-in-Publication Data

Landon, H. C. Robbins (Howard Chandler Robbins). 1926–
    Mozart and Vienna / H. C. Robbins Landon. — 1st American ed.
        p.   cm.
    "First published in Great Britain by Thames and Hudson Ltd., London"
        — T.p. verso.
    Includes bibliographical references and index.
    ISBN 0–02–871317–6 : $22.50
1. Mozart, Wolfgang Amadeus, 1756–1791. 2. Composers — Austria-Vienna —
Biography. 3. Music — Austria — Vienna — 18th century-History and criticism.
I. Title
ML410.M9L239   1991
780'.92 — dc20
[B]   91-7648
                                                                                CIP
                                                                                MN

Contents

List of Illustrations

⚛⚛⚛⚛⚛⚛⚛⚛

Preface

—◦◦◦◦◦◦Q◦◦◦◦◦—

D URING THE LAST TEN YEARS of his life, Mozart lived largely
in Vienna, but before he settled in the Austrian capital in
1781 he had made several visits, starting in 1762, when he
was only six. In September 1767, Leopold Mozart took his whole
family – his wife Anna Maria, his daughter Maria Anna ('Nannerl')
and Wolfgang – and stayed there well over a year, until January 1769.
In 1773, Leopold and Wolfgang made a third visit. This chronicle will
attempt to portray the Mozarts' triumphs and disappointments in the
years from 1762 to 1773, as well as sketching in the background to
Wolfgang's residence in the capital during the decade 1781–91. After
their failure to secure a permanent position for Wolfgang in Vienna,
father and son attempted to do the same thing in Italy, again without
success. In the event, Wolfgang's subsequent career turned out to be
inextricably bound to Vienna, and when he settled there and married,
he soon effected fundamental and widespread changes in the musical
life of the capital.

Since Vienna occupies such a central and important position in
Mozart's career, I thought it would be of general interest to present
substantial extracts from descriptions of the city published in the 1780s,
and thus the central part of this book has been translated from Johann
Pezzl's *Skizze von Wien* ('Sketch of Vienna'). All sorts of fascinating
and revealing details of the city emerge from his lively and topical
writing. Like Mozart and Emperor Joseph II, Pezzl was a dedicated
follower of the ideas of the Enlightenment (and hence a strong
supporter of Joseph's reforms), and in many respects his 'sketch' (as
he modestly entitles it) is a hymn to the same humanitarian principles
that inform Mozart's *Le nozze di Figaro* and *Die Zauberflöte* or Haydn's
string quartets of this period.

Vienna has been a leading creative force in Europe's musical
history from the time of Haydn to that of Alban Berg; and today it
boasts one of the greatest orchestras and probably the finest opera
company in existence. Mozart contributed materially to this tradition,
and I feel sure that many lovers of Mozart's music will enjoy learning
more about the city from a first-hand source published in the composer's

lifetime, embellished here with a selection of contemporary paintings and engravings. It is in that spirit that this brief account of Vienna and its musical and social life is offered.

This book is dedicated to my wife, Else Radant, whose expert knowledge of eighteenth-century Austria and its social history has been a constant source of inspiration and invaluable advice.

Château de Foncoussières   H.C.R.L.
September 1989

NOTE ON AUSTRIAN CURRENCY

In Austria in the 1780s, the principal currency was Gulden/gulden, abbreviated as 'fl.' or 'F.' (Florins – a term used interchangeably with 'Gulden'). The system was based on the duodecimal principle (as in Great Britain before decimalization in 1971). The smaller denomination was Kreuzer (abbreviated as 'kr' or 'xr'), 60 Kreuzer making 1 Gulden. Another denomination widely used was 'ducat' (a silver or gold coin), 1 ducat being equivalent to $4\frac{1}{2}$ Gulden. In 1791, £500 sterling converted to 4.883 Gulden.

Another coin in circulation in Austria in the 1780s was the Groschen, including Polish or Bohemian types of small value and made of copper. The original German Groschen was usually made of silver alloy.

NOTE ON SPELLINGS

In quotations from eighteenth-century sources, notably letters written by Leopold Mozart, proper names and titles are given in the form used in the original context, the more usual or modern version being added within square brackets, e.g. 'Palfi [Pálffy]'. Similarly, the variable use of 'C' and 'K' in German orthography of the period is retained, e.g. 'Capellmeister/Kapellmeister'.

I
The first journey (1762)

WHEN LEOPOLD MOZART realized that his son Wolfgang was a child prodigy and that his daughter 'Nannerl' (Maria Anna) was also endowed with exceptional musical gifts, he decided that he could exploit their musical talents by presenting them at various courts in Europe. His first such venture involved travelling from their home in Salzburg on a visit to Munich where, in January and February 1762, the two children were presented at the court of Elector Maximilian III. It was only natural that Leopold would want to take his daughter, then aged eleven, and the six-year-old Wolfgang to Vienna, so that they could entertain the court of Empress Maria Theresa and her consort, Francis Stephen of Lorraine. The palace of Schönbrunn in the city of Vienna was the centre of Austrian power and influence and in the capital were to be found many wealthy aristocratic and diplomatic patrons whose interest, Leopold considered, could be cultivated, with the prospect of financial profit and enhanced social prestige. He calculated correctly. During the visit to Munich, Leopold had left his wife Anna Maria at home in Salzburg, but for the trip to Vienna, which began in September 1762, he took his whole family with him, as well as a servant, one Richard Estlinger, who was a music copyist in Salzburg. They hired a coach, but undertook part of the journey by boat, sailing down the Danube from Passau to Linz (where they spent one night), from Linz to Mauthausen (where they again spent one night), then on to the pretty town of Stein[1] (another overnight stop), and from there straight to Vienna, where they arrived at 3 o'clock in the afternoon of 6 October.

In 1762, the Imperial capital boasted a splendid court orchestra, a court choir and a court opera company. There were regular performances of French plays at the Burgtheater, as well as French opera and ballet. The day before the Mozarts arrived in the city, Gluck's new reform opera, *Orfeo ed Euridice*, had its first performance. This work at once became the talk of the town and certainly excited Wolfgang's interest. At that time, the prose theatre gave performances of plays by the well-known Italian writer Carlo Maria Goldoni in German translation, and the castle theatre in the royal palace of Schönbrunn put on Hasse's *Il trionfo di Clelia* and a pasticcio in French with new arias by Gluck, both taken over from the Vienna Opera's repertoire. Church music flourished in the Imperial chapel (the Hofburgkapelle), in St Stephen's Cathedral under Kapellmeister Georg Reutter, Jr (Joseph Haydn's erstwhile teacher), and in many other city churches which supported a full-time choir and orchestra. Since May 1761, Haydn had been Vice-Capellmeister first to Prince Paul Anton Esterházy, who died in March 1762, and then to his brother, Nicolaus, who succeeded to the princely title. Nicolaus had confirmed Haydn's appointment in the princely household and was a great source of encouragement to him.

The musical sensations of the 1761–2 season included, in instrumental music, Haydn's first three symphonies composed for Prince Paul Anton – 'Le Matin', 'Le Midi' and 'Le Soir' (nos. 6–8) – which were performed at the Esterházy Palace in Vienna in 1761. These works revealed an intriguing stylistic mixture reflecting earlier *concerto grosso* form while exhibiting forward-looking features (slow introductions, amalgamations of concerto and symphonic styles, etc.).

Vienna was an intensely musical city, encouraged by a highly musical court, every member of the Imperial family being taught to sing or play an instrument with proficiency (Empress Maria Theresa sang complicated operatic arias and her daughter Marie Antoinette received harpsichord lessons from Gluck). In 1765, a performance of a Gluck opera – *Il Parnasso confuso* – at Schönbrunn was directed from the harpsichord by Archduke Leopold,[2] while his elder sisters sang the vocal parts and his younger sisters, including Marie Antoinette, danced in the ballet. Gluck himself trained the young archdukes and archduchesses in their various roles. In 1778, when Queen of France, Marie Antoinette had a painting by Johann Franz Geipel depicting this performance sent to Paris; today it hangs in the Palace of Versailles.[3]

The chronicle which follows is based on first-hand information – fortunately, a great deal is available. A whole series of letters from Leopold Mozart to his Salzburg landlord, Lorenz Hagenauer, have survived. Important entries occur in the diaries of Johann Carl, Count von Zinzendorf, a court official, and there are also passages from two posthumous biographies, for both of which Mozart's widow Constanze and sister Nannerl supplied information: Friedrich Schlichtegroll's *Mozarts Leben*, published in Graz in 1794,[4] and Franz Xaver Niemetschek's *Lebensbeschreibung des k.k. Kapellmeisters Wolfgang Amadeus Mozart* (Prague, 1798).[5]

In a letter to Hagenauer dated Linz, 3 October 1762, Leopold Mozart describes – in his precise, slightly dry but charming fashion – the first part of the journey from Salzburg to Vienna:[6]

You thought, did you not, that we were already in Vienna, but we're still in Linz. Tomorrow, God willing, we shall leave by the so-called ordinary boat. We would certainly have arrived [in Vienna] by now had we not been obliged to spend five whole days in Passau against our will. Furthermore, this delay, for which His Grace the Prince-Bishop of Passau was responsible, cost me 80 fl., which I should have earned in Linz had I arrived sooner. As it is, I have to be content with the forty-odd gulden which I made, after deducting expenses [*deductis deducendis*], from the concert given the day before yesterday.... Wolfgang – but not the girl – had the honour of playing before His Princely Grace, for which he received one whole ducat, *id est* 4 fl. 10 x, in cash, but don't tell anybody; meanwhile, we only pray that our Archbishop [Siegmund Christoph, Count von Schrattenbach] enjoys a long life.... Now for a description of our journey. On the 20th of last month we arrived in Passau at 5 o'clock p.m., and in the morning of the 26th we left Passau with [the] Cathedral Canon, Count *Herberstein*, arriving that same evening in Linz at 5 o'clock.... My children are admired everywhere, especially the boy. Count *Herberstein* has proceeded to Vienna and will bring with him advance fanfares. And yesterday *Count v. Schlick*, Provincial Governor [*Land(e)shauptmann* of Upper Austria], with his wife, left for Vienna. Both were uncommonly gracious to us; they said that as soon as we arrive in Vienna we should attend on them; also that they will tell Count Durazzo [Intendant of the Court Opera] about us and that they will make our arrival in Vienna generally known. To all appearances it looks as if our prospects are pleasing. May God keep us in good health, as hitherto: so far we are all well, although now and again I feel a small twinge of the gout. The children are cheerful, and behave everywhere just as they do at home. The boy treats everyone, especially the officers, with as great a degree of familiarity as if he had known them all his life....

Please ask your wife (to whom we present respectful compliments) to *have four Holy Masses said for us at* [the pilgrimage church of] *Maria Plain*, and as soon as possible. My girl presents her compliments and begs leave to tell your lady wife that she has fulfilled her promise at [the pilgrimage church of] Maria Hilf in Passau. We all prayed to St Lawrence [patron saint of Hagenauer].... We hope you are all in good health....

Following their arrival in Vienna a few days later, the Mozarts became a much discussed and admired family. Zinzendorf's diary entry for 9 October 1762 reads: 'In the evening at 8 o'clock I went to fetch

Lamberg and we went together to Col[l]alto's where *la* Bianchi [the soprano Maria Bianchi, who appeared in the role of Eurydice in Gluck's *Orfeo ed Euridice*] sang and a little boy, who they say is only 5½ years old, played the harpsichord....'.[7] This is a reference to Wolfgang's appearance at the palace of Count Thomas Collalto, a building which still stands, situated next to the Jesuit church known as the Kirche am Hof. Leopold Mozart furnishes many delightful details about this occasion in a letter to Lorenz Hagenauer dated 16 October:[8]

Monsieur mon trés cher ami

On the Feast of St Francis [of Assisi, 4 October] we left Lintz [*sic*] at 4.30 p.m.... On Wednesday [6 October] we arrived in Vienna at 3 o'clock,... Steady rain and wind accompanied us during the trip; Wolfgang caught cold in Lintz, but despite all the disorder, early rising, irregular eating and drinking, the wind and the rain, he remained healthy, thank God... On our arrival, H: [Herr] Gilowsky's servant was already waiting and came on board the ship. He took us to our quarters, but we soon hastened to a tavern to allay our pangs of hunger; before doing so, we had our luggage put away safely in our quarters. Then H: Gilowsky [a family friend] came to pay his respects. Now we've been here for 8 days and don't even know when the sun rises in Vienna: for up to this very hour it has done nothing but rain and there has been a steady wind that brought some snow – we could even see some on the roofs. All the while it was not really very cold, but nippy enough. I must tell you about one thing, and that is, we passed through the local customs office very swiftly and were completely exempted from the main customs. H: Wolferl [diminutive for Wolfgang] saw to that, for right away he made friends with the chief customs officer, showed him the clavier [clavichord?], invited him to visit us, played a minuet on his little violin, and that got us through. The customs officer asked with the greatest politeness for permission to visit us and wrote down our address for this purpose. Up to now, despite the disgusting weather, we have already attended an academy concert at Count Collalto's, also Countess von Sinzendorf presented us to Count Wilschegg and, on the 11th, to His Excellency the Imperial Vice-Chancellor, Count v[on] Colloredo, where we had the honour of conversing with the first ministers and ladies of the Imperial court, to wit: the Hungarian Chancellor, Count Palfi [Pálffy] and the Bohemian Chancellor, Count Coteck [Chotek], together with Bishop Esterházy [Carl Esterházy, Bishop of Erlau] and a lot whose names I didn't remember. Everyone, especially the ladies, was very gracious to us. The fiancée of Count Leopold Künburg [Kühnburg, Chief Equerry in Salzburg] started a conversation with my wife and told her that she is going to be married in Salzb[urg]. She is a pretty, friendly lady, of medium height. She expects her fiancé to arrive in Vienna today. Countess v[on] Sinzendorf is most concerned for our welfare, and all the ladies have fallen in love with my boy. Now everybody is talking about us, and when I went to the opera [Gluck's *Orfeo ed Euridice*] alone on the 10th, I heard Archduke Leopold in his box telling someone in another box all about how a boy had arrived in Vienna who played the harpsichord brilliantly, etc., etc. That same evening at 11 o'clock I received the order to appear at Schönbrunn on the 12th, but next day I received another order changing the date to the 13th because the 12th is the name-day of [Archduke] Maximilian and [hence an eventful] gala day, for, as I learn, they want to hear the children play. Mainly their amazement concerns the boy, and I've not met anyone who doesn't find it inexplicable. . . .

I wrote all this on the 11th with the firm intention of writing on the 12th, after our return from Schönbrunn, and telling you how it all went. But from Schönbrun[n] we had to go straight to [the house of] Prince von Hildeburghausen, and 6 ducats outweighed the despatch of the letter. . . . Now time does not allow me to do more than say in haste that we were received by Their Majesties in an exceedingly gracious fashion, and if I tell you that Wolferl jumped into the Empress's lap, threw his arms around her and covered her with kisses, people will regard it as a fairy-tale. In short, we were there from 3 o'clock until 6 and the Emperor himself came into the antechamber to escort me inside to hear the Infanta [Princess Isabella of Parma, married to Archduke Joseph] play the violin. On the 15th the Empress sent, via the Privy Paymaster, who arrived at our house in ceremonial costume, two court dresses: one for the boy and one for the girl; the moment the order comes, we must appear at court and the Privy Paymaster will come to fetch us. Today at 2.30 p.m. we must attend on the two youngest Archduchesses, at 4 o'clock we go to Count Pálfi's [Pálffy], the Hungarian Chancellor. Yesterday we were at Count Caunitz's [Kaunitz, the Austrian Chancellor], the day before that at Countess Küntzgin's [Kinsky] and later at Count v[on] Ulefeld's [Ulfeld]. . . .

In this letter, Leopold also relates how, by word of mouth, news of the Mozart prodigies reached the Empress (via Archduke Joseph, Countess von Schlick and the young Count Pálffy), resulting in an

Imperial summons to Schönbrunn. Leopold Mozart's friend Gilowsky, who had greeted him on his arrival, was probably Wenzel Andreas Gilowsky von Urazowa (1716–99), court surgeon and *Antecamerakammerdiener* (something like a 'valet of antechamber'), whose son, Franz Xaver Wenzel (1757–1816) would sign the register as a witness at Wolfgang's marriage to Constanze Weber in 1782. (Another Franz Gilowsky was also alive in 1762: Wenzel's brother Franz Anton [1708–70].) It is indeed astonishing how many persons who would play vital roles in the events of Mozart's later life were present at these court galas in 1762 – the future Emperors Joseph II and Leopold II and, of course, Marie Antoinette. A passage in the biography of Mozart by Niemetschek – in this case based almost entirely on the 1794 biography by Schlichtegroll – provides further details of Wolfgang's amazing performances at Schönbrunn:[9]

> One of the ladies of the court assured me that both children made a very great impression; those present at the performances could hardly believe their eyes and ears. Emperor Francis I, that great lover of the arts, was greatly delighted with the little 'magician' (as he was jokingly called). He often chatted with the boy. All the anecdotes mentioned by Schlichtegroll have been confirmed.
>
> Among other things, the Emperor said in fun that it was not such a great art to be able to play, if the keyboard could be seen, but what if the keys were covered? This did not trouble Mozart in the least. The keys were covered and he played just as well as before.[10]
>
> Even that was nothing so extraordinary, if every finger was used when playing, but if he were to play with only one finger, that would be really clever.
>
> Still the boy was not put out – he straightaway attempted it, and to everyone's astonishment, played several pieces in this manner. Even then he showed a trait of his character which he was to retain throughout his life – his contempt for all praise from the nobility and a certain diffidence about playing for them, if they were not also knowledgeable people. When compelled to perform willy-nilly, he would play nothing but trivial pieces, dances, etc. – unimportant trifles. In the presence of experts, however, he was all fire and enthusiasm. . . .
>
> That is exactly what occurred in the presence of Emperor Francis. As Mozart was seating himself at the clavier while the Emperor stood at his side, the young boy said 'Isn't Herr Wagenseil here? He understands.' Wagenseil came in, and the child prodigy

said to him, 'I am going to play a concerto of yours. You must turn the pages for me.'

Perhaps the following anecdote will also add something to this picture of him.

Of all the Archduchesses, the future Queen Marie Antoinette of France took most interest in him, and he had a particular affection for her. When on one occasion he entered the chambers of the late and revered Empress Maria Theresa and was being led around by the young Princes and Princesses, he had the misfortune to slip and fall on the highly polished floor, to which he was not accustomed. Nobody was more eager to help him up than young Antoinette. He was so touched in his little heart that he went straight up to the Empress and praised the great kindness of the little Princess. Who could not love such a child?

The exemplary way in which he handled the clavier, and his knowledge of the art, which he had acquired at an age when most children would not as yet have shown any particular artistic inclination, was admirable enough: surely nothing further could be expected. But this marvellous musical talent, which had been implanted in him by his Creator, knew no bounds and, once it had been awakened, far outstripped any formal instruction. What one wanted to teach him, he already seemed to know. He had only to turn it over in his mind

His lessons served merely as an encouragement and as a help to his general development.

Some years after Mozart's death, a series of notes about the composer appeared in the *Allgemeine Musikalische Zeitung*, published in Leipzig. These were based on information supplied by Constanze, and include the following:[11]

Mozart's wife had a dog, which was very devoted to her. On a walk in the Augarten, they [Wolfgang and Constanze] were chatting about the faithful animal and she said: 'Pretend to hit me, he'll go for you!' – Mozart followed this good advice and as he was doing so, the humanitarian Emperor Joseph was leaving his summer residence [p. 167].

'Well, well, married just three weeks and fisticuffs already?' Mozart related the circumstances and the Emperor laughed. In the ensuing conversation, he asked Mozart:

'Do you remember the anecdote about Wagenseil? And when I played the violin you were among the listeners in the antechamber; and you said 'Pfui, that was flat' or called out 'Bravo!'

Count Zinzendorf's diary entries provide further first-hand information:

> 14 October 1762 . . . To Princess Trautson's. I saw there M^c de Martinitz, the friend of the late M^c de Dünewald. Talked to the Papal Nuncio [Vitaliano, Conte de Borromeo] about the opera [*Orfeo ed Euridice*]. He was very critical of the libretto. On the subject of the little boy who played yesterday at Schönbrunn and today at Vhlefeld's [*sic*] . . .
>
> 17 October 1762 . . . Then to *Thurn's*, where the little child from Salzburg and his sister played the harpsichord. The poor little thing played marvellously, he is a vivacious child, lively, charming, his sister's playing masterly and he applauded her. Melle de Gudenus, who plays the harpsichord well, gave him a kiss, he wiped his face.[12]

On 19 October 1762, Leopold Mozart wrote to his landlord in Salzburg about the increasingly busy social and musical life his family was leading in Vienna:[13]

> You will have received my letter by the previous post. Today I was called in the morning to the Privy Paymaster's, who received me with the utmost courtesy. His Majesty wished to know if I could remain here a little longer. I humbly placed myself at His Majesty's disposal. The Privy Paymaster thereupon paid me 100 ducats, adding that His Majesty would soon summon me again. However I choose to view the situation, in reality it is unlikely that I shall be home before Advent. In any case, I shall apply in advance for permission to extend my leave of absence [from service with the Archbishop of Salzburg]; even if I am able to leave here in a fortnight or three weeks from now, I have to travel slowly because of the children, so that they can have a rest for a few days and not fall ill . . . If I could find a good carriage for an honest price I would be inclined to buy one, so that my children can enjoy greater comfort. Today we were at the French Ambassador's.
>
> Tomorrow we have to keep an appointment at Count Harrach's betwen 4 and 6 o'clock, but I don't know which member of the family he is. I shall find out in good time where the carriage is taking me, for when visiting a noble house we are always fetched by a footman and brought home in the same fashion. From 6 o'clock or 6.30 to 9, we have arranged, for 6 ducats, to attend a grand academy concert given by a rich member of the nobility, and at which the greatest virtuosi who happen to be in Vienna will perform. The nobility invites us 4, 5, 6 to 8 days in advance,

so as not to miss the chance of having us. We are thus expected at the Postmaster-General, Count Paar's, next Monday. Wolferl gets quite enough rides, at least twice a day. On one occasion we went at 2.30 to a certain place and remained there until 3.45; from there Count Hardek [Hardegg] had us fetched in his carriage and we were driven at full gallop to the house of a lady where we stayed until 5.30. From there Count Kaunitz had us fetched to his palace, where we stayed until nearly 9 o'clock. I can hardly write: pen and ink are both terrible and I have to steal the time to write. I can't tell you anything new whatever, for here the [progress of the Seven Years'] war is so little discussed that it's as if there were no war. In my whole life I never saw or read fewer newspapers than in the 4 or 5 weeks that I've been absent from Salzburg....

Do you want to know how Wolferl's dress suit looks? – It's made of the finest cloth, lilac-coloured. The waistcoat is of moiré silk and the same colour as the cloth; coat and waistcoat are trimmed with wide double gold braiding. The suit was intended for Prince [Archduke] Maximilian, and Nannerl's dress was the court dress of a princess. It is made of white brocaded taffeta, with all kinds of trimmings. It is a pity that we shall only be able to use it as an underskirt [*gottillion = cotillon*], but it also has a little bodice. The sheet of paper is full, and time is up. My compliments to everyone in Salzburg, and I am [etc.].

By Leopold Mozart's own admission, the Seven Years' War with Prussia was, evidently, a subject of greater interest to him that it was to the populace of Vienna. Even if his curiosity about the war could not be satisfied, Leopold had a great deal to be grateful for. He had portraits of the children painted showing them in their court dress (see ill. 1). A great shock was to come, however, and in a letter to Lorenz Hagenauer of 30 October 1762 Leopold related how the family had been affected:[14]

Happiness and glass break like a jar of vinegar! For a fortnight I almost had the feeling that our happiness had been just too great; God sent us a small cross to bear and we thank His endless bounty that things turned out as they did. On the 21st in the evening, we were again invited to Her Majesty the Empress: before we went there our *Wolferl* somehow wasn't his usual self, and again when he went to bed, he said he had pains (pardon me) in his backside and feet. When he was in bed, I examined the places where he said he felt the pain; and I found several spots, each the size of a kreutzer [*sic*], which were very red and slightly raised [*erythema nodosum*] and which were painful to the touch. But they were only on both shins, on each elbow, with a few on his posterior; but very few. He had a fever and we dosed him with black powder [*Pulvis epilepticus niger*] and with margrave powder [invented by the German chemist Andreas Sigismund Marggraf (1709–82)]. He slept rather restlessly. The following Friday, we repeated the powders in the morning and in the evening, but we found that the spots had grown; though larger, they were no more numerous than before. We had to send word to all the nobility with whom we had engagements for the next 8 days, and cancel the appointments day by day. We continued to give him margrave powder and on Sunday he began to sweat, which is what we had wanted, for up to then the fever was more a dry one. I happened to meet the doctor of Countess v[on] Sinzendorf (who was not here) and told him what had occurred. He came with me right away. He approved of what we had been doing; he said it was a kind of scarlet fever rash. . . .

Thank God, he is now sufficiently recovered for us to hope he will be out of bed in a couple of days, if not tomorrow . . . I beg of you, do everything in your power to ascertain what His Grace the Archbishop intends to do eventually, and what hopes I can entertain of the position of Vice-Capellmeister [Leopold Mozart was later appointed to this position, in February 1763]. I do not ask in vain. You are my friend. Who knows what I shall do: if I only knew what the future holds; one thing is certain, and that is, I am now in such circumstances that I could just as easily earn my living here.

I still prefer Salzburg to the prospects offered anywhere else: but I must not take a step backwards. I ask you once again: for otherwise I might allow myself to be persuaded by others to do – I know not what. . . .

The Mozart family stayed on in Vienna, flattered by the attentions of the nobility and with Wolfgang's health gradually improving. On 6 November, Leopold wrote to his landlord in Salzburg, thanking him from the bottom of his heart for all his many kindnesses. 'Thank God, everything is now all right', Leopold adds. Two days previously, on the feast of St Charles Borromeo, he had taken Wolfgang to the Church of St Charles (Karlskirche) and afterwards for a walk in the suburb of Josephstadt. In his letter Leopold also wrote:[15]

Yesterday [5 November] we rewarded our good Dr Bernhard [who had treated Wolfgang] with a concert . . . Please, out of love and friendship, exert some pressure on His Excellency Count Spauer [Spaur] . . . You can speak quite openly about the position of

Capellmeister, for he is entirely well disposed towards me. Can you imagine how beneficial it would be for me if I received the appointment while I am still here? — —

Since my arrival here, I have always been addressed as the Capellmeister from Salzburg; and the Emperor himself, whcn he wanted to conduct me to hear the Infanta play the violin, came out and called, '*where is the Capellmeister from Salzburg?*' . . .

Meanwhile, Wolfgang was again making appearances in the houses of members of the Viennese nobility. Count Zinzendorf heard him (writing in his diary 'Le petit Salzbourgeois joua') at Prince Windischgrätz's on 9 November, on which occasion Count Collalto handed Leopold a poem about Wolfgang written by Konrad Friedrich von Pudendorf. Leopold wrote to Lorenz Hagenauer about the poem on 10 November and added, 'you will know what use to make of it'. Next month, the poem appeared in print on Christmas Day.[16] In a postscript to the same letter, Leopold mentions that:

Master Wolferl thanks you for your kind remembrance of his name-day; he was not so satisfied with the Viennese name-day remembrances; too few people appeared to congratulate him, he felt. He wants to know how the harpsichord [*Clavier*] fares – He thinks of it often; for we have not found its equal here. We shall bring with us a sufficiency of new concertos. We have had 10 copied and another 12 are being copied. And all of them are by Wagenseil. . . .

Wolfgang's illness had meant that the Mozarts had no income while he was unable to perform. On 24 November, Leopold writes to Hagenauer:[17]

. . . on account of the boy's sickness we have suffered a setback of 4 weeks; for although, since he has recovered his health, we have taken in 21 ducats, this is a mere trifle, since we have to spend exactly 1 ducat per day on living expenses; and there are other daily expenses as well. Meanwhile, we are in good form. The lady-in-waiting Countess Theresia v[on] Lodron recently conferred a great honour on us; she provided us with a box in the theatre (very hard to come by) and presented my Wolferl with golden shoe-buckles, with gold plates which give the impression of being made of solid gold. On St Elizabeth's Day [19 November] we were at the gala table. The honours and compliments we received from the nobility on this occasion beggar description; it will suffice if I tell you that Her Majesty the Empress called out to me from table [to ask] if the boy had entirely recovered. An account of the Feast of St Cecilia [22 November] will have to wait until we meet, for we shall need many conversations to explain everything that happened. On St Cecilia's Day we lunched with the Imperial Capellmeister v[on] Reitter [Georg Reutter, Jr]. When we arrive home we shall recite the menu to Madame Hagenauer. Yesterday we dined at H: v[on] Wahlau's and in the evening H: Doctor Bernhard fetched us [and we sat] in his box to hear the opera. Thus in God's name one day follows another. We could be entertained as often as we wish by H: Reitter and H: v. Wahlau: but that might be harmful to my children's health, and apart from all else, the carriages are very dear...

In a letter to Lorenz Hagenauer of 10 December,[18] Leopold wrote that he now considered that he would have to postpone returning to Salzburg until Christmas or the New Year. 'But perhaps you have long since come to the conclusion that *all those who come to Vienna are so enchanted that they have to remain there.*' The other reason for staying on in the capital was that members of the Hungarian nobility were pressing them to travel to the old coronation town of Preßburg (now Bratislava) on the Danube. On the Feast of the Immaculate Conception (8 December), which was also the Emperor's birthday, the Mozarts met many Hungarian aristocrats at the great public banquet held to celebrate the occasion. So 'tomorrow (i.e. the 11th) we shall leave for Preßburg,' where 'I haven't the slightest intention of staying longer than a week.' Leopold notes further:

There are many things that might cause us to stay at least another month. For, imagine it, Count Durazzo, musical director of the court here, has not yet persuaded us to participate in his academy or public concert. If we wanted to do so, we could remain here until Lent or Easter and earn a nice sum of money every week. You will think: Vienna makes everyone crazy...

In the event, Leopold Mozart was afflicted with a raging toothache. 'Homo proponit, Deus disponit', he writes resignedly on 29 December from Vienna.[18] He had planned to leave Preßburg on the 20th and to set out from Vienna on 26 December to return to Salzburg. The weather became so cold that traffic on the Danube (including the ferry service across the river) was seriously disrupted. The Mozart family left Preßburg on Christmas Eve at half past eight in the morning and twelve hours later arrived back in their Vienna lodgings. On the way the road was frozen solid, with treacherous ruts and ridges.

As soon as we had arrived in Vienna, our landlady told us that Countess Leopold Kinsky had sent word daily, to ask if we had arrived. I visited her on Christmas Day and she told me she had been anxiously awaiting our arrival and had postponed a banquet she wanted to give in honour of Field-Marshal Daun, who desired to meet us. She therefore gave the banquet on Monday. Now I really must leave here tomorrow, Friday, and hope to arrive, with God's help, on Sunday in Lintz; and on the Feast of the Epiphany, that is 5 January 1763, I hope to stand in your room...

[On the envelope:] For the past few days it has been astonishingly cold, and today it is positively freezing. Her Maj. the Empress has lost another princess, namely the Princess *Johanna who was 13 years old*. She had taken my Wolferl by the hand and led him to and fro in her rooms when we were visiting her.[19]

The young Wolfgang's career had been launched in the most spectacular manner possible within the Austrian monarchy. He had become the darling of the Viennese court and of the Austro-Hungarian nobility. The family journeyed home in the private carriage that Leopold Mozart had purchased in Preßburg; Archbishop Schrattenbach had taken a lenient view of Leopold's vastly over-extended leave of absence and indeed, very soon after the family's return, rewarded his famous violinist with the coveted position of Vice-Capellmeister at the Salzburg archiepiscopal court. This first journey to Vienna had been, in sum, a brilliant success.

II
The second journey
(1767–8)

O N 11 SEPTEMBER 1767, the whole Mozart family set off for
Vienna, accompanied this time by a servant named Bernhard,
who, however, after their arrival, left them to become a lackey
in the service of a Salzburg Cathedral canon, Anton Willibald, Count
Waldburg zu Solfegg und Waldsee.[1]

The family travelled via Lambach Abbey, Linz, Strengberg, Melk
Abbey and St Pölten, and on 15 September they arrived in Vienna,
staying with a goldsmith in the Weihburggasse. Again it is Leopold
Mozart's letters written to Lorenz Hagenauer in Salzburg that provide
first-hand information about the activities of the Mozart family in
Vienna. After describing the trip – they arrived at Melk Abbey
incognito, but when Wolfgang played the organ, the local organist
guessed the identity of the visitors – Leopold continues, on 22
September:[2]

> ... His Majesty the Emperor [Joseph II] has just returned from
> Hungary; and Her Majesty the Empress [Maria Theresa] has her
> monthly devotions in memory of the late Emperor [Francis
> Stephen, who died in 1765]. But every day there is *opera seria* or
> *opera buffa* or a play. On Sunday there was a ball at the Neapolitan
> Ambassador's, tomorrow, the 23rd, there will be, in the [Princely]
> Liechtenstein garden, illuminations, a ball and fireworks.

In his next letter, dated 29 September,[3] Leopold states that they
attended a performance of Johann Adolph Hasse's new opera, *Parthen-
ope*, at the Burgtheater, part of the festivities to honour the presence
in Vienna of a proxy for King Ferdinand I of Naples, who was
betrothed to the sixteen-year-old Archduchess Maria Josepha. Leopold
hoped to participate in the festivities.

> The opera by Hasse is beautiful, but the singers are, for such a
> festive occasion, nothing special. Sgr: *Tibaldi* is the tenor and Sgr:
> Raucini [Venanzio Rauzzini, for whom Wolfgang later composed
> the Motet 'Exsultate, jubilate' (K.165) in Milan in January 1773]
> from Munich is the best castrato. The *prima donna*, Sgra Deiber
> [Theresa Teyber, who would sing with Mozart in the 1780s] is a

daughter of a Viennese court violinist. The ballet, however, was excellent, the principal role being taken by the famous Frenchman [*sic*] *Vestris* [Gaetan Vestris, 1728–1808, Italian in origin].

Is it raining in Salzburg as it is here? It is raining quite horribly here, and incessantly.... Do you know that the Emperor will be travelling *incognito* as far as Naples, and will be away from Vienna for at least 6 months?...

In his subsequent letter, dated 7 October,[4] Leopold very briefly tells Hagenauer that 'on Saturday evening' Archduchess Maria Josepha felt ill and then came down with smallpox.

...You can well imagine the confusion this created.... The pox is of the benign sort, but we must wait and see, for God alone knows what the outcome will be. It is to be expected that this will put paid to our plans, as you will also easily understand.... Everyone here is very fearful of smallpox. God alone can protect us, we recommend ourselves to the general prayers of our friends...

Leopold Mozart was obliged to draw 400 or 500 gulden because they were earning nothing. On 14 October he writes of this,[5] adding '*aut Caesar, aut nihil* [i.e. 'it's feast or famine']... Perhaps we can repay it all in a single day. We've not yet played anywhere at all because we've not yet played at court; I shall be telling you of extraordinary things one day...'.

One such extraordinary thing was that on the Feast of St Francis (the previous Sunday), the Empress had taken her daughter Maria Josepha to the Church of the Capuchins where they confessed and, after taking communion, went into the vaults – traditional burial place of the Habsburgs – and there, in the course of a three-hour service, prayed for their late father, brothers, sisters and sisters-in-law. 'The foul smell, the impressions etc., brought about a marked change in her [Maria Josepha] and on Tuesday smallpox was evident.' In his next letter Leopold tells Hagenauer that the ultimate horror has occurred: Maria Josepha did not after all have a benign pox, but a virulent form of smallpox. On the evening of 15 October, about seven o'clock, she died. This was the second occasion on which a Habsburg daughter betrothed to Ferdinand had died before the marriage could take place (the first had been Archduchess Johanna, 'whom we knew well', added Leopold sadly). Leopold correctly predicted that the Archduchess Maria Carolina would be the next in line for betrothal to Ferdinand (in fact they were married the following year). Leopold thought it a sinister omen that the second festival opera was *L'Amore e Psiche* (based on the story of Cupid and Psyche from ancient Greek mythology) by

F. L. Gassmann, in which the beautiful damsel Psiche attracts the ire of Venus and for a time appears to have been killed by her. During the period of official mourning for Maria Josepha, all theatres were closed for six weeks. Smallpox raged in Vienna and as a precaution, the Mozart family split up: Maria Anna (the mother) and Nannerl stayed in their flat, Leopold and Wolfgang went to stay with a friend.[6]

The Mozarts decided to flee Vienna and the epidemic. On 23 October they departed in great haste for Brünn (now Brno) and after staying two days there, they proceeded to Olmütz (Olomouc), arriving there on 26 October. Wolfgang did in fact contract smallpox; he was nursed at the family home of the Dean of the Cathedral and Rector of the University, Leopold Anton, Count Podstatzky, whose brother was a Canon of Salzburg Cathedral. On 10 November, still in Olmütz, Leopold Mozart could write a joyous letter to Lorenz Hagenauer, explaining the entire episode and its happy outcome:[7]

> ... TE DEUM LAUDAMUS!
> Wolfgangerl has recovered from the smallpox!
> And where? ... in Ollmitz [*sic*]!
> And where? ... At the residence of His Excellency Count Pod-
> statsky.
>
> You will already have remarked from my previous letter that everything in Vienna was topsy-turvy. Now I must relate some particulars which concern only us, from which you will see that Divine Providence so arranges everything that if we place our undivided trust in it, our destiny cannot be adversely effected. You already know the state of affairs the court ... was experiencing, just when circumstances could have been propitious for us.
>
> At this same time, our fears were aroused not a little by another chance circumstance. The elder son of the goldsmith with whom we were living caught smallpox immediately after our arrival, and we heard about it only when he was almost recovered and after the two younger children had caught it as well. I sought another apartment for us as hastily as possible, but in vain. I was obliged to leave my wife and daughter there and I fled with Wolfgang to good friends of mine, where we stayed. The servant remained with my wife ... In Vienna people talked of nothing but smallpox. If 10 children were listed as dead, 9 of them had died of the pox. You can well imagine how I felt; I spent whole nights without sleep and I had no peace during the day. Immediately after the Princess bride's death, I had resolved to go to Moravia, until the first period of mourning was over in Vienna, but we couldn't get away because His Majesty the Emperor talked about us so often that one was

never sure when it might occur to him to send for us. However, as soon as Archduchess Elisabeth fell ill, my hesitation was at an end, for I could wait no longer to take my Wolfgang away from that pox-ridden Vienna...

On Saturday [24 October] we were in Brünn. I went with Wolfgang to pay our respects to His Excellency Count von Schrattenbach [brother of the Archbishop of Salzburg] and Countess von Herberstein. They talked of a concert in which the children could be heard playing and for which plans were actually complete. But I felt a certain inner presentiment which I couldn't rid myself of, that we should proceed directly to Olmütz at once and postpone the concert in Brünn until our return journey. That same Sunday, therefore, I explained all this to His Excellency, who agreed with me, especially since the members of the nobility who were still in the country would by then be back in town. So we packed everything up again and on Monday the 26th we departed for Olmütz, where we arrived somewhat later than expected because during lunch at Wischau our carriage required some attention and the smith took three hours over it. We were annoyed to find that in the Schwarzer Adler [Black Eagle] Inn, when we arrived, all we could have was a bad, damp room, because those which were a little better were all occupied. We were thus obliged to heat the room a little, and that provided the next cause for annoyance; the stove smoked so much that we could hardly see. At ten o'clock Wolfgang complained about his eyes, but I noticed that his head felt warm, with hot and very red cheeks, whereas his hands were cold as ice. His pulse wasn't right either; so we gave him some black powder and put him to bed. He was rather restless throughout the night, and the dry fever continued in the morning. Then they gave us two better rooms. We wrapped Wolfgang in furs and moved with him into the other rooms. His temperature rose; we gave him some margrave powder and black powder. Towards evening he became delirious, and that continued all night and during the morning of the 28th. After church I went to His Excellency Count von Podstatsky, who received me very graciously; and when I said that my boy was sick and I thought he was ill with smallpox, he said that we should move in with him, since he has no fear at all of smallpox. He immediately called his major-domo, had him prepare two rooms, sent him for the doctor and told him to visit us at the Schwarzer Adler....

In the afternoon at 4 o'clock, Wolfgang was wrapped in leather and furs, placed in the carriage and I drove with him to the Cathedral Deanery. On the 29th we saw a few little red marks, but we still doubted whether it was smallpox because he wasn't very sick any more; all he took was a powder every six hours [Leopold adds the precise composition of the medicine], always followed by scabious tea [a traditional herbal remedy used in cases of skin eruptions]. On the 30th and 31st, on his name-day, the smallpox became fully developed [Leopold describes a new medicine which Wolfgang now took]...As soon as the smallpox [eruptions] appeared, the fever completely vanished and, thank God!, he felt quite well again. The pox was generalized and, since he was astonishingly swollen, his nose was so thick that when he examined himself in the mirror, he said 'now I look like little Mayr' [son of a musician in the Salzburg orchestra]...Since yesterday [9 November], the pocks have begun falling off here and there; and all the swelling subsided two days ago.

You see now that my motto is true: *in te, Domine, speravi, non confundar in aeternum* [the closing words of the Te Deum: 'O Lord, in thee have I trusted: let me never be confounded.']...

In the circumstances it was probably inevitable that Nannerl too should have caught the smallpox, but she too recovered, as Leopold tells Hagenauer in his next letter, dated 29 November:[8]

...This very minute I have *just received your letter.*
Iterum Iterumque [Again, and again].
TE DEUM LAUDAMUS!
MY DAUGHTER HAS SAFELY RECOVERED FROM THE SMALLPOX!
A proof that the few pocks she had in childhood were, just as I then thought, not the real thing. She had the pox in such a mild form that she shows no traces of it, and Wolfgang only a few....

With both the children now happily recovered, the Mozart family shortly made their way back to Brünn, where they arrived on Christmas Eve and stayed for a fortnight. They were welcomed with open arms in the Schrattenbach household, and the local nobility proved to be equally keen to receive them. In his first letter of the new year, written on 12 January 1768,[9] Leopold reports that the family had left Brünn for Vienna three days earlier. The roads were covered with snow and, due to many delays, they did not reach the capital until the following day; their lodgings were in a house called 'Zum roten Säbel' (At the Red Sable) on the Hohe Brücke.

Now at last Leopold could make arrangements for an official visit to the Imperial court and, in a letter dated 23 January 1768, he informs Hagenauer:[10]

...The latest that I have to report to you (apart from all of us being in good health, thank God) is that on Tuesday the 19th from 2.30 to 4.30 p.m. we were with Her Majesty the Empress. His Majesty the Emperor [Joseph II] came out to the antechamber, while we were waiting until the distinguished company had drunk their coffee, and personally conducted us inside. Apart from the Emperor and the Empress, there were present Prince Albert of Sachsen[-Teschen] and all the Archduchesses; but besides these royal personages not a soul was present. It would take too long to relate everything that was said and done there. All in all, I must say that you can hardly imagine how intimate Her Majesty the Empress was in speaking to my wife, discussing in part my children's smallpox, in part the circumstances of our big trip [to France and England]; she stroked my wife's cheeks and clasped her hands. Meanwhile, His Majesty the Emperor talked to me and to Wolfgang about music and many other matters...

The Mozarts had, understandably, high hopes concerning the outcome of this interview. However, the Imperial court at Vienna had changed greatly since the Mozarts had made such an impression in 1762. The Empress was now a widow and had largely withdrawn from public spectacles; she no longer attended the opera or plays; her eldest son and co-ruler Joseph II had greatly reduced the expenses of court life and preferred to live unostentatiously. Leopold Mozart began to be worried. In his next letter to Hagenauer, which was many pages long and written between 30 January and 3 February 1768,[11] he reflects that his correspondent is probably wondering 'why our affairs have not improved more rapidly'. In attempting to explain the situation, Leopold starts with Viennese taste; instead of serious music they prefer Hanswurstiada (buffoonery), magic, devils and ghosts (such as appear in Haydn's opera *Die Feuersbrunst*). The second problem is the organization of the Imperial court.

After we had returned from Moravia, we met members of the Imperial family before we had even thought about making arrangements. As soon as the Empress heard what had happened to us in Ollmitz [*sic*], and that we had returned, we were told the day and hour when we were to appear; but what purpose was served by all that astonishing grace, that indescribable friendliness? What was the result? Nothing, except for a medal which is indeed pretty but of such little value that I will not tell you its actual worth. She leaves everything to the Emperor [Joseph II], who enters it in the book of oblivion and is quite certain in his own mind that he has paid us by virtue of his most gracious conversation.

Well, you'll ask, what about the other *noblesse* in Vienna? – What do they do? – They cut down as much as possible on expenses, to please the Emperor. . . .

For the whole Carnival period [preceding Lent], dancing is in the forefront of everyone's mind. Balls are held everywhere, though all of them are open to the general public; there is even *an entrance charge for the Redoute at court*. And who gains by it? – *The court*; for all the dances, *Redouten*, balls and all theatres are rented out. The others lend their names and the profit is split between the Court and those renting it [the space]; so anyone who goes there is doing the court a favour. These are, therefore, the expenditure of the nobility. We are under the protection of the greatest members of the nobility. Prince *Kaunitz*, the *Duke of Braganza*, Fräulein von *Guttenberg*, who is the left eye of the Empress, the Chief Equerry Count Dietrichstein, who is all-powerful with the Emperor, are our friends . . .

Leopold explains that he has not been able to see Kaunitz because the prince is terrified of catching smallpox and 'Wolfgangerl still has many red spots on his face which, though small, are visible when it is cold.' Leopold goes on to explain a much more unpleasant circumstance. He gradually came to realize that Wolfgang's youthful brilliance had created a great deal of jealousy among older composers. They accused him of playing works he had memorized, claiming '*that it is ridiculous to think he can compose, etc., etc.*'. One such critic fell into a trap set by Leopold. He was persuaded to bring along a very difficult harpsichord concerto, which Wolfgang proceeded to reel off to perfection. Finally convinced, the other composer said: '*as an honest man I can only say that this boy is the greatest man now living in this world . . .*'.

Not every professional musician in Vienna was against the Mozarts, however. In this respect Leopold singled out Wagenseil, the distinguished old composer and teacher of the young archdukes and archduchesses, 'but he is sick at home and hence can't help or can do little on our behalf.'

Leopold had formulated a bold plan. He was going to persuade Wolfgang to compose an *opera buffa*. People would say, 'What? . . . today we go to hear a Gluck and tomorrow a boy of twelve sits at the harpsichord and directs his own opera? – Yes, down with all of them!' Leopold adds that he has won Gluck over, 'even if not from the bottom of his heart'. What had happened was that the idea came from none other than Emperor Joseph II, 'who twice asked Wolfgangerl if he wouldn't like to compose an opera and conduct it himself?' Wolfgang said yes, but the Emperor cannot do more since the [Court] Opera is directed by [Giuseppe] Affligio', who was in charge of both the Burgtheater and the Kärntnerthortheater and was known to be a very difficult arch-intriguer. Even so, the strong-willed Leopold resolved to risk everything on such an opera commission. It 'won't be until after Easter, that's clear. I shall write as soon as I can to seek permission to stay here longer. It will not be an *opera seria*, they don't perform *opera seria* here any longer; and it is also not liked, so the work will be an *opera buffa*, not a small *opera buffa*, but one lasting $2\frac{1}{2}$ to 3 hours. There are no singers here for serious opera, even the sad opera *Alceste* by Gluck was performed by a whole collection of *opera buffa* singers ... and there are excellent singers to be had.' Leopold names the future stars, and ends his letter by saying that an opera composed for the Vienna Court Theatre would be the best 'credit' for Germany as well as Italy.

Such were the circumstances in which Mozart's first full-scale Italian opera, *La finta semplice*, was born; it was to be a still-birth, however, accompanied by harrowing pains. Leopold Mozart had been away from Salzburg for months, and in a decree dated 18 March 1768, Archbishop Schrattenbach ordered that his salary be stopped. In fact, Leopold received no income from March to December 1768, but apart from taking this action, the archbishop tolerantly allowed him to seek his fortune in Vienna. Indeed, Leopold had many friends. On 27 April 1768, Marie Thérèse Geoffrin, whose salon in Paris was famous, wrote to the Chancellor, Prince Kaunitz, recommending him to afford the Mozart family his patronage,[12] and this he did, not only immediately, but also when Wolfgang moved to Vienna in 1781.

On 30 March, Leopold was able to write that 'The ice is broken! not only on the Danube but in our circumstances. Our enemies are vanquished! NB: *here in Vienna*.' But he added, cautiously, 'nothing can happen instantly.'[13]

Among acquaintances of the family in Vienna was one who would turn out to be of crucial importance to Wolfgang's career in the 1780s: the wealthy and influential Russian Ambassador, Dimitri Mikhailovich, Prince Galitzin (1721–93), who held that office from 1762 to 1792 and who was well known for his philanthropic activities.[14] In the same letter of 30 March Leopold notes that 'last week' there was a grand concert at Galitzin's (for the Mozarts), attended by the Dean of the Cathedral and Count von Wolfegg. Leopold then adds, 'The opera is also proceeding well. But perhaps it will be possible to perform it only after the Emperor returns from Hungary.'

Soon it was getting warm in Vienna, and on 11 May Leopold asks Hagenauer to send him summer clothes for his family (he gives a detailed list – *my suit of Lyons silk, my suit of red cloth ... and Wolfgang's light-grey camlet suit, my wife's and daughters' Persian silk dresses and a lady's hat with a veil in front*, located in the large round hatbox...').[15]

A few weeks later, it seems that things were again not going so well. On 29 June Leopold informs Hagenauer that 'We are all otherwise, thank God, in good health: but envy comes at us from all sides. But you know I remain true to my old motto: *in te, Domine, speravi etc.* [= Te Deum]; *fiat Voluntas tua etc.* ['Thy will be done' = Lord's Prayer]...'.[16] The full details of the trouble were revealed a month later, in a mammoth letter to Hagenauer dated 30 July:[17]

...Concerning our long sojourn in Vienna, we are highly displeased. Yes, nothing but our honour keeps us here, otherwise we would have been in Salzburg long ago. But would you really want to have the whole of Vienna saying that Wolfgang couldn't finish the opera; or [claiming] that the result was so wretched that the work could not be performed at all; or that he didn't write it at all, but the father, etc.? Would you want us to look on with *sang froid* while such slanders were circulating in all countries? Would that redound to your honour or for that matter, to that of your gracious Prince [Schrattenbach]? You will ask: *what does His Majesty the Emperor say about it?* – Here I can only touch on the matter... If I had known then what I know now, and I could have foreseen all the events that took place, Wolfgang would not have composed a single note and would have been home long ago. The theatre is rented or rather loaned out to a certain Affligio: each year he has to pay 1,000 f: to people whom the court would otherwise have to pay; the Emperor and the whole Imperial family pay nothing when they attend. Because of this the court can say not a word to this Affligio, for he undertakes everything at his own risk...

His Majesty asked our Wolfgang if he wouldn't write an opera and... would like to see him direct the opera from the harpsichord. His Majesty had this passed on to Affligio, who drew up a formal contract with us for a fee of 100 ducats. The opera should have had its first performance at Easter; the poet [Marco Coltellini] was the first to cause delays, in that he had to make necessary changes and postponed doing so, the result being that we didn't receive two of the revised airas until Easter. It [the première] was soon set for Whitsuntide and then postponed until His Majesty returned from Hungary. At this point, however, the mask fell from the face. — — — Meanwhile, all the composers, with Gluck at their head, did all they could to undermine the opera's prospects. The singers were got at, the orchestra was incited and every means employed to prevent this opera being performed. The singers, who hardly knew the notes, and some of whom have to learn everything by ear, were now persuaded to say they could not sing their arias, which they had previously heard in our rooms, approved, applauded and agreed were right for them. The orchestra is supposed to have said they would not like to have a boy as a conductor, and a hundred such things. Meanwhile, others put it about that the music was not worth a farthing; others said the music does not fit the words and goes against the metre, because the boy doesn't understand Italian well enough . . .

Leopold said that he had proof that Hasse, 'the father of music', and the librettist Metastasio had vouchsafed that thirty operas had been performed in Vienna that did not match up to *La finta semplice*. Leopold then had someone open any volume of the works of Metastasio and indicate an aria [sc. verse], which Wolfgang would then compose in full score, committing the notes to paper without hesitation. This he did in the presence of Kapellmeister Bonno, Metastasio, Hasse, the Duke of Braganza and Prince Kaunitz. Meanwhile, another opera was put into rehearsal and Wolfgang's was supposed to follow it. Leopold said that if the new work had been an *opera seria* he would have packed his bags, gone to Salzburg and begged Archbishop Schrattenbach to stage it, but as it was an *opera buffa* he imagined that the archbishop would not think it seemly to perform it at his court.

The crux of the matter was that neither Kaunitz nor Joseph II could simply *order* Affligio to stage the opera. The court had persuaded Affligio to engage French actors, involving expenses of 70,000 gulden p.a., and as a result his financial returns had been less than expected. Affligio claimed that it was Kaunitz's fault – he could hardly have said that it was Joseph's – and Kaunitz hoped to persuade the Emperor to support the French theatre and compensate Affligio by making up the shortfall at the box-office. When half of musical Vienna tried to tell Affligio that he would do better to forget about putting on *La finta semplice*, the Italian was only too ready to lend a receptive ear.

On 13 September 1768, Leopold writes, distractedly, '*Day before yesterday it was a year, 11th September, since we departed from Salzburg. Could I have ever dreamed then that I would spend a year in Vienna? – But who can answer for such a trick of fate?*'[18] He awaited the arrival of Joseph II in order to expound his grievances on the morning of 21 September, in the course of a personal audience. However, the Emperor could and would do nothing to make Affligio stage *La finta semplice*.

Even if the Italian opera were now doomed, all was not lost. One positive development was that Wolfgang composed a one-act German *Singspiel* entitled *Bastien und Bastienne* (K.50), which was performed in

September or October in a kind of garden pavilion at the house of the famous 'electric Doctor' Anton Mesmer, who was soon to go to Paris and become internationally known for his cures effected by means of 'magnetic rays'. And there was even better news.

A new orphanage church, the Waisenhauskirche, was being built on the Rennweg, and at great speed. The foundation stone was laid on 21 March 1768, and the Mozarts visited the institution's director, Father Ignaz Parhamer, there on 12 September. The consecration took place later that year, on 7 December, the Feast of the Immaculate Conception, in the presence of Empress Maria Theresa, Emperor Joseph II, the Archdukes Ferdinand and Maximilian, and the Archduchesses Elisabeth and Maria Amalia. The entire music for this occasion was composed by Wolfgang.[19] According to Leopold's letter to Hagenauer dated 12 November, the works consisted of 'a solemn Mass, an Offertorium, and a trumpet concerto for a boy'.[20] The Mass is apparently identical to the very elaborate setting in C minor-major (K.139) with four trumpets and drums, whereas the Offertory appears to be lost, as is the trumpet concerto. The event was reported next day in the *Wienerisches Diarium*,[21] where special mention is made of the fact that 'The complete music performed by the orphanage choir during the mass was composed by Wolfgang Mozart, twelve years old and well known on account of his special talents... it was received with general applause and astonishment, and was conducted by him with the greatest precision, as also were the Motets.'

Wolfgang was rewarded with a noble present from the hands of the Empress herself. The church was filled to overflowing. His reputation was fully vindicated and – as his father wrote a week later – the family could leave Vienna happily before Christmas.[22] The Mozarts were at Melk Abbey on 28 December, where Wolfgang played the organ and was given a banquet by the choirmaster, which the Abbot also attended.[23]

Archbishop Schrattenbach proved to be a magnanimous patron. He welcomed the Mozarts back to the archiepiscopal court in Salzburg, and on 1 May 1769 he even had *La finta semplice* performed in his palace. Michael Haydn's wife, Maria Magdalena (*née* Lipp), for whom Mozart would later write so many beautiful solos in his church music, sang the part of Rosina. In the printed libretto, specially produced for this occasion at the archbishop's expense, there is a note recording the 12-year-old composer's contribution: 'La Musica è del Signor Wolfgango Mozart, in Età di Anni dodici'.

The city of Vienna offered wonderful opportunities for musicians, but, as Wolfgang was fast learning from his own mixed fortunes there, it also harboured many intrigues.

1 *Mozart wearing the lilac-coloured court dress with gold-braid trimmings (originally made for Archduke Maximilian), presented by Empress Maria Theresa after the Mozart family had been received at court in October 1762 (see p. 17); the painting was executed some months later, probably by Pietro Antonio Lorenzoni.*

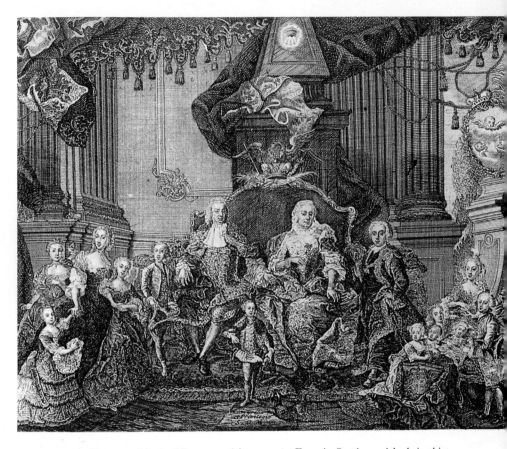

2 *Empress Maria Theresa and her consort Francis Stephen with their thirteen children in 1760. To the right of the Empress stands their eldest son and heir Joseph and to the left of the Emperor is their second son, Carl Joseph (who died in 1763).*

3 *Emperor Joseph II (seated) and his brother Leopold, Grand Duke of Tuscany, portrayed by Pompeo Girolamo Batoni in 1769 during their visit to Rome.*

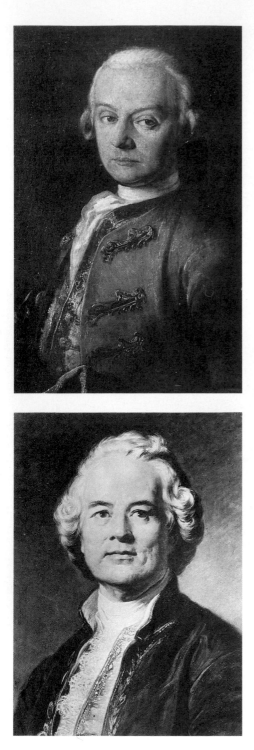

4 *Leopold Mozart, whose letters are a vital first-hand source of information about the family's travels and their successes and misfortunes when absent from Salzburg.*

6 *Franz Anton Mesmer, the 'electric doctor' at whose home in Vienna Mozart's early* Singspiel *entitled* Bastien und Bastienne *(K. 50) was performed in 1768 (see pp. 31f.).*

5 *Christoph Willibald Gluck, court composer and one of the principal musical figures in Vienna in Mozart's time. Shortly after the family arrived in the autumn of 1762, Leopold attended a performance of Gluck's* Orfeo ed Euridice *at the Court Opera (see p. 13).*

7 *St Stephen's Cathedral, the massive Gothic building dominating the city centre of Vienna (see also ill. 10). Here Wolfgang and Constanze Weber were married in 1782 and, had Mozart lived a few years longer, he might have succeeded to the important post of Cathedral Chapel Master (see p. 198).*

8, 10 (Above) *View of the landscape around Vienna seen from Nußdorf, a village lying to the west of the city. The wooded islands created by the arms of the Danube are clearly distinguishable (see Pezzl, sections 1, 85).* (Opposite) *Bird's-eye view of the city of Vienna by Joseph Daniel Huber, 1769–74. The ramparts (Bastei) can be clearly seen and the Cathedral provides a central focal point. In the foreground are sections of the Danube* (right) *and its tributary, the River Wien* (left); *see Pezzl, sections 142, 85.*

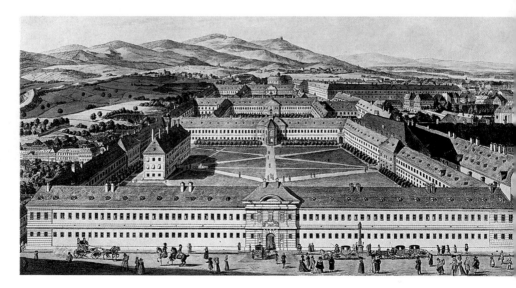

9 *The General Hospital, Vienna, completed in 1784; still serving its original purpose today, this was one of the major new institutional buildings dating from the reign of Joseph II (see Pezzl, section 53).*

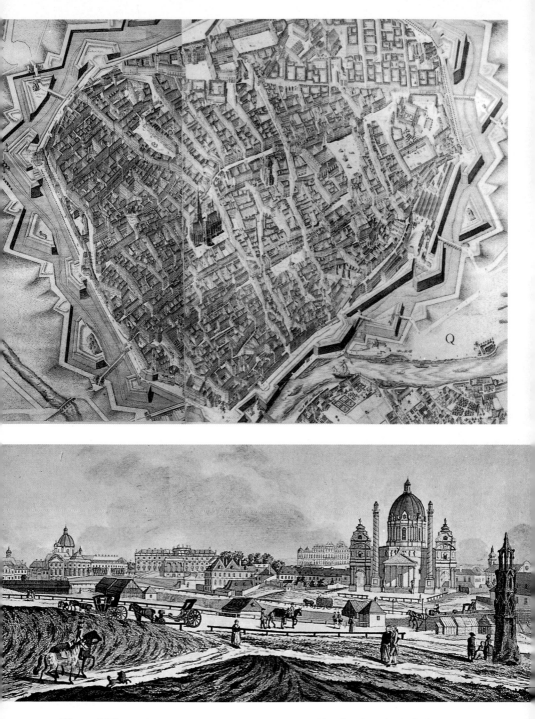

11 *View of Vienna from the Glacis, outside the city walls, showing the Belvedere, the Schwarzenberg Palace and the Karlskirche, all listed by Pezzl among notable buildings in the city (see sections 4, 79).*

III
The third journey (1773)

IN THE PERIOD between 1769 and 1773 Wolfgang and his father visited Italy three times: the first trip lasted from 12 December 1769 to 28 March 1771, and they went to Rovereto, Verona, Milan, Parma, Bologna, Florence, Rome and Naples, as well as many places in between. During this Italian visit, Wolfgang composed most of his first string quartet (at Lodi in March 1770). In the course of their return journey the Mozarts spent three months in Bologna, where Wolfgang studied counterpoint with Italy's most celebrated musical theoretician, Padre Giovanni Battista Martini (1706–84). But the principal reason for the extended sojourn in Italy was the composition of the opera *Mitridate, Rè di Ponto* (K.87), commissioned for performance in Milan, then under Habsburg rule (Archduke Ferdinand of Austria was Governor and Captain-General of Lombardy; the third son of Empress Maria Theresa, he was soon to be married to Princess Maria Beatrice Ricciarda d'Este of the House of Modena). The opera was performed in the theatre of the grand ducal castle in Milan on 26 December 1770.

The second Italian visit lasted from 13 August to 15 December 1771, and it resulted from a commission issued by Empress Maria Theresa to compose a 'serenata teatrale', *Ascanio in Alba* (K.111), to be performed in honour of her son Ferdinand's marriage. The new work had its première in Milan on 17 October 1771.

The third visit to Italy, which lasted from 24 October 1772 to 13 March 1773, originated in a commission to compose the opera *Lucio Silla* (K.135), first performed on 26 December 1772. *Lucio Silla*, which was Wolfgang's greatest dramatic work to date, was an enormous success; after its première at the Milan Court Theatre, it was repeated

12–14 *Opposite.* THE URBAN SCENE
View of the Graben, one of the principal city squares, compared by Pezzl to the Piazza San Marco in Venice (see section 126). Mozart lived here 1781–2 and, after his marriage, for several months in 1784 in the well-known Trattner House, part of which is visible in the right foreground. Above are seen the postman and night-watchman from the series of street cries ('Kaufrufe') of Vienna drawn by Christian Brand and published as engravings in 1775.

more than twenty times. Among the soloists was the castrato Venanzio Rauzzini. Wolfgang (and of course his father Leopold, who accompanied him on all three journeys) hoped to secure a position at the court of Archduke Ferdinand, who indeed wanted to engage the young Salzburg musician. Maria Theresa, however, in a now (in)famous letter, put paid to any such idea. On 12 December 1771, after the successful performance of *Ascanio in Alba*, she had written: 'you ask me if you may take the young Salzburgian into your service. I don't understand as what, or why you have need of a composer or such useless people. If that gives you pleasure, I will not stand in your way. What I do say is that you ought not to engage useless people and should never confer titles on people of that sort, who will represent themselves as belonging to you when they run about like beggars; besides, he has a large family'.[1] Understandably, Ferdinand quailed before this onslaught.

Wolfgang also composed six string quarters (K.155–60), modelled on those of Haydn's set, op. 17. In the event, however, Leopold and Wolfgang were frustrated in their hopes of finding an appointment for Wolfgang in Italy. *Lucio Silla* may have found great favour in Milan, but the work's success remained purely local. (This situation was to be repeated several times in the course of Wolfgang's career: *La finta giardiniera* [K.196], first performed in Munich on 13 January 1775, hardly achieved more than a local success, and a more notable example was the case of the magnificent *Idomeneo, Rè di Creta* [K.366], performed in Munich in 1781 and, apart from a single semi-private performance given in Vienna a few years later, consigned to oblivion during Mozart's lifetime.)

Leopold thought that he might have more success in securing for Wolfgang an appointment at the Imperial court in Vienna; and to this end father and son set out on 14 July 1773. The new Archbishop of Salzburg (Hieronymus, Count Colloredo, appointed in March 1772) was absent from the city at the time of their departure.

Leopold's first letter from Vienna, dated 21 July 1773, records their visit to Dr Mesmer's beautiful house (and garden) in the suburb of Landstraße.[2] Since his last visit Wolfgang's appearance had changed so greatly that no one recognized him: Leopold would send him into the houses first alone, and he then followed immediately. On this occasion Dr Mesmer played 'very well' on a glass harmonica, for which he had paid 50 ducats; Mozart, who could play the instrument, would later write exquisite music for glass harmonica to be played by Marianne Kirchgessner in 1791.

Then came the official audience with the Empress, as related by Leopold to his wife on 12 August 1773:[3]

... Her Majesty the Empress was, it is true, very gracious towards us, but that is all, and I shall have to tell you about it when I return.... On the feast of St Cajetan [7 August] the reverend Fathers [of the Theatine Order] invited us to dine and to attend Mass, and since the organ wasn't such that it was suitable for a concerto, Wolfg: borrowed a violin and a concerto from H: Teiber [Anton Teyber or Teiber] and had the audacity to play a violin concerto. – At the church of the Jesuits [Kirche am Hof] a Mass by Wolfg: was performed in the octave of the feast of St Ignatius [14 August], namely the P: Dominicus Mass (K.66, originally composed for his friend Cajetan (Dominicus) Hagenauer, O.S.B., who had entered St Peter's Monastery in Salzburg five years earlier]. I beat the time and the Mass was astonishingly success- ful. ...

At the end of his father's letters, Wolfgang would add his own light-hearted and nonsensical postscripts addressed to his sister in Salzburg. On 14 August, for example, he wrote: 'I hope, my queen, that you are enjoying the highest degree of health and that now and then or rather, sometimes, or perhaps occasionally, or still better *qualche volta* as the Italians say, you will sacrifice some of your most important and urgent thoughts to me ... '[4]

At this point Wolfgang was busy on a series of string quartets (K.168–173) modelled on Haydn's recently composed set, op. 20, as well as studying all the latest trends revealed in the music then in circulation in Vienna. His hopes of obtaining a formal appointment were slender, but his musical experiences in Vienna in the high summer of 1773 were immensely rewarding, as will be evident below. 'Should the archbishop remain away for long, we won't rush home,' adds the prudent Leopold in a letter of 21 August.[5]

Leopold was somewhat shocked when he learned that the Jesuits were to be suppressed by Joseph II. 'The public is very much affected,' he wrote on 4 September,[6] but apart from several descriptions of the mechanics of closing down Jesuit institutions, Leopold's letters from Vienna (and Wolfgang's chatty insertions addressed to his sister) reveal very little of what was actually transpiring from a personal and professional standpoint.

Whatever Leopold's plans may have been, nothing came of any of them, and at the end of September he and Wolfgang returned to Salzburg. Earlier, both had had an audience with Archbishop Col- loredo, who visited the Imperial court at its summer residence in Laxenburg (a comfortable half-day's journey by coach south of Vienna) from 31 July to 11 August, and on 12 August received permission for their leave of absence to be extended, Wolfgang having been engaged as *Conzertmeister* on 21 August 1772. Apart from the newly composed string quartets, Wolfgang completed several impressive numbers as incidental music for the play *Thamos, König in Ägypten* (K.345), music which was to be further revised in 1779–80 (and in between as well). It is mentioned in a letter sent by Tobias Philipp, Freiherr von Gebler, the author of the play, to the writer Christoph Friedrich Nicolai in Berlin on 13 December 1773: '... I ... enclose in any event the music for Thamos, as it was recently set to music by a certain Sigr. Mozzart [*sic*]. It is his original conception and the first chorus is very beautiful.'[7] The production of the play with incidental music, given at Preßburg (present-day Bratislava) by the Carl Wahr Troupe on 11 December 1773 and attended by Archduchess Marie Christine and her husband Duke Albert of Sachsen-Teschen, is believed to have been the first performance of Mozart's choruses and interludes, performed by an orchestra reinforced by the addition of various instruments, noted the *Preßburger Zeitung* in its report.[8]

IV

Mozart and the 'Sturm und Drang' school

W HILE MOZART was in Vienna in the summer of 1773, he became acquainted with a vast quantity of new instrumental music written by other Austrian composers since *c.* 1768, especially Joseph Haydn, and also including works by Florian Leopold Gassmann, Johann Baptist Vanhal and Carlos d'Ordoñez, among others. Collectively, these works, usually in minor keys and employing extravagant musical language with exaggerated dynamic marks, are now referred to by the name of a parallel, if slightly later, movement in German literature – '*Sturm und Drang*' (storm and stress). Since this school, and particularly Haydn's music of this period, were to have a profound influence on Mozart's output, a brief examination of the German movement will help to set the scene.

The American Revolution of 1776 coincided with the appearance in print of a theatrical piece by Friedrich Maximilian Klinger (1752–1831) entitled *Wirrwarr* ('Confusion'), later that same year renamed *Sturm und Drang*; it is no accident that part of the play's action is set on the American Continent. Klinger's play, then, gave its name to a whole literary movement.

Sturm und Drang proved to be a young men's movement – the eighteenth-century equivalent of the 'angry young men' of the 1950s. In 1776 Klinger was twenty-four, and Goethe was the same age when his play *Götz von Berlichingen* was published in 1773, to be followed a year later by *Die Leiden des jungen Werthers*, which made him a celebrity overnight and created an entire 'Werther' school – and also, incidentally, a new trend in dress: the so-called 'mode à l'anglaise' was known in Germany as 'Werthertracht' – blue frock-coat, yellow waistcoat, boots. It was both simple and nonchalant. Part of the *Sturm und Drang* movement took its tone from the Rousseauian concept of 'back to nature'; part turned away from French literary models and looked towards England, not just the plays of Shakespeare but also Oliver Goldsmith's *The Vicar of Wakefield*, which the heroine of *Werther*, Charlotte, admired; and especially James Macpherson's brilliant poems claimed by him to be the work of a Gaelic bard named Ossian (*Temora*, 1763). These Ossian poems had a profound influence on Austro-German thinking. The 'Ossianic' spirit, with its evocation of winter storms, wild sea-cliffs and clouds scudding across a desolate landscape, was the essence of the new literary feeling in Germany.

As a movement, *Sturm und Drang* was essentially egocentric ('Ich-bezogen'), concerned with the search for personal happiness; but suicide (as in *Werther*), frustrated Romantic love, overblown passions, the delineation of a lone individual pitted against society (Goethe's *Götz*) and a certain disorganization of plot and content (sense and sensitivity overruled by passion) were all aspects of its literary manifestations.

The curious thing was that most of the leading writers associated with the movement later turned their backs on the principles it had espoused: Klinger pursued a military career in St Petersburg and scoffed at his earlier passion. One of the more sympathetic aspects of *Sturm und Drang* literature was its occasional ability to laugh at itself, at its tragic gestures and beautiful souls. Goethe, while engaged on the first version of *Werther*, made fun of the back-to-nature cult in a drama entitled *Satyros*.

Just as the literary movement in Germany had its predecessors abroad, such as the Ossian poems of 1763, so also did the Austrian musical crisis, both abroad and within the lands of the Habsburg monarchy. The wilful and eccentrically brilliant C.P.E. Bach furnished one such work in the Harpsichord Concerto in D minor (Wotquenne 23) of 1748, which in turn derives from his father's trenchant D minor Harpsichord Concerto (BWV 1052). In Austria a seminal model was the D minor finale of Gluck's ballet music to *Don Juan* of 1761, in which the hero is consigned to Hell (Gluck used it later as the Furies' music in the French setting of *Orphée*).

Before proceeding further, it is necessary to explain, if very briefly, the transformation that the use of the minor key had undergone in the previous two decades. This transformation applied largely to instrumental music of the Italian and Austrian (south German) schools, but not to the north German school or to opera, in which (especially in *opera seria*) minor keys were almost always used to express passions, even in this relatively 'dark period'. The Italians, such as the 'reform' composer Tommaso Traetta, were, throughout the early 1760s, using minor keys as vehicles for expressing emotions. A Swiss scholar has summed up the new use of minor keys as follows:[1]

> A symphony in the minor means something out of the ordinary for a symphonist of the eighteenth century. The minor, as the tonality of the outer movements, is the vehicle for the expression of passion or grief. This is in contradistinction to a large number of thoroughly festive, joyous concertos of the Baroque era (cf.

Vivaldi: Concerti Grossi [op. 3, nos. 6 and 11] in A minor, D minor). Philipp Emanuel Bach, on the other hand, uses minor tonality wholly to serve the expression of passion, perhaps most persuasively in the clavier concertos, for example the Clavier (Harpsichord) Concerto in D minor.

Professor Wilfrid Mellers has drawn attention to another important point:[2]

> The tempestuous features in these works strike one's attention immediately; one should not overlook the fact that they also represent a significant development in Haydn's humour. The funny elements in his earlier work were in the main a simple *buffo* frivolity. Such comic movements as occur in the *Sturm und Drang* works tend – in an abrupt contrast of key, a melodic ellipsis, a sudden pause or contraction of rhythm – to startle as much as to amuse. Procedures that may in some contexts be drama are in other contexts wit: an intense levity that entails a recognition of 'other modes of experience that are possible', and therefore an awareness of instability. Consider the approach to the coda of the presto in Symphony No. 52 in C minor:

> All through Haydn's mature music – and in a more poignant way in Mozart's also – one finds this precariousness: the sudden defeat of expectation, the interruption of a norm of behaviour, whether of tonality or of melodic, harmonic, or rhythmic formula. One does not usually find this quality in composers who lived before the Age of Reason, in an age of Faith, whether in God or the State. Bach and Handel are sometimes comic, seldom if ever witty.

The reference to precariousness is another way of saying, perhaps, the irrational; and with that word we are back to the German literary movement. The eccentric, the irrational, in works by writers such as

47

Klinger or Lenz have their direct counterpart in works by Haydn (and his followers) of the epoch. In the finale of Symphony no. 46, the Minuet that precedes this movement is suddenly reintroduced: the effect thus produced is so bizarre as to be almost unsettling. Playing a minuet (and trio) first forwards, then backwards (as in Symphony no. 47) is also highly eccentric, as is the clever introduction of 4/4 time into a 3/4 movement (as happens in the third movement of Symphony no. 65). The irrational is present in many and often very subtle ways. Consider the 'Farewell' Symphony (no. 45),[3] which is perhaps the greatest single symphonic work of this period: it is in the key of F sharp minor, which is almost without parallel in the whole of the symphonic repertoire, and in order to perform the work Haydn's horn players had to have new half-tone crooks specially forged. In the first movement, the secondary theme makes its appearance not in the exposition, but in the middle of the development. Its D major lyricism and poignancy are in pointed, even violent, contrast with the fatalistic, striding-down-the-chord first subject, whose accompanying syncopations become an all-pervading element of the whole movement. And that beautiful second subject never appears again. This is irrationality at its must subtle but also at its most upsetting.

Turning to the music of Haydn's contemporaries during this period, a particularly striking feature is the large number of *Sturm und Drang* symphonies by Johann Baptist Vanhal, as evidenced by the thematic catalogues (of music for sale in ms. and print) of the Leipzig music publishers Breitkopf & Härtel for the years 1770–73. These list Vanhal symphonies in C minor (1770), E minor (1770), D minor (1771), G minor (1771), A minor (1772) and another in E minor (1773). Except for the symphonies in C minor and D minor, all these works contain the full range of Haydn *Sturm und Drang* characteristics. Vanhal makes use of repeated semiquavers, pounding quavers in the bass line, wide skips in the themes, sudden pauses (fermatas), silences, exaggerated dynamic marks (crescendos, off-beat *forzati* or accents), and all these features will appear in Mozart's first large-scale *Sturm und Drang* symphony, no. 25 (K.183) of 1773. There are four horns in Haydn's G minor Symphony no. 39 (*c.* 1768) and four in the Vanhal G minor symphony listed in the Breitkopf catalogue of 1771 – two in the tonic (G) and two in the relative major (B flat *alto* or high B flat). There are also four horns in Vanhal's D minor Symphony of the same year. It is also interesting to observe that Mozart's late G minor Symphony no. 40 (K.550) of 1788 started life with four horns, which the composer reduced to two: originally there were to be two in the tonic and two in the relative major (B flat *alto*). Writing for four horns was a regular part of the *Sturm und Drang* G minor equipment.

Although Haydn's and Vanhal's *Sturm und Drang* period ended rather abruptly, this was not to be the case with Mozart. He composed the for him very uncharacteristic, but for *Sturm und Drang* music very typical, Symphony no. 25 (K.183) immediately after his return to Salzburg from Vienna in 1773; the autograph bears a date (erased) indicating that it was completed in October of that year. After K.183, Mozart never entirely dropped this type of exaggerated language. While still in Vienna, he had written six string quartets (K.168–73) modelled on Haydn's op. 20 composed in 1772; the sixth in Mozart's group is a D minor work in the manner of Haydn's minor-key quartets of op. 20, ending (as do several of Haydn's) with a fugue. Later, however, when Haydn, Ordoñez and Vanhal had stopped writing *Sturm und Drang* works, Mozart would frequently return to this kind of language – the Piano Concertos nos. 20 in D minor (K.466) and 24 in C minor (K.491), the Quintet in G minor (K.516) and the Symphony no. 40 in G minor (K.550) are just some of the best-known works from his later years incorporating many of the most trenchant *Sturm und Drang* features.

Mozart has certainly assimilated into his style many of the elements in the *Sturm und Drang* style of Joseph Haydn and his contemporaries, several of whom have already been mentioned; another example is a sombre and raging D minor work by Michael Haydn – the *Introduzione*, with four horns, to *Der büssende Sünder* of 1771 – a work composed, as it were, on home ground in Salzburg. As noted above, Mozart never abandoned the style entirely: it remained, hovering in his subconscious mind, ready to be called upon whenever circumstances demanded its use. To take two examples from 1791, what are the Queen of Night's second aria, 'Der Hölle Rache', in *Die Zauberflöte*, or the 'Dies Irae' from the *Requiem* if not sublime and sublimated instances of D minor *Sturm und Drang*? There can be no doubt that Mozart's later style was profoundly influenced by the music he heard and studied in the course of the long and otherwise fruitless summer of 1773 which he spent in Vienna. The city was not as frivolous as Leopold Mozart sometimes liked to imagine: Austria has always had a dark side to its character, and Wolfgang was soon to make that aspect his own in a new and unique way. *Sturm und Drang*'s slightly rhetorical anguish was to become Mozart's personal sorrow.[4]

Thus it may be seen that the now-famous 'little' G minor Symphony no. 25 (K.183) occupies a central but curiously atypical place in Mozart's music of the mid-1770s. It is a work as unlike its roughly contemporaneous symphonic companions, nos. 28 and 29 (K.200, 201), as is the Symphony in G minor, op. 6, no. 6, in the catalogue of J.C. Bach's orchestral music. Both are 'single shots', in the case of Bach never repeated and not repeated in this particular fashion by Mozart. Alfred Einstein writes:[5] 'In [K.183]...the choice of key alone transcends the boundaries of simply "social" music, and even contradicts the nature of such music. What purpose of the day can this document of impetuous expression have served?' In some ways, this is a work that, because it reveals a certain lack of balance, can only be described as un-Mozartian. But it is not entirely atypical. Wilfrid Mellers writes perceptively:[6]

> The little G minor symphony, K.183, is fascinating both for its resemblances to and differences from Haydn's minor moods in his *Sturm und Drang* compositions. It has the same passionate repeated notes and brusque changes of dynamics which [may be observed] in Haydn's G minor Symphony (No. 39). But whereas Haydn is fierce, Mozart is melancholy; and the difference consists in the sweetly singing quality of Mozart's themes as compared with Haydn's explosiveness, and in the persistently sighing appoggiaturas:

Archi
[Allegro]

This does not mean that Mozart's melancholy is limp. It is acute, because it is already inherently dramatic. It is worth noting that whereas Haydn and C.P.E. Bach and Beethoven – who were not *primarily* lyrical composers – prefer to unify their material as closely as is consistent with their dramatic intentions, Mozart and J.C. Bach, who naturally think lyrically, can afford to introduce more obvious contrasts between their themes. Even Mozart's A major Symphony, K.201, which is a radiant piece, places sinuously chromatic melodies alongside airily dancing *buffo* tunes: and contains the longest and most exciting development that Mozart had yet created.

'Storm and Stress' was, however, an element inherent in Mozart's temperament, rather than absorbed from without.

V

Mozart and Vienna in
the 1780s

───────◦◦◦◦◦◯◦◦◦◦◦───────

T HE CIRCUMSTANCES of Mozart's move from Salzburg to
Vienna have been told often enough. Briefly, they are as
follows: called to Munich to prepare and conduct the first
performances of *Idomeneo* in early November 1780, Wolfgang overstayed
his leave of absence from the Salzburg archiepiscopal court and his
employer, Archbishop Colloredo, who was on a protracted stay in
Vienna, insisted on having the services of his most talented *Conzertmeister*
available to him in the Austrian capital. Mozart duly arrived in
Vienna on 16 March 1781.[1] Immediately caught up in a whirlwind
of musical activity resulting from the archbishop's concert-giving
requirements, Wolfgang found his own aspirations thwarted. The
disagreement between the two men came to a head in May and Mozart
was summarily dismissed. With his new-found independence he could
now launch himself into concert-giving, teaching, composing and
performing, especially his own piano concertos.

To achieve a detailed reconstruction of life in Vienna during the
decade 1781–91 is not as difficult a task as it might at first appear. Apart
from an infinite variety of contemporary paintings and engravings – the
series commissioned by Artaria & Co. and published in the form of
coloured engravings is particularly striking – there exists a very valuable
printed description of Vienna which appeared under the title *Skizze von
Wien* ('Sketch of Vienna') in six instalments or parts (*Hefte*) from 1786
to 1790; indeed, so successful were they that by the time the 1790
instalments were appearing, the first parts were already being reprinted,
and the complete work ended up as a two-volume publication consisting
of 974 pages in octavo format. Although the work was published
anonymously, it was common knowledge that the author was Johann
Pezzl (1756–1812), a supporter of Joseph II's reform policies.

As a true son of the Enlightenment, Pezzl became a Freemason,
joining Mozart's lodge 'Zur Wohlthätigkeit' ('Beneficence') in March
1784. Born in the same year as Mozart, Pezzl was no dry chronicler,
but a perceptive and often witty observer of Josephinian Vienna. His
short sections – a total of 169 originally identified by roman numerals –
covered every aspect of the Imperial capital and life in the city and
its suburbs.

This part of the present book is an abridged translation of Pezzl's uniquely valuable documentation of Vienna in Mozart's time. As an aid to the reader, explanatory interpolations and comments have been added within square brackets, and summaries of sections that have been omitted or abridged, as well as original footnotes by Pezzl, are similarly shown. A general guide to the Austrian currency in use in Mozart's day is given on p. 8.

JOHANN PEZZL

Sketch of Vienna

1786–90

Silhouette portrait
of Johann Pezzl
by Hieronymus Löschenkohl

PART ONE: 1786

1 *Situation*

...On the southern bank of the great River Danube is a hill of middling size, on which there were fortifications in Roman times; the Danube formed the boundary between the Roman province of Pannonia and the lands of the barbarians, and on that hill stood the outpost called Vindobona, later to become Vienna.

The surrounding countryside is famous for its many beauties, starting with the pretty wooded islands on the north side of the Danube, forming ten arms [now regulated]; from the top of the hill called the Kahlenberg [bare mountain], there is a beautiful view across the Danube at dusk. Towards the south are ranges of green hills; towards the east lies open countryside, flat and fertile...

If one wants to obtain a bird's-eye view of this pleasant landscape, one can climb the tower of St Stephen's Cathedral, or walk up the Kahlenberg, or take up station in Count Cobenzl's country house on the hill which now bears his name [and where Mozart loved to visit] or in the country house [near Dornbach] belonging to the [Russian Ambassador] Prince Galitzin [Mozart's patron in 1784]. Splendid views of Vienna are also to be had from the gallery of the [Chancellor of State] Prince Kaunitz's pavilion in the suburb of Mariahilf, or from the upstairs windows of the Belvedere Palace.

Until quite recently it was the custom to print a plan of Vienna and its outskirts on fans for ladies. It is a pity that this practice is no longer in vogue, for it used to provide the best opportunity, when one was in a carriage with one's lady, trotting out in the direction of Nußdorf, Laxenburg or Dornbach, to teach her the rudiments of geography and to some extent about her mother country....

2 *Summary*

...The city, with its handsome and regular fortifications, forms the centre, surrounded by its suburbs, and the middle of the city itself seems to me to be the site of St Peter's Church.... The so-called Esplanade, or the open space between the city and the suburbs, has been, since 1781, planted with avenues of horse chestnut trees. The principal avenue forms an almost complete circle around the whole city, from the Mauth-Tor [Customs Gate] to the Neues Tor [New Gate] ...

If one considers the enormous expansion of the twenty suburbs, one is astonished at the countless number of buildings which have been in existence for only a hundred years; in 1683 the suburbs of Vienna, besieged by the Turkish armies, were put to the torch by our commander, Starhemberg; the barbarians completely devastated anything which the flames had not already consumed.

The healthiest suburbs are Mariahilf and Landstraße, they are at a slightly higher altitude and enjoy clean air, and there are fine views of the lower-lying surroundings. The least healthy of the suburbs are probably Weißgerber [Tanner's Quarters] and Roßau. ...

Vienna's climate is very varied. The place is beset by winds from the north and the east; the air is very sharp, and dry rather than humid. Even if it has rained all night, clouds of dust rise again by midday.   **3   *Climate***

This constant dust in warm weather is one of Vienna's great plagues. It is the dried-out dust of chalk and gravel, it irritates the eyes and causes all sorts of lung complaints. Servants, runners, hairdressers, coachmen, soldiers, etc., who have to be out on the streets a great deal, often die of pneumonia, phthisis, consumption, chest infections, etc.

An outsider who has not seen this dust with his own eyes can hardly imagine what it is like. Many carriage wheels and horses' hooves, incessantly passing along the streets at all hours, stir it up and if there is a little more wind than usual, the city, the suburbs and especially the Esplanade are covered with it. If you leave your house at eight o'clock on a Sunday evening after a lovely warm day, it is like entering a fog; one can only make out the lanterns flickering through the dust; and if one leaves by one of the city gates, a dense dust-cloud covers the whole Esplanade. In a few minutes, one's shoes, clothes and hat are covered with dust. The wheels of sixteen thousand carriages and their horses' hooves, plus an army of more than two hundred thousand pedestrians, have covered Vienna in fog. The worst situation occurs when, after several warm days, a strong wind springs up.... the dust penetrates mouth, nose and ears... and one's eyes weep....

The water drunk by the Viennese is not the best; it acts like a purgative and any foreigner who has been here for a few weeks usually suffers from diarrhoea for a month.... As in Paris, the exhalation of the city can be clearly felt.

In winter the thermometer reading in the city is always $1\frac{1}{2}°$ to 2° [Celsius] higher than in the suburbs and beyond the *Linie*. During the height of summer the temperature is usually 25° to 27° and on cold winter days 10° to 12° below freezing.

4 *Physiognomy of the City*

The city and its suburbs are laid out in a kind of circle, the circumference of the whole being about four German miles [some twenty English miles].... The entire inner area, that is the sections within the *Linie*,... is illuminated by some 2,500 street lamps [Author's note: In the city all year round without exception, on the Esplanade and in the suburbs when there is no full moon].

The term 'Linie', referring to the line which encircles the whole, dates from the beginning of this century [i.e. the eighteenth], when trench-works and walls were established to form a 'line' to counter the Hungarian rebels [*Korruzen*]. Nowadays it is used to foil dealers in contraband goods...

London is supposed to have 120,000 houses, Paris 50,000, Amsterdam 26,000, Berlin 10,000 and Vienna only 5,500. In London one reckons on [an average of] nine persons to a house, twenty in Paris, eight in Amsterdam, fifteen in Berlin, and in Vienna forty-seven. However, the number of houses in the suburbs of Vienna cannot be accurately established. If in the course of a summer one has not visited places like Upper Neustift, or along the River Wien, or the Währingergasse [*sc.* Währingerstraße],... and then one walks around them in the autumn, one will quite often find whole streets of new houses which have suddenly sprung up where previously there was nothing.

As far as the city itself is concerned, it has long since reached its full capacity... Every square foot is covered with stones and bricks and Lady [Mary] Wortley Montagu very naively but very accurately writes [in a letter published in her correspondence, London 1763], 'As the town is too little for the number of people that desire to live in it, the builders seem to have projected to repair that misfortune, by clapping one town on top of another, most of the houses being of five, and some of them six stories.'

For some time, the names of the streets and squares in the suburbs have been marked. In the first weeks of the year 1784 the same was done in the city, for the convenience of the local populace and especially of outsiders.

Vienna is not remarkably beautiful, but it is much more beautiful that it is reputed to be abroad. Some geographers, who have never been here, describe it as narrow, dark and old-fashioned. Indeed, there are houses where on the ground floor you have to keep a candle burning all year round, and where in winter you need artificial light even when lunching on the first [U.S., second] floor, but such houses are in narrow alleys, through which no carriage can pass.

Vienna is nonetheless very solidly built and could withstand a very heavy bombardment and sustain much less damage than many a brilliant and modern city. The cellars in some houses have as many levels below ground as there are storeys above.

This wonderfully strong method of construction means that one can the more easily dispense with fire insurance. If fire does break out, the people in the neighbouring houses – those next to the one on fire – remain quite unconcerned, and in streets further removed one hears the fire brigade's arrival with equanimity.... Within living memory, there has been no instance of a single storey of a house in the city being destroyed.

The principal building in the city is the Imperial Castle [Hofburg; see section 33] which, as is well known, has an undistinguished exterior, but inside is worthy of a great monarch. The joke of a pamphleteer who wrote that 'the Emperor's horses are better housed than the man himself' is literally true.

Among the fine buildings of the first rank are the Imperial Chancellery [Reichskanzlei], the Imperial Library, the Belvedere, the building which houses the High Courts (where Prince Eugene used to live), the Schwarzenberg Palace on the Rennweg, the building of the new Josephinian Academy of Surgeons [Josephinium] in the Währingergasse, the Hungarian Chancellery, the Lobkowitz Palace, the Imperial Stables, the Karlskirche, the Liechtenstein Palace in the city and that in the Roßau suburb [all these buildings are extant, 1990].

Among the buildings of the second rank are the University, the War Ministry, the State Chancellery [Staatskanzlei], the Bohemian-Austrian Chancellery, the City Hall [altes Rathaus], the Palace of the Hungarian Noble Guard, the former Theresianum, the Invalids' Palace; and the palaces of the [noble]

Esterházy, Kaunitz, Dietrichstein, Auersperg, Starhemberg, Batthyani, Kinsky, Harrach, Schönborn, Khevenhüller, Trautmannsdorff, Pálffy and Paar families, as well as those of many other wealthy and important families who have resided here for centuries [most of the buildings listed still survive], some two hundred in all. Their exteriors are not always very splendid, but within they combine in interior decoration and furnishings all the creations of our refined [eighteenth] century in superb magnificence . . . and graciousness.

Most of the handsome houses stand in a little-frequented part of the city – the Herrengasse, the Hintere and Vordere Schenkenstraße, the Wallnerstraße and the Teinfaltstraße; in short, in the district between the Castle and the Schottentor [Scottish Gate]. It is a pity that not one of these palaces faces on to a central street.

The cost of construction of the new palace for [the banker] Count Fries on the Josephsplatz – now completed – was estimated at 400,000 gulden. The court furniture-maker delivered goods to the value of 60,000 gulden, and the mirror-manufacturers charged 15,000 gulden for mirrors on the walls.

The Trattner House on the Graben, which accommodates some 600 people [including the Mozarts in 1784], brings in an annual rent totalling 32,000 gulden, and it is a remarkable fact that its owner, who came here thirty years ago as an insignificant printer from Hungary, now has a business with an annual turnover of some 300,000 gulden [Trattner's daughter Therese was a pupil of Mozart].

Among the other important buildings in Vienna are the six large barracks for the infantry, cavalry and artillery, and also the enormous General Hospital [see section 53].

5 Reduction of Monasteries

In the Vienna of yesteryear, when it was considered impossible without monks and nuns to lead a Christian life, or to die in a state of grace, the monasteries and nunneries played an important role.

These prisons occupied nearly a sixth of the city. In the past six years, as everybody knows, their numbers have been greatly reduced [as a result of the Josephinian reforms]. If any proof were needed to demonstrate monastic life in all its degeneracy, one would only have to print the protocols of the complaints and depositions against many convents and abbeys which the government has filed during the last five years.

Montesquieu's axiom was once again confirmed: all aspects of ruined passions are nowhere more stirred up and stretched to breaking point than in these unnatural surroundings.

The monks had a thousand ways of making their life easier, and yet on 1 February 1781 the government commission found, in the subterranean prisons of the Capuchin [Franciscan] Monastery on the Neuer Markt [New Market], four fathers, one of whom had been imprisoned for eleven years, another for thirteen, a third for sixteen, and finally Brother Nemesian for no less than fifty-three years of his life.

And as for the nuns! A man who knows about such things assures me that when they suppressed the L . . . . . Convent, they found evidence of such misery that, said my correspondent, if he could have a pin for every tear shed, he would be a rich man. Not just trifles like scratching and slipper fights, for the desperate girls often had recourse to much more serious excesses – all terrible, all true. . . .

Meanwhile, the Trinitarians, Blackfriars, Theatines, the Dorotheans, have disappeared. The Minors have been banned from the city, the former Royal Abbey has been turned into a residence [the palace of Count Fries], the nuns of the Heavenly Gate and those of the St Nicholas Order have been secularized, and where the Sisters of the Seven Beeches sewed amulets, others now produce stockings and nightcaps; and where the Jacobean Sisters whined their antiphons, the directorate of the Tobacco Industry now does its sums.

6 The Suburbs

A great sense of rivalry exists between the citizens of the city and those of the suburbs. The city tailor looks down his nose at the suburban seamstress; the city cobbler engages two assistants from the suburbs to do repairs in his name... This practice, whereby a well-known master in town engages colleagues from the other side of the gate to help with excess work, is very common.

The new citizen opens his workshop first in the suburbs with no greater wish than that after some years he will be a master in town. The young journeyman who begins work in the suburbs considers that he has made no mean progress if, after nine months, he arrives in a city workshop, to the secret envy of his colleagues.

This ambition is not altogether groundless, either. Everything that is important, grand, noble and wealthy finds its way into the city – the suburbs are the domestics serving the lady of the house enthroned in their midst. There are few inhabitants of the suburbs who do not go into town at least once a day, whether to seek patronage, to do business, to collect cloth for making dresses, to deliver their wares, to raise money, or to go to the theatre, visit friends . . . enjoy their chosen pleasures.

Living costs in the suburbs are considerably cheaper. An apartment which will cost you 200 gulden in town can be had outside for 120. Restaurants, hairdressers and cobblers cost a quarter less than in the city. . . . For this reason up-and-coming artists, *rentiers*, white-collar workers, young married officers, etc., live in the suburbs. . . . But those who live there must take into account having to go into town every day: either the dust clouds will ruin your lungs or the hackney-carriage your pocket.

The finest suburbs are the Leopoldstadt, Mariahilf, Landstraße, Wieden. But none of the streets is paved and the houses usually have no more than three storeys.

7 Proposals

[Pezzl suggests planting trees in the Josephsplatz; this was never done. He suggests removing the 'tasteless booths' surrounding the Cathedral; they were later removed. He wants the butchers' stalls on the streets, Lichtensteg, Kärntnerstraße, etc., removed; this was done. On the subject of the remaining monks, he wants the Scottish brethren banished to Scotland or at least outside the *Linie* and their buildings turned into living quarters for two thousand people; he suggests that the Dominican Friars be sent to Spain and their monastery made over to the people for apartments (both orders remained). He suggests the same for the Franciscans, but adds a footnote stating that their garden has been sold and houses put up on the site. 'Let the Capuchin Fathers leave the Neuer Markt in procession with cross and flags'; their presence is ridiculous. The Capuchins, too, remained, but a footnote announces that their garden has been used for new houses.]

8 Plan of Vienna

. . . Population: at least 270,000, a conglomeration of all European nations. . . . A continuous bustle of people, horses and waggons. . . . a numerous, wealthy and brilliant nobility. . . . A very prosperous middle class. . . . A financial turnover of eighteen million [gulden p.a.].

Seat of the first among the reigning monarchs of Europe, who by his activity shows himself worthy of the throne which he occupies as head of the Austrian states, of an empire which is in the first rank and among the most powerful on earth.

In truth, Vienna has great advantages. In every respect it can stand comparison with the principal capitals of Europe, even if its population is not as numerous as those of London and Paris. Perhaps the very fact that it is not so crowded is one of its advantages.

There is no class of people that cannot find its own particular circle in Vienna.

Is your husband a politician? – The ministers are here; and the foreign ambassadors of all the powers, each of which generally sends its best man to this court; here you can find a full range of political ideas, views and speculations. It is also known that the Imperial Court Council [*Reichshofrath*] provides a permanent school of ministers for the German nations.

Is he a soldier? – Here, he will be quite in his element. The Austrian armies, now held in respect by the whole of Europe, are given their directions and derive their strength from here. Everything concerning the economics of war, tactics, etc., is decided here. The great Austrian generals are well known. On state occasions the Emperor always appears in the uniform of a Field Marshal.

Is he from the world of the arts? – Science and fine arts are encouraged here – history, philology, medical science, botany, mineralogy, chemistry, physics, surgery, diplomacy, government economics, etc., all have their masters....

Does he have business interests? – The ports of Trieste and Ostend [the latter then under Habsburg rule as part of the Austrian Netherlands], the commercial treaties with Russia and the Pforte [in Istanbul], the increasing scope for the silk and tobacco industry in Hungary, the facilitation of internal and provincial trade and the fact that many foreign wares and goods are forbidden entry – all this gives him the opportunity to study the situation and take advantage of it.

Has he sworn allegiance to the Church? He will still find a place. Does he defend the interests of Rome, of superstition, or intolerance?... He will be welcomed with open arms by masses of those who have survived from the previous decade and who share his opinions.

Does he seek a position at court, or an office from the hands of the rulers? Here is the source of all honourable positions, of grace and favours. In the furthest corners of Transylvania and

Bukovina, in Brabant and in Lombardy, neither president nor doorkeeper is appointed unless he has found favour here.

Does he wish to lead an independent life? The great city is the true home for philosophers. No one here reckons his income or measures his food and drink. He can live twenty years in one house and no one above him, below him or next to him will pry into his affairs, as would happen in a small town....

Is he rich? – For a few pieces of gold he can have anything he desires to satisfy his senses, his comfort and his humour. Chocolate made in Milan; pheasant raised in Bohemia; oysters fished in Istria; wine from the cellars of Tokay – all await his command. The horse that grew up by the Thames or in Andalusia; the sable hunted in Siberia; silk woven in Lyons – all these are available any time, to make his life more pleasant. Works of art and music from Italy, France's fashions, Germany's books, appear at his purse's command, as if by rubbing Aladdin's lamp.

Has he only modest means? Nowhere else can he manage as easily as here. For 12 gulden p.a. he can find a little room in the suburbs. A cook-shop will furnish him lunch for 2 groschen, a second-hand clothes shop will provide his needs for a pittance. Meanwhile, clad in his greatcoat, he visits the magnificent palaces and pretty gardens, and walks alongside generals, ministers and princesses, whose countenances the wealthiest provincial citizen looks for in vain.

There is a darker side to this attractive picture, however. Excesses, intrigues, frauds, hypocrisies and depravities exist cheek by jowl with wisdom, generosity and *bonhomie*.

Whatever mankind can produce in an area covering 11,000 square miles [German] – be it bad or good, noble or shameful – you will find quintessentially in the capital city.

9
*In Defence of
Great Cities*

It is said that London and Paris are monstrously disproportionate to the size of their respective countries. In the case of London this cannot be denied. A population numbering 900,000 souls – though there are reasons for believing that this figure, as usually cited, is exaggerated by 200,000 – make up a rickety head for a body consisting of not more than 7,000,000. Paris, with 700,000 people, is in better proportion when compared to a population of 24,000,000 for the whole of France. Perhaps there are in Paris 200,000 too many, but half a million would seem to be a sensible proportion.

One would like to see the population of Vienna [earlier given at 270,000] reach the above figure [half a million], considering that the population of the Austrian states has already passed 22,000,000 and, in view of the continuing system of peace, is soon likely to grow considerably.

Whatever one may say against wealthy and populous cities, I consider them good and useful, indeed necessary. Moralists, teachers and fathers have brought forward objections – degeneration of morals, luxury in offensive profusion, extravagance, insolence and harshness on the part of the great and rich, suppression of the poor and weak, mockery of religion and virtue, and a single-minded pursuit of sensuality and lasciviousness.

As soon we no longer incline to the views of that dreamer Rousseau, to wander through the forest on all fours like our friends the animals and to live in a hollow tree, existing on water and acorns; as soon as we admit that law and order, arts and sciences, culture and reflection, society and improvement – that these are the true and only roots of human society – then one must have respect for large cities. These are the only means to develop our natural forces, to teach us that we have a soul . . .

Long live great cities! They make people out of barbarians, and this benefit reduces all critics to silence. What do these terrible deeds of the great city consist of? That one treats love in a slightly more easy-going way; that one laughs at the platitudes and idiocies of the Philistines; that one has carriages and servants; that one enjoys a good table, and the theatre; and that one lives not just for work but for pleasure. Such are the principal sins of great cities. . . .

10
The Emperor

Anybody misled by the chronicles of former Austrian rulers into believing that Emperor Joseph is hidden out of sight in his castle, would be greatly mistaken. No other living sovereign has so often traversed his own lands, as well as many foreign states. From the Pyramids to the Krim, from Naples to St Petersburg, the Emperor has crossed and recrossed our part of the globe, and has examined everything of significance *en route* with his penetrating eagle eye. . . .

That is why his features are tanned, and that is the reason for his rather weakly if well-proportioned body being best suited to wearing, of all clothes, the green uniform [of a Field Marshal].

In the political world, the monarch occupies approximately the same position as the rainbow in the physical: everyone sees the same object, but each in a different way. One sees him as a soldier; the other as a law-giver; a third as a good economist; a fourth as an altogether too strict housekeeper; some see him as the enlightened reformer of the Church; others as the reducer of general devotion and Church rights; for some he is a benevolent father to his country; and for others an over-zealous state reformer.

The civil servant, the officer, the Orthodox priest, the nobleman, the scholar, the artist, the citizen, the peasant: each judges him according to his own ideas, and on the basis of the momentary advantage or disadvantage which he believes has resulted from [the Emperor's] measures.

The philosopher regards him with *sang froid*, silently considers his deeds and collects opinions, placing them in the archives of mankind, so that posterity may have an accurate picture of this truly extraordinary prince.

11
Prince Kaunitz

Except for [Empress Maria] Theresa and [Emperor] Joseph, no one in the last thirty years has excited the attention of the Austrian public more than the Minister of State, Prince Kaunitz.... and not just the Austrian public, but the greater part of educated Europe has shown this Minister respect and love, and this out of deep inner conviction. In fact, Kaunitz is unique of his kind: such honesty, disinterest, his noble and grand manner which colours all his actions, are found in few ministers.

Kaunitz is of noble build; he must have been extraordinarily handsome in his youth....

12 *Population*

The city has 1,310 buildings, and the suburbs 4,347, making a total of 5,657. The number of buildings in the suburbs grows annually and substantially. There is constant argument as to the exact size of the population of Vienna. Some time ago [Ignaz] de Lucca supplied the following figures:

City	52,053
Suburbs	156,989
Clerics	2,139
Military	12,530
Greeks and Jews	3,550
Foreigners	27,000
Total	254,261

[Pezzl points out that other authorities, e.g. Christoph Friedrich Nicolai, have considered these figures too high. For his part Pezzl considers them too low and adds that de Lucca seems to have changed his mind; in his latest writings he gives the total population as 268,000 in 1786. Pezzl believes the correct total to be 270,000.]

Each year there are usually 11,500 deaths, and about 10,000 births.... Published statistics [in the *Hamburgisches politisches Journal*, February 1786] reveal comparative figures for the year 1785 as follows:

	Paris	Vienna	Berlin
Deaths	20,365	11,603	4,961
Births	19,919	10,559	4,952
Marriages	5,234	2,488	865

Paris's population is reckoned to be 700,000, Berlin's 140,000....

Berlin has an excellent system for increasing its population: its citizens are exempt from military conscription.... If the Emperor were to free Vienna from conscription, the size of the population would rise to half a million in ten years, and in twenty years' time the boundaries would have to be extended beyond Nußdorf on the one side and Schönbrunn on the other. But the Emperor, on the contrary, does things which in fact limit the size of the population in Vienna: he transfers each of the Princesses – his sisters – with her retinue to some provincial town; he gives neither gala days nor other brilliant feast days, etc. Notwithstanding, the population grows steadily, as may be seen from the continous buildings of dwellings in the suburbs.

A pleasant feast for the eyes here is the variety of national costumes from different countries. The city is not limited to the usual German costumes, all alike, as in most European cities. Here you can often meet the Hungarian, striding stiffly, with his fur-lined dolman, his close-fitting trousers reaching almost to his ankles, and his long pigtail; or the round-headed Pole with his monkish haircut and flowing sleeves: both nations die in their boots. – Armenians, Wallachians and Moldavians, with their half-Oriental costumes, are not uncommon. – The Serbians with their twisted moustaches occupy a whole street. – The Greeks in their wide heavy dress can be seen in hordes, smoking their long-stemmed pipes in the coffee-houses on the Leopoldstädter Bridge. – And bearded Muslims in yellow mules, with their broad, murderous knives in their belts, lurch heavily through the muddy streets. – The Polish Jews, all swathed in black, their faces bearded and their hair all twisted in knots, resemble scarecrows: a living satire of the Chosen Race. – Bohemian peasants with their long boots; Hungarian and Transylvanian waggoners with sheepskin greatcoats; Croats with black tubs balanced on their heads – they all provide entertaining accents in the general throng.

It is a fact that no family can preserve its national origins beyond the third generation. The [foreigners] come in droves to Vienna to seek their fortune (which in part they find), and become naturalized. The original Viennese have disappeared.... This very mixture of many nationalities here produces an endless babel of tongues which distinguishes Vienna from all other European capitals....

The native languages of the Austrian Crown Lands are German, Latin, French, Italian, Hungarian, Bohemian, Polish, Flemish, Greek, Turkish, Illyrian, Croatian, Wendic, Wallachian and finally Romany.

13 *Appendix to The Population*

This section – of great importance – deals with horses and dogs. In Vienna there are more than 3,000 coaches belonging to the nobility, 636 numbered hackney-carriages [*Fiaker*], 300 so-called coaches for hire [*Lohnkutschen*] and about 300 country carriages and chaises belonging to private individuals [see section 71]. Cabriolets are not customary here [but one is shown in a well-known engraving by Johann Ziegler, published by Artaria & Co. in 1783, showing Joseph II and the Director of the Court Opera, Count Orsini-Rosenberg, riding in a two-horse carriage of this type].

There are 9,500 riding and draught horses within the *Linie*. The degree of fondness for these beasts borders on the exaggerated. Many a saddle-horse is traded for 2,500 gulden, and some princely houses have 80 or 100 in their stables.

The dangers are endless, particularly in the main streets; and more so on holidays than on ordinary days. If on a Sunday evening you go and stand in the Stock-im-Eisen-Platz, in the Graben or in the Kohlmarkt, between eight and ten o'clock you are in the midst of a thunderous clatter. Carriages press through every gate: everyone who has been out in the country, in the suburbs, in the Prater and Augarten, is rushing home. A man from the provinces who is in town for the first time, crawls along in front of the houses like a thief, and at every coachman's cry fancies himself crushed under wheels and horses' hooves.

In fact, the number of accidents attributable to wheeled traffic is – in view of many waggons and by comparison with other large cities – very small. The average number of people run over [and killed] annually is only 3½.

The hackney-carriages are not, as is typical of Paris, miserable, falling to pieces, dirty, closed with wooden slats and drawn by worn-out hacks. Plush and lacquer lend them comfort and a nice appearance; and for 18 ducats [81 gulden] you can have a pair of lively little horses from neighbouring Hungary....

Mr de Lucca gives a total of 30,000 dogs of all kinds. I think Mr de Lucca has calculated 6,000 dogs too many, but even if there are only 24,000 and each of them eats but a quarter of a pound of bread daily, that amounts to 6,000 pounds of bread. Apart from dogs owned by butchers, gardeners and waggoners, the rest are a real pest for the public, and this leads me to suggest levying an annual tax, for the benefit of the Poorhouse, on these useless food-consuming beasts.

The worst aspect of all this dog business is the vile, mindless love with which these darlings are treated.... The miserable beasts sleep on pillows, are bathed periodically and cleaned; they are fed with chicken broth, chocolate and pheasant; and servants and chambermaids are put to trouble and even mistreated on their account....

14 Consumption

Writers like to lament the condition of farmers, etc. near a large city, forced to sell their wares to city dwellers; ... but in fact it is precisely these country people who have the fattest cattle, the best houses and the finest gardens, vineyards and fields in the vicinity.... It is a fact that Vienna's stomach is enormous, swallowing up the produce of all the neighbouring provinces – all the better for them! ...

Austria itself provides wine, wood, calves, salt, eggs, milk, butter, vegetables, dried beans, fruit and poultry. Hungary: an inexhaustible number of oxen among which (miracle!) there is not one black or brown; pigs, lambs, fish, tobacco, wheat, wine, poultry, hay. Bohemia and Moravia: venison, pheasants, fish, eggs, wheat, poultry, straw. Styria: oxen and capons. Milan: cheese and silks. Trieste: oysters and turtles. Tyrol: fruit and wood. The Netherlands: cloth, textiles and lace.

In 1783, Vienna consumed the following...:

Oxen	40,029 head
Cows	1,110 —
Calves	63,856 —
Sheep	7,724 —
Rams	35,400 —
Lambs	169,912 —
Pigs	80,650 —
Sucking pigs	16,906 —
Dried beans, peas, etc.	40,526$\frac{3}{8}$ *Metzen*
	[1 *Metz* = 3.44 litres]
Wheat and rye	119,603 —
Barley	88,002 —
Oats	521,081 —
Fine white flour	723,990$\frac{5}{8}$ *Strich*
	[a Bohemian measure
	= 93.6 litres]
Ordinary household flour	194,711 —
Rye flour	972,518$\frac{1}{2}$ —
Hay	20,660 waggon-loads
Bundles of straw	1,265,180 —
Tallow	20,940 *Zentner*
	[hundredweight = approx.
	50 kg]
Firewood	297,133$\frac{1}{2}$ *Klafter*
	[fathom cords; 1 cord
	= 216 ft^3 or 18.5 m^3]
Wine	494,044$\frac{1}{4}$ *Eimer* [liquid-measure kegs]
*Beer	4,447,574$\frac{1}{4}$ —

[*The figure quoted was exaggerated approximately tenfold – see Pezzl's correction in section 58.]

15
The Kind of People and What They Wear

The native Austrian is of medium height, though taller rather than shorter, ... and generally good-looking. In Vienna itself pure native blood has been so diluted with that of other nations that it has become a rarity. The typical Viennese, as he has existed for some time, is endowed with a characteristic long pointed chin.

The Hungarians are characterized by somewhat high cheekbones.

Viennese ladies – who qualify for this description better because most of them were in fact born here – are nicely proportioned, of a vivacious temperament, quick-witted, light-footed, slim, of slender build, with a pale complexion and fine skin. They age rather quickly, however, their skin becomes slack and in their old age they show a tendency to plumpness.

The clothing of both sexes follows closely the decrees of the latest fashion, with all the advantages and lapses of good taste this fickle goddess brings.

Gentlemen nowadays wear everything short and close-fitting. Their hair-dress is flat. Enormous belt-clasps [*Pferdeschnallen*] are still worn, but they are a few inches shorter and smaller. In general, tall old-fashioned Anglo-Saxon hats remained in style for only six months; now the fashionable headgear is the small, round, English sort. The wearing of two watch-chains is getting less common once again. Laced shoes and striped stockings are becoming popular, stockings matching the colour of your clothes being the latest fashion. For everyday wear, red and dark-green frock coats are preferred. Rings are now set with cameo portraits of famous men. Swords are inlaid with brilliants.

And as for the ladies! Who can count their fancies, what pen is agile enough to capture their thousand changes, to put down on paper all those little nothings which form the basis of feminine attire? . . . One thing is certain: in our age the fair sex is dressed in a manner that is incomparably more natural, more tasteful, lighter and more attractive than previously.

The fabrics are not as heavy, as expensive or as durable; but because of their lightness and cheaper price they are changed more often, and replaced by new ones, and thus have a more varied, cleaner and always fresher appearance.

The country hat with its thousand kinds of ribbons, flowers, garlands, lace, feathers, decorative pins, etc. – how much more charmingly does it flatter the wearer compared to the former stiff head-dress! . . . How like nymphs are those vivacious girls with their white summer dresses and a ribbon around their waists as they float across the Promenade. . . . And the furs in winter – my favourite form of dress – what Grecian simplicity they have! How they complement the charms of a rounded bosom! . . .

Alas, all these charms, all those beauties are ruined by the frightful, clumsy and accursed hooped skirts [*Buffanten*]. Never did an invention do more to destroy charm and grace than this monstrous contrivance. Even the slimmest girl is transformed by it into a herring-barrel...

Ladies in high society have now begun to divest themselves of this burdensome piece of baggage, and thus to reveal their natural charms. [In a footnote Pezzl adds: 'By 1787 all hooped skirts had disappeared.']

The costume of the famous Viennese housemaids has certain advantages over that of the ladies themselves. The [style of] dress of bourgeois ladies and their daughters is rich, but somewhat stiff.

16
The Nobility of the First Rank

The three classes of the nobility generally considered as being of the first rank are princes, counts and barons. It is natural that in a place like Vienna there should be a numerous nobility, attracted by the throne, business and high society... and many persons of rank come here from all the provinces of the Austrian Crown Lands.

Yet in this regard Vienna does not have the advantages of London or Paris: in those countries every nobleman, from even the furthest parts, journeys to his capital at least once in his life, if only to say he has been there. This maxim does not obtain generally in Austria.

Members of the nobility in Vienna who come from the Netherlands, Lombardy or Styria are comparatively far less numerous than those from elsewhere. These families keep to their own provinces, partly because of the distance, partly due to indolence, partly for economic reasons, partly out of wilfulness. They have declared Brussels, Milan and Graz their territory, and there they live and move in comfortable self-sufficiency....

In Vienna, as in other European courts, one used to have no better occupation for the nobility than to use its members for festive occasions – papering the audience chamber, filling processions and solemn entrances with lines of periwigs. In this way the most embroidered dress, the most glittering uniform could make the greatest impression.

These times are no more. No longer do old parchments and new clothes attract the favour of the monarch, the right to positions of honour, or the public's respect. A cavalier of ancient lineage and no merits may ride in a coach-and-six, give banquets, occupy the best boxes in the theatre, keep a great house; no one minds about this, but if because of it all he thinks himself a great man and demands respect, he won't get it. Nowadays a ne'er-do-well and dissolute scion of princely or baronial lineage is accorded no respect by the genuine aristocracy.

And how could it be otherwise? Among the nobility of the first rank are those whose own merits are a credit to, as well as a reflection of, their august rank, and who, through their demonstrable talents, their holding of most important appointments, through the trust placed in them by the monarch and through their influence on the administration, ... have made most worthy contributions to the well-being and safety of the state.

Except for some princely families in the Netherlands and Lombardy, the heads of most other princely houses in the Austrian Crown Lands either live permanently in Vienna or spend at least part of the year there. These [princely] houses are: Auersperg, Batthyany, Clary, Colloredo, Czatorisky, Dietrichstein, Esterházy, Grassalkowics, Kaunitz, Khevenhüller, Kinsky, Li[e]chtenstein, Ligne, Lobkowitz, Paar, Palm, Poniatowsky, Schwarzenberg, Starhemberg and Sulkowsky....

The list of counts and barons is too numerous to find a place here. Most of those from Upper and Lower Austria, Bohemia and Hungary, who are wealthy and distinguished, come to live in the residence [Vienna].

Considering the ease with which the born cavalier can train himself to become a useful citizen; the time and money he has at his disposal; the education he enjoys; the care with which he is given excellent teachers and books; and the encouragement, applause and reward which are constantly his – all advantages that a bourgeois young man so seldom enjoys; if, after all this, he still grows up to be a ne'er-do-well, one clearly has every right to despise such a man. And this seems to accord with the sentiments of the real aristocracy too, for they appreciate a bourgeois scholar, artist and businessman much more than a useless nobleman.

But let us be fair. Intelligence, wit and knowledge are not just the inheritance of men. Among the nobility of the first rank in Vienna are ladies who are truly sisters of the Muses and Graces....

17
*The Nobility
of the Second
Rank*

...This is the class of the newly created barons...those otherwise referred to as *Honoratiores* – such as councillors, commissioners, doctors, also bankers and business people. The class contains a nucleus of businessmen who assist the leading figures in affairs of state [literally, in Pezzl's phrase, the state's stars of the first magnitude], who are the cogs of the machine, as it were; they are liked and respected for their patriotism, honesty, diligence, discernment and hard work....

Membership of this group (unlike the carefully restricted first *noblesse*) is open to honourable but non-titled sons of the earth, hence it embraces so many different classes of the public and is pluralistic in outlook. Here we must single out the merits of several ladies of these houses, who combine a male intellect with feminine grace and are thus doubly attractive. I would name them if their modesty allowed,...these pupils of the Muses whose deportment is as instructive and tasteful as it is charming; in their houses one does not yawn with boredom over miserable card parties. Intimate musical entertainment, good conversation among friends, literary novelties, discussions about books, travels, works of art, theatre, interesting pieces of news, daily events, all related with spice, judged and illumi-nated – such are the entertainments that shorten the winter evenings of such a familiar circle. There, one makes the acquaintance of most local scholars, as well as those from abroad who happen to be passing through Vienna.

It is hard to believe, but these ladies suffered the same fate as that of Mesdames Geoffrin and Necker in Paris. Some small-minded people stirred up intrigues against these ladies, saying that they managed *bureaux d'esprit* [intellectual clearing-houses]. These fishwives should realize that it is a real compliment for a lady to preside over such a *bureau d'esprit*, when so many other women preside over *bureaux de sottise* [slander houses].

18
*The Man in
the Street*

I am referring here not to the rabble but to the bourgeois or, to put it more precisely, professional men, tradesmen, lower-ranking court servants and servants of the nobility, shopkeepers; in short, the usual kind of people between the nobility and domestic servants.

In Vienna, the man in the street is upright, polite, open-hearted, obliging, sincere, tractable, willing, and a good patriot, even if he doesn't applaud the Emperor when he sees him on the streets, out walking, or in the theatre. He despises cunning, humbug, avarice, arrogance, slander, meanness and mistrust of foreigners. He is fair and punctilious in his daily affairs, accommodating with his neighbour, and friendly and well-disposed towards foreigners. His guiding principle is: live and let live. . . .

The Viennese has one deeply rooted weakness, and that is his attachment to clerics and devotions. He could be excused for adopting this attitude, considering how powerful, how numerous, how penetrating, how cunning the venerable clerics have been until very recently; and how unified and indefatigable they were in setting out to make the poor laity wholly the machines and tools of their intentions, and the property of the Church.

But, honest Viennese citizens, the time has come for you to free yourselves from this mistake! Don't you see that wheat and wine continue to be produced even if you have no Blackfriars or Whitefriars, no Dorotheans and hardly any nuns? . . . Have you less work, are you paid less because you are no longer registered with . . . all those Brotherhoods? Is your life any less long or healthy because you are not buried with pomp and circumstance attended by endless processions of friars, crosses and banners? . . . Are your wives less fertile, your daughters less beautiful because you don't attend a hundred little chapels and chant twenty litanies, rosaries and vespers? . . .

The Viennese love banquets, dancing, shows, distractions. On holidays they love to walk in the Prater and the Augarten, to attend animal-baitings and firework displays, to go into the country with their families and sit down to a well-appointed table. These sins, which some people consider so offensive, are in my opinion easily forgivable. Since living in Vienna, except for rent and firewood, costs very little compared to other capital cities, it is obvious that tradesmen do not overcharge their clients, and since ordinary citizens do not usually go bankrupt, but on the contrary are well off, one must conclude that people are well able to afford their pleasures.

Then what is so reprehensible about these pleasures? Lecture a Westphalian or a Swede about thrift and frugal dishes: the nature of his country determines that; but do not begrudge the citizen of Vienna, living in superabundance, his table, for it makes him happy and well disposed, and what more could one wish for? It's even worse if one censures the Viennese when, out of the fullness of his heart, he sometimes says: there is only one Vienna! . . .

73

It's no wonder, then, if the Viennese considers his native city a paradise. He has just as much right to think so as the Parisian, the Spaniard [*sic*] and the Berliner.

19 *Living Requirements*

...Let us draw a line between the prince, with half a million [gulden] at his disposal every year, and the disabled daily worker, who makes do with five-and-twenty gulden; between the countess who is free to spend a thousand gulden a day, and the seamstress in the suburbs who earns $3\frac{1}{2}$ kreuzer for a long day's work. Who then, given these examples, would dare to determine a sum for living requirements?

Such extremes of fortune do not come into the reckoning, nor do conditions of a similar nature ranging between annual incomes of 200 gulden and 100,000 thaler. I propose to give a list of living expenses...for middle-of-the-road needs.

Assuming that you have no family, that you are not employed in a public office, that you are not a gambler, and that you do not keep a regular mistress – these are things which cause complications and require a certain type of wardrobe, and also involve a great deal of continuous, unregulatable expenses – you can live fairly comfortably in Vienna for the following annual outlay, which will enable you to move in respectable middle-class circles:

Rent	60 fl.
Firewood and light	24 "
Winter suit	40 "
Summer suit	30 "
Suit for visiting	60 "
Smaller items of clothing	30 "
Laundry	10 "
Food	180 "
Household service, hairdresser etc.	30 "

Total = 464 fl.

I leave to your imagination and your purse the question of how much you wish to spend on theatres, parties and private pleasures. You can manage quite comfortably on 500 or 550 gulden.

In Vienna you can very easily reduce the costs of food and parties [see also section 147], or at times even save them entirely, because the Viennese are extremely hospitable. If you are worldly, have travelled, are decently dressed and can hold your own in conversation, you don't need to worry much about your own table. There are many houses of the nobility of the first and second rank, ... whose owners consider it a pleasure to invite you with all sincerity to participate in their treats and amusements.

All travellers have been in general agreement about this Viennese hospitality ... [one writer] Archenholz admits candidly that among all the Italians only the Milanese show true hospitality, and that is because they are Austrian subjects and have learned from the Viennese. ...

Viennese hospitality is the ruin of the local restaurants. And in fact they are nothing special for such a city, nor can they be, for any foreigner of some name and standing dines out only on the first day, and at the most he only stays three days in an inn: as soon as he has arrived and has paid social calls in town, his acquaintances invite him to their table and he leaves the inn.

That is how it has been up to now. But I have the feeling that in the future there will certainly be, not a total revolution, but significant changes, in the virtues of hospitality. The severe economic reforms of the sovereign; and the cynical and profligate behaviour of some malicious foreigners here will, I fear, gradually give the Viennese good reason to be less fulsome in their invitations.

In recent times there have been four dangerous political crises for Vienna; the year 1683, when the city was almost forced to surrender to the Turks; the period 1704–8, when the Hungarian rebels under Rakoczy [Prince Francis II Rákoczi] and Tekely [Count I. Thököly] reached the gates of the city; the year 1741, when Bavarians and French troops captured Linz and pushed on towards Vienna; and finally the early part of May 1757, following the defeat [of the Austrians by the army of Frederick the Great] at the Battle of Prague.

These were the most disastrous periods for the inhabitants of Vienna –and with good reason – for fear and confusion reigned in the city. Fortunately, they survived all these crises without going under. Now these events have been forgotten,

20 *Hospitality*

21 *Political Character*

and were it not for the Turkish heads painted on some houses, one would hardly recall their former visit.

The Viennese today have only a vague, though ever-present, realization of the present strength and security of their state. They tremble before no one, in the firm conviction that their ministers and generals will see to it that no hostile army approaches their boundaries ever again.

Otherwise they let their ruler do as he sees fit. He has touched several very sore spots, but they have not made sour faces, at least not openly. For the Viennese public it was a matter of total indifference that the so-called heretics were tolerated, monks and nuns secularized, church music abolished, devotions curtailed, saints dethroned, and a visit by the Holy Father Pope [Pius VI, in 1782] wished on them. The Viennese accepted it all with happy indifference: and if the monks and bigots had not crept around all the houses and taken such pains to stir up trouble with the faithful, to slander the new measures of the sovereign, to circulate various abusive pamphlets and to embitter to the fullest extent the hearts of all and sundry, the voicing of dissatisfaction and slanderous comment would not have been heard even in private society.

Some writers were correct in noting that the Emperor's [Joseph II] unexpected and unprepared reforms would not have been received as easily in other countries as they were in Austria. This shows the easy-going outlook of the typical Viennese, which is so characteristic that an agitator would surely have no luck in Vienna.

22 *Moral Character*

They are nice people, the Viennese. On this point, too, there is general agreement among commentators. The city dweller's character is gentle, nimble, good-hearted, well-bred, pleasant, companionable, adaptable and sympathetic. An enviable *bonhomie* exists among all classes of people, without exception; the mild climate, general prosperity, tolerant government and opportunities for everyone to earn their daily bread all being contributory factors.

It is true that the soft character of the Viennese is not calculated to produce heroic virtues. But who needs heroic deeds in this day and age, in our condition? Our state machines run like clockwork, and even our bourgeois everyday existence is so methodically organized that big, exceptional explosions of head and heart would cause more confusion and evil than profit and grace.

The people of Vienna are very sensual, a characteristic which the fertile nature of the country accounts for. This has always been the case with peoples who live under a mild sky and on a bountiful soil. . . .

Formerly it was thought that the Viennese were incapable either of great virtues or of great sins, and some clever observers have pointed out that among any six criminals publicly punished in Vienna, four were usually foreigners and their crimes the more serious. I do not know the former Viennese, but if uncouth crimes are evidence of a strong national spirit, the present-day Viennese are, judging by some recent examples, not wanting in violence and energy. . . .

One evil which the Viennese used to be regarded as hardly capable of committing, and which was actually very rare was suicide, but now it has become rather frequent not only here but throughout Europe. It is now to be encountered among all classes, although with good reason the police keep such cases secret as far as they can.

**23
Dandies of
Both Sexes**

The male Viennese dandy must know where the best wine is sold and where church festivals are taking place. – How much a game of *carambolage* [billiards] costs. – Where the best bowling alleys are to be found. – Which dog is best for a solo kill in the baiting amphitheatre. – Which hackney-carriage is quickest. – He must know, as a clerk, how to act the court councillor. – In society he must play the clown. – He must know the *chronique scandaleuse* of the city and the going rate for the courtesan. – He thinks that there is no better place to live than Vienna. – He thinks he's an Englishman when he gives picnics, drinks punch and wears a round hat. – He hopes to receive a government appointment simply because he is a native Austrian. – He hopes for a *terno* [a draw of three numbers] in the lottery to improve his finances. – He loves his darling Vienna with its tower of St Stephen's [Cathedral] – loves his *Heiligenstriezel* [akin to Hot Cross Buns], his Advent sausages with vermouth, his blessed Easter ham; loves all foreign idiocies; loves holidays and all the days when he needn't work.

His joys are: a Styrian capon with sauerkraut or mussels. – A trip in the country. – The National Theatre in the Leopoldstadt. – Animal-baiting and ox-quartering. – A dance hall.

For him deadly sins are: a sensible discussion. – A useful book. – Hard work. – A bad meal.

He considers it extremely bad form: to stay at his office one minute longer than the time specified; not to attend a party; not to eat *Krapfen* [fritters] during Carnival.

The female Viennese dandy must know:

What the current fashions are. – Who is the best for German dances. – Where the best ices are to be had. She must be able to calculate the merits of her lovers by the number of decorations they are wearing on their waistcoats.

She thinks it is sufficient for her to be Viennese in order to find a husband. – She thinks it an honour to be visited by men of high rank. – She hopes to become a *grande dame* and, as a lady, to do as she pleases.

She loves any man who pretends to be a count or a baron; everyone who wears boots and spurs, and understands horses; and every male hand bearing a diamond ring.

Her joys are: pretty clothes and an equipage. – Unhurried *toilette* after a long sleep. – A little bit of scandal. – Costly presents, even those given by her husband.

For her, deadly sins are: a face without make-up. – Not to be the most important person on a sofa. – To enjoy good health throughout the year.

She is guilty of foreign sins: by her *poches, bouffantes, culs postiches* [purses, hooped skirts, false posteriors]. – By the French education which she procures for her children through foreign abbés and runaway governesses....

Vienna is a world of its own, and a simpleton there lives his life unconcerned about anything else outside. He rises, is clothed and has his hair dressed, goes to the office, rides in the Prater, sits down at table, visits a coffee-house, attends the theatre, a social gathering, a supper, and goes to bed; there you have his whole life's story. Everything waits on him at a certain hour; and if the hairdresser, caterer and waiter are quick with their duties, if the horse isn't badly shod and Madame Storace [the singer and friend of Mozart] hasn't caught a cold, and if a thunderstorm hasn't ruined his promenade or a domestic problem disturbed his evening society, this man is not interested in what happens in the rest of the world.

How many Viennese have never in their lives ventured beyond the Lusthaus [pavilion in the Prater] or the outer Danube bridges; and how many countless more never go further than the inns of Simmering, Nußdorf, Penzing and Dornbach [Viennese suburbs]?

Hence the narrowness of their ideas. But such a world is unavoidable for many an individual, and good for him!

Here is one of the great passions and principal preoccupations of dandies of both sexes. Twenty and thirty years ago, if one knew of no better way of spending the time not devoted to conducting business, or of whiling away cold, rainy evenings, the entire *beau monde* of Vienna crowded round those magical three- or four-cornered tables. Those players became stiff, speechless automatons for many hours on end, their sole actions consisting of mechanically flipping through a pile of coloured pieces of paper.

24 Gambling

One must concede, however, that to some extent the court itself set the tone of this passion for gambling. In addition, stupid ambition compounded this folly. It was a feature of high society. It was found to be (I know not why) excellent, lofty, brilliant to lay whole rolls of gold coins on an ace, to boast of one's gambling losses, even to tell the whole world that one's house had been brought to ruin at the tables.

This miserable insanity attracted a huge, profligate swarm of professional gamblers, adventurers, fortune-hunters and swindlers to Vienna, mostly from Italy and France: their income and property derived from cards and dice; they made a living from the young Viennese nobility's passion for gambling. The fortune of many a high-living household depended upon a gambling table with some pretty wenches around it.

Anyone can see at a glance that in recent times Vienna has changed considerably in this respect. Punishments for playing games of chance were meted out with severity, the card-sharpers were chased away or left of their own accord, and bankruptcy brought about as a result of gambling debts has practically ceased to exist.

The more intelligent members of society have begun to choose more honourable and intellectual pursuits – household theatre, music recitals, friendly conversation gradually replaced gambling; and if a playing card does occasionally make an appearance, it is to gratify society's weakness.

This behaviour is found only in high-minded society, however, which is small in numbers. A large segment of the great and less-than-great still spends many hours every evening with the Queens of Hearts and Spades.

25 *Lottery*

Though still permitted, this is the most widespread of all games of chance, and the one that does the greatest possible harm, because it never stops and is indulged in by all classes of the population; and it is the neediest for whom it holds the greatest fascination.

It was established in Vienna in 1750, and up to the end of 1769 it attracted 21,000,000 gulden, of which 3,460,000 went to the court and 2,080,000 to the staff running the lottery; while 7,000,000 were paid out to winners. Hence within nineteen years more than 8,000,000 went into the pockets of the lottery's organizers and lessees. Calculated on the basis of these figures, some 20,000,000 gulden must have been gambled [in the seventeen years] since 1769, making a total of 41,000,000 gulden in thirty-six years. . . .

The owners of tobacco shops hang whole sheets of numbers outside their doors to entice the avaricious. People tear off a few numbers of their choice, placing their hopes of future prosperity on them. A large number of people make it a habit to place a certain sum on the lottery every month of their lives. Every year they spend 6 gulden in this fashion and win 45 kreuzer. Enough! They've won, haven't they?

The worst aspects of this kind of gambling in general are that it corrupts civil servants, so that they put their hand in the public till; that it causes heads of households to reduce their families to penury; that it encourages domestics to become thieves. . . .

26 *Thirst for Titles*

. . . In former times a thirst for titles caused chaos within Viennese society. One recalls the amusing anecdote in Lady Montagu's letters, when during Leopold's reign two ladies riding in their open carriages came face to face in a narrow street one evening and remained there without moving until two o'clock in the morning because neither would yield to the other on account of rank and title. Nowadays the Viennese are above such pettiness. . . .

The more senior titles [see section 16], which are coupled with a real rank and position, enjoy a legal stability.

Lower down the social scale a kind of tacit agreement has produced the following grades: a woman of the lower classes is always addressed as 'Frau', as are the lowest tradeswomen. After 'Frau' comes 'Madame', and after 'Madame', 'Frau von'; these two latter are used for wives of merchants, wives of lesser government clerks, of artists, well-to-do professional men and house officers of great families. The wives of gentlemen in all higher official positions, also of great merchants, are always addressed as 'Your Grace'; their daughters as 'Fräulein'.

The bourgeois daughters of less grand families are also called 'Jungfern' [Mademoiselle]. Ladies' maids, even cleaning women and chambermaids have banned that old-fashioned word from their vocabulary; they want to be called 'Mamselle'.

Men of the lower bourgoisie are called 'Herren'. The salesman in the shop, valet, etc., the middling professional classes are 'Monsieur'. All those people between the professional men and the barons are addressed as 'Herr von'. This title is very widely employed, and the one which is in the most common use in Vienna.

Without doubt one could raise many objections concerning the legality of these titles; one could write satires about them. But they have become accepted, and the modest man follows the customs of the country.

It has often been remarked that in the German language there is no word which describes the class of men known in England as 'gentlemen'. In Vienna, the title 'Herr von' has exactly the same significance as the English 'gentleman'.

... I shall take an ordinary weekday in the middle of spring or autumn for analysis.

**27
The City's
Daily Order**

Between 6 and 6.30 a.m. the humble servant girls from the kitchens of the great houses and from the chambers of the bourgeois homes come tripping alone in their casual morning dresses, paternoster in their hands, on their way to church. Their lovers, the coachmen, stable-boys, hussars of the guards and porters likewise do not fail to attend, thus combining religious observance with their own hearts' desire. On the way home, breakfast will be eaten in a modest coffee-house, and usually it is the girl who treats her moustached admirer.

Meanwhile, there is growing activity on the Hof, in the Freyung, the Wildprettmarkt, the Fischmarkt, Seilerstatt and the Bauernmarkt. The women selling herbs, fruit, milk, eggs and poultry have set up their stalls and ranged themselves into long lines, displaying their wares for sale. The same thing happens at this hour in the main streets of all the suburbs. A whole stream of cooks descends on these stalls and takes away great piles of vegetables, fruit, butter, eggs, chickens, ducks, capons, pigeons, turkey-cocks, pheasants, rabbits, game, etc. About 8 o'clock the wives and daughters of lesser government clerks, of artists, of house officers of the great families, trot along, wearing a faded bonnet and cape, fan in hand, to the same places and, displaying a ridiculous mixture of pride and niggardliness, order their daily necessities. One hears an amusing exchange of courtesies and affronts. The voices of most of the market-women seem half-hoarse, but very sharp withal, attacking one's eardrums with piercing insistence; no professional speaker could ever compete with their voluble tongues. The greatest noise surrounding these markets lasts until 10 a.m., after which it subsides.

No carriages of distinction arrive on the streets before 9 o'clock; only the occasional hackney-carriage brings a wealthy bourgeois family, or a household secretary from the suburbs. But the streets are still crowded with waggons of every kind carrying wood, cloth, beer, meat and other goods, as well as other transports.

At 8:30 a.m. an army of some 1,500 dicasts marches out ... its battalions are made up of secretaries, registrars, adjuncts, clerks, transcribers, wholesale dealers, draughtsmen, supernumeraries, etc. After them follow 300 carriages with chancellors, vice-chancellors, presidents, vice-presidents, archivists, judges, etc., all of them heading for government offices....

Towards 10 o'clock the main streets become particularly busy. People drive to breakfast, to visit the hairdresser. The coffee-houses fill up. Between 11:30 and 12:00 noon the devout *grand monde* walks or rides to church. The better class of courtesans, whose wardrobe is sufficiently brilliant to survive the midday glare and the lorgnettes of the curious, likewise choose this hour to go to church. Their preference is for St Stephen's Cathedral or St Michael's, which edifices they patronize because both are reached via the Graben and the Kohlmarkt, where since time immemorial the markets for gallantry were held.

Meanwhile the dandies, dawdlers and strollers have planted themselves on the Graben and in front of the Coffee-house 'Milan'. They are waiting, spy-glass in hand, for the 'Ite missa est' to sound in the two neighbouring churches, so that they can inspect the ladies as they return from their prayers.

At noon the dicasteries send their workers back again. They use their time either for a short visit to the lady of their heart or they stroll about for half an hour – in both cases to take a little exercise before lunch and to whet the appetite.

Between 12:00 and 1:00 p.m. you can see many carriages with four or six horses, driving out towards the [suburb of] Leopoldstadt. These are the ladies of distinction who are taking a drive in the Prater with their friends or children, so as to enjoy the spring air and to provide a break in their interminable sitting-about.

The ladies of the middle class use this time of the day to take the air on the Bastei [city walls], and their appearance between 11:30 and 1:00, when the weather is fine and mild, is very splendid, and calculated to outwit the watchfulness of many a mother.

The common man eats at 12:00, the middle classes and government officials (who have to be back in the office at 3:00) at one o'clock, the upper class at two o'clock, and some of the highest nobility even later.

After 1:00 p.m. the pedestrians on the streets dwindle to a trickle, but there are still many carriages about, taking councillors home from government offices for lunch. At 2:00 it is very quiet and the streets are deserted. Everybody is at table, or drinking a cup of black coffee after lunch, or reclining on a sofa to aid his digestion. At 3:00 the dicasts hasten back to their inkwells.

About 4:30 p.m. the activity starts again. People, horses and waggons fill the streets. Half are rushing to their work and business occupations, the other half to their amusements. This is the time for afternoon promenades. People walk, ride on horseback or in carriages, on the Bastei, to the Belvedere, the Augarten, the Prater, to the Lusthaus [in the Prater], to Schönbrunn, Hernals, Währing, etc. It is the time for dawdlers; the ladies with their friends – the husband will follow somewhat later. Those who love the theatre can enjoy this promenade and still go to the theatre afterwards.

After 6:00 the streets of the city are at their noisiest. Government offices close, and workers in the suburbs lay down their tools, it is nearly time for the theatre. The hour for soirées is approaching. The majority of manual labourers stop work at this hour. Many small shops and stalls close.

The army of office workers flows forth on to the streets again. The inhabitants of the suburbs who work in town press their way out through the gates. The *grand monde* sets out at a gallop, their horses' hooves striking sparks on the paving stones, for the playhouses and the salons of society. The bourgeois betakes himself to the beer-house or to his neighbour. Those countless women who display and carry about all manner of objects in the streets pack up their stalls, put their carrying basket on their backs and swell the number of people blocking the passages.

If a new opera or play is being performed, the racket of the carriage-wheels, the stamping of the horses and the barkings of the coachmen as they cross the Graben and the Kohlmarkt combine to produce a hellish concert. You cross St Michael's Square at your peril, for here carriages are driving from all four sides. The number of pedestrians in this part of town is also so great that you must be sure not to have very delicate loins and nostrils if you risk being here at this hour.

This confusion lasts until 7:00; thereafter a general stillness descends. Only a few pedestrians are about, wandering as if lost through the main streets. As soon as darkness falls, those girls of the oldest profession who are too poor to dress sufficiently attractively to show themselves at noon make their appearance. The usual haunts of these birds of passage are the Graben, Kohlmarkt and the Hof, and they are present only until ten o'clock. These pathetic creatures, so badly treated by some theoretically strict moralists, deserve as much pity as contempt, for their way of life is, despite any outward appearance of cheerfulness, surely one of the most miserable. Compared to the street girls of other cities, those of Vienna are not as bold and brassy; they don't grab at your arm and rush after you through the mud as happens in Paris; all they do in order to hook you is to direct a fiery and inviting look towards you.

After nine o'clock the racket begins again. The theatre is finished, the soirées break up. This activity doesn't last long: the carriages hasten homewards, the pedestrians soon disappear.

At ten o'clock all private houses are closed up. They say it is a police rule. For a large city with such big houses filled with so many people, this custom has many advantages; without it, many sorts of riff-raff, thieves, pickpockets, marauders, etc. could creep into the spacious courtyards and passages of the larger buildings and make it much more difficult for the police to maintain the astonishing level of quiet and safety that now prevails. On the other hand, this rule creates the disadvantage that every house-dweller must be back at his front door by the stroke of ten, otherwise he will have to pay the usually not very polite porter a groschen to let him in.

From 10:30 p.m. on the cavalry patrol the streets of the city and the suburbs.

For anyone who has witnessed the daytime racket of the city, with its crowds of people in the streets, it is difficult to appreciate how extremely empty and silent the entire city is after 11 o'clock. At this hour you can walk the breadth of the city and encounter hardly more than fifty persons as they creep out of a few taverns and coffee-houses. I think there are two reasons for this: one is that most of the people living in the suburbs who work during the day in town have returned to their homes outside the city by nightfall; and secondly, the closing-up of houses at ten o'clock drives many people home before that hour so that they can save themselves the porter's groschen.

Between midnight and 12:30 a.m. there are still some carriages returning from supper in the great palaces. The lowly citizen who is already asleep is awakened from his slumbers by the rumble of the wheels; and his modest better half is not displeased by it. Many a young Viennese owes his existence to the nightly thunder of passing carriages.

At two o'clock the lanterns of the city are extinguished, and four hours later the same circus begins again.... At the height of summer and in the depths of winter things are slightly different. In the summer the palaces are empty, when their owners go off to Bohemia, Moravia, Hungary, or the flat lands of Austria. In the winter they foregather in Vienna once again, renew acquaintances, love-affairs, arrange marriages, form friendships. Winter is the soul of cities and gives them a new lease of life.

28
Sundays, Holidays

The *grand monde* no longer knows the difference between holidays and working days. The idlers of this class make every day of their lives a holiday, that is to say, every day is for rest, relaxation and pleasure. The industrious among this class sit at their desks even on holidays, and watch over the affairs of state. The structure of the political machine requires it.

It is a quite different matter for the vast numbers of ordinary people. One has to thank religion for having introduced certain days of rest during which the farmer, the artisan, the journeyman may halt his gruelling labour without fear of committing a mortal sin. . . . Every Sunday and holiday is for the Viennese of the middle and lower classes a much-loved and welcome day. The morning is devoted to church-going, and the congregations are enormous, a fact which contradicts the claims of those who always maintain that religious observance is in decline. If the Emperor is in Vienna, he and his nephews set a personal example of public worship.

The aristocracy attends the Church on the Hof, the Italian Church [Minoritenkirche], St Stephen's Cathedral and St Michael's. High society entertains a clear and undivided veneration of St Michael: between 10:30 and 12 noon one sees the most magnificent equipages, the proudest horses, the most richly liveried runners, hunters, hussars, heyducks waiting outside the doors of St Michael's and escorting their lords and ladies there. This attracts a crowd of curious onlookers . . .

Apart from taking a walk in the Graben or on the Bastei, there is no pleasure-seeking in the morning. But in the afternoon: ah, that is the time worth waiting for, not to remain within the walls of Vienna, but to go out, visiting the Prater, the Augarten, the Belvedere and the nearby villages. The Prater and the Augarten are the most frequented places for public recreation, because both can be reached on foot. Anyone who so desires drives to the Lusthaus, to Schönbrunn, Dornbach, Nußdorf, Währing, to the outer Danube bridge. Others, who prefer to enjoy a real day in the country and escape the crowded city, trot away at seven o'clock in the morning to Korneuberg, Purkersdorf, Laxenburg, in the Brühl, etc., and return at nightfall.

Some eccentrics affect to avoid these public places especially on Sundays. But because it is on these very days that the greatest numbers of happy people are together, and because a large circle of satisfied people constitutes, in the eyes of the wise man and the philanthropist, the noblest of all spectacles, the true philosopher does not disdain such a scene.

29
The Twelfth of September

What a day that was in the year 1683! It was also a Sunday – the most remarkable, the happiest Sunday in the annals of Vienna. As soon as the first rays of sunshine lit up the summit of the Kahlenberg, you could see the armies of the Christian allies on the move. They advanced down the mountainside; the Turks were soundly trounced, and Vienna was freed forever from their attacks.

I witnessed the last celebration commemorating that perilous day in 1783, the centenary year, and in fact the cowards of Istanbul are no longer worthy of the gunpowder exploded in their memory. . . .

The last remaining gala day! – Under Emperor Francis and Maria Theresa there were still many such days and under Charles VI and Leopold too many. For my part, I am personally convinced that the monarch of a great, rich and mighty country should encourage splendour of his court. In this way he infuses a certain warmth in the hearts of his subjects, by treating his fatherland as important, prosperous and deserving of respect. At the moment of this splendid celebration, ordinary people do not give a thought to the fact that it is they who must pay for it all; on the contrary, they rejoice that their sovereign can appear in such a magnificent fashion; they consider themselves part of the glittering spectacle, and their expression says to every foreigner who admires the splendour of the court: it's true, is it not, that our prince is a great and mighty man.

30 *New Year's Day*

The First of January has been chosen for such an annual ceremony. The Royal Bodyguards [cf. section 122] and the directors of the principal offices of state attend court in full-dress uniform between ten and twelve in the morning, followed by the ladies and gentlemen of the aristocracy in all their finery.

The German Guard, as the oldest, has pride of place; its members are worthy and venerable gentlemen, whose rich uniforms give them an appearance of great dignity.

In second place comes the Hungarian Noble Guard. It is possible that somewhere in Europe there are bodyguards with richer uniforms, but this corps is unsurpassed anywhere for general appearance, suitability, dress and withal a martial mien. Man, horse and armour seem to have been made one for another and especially when mounted they have an exceptionally graceful character, no other uniform being lighter, more attractive, manly and martial than that of Hungarian military dress. The young men come from noble families and are specially selected for their build: they ride white Hungarian horses and their shabracks [saddle-cloths] are green with silver edging and bear the monogram of their king. Their uniforms are red with silver, their weapons a large, curved Hungarian sabre; over their shoulders hangs a tiger-skin, on their heads they wear a tall cap of rough fur adorned with a plume of white feathers. Their commander is Prince Nicolaus Esterházy, one of the most magnificent vassals in the whole of Europe. His family jewels, with which his uniform is embellished on this occasion, are worth over half a million [gulden].

The Galician Noble Guard, newly established a few years ago and usually known as the Polish Bodyguard, consists of scions of the Galician nobility. In some respects its members are even more richly clad than the Hungarians: their horses are brown, their uniform the Polish national dress, dark blue trimmed with red and with gold borders; a tiger-skin likewise thrown over their shoulders, on their head a very neat white, fur-lined cap. The hairstyle is not the usual shaven Polish head, but worn long without side locks and formed into a chignon behind and under the cap. Their arms, apart from the large Polish sabre, consist of a long lance from which flutters a pennant in black and gold taffeta. The guardsmen are all fiery young heroes, whose youthful and fresh looks, as well as their physical characteristics, differentiate them clearly from the Hungarians. The commander of the Polish Bodyguard is Prince Adam Czatorisky, one of the most distinguished and wealthy Polish magnates, and a man much appreciated in Vienna.

Following the guardsmen come the Lord Equerry and the Lord Master of the Hunt, both on horseback, with a long train of people from their respective departments, proceeding slowly into the castle.

Then there follow the nobility of the first rank and the foreign ministers. If you want to see Vienna's most magnificent carriages, horses, trappings and liveries, you must take your place in the castle square on this day. There are very costly and brilliant objects among them, but not as many, or as expensive, as in former times....

15 *The façade of the Jesuit church (Kirche am Hof), with Pope Pius VI blessing the people of Vienna on Easter Sunday, 1782. The Pope had come personally to Vienna in response to the religious reforms, including the closure of monasteries and the issuing of the Edict of Toleration, introduced by Joseph II, but was unsuccessful in his attempts to restore the primacy of the Catholic Church in Austria (see Pezzl, section 65).*

16 *Relaxation in the Prater was a regular feature of Viennese life in the 1780s. In this engraving some of the coffee-houses providing refreshments can be seen on the left; the crowds of strollers and pleasure-seekers include gentlemen wearing the fashionable round 'English' hat, as well as those with the traditional tricorn hats (see Pezzl, sections 15 and 104).*

17, 18 *Pezzl's comments concerning feminine attire in the 1780s include (in section 92) approval of the typical dress of chambermaids, as seen (left) in an engraving of 1786, and disapproval of the wearing of hooped skirts in fashionable circles (see section 15), a practice which died out by 1787. A satirical engraving (opposite) by Hieronymus Löschenkohl, c. 1784, pillories the idea of 'upholstery' concealed beneath ladies' skirts and alludes to the current fashion for balloon flights (see Pezzl, section 37), initiated in France by Montgolfier, Blanchard and others and including an abortive attempt by Stuwer in Vienna.*

19–25 *View of the Neuer Markt, with the Schwarzenberg Palace in the background, partially hidden by the façade of the Mehlgrube, in which Mozart gave subscription concerts and which also served as a ballroom (see Pezzl, section 81). Market stalls were ranged in long rows, offering all kinds of fresh produce. The inset figures show street-sellers from the series published in 1775 based on drawings by Christian Brand. The individuals (from bottom left) are offering: hats, beer mugs and jugs, Italian sausages, lemons, snails and eggs.*

26, 27 *A performance at the Burgtheater* (left), *the principal Viennese theatre where one of the leading actors in the early 1780s was Friedrich Ludwig Schröder* (below), *seen here in the role of Falstaff.*

28 *High Mass celebrated with the accompaniment of an orchestra and solo singers, a practice common in Vienna until banned by Joseph II as part of his religious reforms.*

29, 30 *Two extremes in popular entertainment are represented by the graceful balls held in the large Redoutensaal (as depicted in a coloured engraving of c. 1800), especially during the Carnival season, and (below) the animal-baiting displays put on at the amphitheatre on the outskirts of the city (see Pezzl, section 57).*

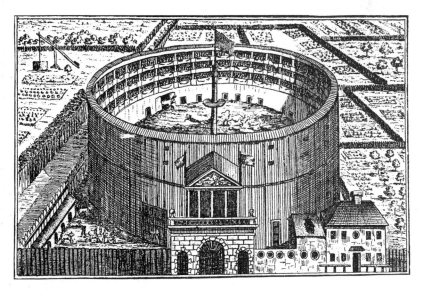

31, 32 *Penal reforms instituted by Joseph II included punishment by public example for a variety of offences, including convictions for prostitution. An engraving by Hieronymus Löschenkohl shows prostitutes having their hair cut off and being led off in groups to sweep the streets (see Pezzl, section 96). In a night-time scene* (left) *illustrating the* Taschenbuch für Grabennymphen auf das Jahr 1787, *prostitutes are shown seeking clients in a Vienna square (see Pezzl, section 126).*

PART TWO: 1786

.[This section, largely devoted to rebutting assertions made by   31
C. F. Nicolai in Berlin, has been omitted.]

The Imperial court in Vienna has its own curious organization,   32   *The Court*
especially under the present government. It differs widely from
the courts at Versailles, St Petersburg and Madrid. . . . [Pezzl
describes the insidious courtiers with 'poison in their breasts
and honey on their lips', who are the power behind many such
courts.]

If you go to Vienna and ask about people of this kind,
nobody will understand you. Neither the monarch nor the
heads of government will tolerate creatures of this sort. Indeed,
there are at this court no positions or titles that would enable
anyone to play the courtier in this conventional sense.

A spectacle of a special sort is revealed by a careful study of the
history of certain European courts, examining how favourites,
women and priests operate within them; how generals are
created and destroyed; how the prince lives so insulated from
his people by courtly surroundings, how he knows his people
so little, and they him, that he might as well be 3,000 miles
away from them.

The nature of the court in Vienna is simplicity itself. The
Emperor is the soul of all his departments; he wants to hear
and see everything personally; he is available to anyone,
regardless of rank or name, nearly every day. Rapid changing
of ministers, secret subversion of the laws of the land, protection
without reason and merit, political jealousies, devious intrigues
and all such petty machinations are matters which are either
unheard of at the court of Vienna or disdained.

This simple and open way of doing things is certainly not
to some people's taste, of course, because it does not suit
everybody either to act or to be treated in a straightforward
manner.

The character of the German nation was always inclined to
be rather serious. It is good that in this matter the court
generates a kind of respect, for such things have an influence
on people's way of thinking.

33   *The Castle*   I will refrain from describing the exterior of the buildings, which, as is well known, is less than impressive.

There was a time when [Francis and Maria Theresa], an Emperor and an Empress with [a family of] sixteen princes and princesses, lived in this castle. One can imagine how many people would have been needed to serve them – the Lord High Stewards, the Lady High Stewards, gentlemen and ladies of the bedchamber, gentlemen and ladies in waiting, etc., etc.; in short, a whole army of castle personnel. One can appreciate what a lively atmosphere there must have been in the Imperial castle. Contemporary eye-witnesses say that it was like a *perpetuum mobile*, a sort of human ant-hill. A few statistics will serve to illustrate the point: every year twelve thousand fathom cords of wood were consumed by the court; and the court stables were filled to capacity by 2,200 horses.

Compared to those times, the castle is a dull place nowadays. With the exception of the hours when church services are held on Sundays, one never sees a living soul in the windows of the middle building on a normal working day, apart from the guardsmen of the three nations [German, Hungarian and Polish, see section 30].

The Emperor is away travelling for nearly half of each year, and when he is in Vienna he resides more frequently at Laxenburg or in the Augarten than in his castle.

Ever since Archduke Francis and Princess Elisabeth began living in a part of the castle [following their marriage in 1788], the place has become livelier again. May it one day return to its former populous state! What a heartening sight for the good Viennese it would be if once again there were to be an Imperial couple blessed with sixteen offspring! In any royal house, a monarch without his better half is always a rather shadowy figure [Joseph II had been a widower since 1767; he became Emperor in his own right on the death of his mother, Maria Theresa, in 1780]. The castle has been the scene of some curious and remarkable events. Here, in 1463, Frederick III was besieged by the citizens of Vienna, and in the end he was so famished that, had it not been for a few chickens smuggled in by a sympathetic student, he might have died of starvation. In 1619, Ferdinand II, saddened by rebellious Bohemians and his other vassals, consoled himself with a crucifix inscribed with the following Latin words: *Ferdinande non te deseram* ['I will not forsake you, Ferdinand']. In 1782, Pope Pius [VI] Braschi spent a month and a half here, and he had that same crucifix in his room. . . .

One of the most interesting parts of the castle is the so-called Controller-Corridor. Anybody who wishes to petition the monarch in person, to seek a favour, to defend his interests, to ask for protection against the peremptory decisions of a petty official, to suggest improvements for a public office, and so on, presents himself here. When the Emperor is in Vienna, one sees him giving over the whole day to granting audiences to all sorts of people. Men with projects, officials in penury, widows, orphans, ex-monks, ex-nuns, officers, factory-owners, farmers – they all address him; most carry a petition in their hand, others address him *viva voce*. Everyone waits expectantly: the door opens, the Emperor comes out, the crowd surrounds him; he is presented with petitions, his all-powerful signature is requested. Anyone having a short, verbal petition says what he has to say right here in the corridor. If his business requires more time, a nearby room is available, and there he can unburden himself in private.

The Emperor repeats this appearance four or five times a day. It is self-evident that not everyone can leave the Controller-Corridor fully satisfied, for what monarch can satisfy all the wishes of his subjects, or attend at once to all their complaints, or comply with all their demands?

Nevertheless, it is a great comfort to know that the monarch can be addressed face to face, even by a person in threadbare clothes or bearing the most unpleasant petition. How many royal houses in Europe are accessible to labourer and first nobleman alike?

34 The Key of a Gentleman of the Bedchamber

[To hold] the I.R. [Imperial Royal] key of a Gentleman of the Bedchamber has long been the ambition of all noble houses who wish to be considered among the oldest and most respected, and this situation will go on growing. The keys were distributed by previous governments in countless numbers. Throughout almost the whole of Europe, and particularly in Germany, one encountered cavaliers wearing the gilt key adorned with the double-headed eagle on the corner of the right-hand coat pocket, who enjoyed the honorary title of an Imperial Gentleman of the Bedchamber, even if they had never laid eyes on either the Emperor or his bedchamber.

This etiquette will gradually fall into disuse. The Emperor

no longer distributes any new keys, and has those already in circulation withdrawn upon the death of their owners. He has thirty-six gentlemen of the bedchamber in actual service, quite sufficient for the performance of necessary duties. Duty periods last for eight days on a twice-yearly basis.

35   *The Police*

A hundred years ago, this department was still hardly known by name. In those days the very idea of the smooth and secret workings of today's police was totally unheard of.

Nowadays the police have earned widespread sympathy. They are not as excessively nasty as the Parisian police and, although some of their procedures have been adopted here, the police still fulfil their duties in the best possible fashion, concerning themselves with order, peace and safety; they look after the necessities of city life; they flush dangerous persons and criminals from their secret lairs; they protect the humble from the insolence of the great. They provide a tolerable support for the needy, the helpless, the abandoned.

Among the police's duties are: the lighting in the city, cleaning the streets, prevention of public quarrels and fisticuffs, supervision of weights and measures, etc., upkeep of pavements [U.S. sidewalks], confiscation of contraband, and so on. . . .

The Director of this department is Herr von Beer, who enjoys the reputation of carrying out his generally unpleasant duties fairly, with magnaminity and humanity. It is a great credit to him, and this is not mere flattery, for public opinion does not confer the same praise on all his subordinates.

He presides over an army of some 150 police inspectors, partly operating within the city limits of Vienna, the rest in Prague, Linz, Graz, Brussels, Trieste, Preßburg, Brünn, Ofen [Pest, now Budapest], Lemberg, Innsbruck, Freiburg, etc. Regular exchanges between him, at the centre, and the others circulate all the news which might affect public security. In vain does the criminal flee from the capital city to a remote province: a warrant for his arrest follows him, and will often have preceded him; hardly has he arrived in some distant Hungarian or Polish small town, than he is identified from the description that has been sent on ahead of him and arrested.

To the corps of police personnel belong about 300 armed militia, each man having a numbered cartridge-pouch by which one can identify him if one has some reason to complain about unfair treatment. Pity that most of these men are somewhat old for the job, which requires agility, strength, courage, cleverness and a great deal of physical stamina to be able to survive both the heat of summer and the extreme cold of winter nights.

In 1783 an official decree ordered that the armed militia be accorded the same status as other military units. In vain: public opinion cannot be swayed just by issuing a decree, and never will it consider the worth of a police battalion equal to that of a field battalion....

It is a disheartening thought for every upright citizen that, in order to fulfil their duties quickly and efficiently, the police of our great cities need to employ a swarm of *mouches* [paid informers]. This vermin penetrates all circles of society..., laying its eggs for preference in restaurants, coffee-houses, traiteurs, gardens... and all places of public recreation....

There is no way to escape from it: it sits at the gambling tables, dances at balls, breakfasts in the Augarten, listens in the theatre, holds bold discourses at soirées, flirts in the chambers of prostitutes, lurks in dirty beer-houses.

It is not as widespread as in Paris, but if a gathering wants to be free of it, those present must be thoroughly checked and their numbers restricted....

Despite this all-knowing, all-registering, all-hearing police activity, there is nevertheless in Vienna a most unconstrained freedom of speech, found not only in private houses, but also in public squares and places.

36 Freedom of Speech

If one compares the free tone that prevails here, in the spoken word as well as on the printed page, with most of the supposedly free states such as Switzerland, Venice, Genoa, etc., one can only laugh heartily at the vaunted claims of those people who imagine themselves to be free. If one considers the timid whispering that goes on in many a small residence of many a small princeling in many a small country, one may count oneself lucky to be living in the capital city of a great and mighty prince....

There are, for sure, good reasons for this situation. The existence of our republics today is extremely precarious: they are weak within and weak without, and a small group of outspoken hotheads can bring disorder to any ill-defended state. And as far as certain princelings are concerned, they often have such petty whims, such petty passions, such petty principles in the conduct of their lives, that they know of no other method of gaining respect than by crowning their actions with pettiness and the suppression of free speech among their subjects.

Things are quite different in a great state. What does the ruler care about the whims of the inhabitants of his capital? ... In the press of several hundreds of thousands, the boldest declamation is a voice crying in the wilderness, which at best provides amusement in a coffee-house and is instantly forgotten, without having made an impression on even a tiny percentage of the public. ...

During the lifetime of the present government, there has been no example of anyone getting into difficulties with the police on account of speaking freely. Without doubt this is the clearest proof of the wise decision taken by the government in this respect. It reflects honour on the government which, if it appreciates its advantage, will continue to adhere to these principles.

The person of the monarch, politics and religion are the three topics on which many a latter-day Demosthenes has come to grief and lost his peace of mind, his fatherland or his liberty. Not so here. Emperor Joseph ignores the ill-tempered shafts directed at his person by some malcontents. Politics are nowadays conducted and planned in such impenetrable secrecy that all those who think they have a special understanding of this science, and hence discuss it, tend to make themselves look ridiculous and to amuse rather than worry the government. As to religion, it is never treated roughly by a sensible man armed with his five senses; and when in some dirty, dark and remote tavern a tipsy individual utters crude and blasphemous remarks, it is obvious that his outburst is due to drink and he is simply regarded as ridiculous by others present.

I wish that freedom of speech will never be subject to more restriction than it is today. Of course there are occasional cases which require that tongues be forcibly silenced – and that obtains in all countries and under all forms of government – but they are few and far between, the result of exceptional circumstances and situations. ...

37   *Curiosity*   [Pezzl suggests that the Viennese share the innate curiosity of the inhabitants of all great cities; the large crowds on the street relish any exceptional occurrence and seem to be fascinated even by trivialities, such is their avid curiosity.]

...The Viennese have often paid a heavy price for their curiosity.... The two most recent hoaxes of this kind were perpetrated in 1784. First, the already wrinkled Hyam, a performer of equestrian feats, promised that on 10 May, after displaying his riding skills he would make three balloons rise, the third carrying a person or, if the winds were unfavourable, a ram. Naturally, he drew big crowds. What happened? First there was a little bubble of a thing the size of a toy balloon, which flew away. Then came the balloon that was supposed to carry a person or a ram into the air; and what was that? A ball of rubber-coated yellow taffeta about five feet in diameter, from which was suspended an empty wooden cage so small that not even a goose would fit inside it.

Later that year, a certain Swiss named Boden promised, in public placards, that on 8 August he would cross the Danube on foot near the Tabor bridge. The novelty of this enterprise attracted large crowds once again. Boden had shoes made of cork; he stepped on to the water, staggered a few steps, lost his balance and fell head over heels into the river. He was pulled out. Trembling and dripping with water, he made a second attempt and fell as before. Then the police had to protect him from the fury of the exasperated crowd.

Who deserves to be exposed to ridicule for such goings-on? Certainly not the curious onlookers. But the police ought to appoint a commissioner to investigate the practical possibilities of the experiments and machines produced by such artists before they are allowed to take money from the people by displaying placards in public places....

There is another kind of curiosity in the empty, idle and blunted brains of certain people, which is vile and despicable. This was manifested in two recent events. In March 1786, a murderer was broken on the wheel. This tragic performance was for the present generation of Viennese something novel: it attracted crowds of people, and not just the riff-raff, but many of the supposedly better class who lay claim to education, honour and intellect. To quote from a pamphlet which appeared at the time: 'The procession to the place of execution was more in the nature of a donkey-train than an exercise of the harshest justice. Our young Cavaliers rode in front of the executioner's waggon and cleared the way with their canes; even ladies on their English steeds crowded round....' [*Über die Wiedereinführung der Todesstrafen* (Concerning the Re-introduction of the

Death Penalty)]. The writer was right to be so blunt concerning this affair....

Alas, the ladies and gentlemen are not to be converted. A few months after that occurrence, a seventy-year-old greybeard of name and rank was condemned to the pillory for embezzlement. And lo and behold, there were the knights in faithful attendance!

The rabble may be forgiven for attending such exhibitions of justice, first because the rabble is what it is, and second because the purpose of justice would be lost if the person being punished is entirely without a public audience, hence deprived of any feelings of shame and repentance.

But what people of higher education and upbringing are doing at such events is difficult to explain. When Damien [the man who attacked Louis XV] was executed, all the windows overlooking the place of execution [in Paris] were rented for 2 *louis d'or* each to the *beau monde*, two months in advance of that most appalling of appalling executions [they burned off Damien's right hand, cut holes all over his body and filled them with boiling lead, and pulled him to pieces with four horses, having first severed his tendons]. Alas, that is what happened. But such ill-breeding in Paris does not excuse the same behaviour among the Viennese.

I can imagine two reasons why people of a certain standing should want to attend such displays: either they actually enjoy the sufferings of their fellow-men or they require such living examples for their morale. In both cases I pity them just as much as the guilty person, and I despise the first more than the second.

38
Extravagance and Expenditure

Other times, other opinions.... Twenty years ago the court here was all in favour of promoting extravagance and expenditure in every possible way.

He [Emperor Francis Stephen] himself set a shining example. Feasts, gala days, gambling, countless personnel, lavish salaries and pensions, pleasure trips and outings, and a certain liberal generosity when it came to giving, in royal fashion, rewards for services rendered – all this was characteristic of the Austrian court. Everyone who moved in that circle was affected in some way; these were the good times.

The nobility followed the court's example; and since there were many extremely well endowed families among the aristocracy, they could afford to do so. Every great house in Vienna set up its own small court, in which magnificence, extravagance, luxury and a permanent state of gratification and pleasure obtained. This side of the Viennese nobility was generally regarded with astonishment throughout Europe, and was imported into foreign courts by our ambassadors and business people. There was almost no limit to the splendour of the aristocracy, displayed at [Imperial] elections, coronations, marriages, etc. held in Frankfurt and Vienna.

... Today [1786] the outward appearance of the court has totally changed: its watchword is economy [see section 44]. There is no longer any question of grand, noisy celebrations and, all in all, the court makes no impression as far as expenditure is concerned. Except for Corpus Christi [see section 149] and the Feast of St Stephen [26 December], when the Emperor (if he is here) shows himself in a kind of state procession, one would hardly be aware of his presence in Vienna at all, were it not for his occasional appearance in a two-horse chaise painted green, driving to the Augarten. ...

If the court, by its reduction of expenditures, had intended to set an example for the nobility to follow, one is bound to admit that this expectation has been only partially fulfilled. It is common knowledge that there are about a dozen princely houses in Vienna each having average yearly expenditures in excess of 200,000 gulden; indeed, there are among them some, like the Li[e]chtenstein, Esterházy, Schwarzenberg, Dietrichstein and Lobkowitz families, which disburse sums ranging from 300,000 to 700,000 gulden. The rest, less wealthy, spend between 80,000 and 150,000 gulden.

To the princely households must be added the much greater number of those belonging to counts, who spend between 50,000 and 80,000 gulden p.a., as well as an even greater number who spend annually between 20,000 and 50,000 gulden. Some families first ennobled as barons under Maria Theresa were able, during the Empress's difficult wars, to amass great sums through commerce, supplying the army and entering into all kinds of other important transactions; and they now enjoy this money in peace and comfort. And finally there are the houses of agents, bankers and businessmen whose annual expenses run to some 10,000 to 12,000 gulden.

Which categories of expenses in these grand houses call for the greatest outlay, it is difficult to say. The categories are: the table, clothing, horses, servants, pleasure-parties. . . . If in such a house the table costs 30,000 gulden annually, the upkeep of the stables would amount to 24,000. If one prince rides out with a retinue of eight to ten persons, another will own diamond-studded buckles on his shoes worth 30,000 and wear a pair of watch-chains set with brilliants worth 18,000 gulden. If a countess receives the latest fashion designs every post-day from Paris, it is likely that each week she will give a grand *souper*, put on a concert, or take an excursion, etc. . . .

Anybody without at least 20,000 gulden to spend each year makes no impression in Vienna; that is, he can live quite comfortably, but receives no attention. . . .

In general one can say that today the main expenses for men are their horses and, for the ladies, the dressing table. Playing for high stakes is becoming very rare, and the dinner table is notable more for its modern delicacies than for being overladen, as used to be the habit.

39   A Great House

. . . In Holland, Switzerland and the Holy Roman Empire, there is many a burgomaster whose entire staff consists of a manservant and a maid: the first is valet, lackey, runner and porter all rolled into one; on Sundays he follows his master to church wearing a livery with wide sleeves, and on Monday he splits wood; the girl acts as chambermaid, cook, washerwoman, and so on, as circumstances require. In those lands nobody considers that the person of the burgomaster or the alderman could deserve or require more respect and more servants, and in those states such a situation is quite accepted. . . . But in Vienna a grand gentleman has to live quite differently, and here that is considered appropriate.

I shall not describe one of the very great princely households, but one of more modest dimensions, on a par with the establishment of a wealthy count. If this family does not own a house in town, it must expect to pay at least 5,000 gulden in rent. The mistress of the house requires two lady's maids, a *valet-de-chambre*, a wardrobe-maid, two chambermaids, a parlour-maid, a scullery-maid, a runner and three flunkeys. The master of the house has a secretary, a valet, lackeys, huntsmen, runners, hussar bodyguards and two flunkeys. For the general running of the house there are: a major-domo, a man in charge of table-linen and silver, two manservants for cleaning the rooms, two porters, a concierge or gate-keeper. The kitchen

staff includes a chef, a confectioner, a pastry-cook, a master of
the roasts, together with the usual complement of kitchen hands,
pot-cleaners, kitchen-servers, scullery-maids, and so on.

The stables call for a master-of-the-horse, a riding master,
two coachmen, two postillions, two outriders, two grooms, four
stable-boys, etc. They are responsible for: one parade carriage,
two travelling coaches, sundry carriage-horses, chaise-ponies,
five or six riding horses, three or four hacks and some work-
horses, etc.

Three different kinds of table are prepared daily; one for
the lords and ladies, one for the so-called house officers [as
Kapellmeister in the Esterházy household, Joseph Haydn was
classified as a house officer], and one for the servants.

The best-paid posts are those of major-domo and chef (also
known as the Controller [of the kitchen]). They act as buyers
for all the usual necessities of the household, and do the
bookkeeping: the great families in Vienna are generous, and
are not difficult or strict overseers. It is thought that there are
a total of 20,000 male and female household servants in Vienna,
and this figure is surely not exaggerated. . . .

40 Consumption of Wood

[Pezzl states that Vienna's heating requirements are mostly
provided by burning wood. The Viennese hardly realize that
other fuels exist, and Pezzl wishes they could continue burning
wood, but forecasts, quite correctly, that fifty years hence things
will be different, by which he is presumably suggesting that
coal is the fuel of the future.]

Vienna requires 300,000 fathom cords of wood every year,
most of which is transported by water. . . . There are many
households which consume a whole cord of wood every day
throughout the winter. In one particular great princely household 650 cords were consumed between May 1784 and May
1785; . . . 100 stoves were in daily use in the cold months.

Two years ago, wood had a fixed price. H.M. the Emperor,
who prefers a free economy to operate in every aspect of business
and commerce, removed controls on the price of wood in order
to bring the price down through competition. But this good
intention was not realized, and since a higher tax was imposed,
the price of wood has risen. A cord of hard wood costs at
present – January 1787 – 8 fl. 30 kr., soft wood 5 fl.

[Pezzl points out that more trees are being felled than can
be replaced; in the last 100 years the price of wood has risen

tenfold. The Viennese seem not to realize that in countries like Holland and England peat, anthracite, straw, etc., are also used for heating. These alternatives, Pezzl notes, do not produce such a pleasant or healthy warmth as wood, and he asserts that 'London is shrouded all year round in its coal fog'. He concludes by expressing the hope that Vienna may long be spared this stench.]

41 *Banknotes*

... In Vienna this kind of paper money is called 'Banco-Zettel' [banknote]. In June 1785, all old banknotes were called in and new notes valued at twenty million [gulden] were put into circulation. The smallest denomination of these notes is 5 gulden, followed by those for 10, 25, 50, 100, 500 and 1,000 gulden (the largest denomination).

These notes were formerly in circulation only in the German Crown Lands, in Hungary and in Bohemia; since the new ones were introduced, they circulate also in Galicia [Poland] and in Lombardy.

From the first the public did not take to these notes, and because merchants in particular tried to avoid accepting them, the court issued a decree requiring business people to pay half their taxes in banknotes. Although this law is still in force, it is no longer necessary, because merchants have come to realize how useful the notes are, better for mailing than coins....

[Although great care was taken to print the notes in such a way that they would be more difficult to forge than previously, and although counterfeiting was punishable by death, there were soon forgers at work again. The court had announcements published in the press offering a reward of 1,000 gulden in cash to anyone who identified a forger, plus immunity for the informer if also implicated in the crime.]

42 *Changes*

[In this section Pezzl traces one of the changes that occurred after Joseph II began to reign alone in 1780, following his mother's death: beforehand bigoted persons could profit from their hypocritical actions; they received titles, positions and even money; they also persecuted those who did not agree with them. With the introduction of Joseph's reforms, however, these Tartuffe-like figures began to disappear and lose all their evil influence.]

... It has been often and seriously suggested that the theatre serves as a school for manners. I am not able to determine its former influence; but in our own age it is certainly not that. But if any theatre were to have an influence on the morals of the public, that would be true of our National Theatre, for it is always well attended, despite having suffered the considerable and deeply regretted loss of the much-loved Katharine [*sic*] Jacquet and of [Friedrich Ludwig] Schröder [Katharina Jacquet died in 1786, Schröder left Vienna in 1785].

Without wanting in any way to underrate the splendid services of most theatre personnel, I declare [the actor Franz Carl] Brockman[n] [in 1786 a member of the original cast of Mozart's *Der Schauspieldirektor*] to be my hero. Everybody has his own preference, so why should I not have mine? But I prefer my Brockman[n] in comic roles... In tragic roles, especially in foreign costumes, his talent (although always great) is not so striking.

The English, after 250 years, have still not grown tired of repeating their original Shakespeare plays. Also the French, after nearly 150 years, continue to perform the plays of Corneille, Racine and Molière, even though some of the latter's works have lost much of their interest nowadays because the original characters he portrays have disappeared from our present-day world. Compared to these nations, we Germans are far less fortunate. We have no playwright who has written so many and such excellent pieces that one can fill a stage with his works one after another for a fortnight. Lessing, Goethe, Weiße, Großmann, etc. have each written two, at the most three, excellent pieces. – The masterpieces of monstrosity by Klinger, Lenz, Schiller etc. are (as you might expect) banned. – The mediocre pieces by Stephanie, Schröder, Bock, Brühl, Wezel, Jünger etc. can be performed quite tolerably once or twice, but that is all. Altogether the German public seems to hanker after greater variety than do its neighbours.

To encourage playwrights, the well-known device has been introduced here, whereby box-office receipts for the third performance of a new play are given to the writer. If the house is well attended, the poet can earn some 500 gulden, because he receives nothing at all from all the boxes and other seats which have been subscribed for the entire year. However, for a whole year he receives free entrance to the noble parterre [front stalls]. Of course one has to realize that [a fee of] 100 ducats [450 fl.] is not going to command any masterpieces of genius, but this honorarium (the usual one for a play) is still quite respectable.

It is a pleasure to sit in the parterre before the curtain goes up. The members of high society are present in their finery, their expression pleasing and agreeable, in keeping with the well-known maxim: *Spectatum veniunt, spectentur ut ipsae* ['They come to see and to be seen']. All around, a collection of notable men: ministers, whose mien speaks of important plans, generals with scars gained in fighting for the fatherland. To see these people and especially everyone who otherwise wears a serious expression suggesting a preoccupation with affairs, shedding their troubles and laughing, flirting, teasing, joking, amidst a group of friends – that is something I treasure as much as seeing the actual spectacle on the stage.

A part of the parterre [audience] has adopted a mean and nasty habit which verges on the insolent. When, during a play, derogatory remarks are made about the aristocracy, these empty-headed people applaud. Now everyone knows that there are some aristocratic creatures who have behaved in a silly way (and perhaps *are* silly), but taken as a whole the class is honourable. Therefore, dear Viennese public, respect the nobility; consider that it is largely responsible for your livelihood, protects you against foreign enemies and on the whole increases your prosperity.

Ten years ago the theatre was an altar, before which everyone of good taste burned incense. This religion emanated particularly from Gotha and Hamburg. Plays and playwrights were made out to be so important that the world's well-being depended on them: medals were struck in their honour, people wrote books about them by the thousand, drama was the sole topic of discussion, and actors and actresses saw themselves as utterly indispensable to the state. This paroxysm is now past; nowadays the theatre is judged to be no more and no less than what it really is – a pleasant, decent and tasteful amusement.

44 Concerning Love

[Pezzl speaks of love in olden times, when knights slew giants and dragons and tilted at windmills to win a lady's favours. At the beginning of the (18th) century, this kind of romantic love was still a powerful force: people married for imagined happiness and the physical charms of this or that modest but pretty girl. The last sparks of this kind of romantic love were to be seen in the preceding decade in some corners of Germany. It was particularly suited to Protestant theological candidates growing up in a stiff German town. Even this madness has now disappeared; it never took root in Vienna or in any large city where one knew the ways of the world and how to live.]

All the same, so-called true love is not entirely unknown here. It is to be encountered frequently among the middle and lower classes and among poorer people. The lowlier servants of average-sized and smaller houses also tend the flame of old-fashioned love, but less assiduously than the young sons and daughters of minor artisans. These children of nature, who have no concept of what so-called prosperity is, and whose impulses are, with the exception of the Sixth Commandment ['Thou shalt not commit adultery'], unfettered, enjoy the delights of love without inhibition and to their hearts' content. When they have chosen each other, they go around hand-in-hand and, unsupervised and unconstrained, are to be seen together on the dance floor, out walking, in the gardens or in the taverns. Their parents, far from standing in their way, are pleased that they have found each other and spend Sundays and holidays together. And if things get too serious, well, the priest comes and joins them; all their cousins, aunts and uncles, and godparents help them gain a livelihood; and thus they (as it were) live happily ever after.

Things are quite different in elevated social classes: there, love has disappeared. For such people, all attachments are determined by calculating fathers or ambitious mothers, and the young pair are simply the means by which the parents realize their intentions. If it happens that a couple from the great noble houses comes together through a genuine reciprocal attraction, this is a very rare exception to the general rule.

People from the middle class, from the lesser nobility and the families of councillors, seek from love and the ensuing marriage either a position, or capital, which will enable them to live comfortably. Since these intentions are quite open, and the bride fully realizes that matters turn not on her person, but on an important matter of secondary interest, she entertains no illusions about her husband's true affections and is in no wise disappointed in her expectations. She marries him because by doing so she can become a matron, live more easily and be mistress of the house ... where she reigns and where she may also cause infinite confusion; but now she has the choice of a lover who will provide compensation for her husband's bored indifference.

All in all, that grand passionate love – a principal occupation of our grandfathers – has become invisible in our age. The common man, who occasionally still loves, finds in the goodhearted kindness of his girl everything he could wish for. The man of more refined tastes does not know the former explosion of love, he is never motivated by it sufficiently to indulge in those outbreaks of wild passions which sometimes still occur in smaller towns. No Viennese of fine society will ever play the Werther [in Goethe's play of thwarted love and suicide] or the Tarquinius. For many years now we have never had more than the very occasional case of jealous love; one such as an apothecary who blew himself up because his lady bestowed her favours on another.

[Pezzl concludes that the Viennese considers it ridiculous to treat love as a major occupation or an intellectual pursuit. A woman deserves attention if she bestows on men the literal gift of love, but if she thinks this entitles her to consider men as her slaves, the tools of her whims and fancies, she is mad and ought to be consigned to the realm of fiction.]

45 Gallantry

Gallantry, flirtation (or what the Austrians call 'spooning') has taken the place of love among the *beau monde* and in fine society. Today the great passions of women of the upper classes are, I believe, roughly in order of importance as follows: vanity, jealousy, distraction, love-making, etc.

Vanity occupies the first place, that is agreed. Any man who is able to satisfy its demands consistently and urgently can be assured of displacing any rival for the affections of his goddess. Another axiom is that a lover who owns carriages and horses is more successful in conquering his lady love's heart than any pedestrian.

Chloë seeks the most energetic exponent of the German dance, Emilie the most tenacious gambler, Daphne the latest fashions, Philine the best boxes in the theatre, Amarante precedence at balls, and so forth. If you can play the fiddle to those tunes, good for you! You will receive the lady's favours in preference to twenty others whose merits are no more than the dubious advantages of a good head and a stout heart.

One of the sweetest shows of vanity among some ladies is collecting as many slaves as possible, harnessing them to their triumphal carts and parading them in the pleasure-haunts and theatres. Since Vienna has never lacked for a host of empty-headed individuals with nothing better to do than amuse themselves dawdling at the dressing table or in a box at the theatre with the ladies, or who can offer them an arm in the Augarten or the Belvedere,... there has never been a shortage of such creatures. This situation soon gives rise to perjury; they tear themselves away from one carriage so that they can be harnessed to another, secrets are passed on in whispers, and at least half of them are believed because it is thought the game must be worth the candle.

Naturally, because of this capricious vanity, men have had to become accustomed to the inconstancy and disdain shown them by women, which is nowadays all the rage among a certain class of people. Since it is evident that one is simply dealing with puppets, teasing them and playing with them is all anyone wishes to do. One flatters their whims for a while until one has achieved one's objective; then one laughs over the vain little creature and leaps out of her arms into those of the next one, where the same game is played over again, with the same conclusion...

Thanks to our malleable morals, our inclination to laugh at everything, our refined way of thinking, we have been freed from the desperation of unrequited love.... Nowadays there is no more pathetic figure than a languishing lover. If you lust after the one with the turned-up nose, or the one with the willowy figure, or the one with the talent for flirtatious teasing, or the one with the gift of revealing her feelings, or simply a neat foot, an undulating bosom – well then, take the plunge, kindle the flame of your goddess's vanity and satisfy it. You've won her. But avoid worshipping her too long at the same altar, for if you are unstylish enough not to look for a change soon, you might get on your goddess's nerves; withdraw before you both get bored; excite her jealousy and you will be able to knock on the same door again if that is your fancy; on the other hand, once boredom sets in, the bonds are broken for ever.

[Such conduct, continues Pezzl, means that any girl of unimpeachable virtue can remain completely safe. If she doesn't want to give in, one leaves her alone, silently admiring her virtue, and moves on....] Acts of violence, absconding with girls and the like, which were not infrequent in previous centuries, are things for which it is no longer necessary to mete out hideous punishments: we are more broad-minded and gallantry has contrived to alleviate emotional strains and fulfil our desires.

But woe betide a well-known flirt if she suddenly decides to become a prude! Her punishment is general mockery....

46
Reduction in the Number of Marriages

...The number of marriages has declined generally: any geographer or statistician can demonstrate this with the aid of birth- and marriage-certificates. This situation is particularly applicable to large cities, and is a fate that has also befallen Vienna.

What has given rise to this unnatural state of affairs? Some factors are clear enough for anybody to observe: women's vanity, their love of finery, their endless search for amusement, their infinite needs as they imagine them – all these have made many a man steer clear of the joys of the marital bed. In such fashion does the female sex bring punishment upon itself, thanks to its own exaggerated vanity! On the other hand, many women are held back from marrying because of the curtailments and uncertainties of pensions. Some positions in the houses of the great are subject to a condition that those who hold them remain single. A significant number of people in this situation remain unmarried, as also do artists and others not bound by bourgeois values.

Finally, the fact that our marriages cannot be dissolved is also a warning signal for many a man who loves his peace of mind and health. Unfortunately, the holy sacrament is like a lucky dip: for every one success there are nineteen misses.... The only method of solving these marital problems – namely a dissolution of the marriage – is utterly inadequate and badly calculated. The two dissatisfied partners separate and, not being allowed to remarry, live in a condition of suspense, and their uncomfortable, depressing loneliness drives them to new states of confusion.

Maria Theresa was well known for her strong advocacy of marriage. She was as severe in dealing with non-sacramental enjoyment of love as she was a supporter of that sanctified by the sacraments. She conferred many a position and many a pension simply in order to bring a loving couple to the marriage bed. She also did more than merely provide the languishing maiden with a husband or the love-sick young man with a wife: she cared for the whole world of impecunious young things who entered her sphere of influence: it is common knowledge that she paid for the upkeep of more than 3,000 needy children.

It is an undeniable fact that certain ordinances in our national economy have contributed to the reduction in the number of marriages; and that with a certain amount of not very great sacrifices, this situation could be improved quite easily.

47
*Wrong
Conclusions*

While admitting this, there may be many people who would see no great advantages arising from a greatly increased number of marriages in the city, in that the resulting children would constitute a generation of frail weaklings, some born with incurable diseases; by contrast, the population in country areas would provide the real flower of the nation.

This assertion is true, but the conclusions that have been drawn from it are false. it is well known that in great cities the number of deaths exceeds the number of births [see section 12], and that the resulting loss of population must be made up by importing people from the country. The fewer the marriages that take place in the capital, the greater the number of people who must be imported from the country. The weakling born in the city is in truth a pitiful specimen, yet strong enough for the city's needs; and if the numbers of urban weaklings are insufficient to fill essential positions, then it becomes necessary to introduce more robust people from rural areas, and they in turn are permanently lost to agriculture and the country population.

The population of the city must have its full complement, and it is therefore a matter of no little importance whether a thousand people, more or less, are born there each year, because their numbers may have to be made up from outside by a thousand country folk, who are thereby obliged to renounce forever the furrow and the plough and thus deprive the country of their strong hands and healthy progeny....

A dwelling is one of the most expensive and most important considerations in Vienna.

48
*Dwellings and
Rented Lodgings*

The largest private building within the *Linie* is the Starhemberg free-house which stands outside the Kärntnertor, as one approaches the suburb of Wieden. Emperor Leopold donated to Count Rüdiger Starhemberg, as a reward for his courageous defence of Vienna against the Turks, the land on which the house stands, removing the building from the customary jurisdiction of the City Magistracy, and granting it freehold status exempt in perpetuity from all tithes and taxes. It is a highly important part of Vienna, for although the façade on the street side does not appear to be very extensive and the house is only two storeys high, experts maintain that it is large enough to accommodate at least 3,000 people. At present this house provides its owner with an annual income of 15,000 gulden, and thus it is worth as much as many a county within the Holy Roman Empire.

There are several other stone counties of this kind in Vienna. The Trattner House is known to earn as much money as, for example, the principality of Hechingen in Swabia. A house for a cavalier's family of the first or second rank costs 5,000 to 6,000 gulden p.a. And a house of the same size which is arranged not just for one large family to live in, but is divided into several apartments for middle-class and bourgeois people, brings in even more. For this reason people who have purchased monasteries that have been dissolved do not turn such buildings into magnificent palaces, but convert them to provide fifty or so bourgeois dwellings, workshops and stalls....

The larger bourgeois houses on the Graben, the Kohlmarkt, Hof, Stock-im-Eisen-Platz or in the Kärntnerstraße yield 6,000 to 8,000 gulden each year. A mere shop on the Graben or the Kohlmarkt costs 700 to 900 gulden in rent. An ordinary dwelling for a family owning one carriage and two horses, situated on the first or second floor, in an average street, costs 800 to 1,100 gulden.

If I am not mistaken, it was Emperor Charles V who introduced, from Spain, the practice that every householder was obliged to make available his second [U.S. third] floor *gratis* for the billeting of court officials. This custom persisted until Maria Theresa's death and was for male and female favourites at court a rich source of gifts, because the more extravagant the favour granted, the more attractive the apartment received. The Emperor [Joseph II] removed this obligation, so onerous to the house-owners, and substituted an annual levy in cash, a system by which all house-owners profited, however, most by half, some by as much as two thirds, because although they now have to pay the court some 300 gulden for the apartment, they rent it out for 700.

The ground floor of almost all houses in Vienna is not lived in, but serves as space for shops, taverns, stables, workshops, storage places, apothecaries, coffee-houses, etc. The floors below street level [i.e. cellars] are not counted, only those above the first flight of stairs. The first [U.S. second] floor, although enjoying the advantage of being reached by only one flight of stairs, is not considered the best part of the house because the rooms are harder to heat on account of the vaulted [sometimes empty] ground floor below, also because they are affected by dust from the street, the smells of stables and sewers, and the noise of wheeled vehicles passing outside or entering and leaving the house [courtyard]; furthermore, in the narrower streets these apartments receive the least daylight and are more expensive in terms of lighting costs.

The second [U.S. third] floor is considered the most comfortable [as in Mozart's flat in the Camesina-House in the Domgasse], hence the dearest. On this basis rent payments decrease the higher one mounts: the more stairs you climb, the cheaper it gets, the better the air and the finer the views; but it is hard work carrying the necessities of life, wood, water, etc. to these heavenly heights, and while the number of steps brings a reduction in rent, it increases the price to be paid for delivery of goods carried up 150 steps ten times a day.

Anyone wanting to stay a few weeks in Vienna looks for a room to rent on the second day after arriving. Handwritten notices (mostly with abominable orthography) hang on the doors of many houses all year round, advertising whole apartments or single rooms and small chambers. These notices are at their most numerous for fourteen days after St George's Day [23 April] and fourteen days after Michaelmas [29 September], the two dates on which it is customary for half the city to change quarters. Anyone without a family who wishes to live cheaply takes a single room. In the city the cheapest price for rooms on the first, second and third floors is 1 ducat monthly. For that you get a little room, 120 square feet in area, containing a bed, a chest of drawers, a rickety table and a pair of old chairs: the only view is into an airless courtyard or a narrow street. If you desire a room with two windows looking on to an airy street, equipped with some furniture and a proper entrance, you will not find one for less than 2 ducats a month. The maidservant of the house, who makes the bed, cleans the room, and possibly also prepares breakfast, earns 8 groschen per month. All these prices apply only to the city proper; in the suburbs everything is at least a third cheaper.

In the top floors of city buildings, in garrets and in attics, nestle the poorest type of tailors, copyists, gilders, music copyists, wood-carvers, painters, and so on, who require a great deal of regular light to do their work. These attic floors are often crawling with hordes of children, whose numbers and constant requirements often worry the poor father to the same extent as the rich and distinguished man living on the second floor below has his worries about not being able to find a sole heir for his family.

49
Wine-cellars

When the poor man who has spent whole days in his attic, sometimes half a week at a time, hard at work and with only his wife and children for company, manages to scrape together a few groschen, he climbs down in the evening from his tower to the street, stands for a while under the street door watching the passing crowd and then descends another thirty steps to a wine-cellar below street level.

The usual wine-cellar in Vienna also serves as a tavern, where the lower classes gather in the evenings to eat their supper. You sit ten ells under the street in a bomb-proof subterranean vault, where candles are always burning. The atmosphere of this den is filled with the smell of wine, so that you absorb wine not just from the glass, but through the nose and throat, which means that the guests in these cellars become tipsy much sooner than they do elsewhere. Wine is sold from 6 to 16 kreuzer the *Maß* [about a quart], and cheese, cold fish, sausages, etc. are also served. The tapsters are dirty louts smelling of wine-dregs, whose complexions are either copper-red or deathly white because they are swimming in wine and hardly ever get out into the fresh air.

The best known of these cellars is the one beneath the Tuchlauben [a street], the so-called Seizerkeller, which used to belong to a monastery and is now the property of a wealthy citizen. Here one sits between enormous vats fitted with iron hoops as wide as a man's fist, and if, all of a sudden, those hoops were to give way, their contents would flood the entire cellar and drown the guests in a lake of red and white wine. The cellar guardians seem to have fallen out with the sun; they never see its light, but live in omnipresent darkness in their underground labyrinth of wine.

Every year some 18,000 candles are burned in this cellar.

In Vienna almost as much beer is drunk as wine – something one would hardly expect in the capital city of a wine-producing country, such as Lower Austria is. There must be some truth in what many people maintain: since they don't want a hot meal in the evening, they have only to choose between a glass of wine or a glass of beer, either of which is served with a piece of bread accompanied by cheese, cold meat or the like. The cheapest wine costs as much as medium-priced beer; this wine, at 6 kreuzer the *Maß*, is (as you can well imagine) rather tart and sour. Instead of satisfying you, it actually increases your hunger because of its biting and gnawing force, and it makes you feel hot and thirsty in the night. By contrast, an identical amount of beer gives you more nourishment and with its soporific ingredients promotes a deep and peaceful sleep. And in this knowledge people consume, especially in the summer months, much more beer than wine.

Actually, it is not just the neediest class that eschews the wine and congregates in the beer-houses; though they might prefer a glass of wine, lackeys, students, artists, office workers, average citizens also spend their evenings in beer-houses, which, as a result, are much better furnished than wine-cellars. Some of them have damask wall-coverings and are fitted out with marble tables, mirrors on the walls and chandeliers of crystal glass.

Together with the coffee-houses, these beer-houses are the haunts for political discussion. Those frequenting them fancy they know something of the cabinet's mood, and the less they understand about the world's affairs, the more they try to put matters to rights... alliances are formed, fleets sail out of harbours, armies march, potentates die or go on travels, and so on. The livelier the discussions, the better the beer tastes.

There are vast numbers of these houses. When they removed the tax on wine, but not on beer, this was presumably to reduce the consumption of the latter, and to woo the Austrians back to their natural drink: wine.

50 *Beer-houses*

The Emperor, who in the course of his many travels has examined everything that is worthy of the attention of a thinking person and especially of a monarch, during his stay in Paris visited the school of Abbé l'Epée, and decided to create a similar institution in his own capital; and this he did.

51
Institution for the Deaf and Dumb

119

The institution now consists, thanks to the Emperor, of three houses. The home for the deaf and dumb, on the Dominican Square, bears an inscription [with the date 1784]....

The institution's director and leading teacher is Herr Stork, secular priest. The number of deaf-and-dumb pupils to be educated *gratis* has been fixed by H.M. at thirty... Anyone seeking a place for a deaf-and-dumb pupil over and above this number pays a modest annual fee of 100 gulden for bed, board, clothing, education and everything else.

[There follows further description of the organization, some criticism of the subjects being taught, e.g. speculative questions in religion, and a description of the printing plant installed for the pupils. Pezzl wonders, moreover, why they have to go to morning prayers at 7 o'clock followed by chapel: 'Why the daily attendance at Mass when they have already said their prayers at home?', he asks. Similar criticism is made concerning a daily walk lasting an hour, which Pezzl considers a waste of time for anybody who will earn a living by manual work. In a footnote he adds: 'The daily walks have been reduced to three times a week, but daily attendance at Mass still continues, despite well-intentioned reminders.']

52
*The General
Seminary*

[In former times priests were able to live, teach and preach unfettered by any outside influences. In line with Joseph II's reforms, and to force the priesthood into a system supervised by the state, general seminaries were established; that in Vienna, founded by the Emperor in 1783, was housed in the buildings of the former Jesuit academic college. Seminarists must spend five years here; apart from theoretical studies, one of the activities on which special emphasis is placed is preaching.]

53
*The General
Hospital*

In the suburb known as Alstergasse [Alservorstadt today] stands the largest of all public or private buildings in the whole of Vienna. It bears the superscription: 'Saluti et Solatio/ Aegrorum./Josephus II. 1784'. Formerly there were several hospitals in various parts of Vienna. They were all merged to form this single centre. The extent of its buildings is enormous: it contains several courtyards, some with rows of linden [lime] trees, and accommodates up to 3,000 patients, each with his or her own bed, together with the necessary doctors, nurses, etc. [This impressive building still serves its original purpose; see ill. 9.]

Anyone with the means to pay is charged the following fees during his stay in this hospital: first class, 1 gulden daily; second class, $\frac{1}{2}$ gulden; third, 10 kreuzer. A person bringing a note from the parish priest and district magistrate certifying his or her genuine poverty receives treatment *gratis*.

Those competent to judge the hospital's appointments, sick-nursing, cleanliness, etc. unanimously consider them to be of the highest possible standards, and the pharmacy to be fully and excellently equipped. The general administrator and director is Doctor [Joseph von] Quarin, well known for his publications and his achievements. Maximilian Stoll, one of the greatest doctors alive today in Europe, gives his seminars at the patients' bedsides, teaching physicians and surgeons....

Associated with the General Hospital is a lying-in section. At last they have rid themselves of the old prejudice about a girl who in the throes of a love affair commits an indiscretion but whose reward for so doing is to present the state with a citizen; in the old days such a girl was publicly repudiated and left alone to suffer her desperation and uncertainty. This lying-in house is excellently appointed: the embarrassed girl can, if she wishes, enter veiled and using an assumed name; she can become a mother anonymously and leave anonymously. Viennese girls seem to take full advantage of this institution: in the first year of its existence some 800 children were born there.

In another corner of the hospital is the newly built Insane Tower. [While pitying the plight of the insane, confined to the tower, Pezzl criticizes the fact that, for those on the mend, the small inner courtyard is too small as a place for outdoor exercise, and comments that a small garden or an open grassed area would be of immense benefit.]

In Vienna, no corpse may be buried until it has been examined by a judicial commission. This commission, which consists of a physician and a surgeon, is called *Todten-Schau* [Post-Mortem Examination]. Every doctor must, on the death of a patient, leave a written description of the manner of his death, which the commission then considers. This very useful institution has the following principal duties: it decides what is to be done with the bed and clothes of the deceased. If death was the result of a suspicious illness, it has the bed taken away and either burned or thoroughly cleaned; or the relatives are given instructions about what should be done with it. This board

**54
*Coroner's Office
and Lists of
the Deceased***

examines the corpses of those who have died suddenly when not under a doctor's care, to discover whether the deceased might have been given an overdose of sedatives, or met with a violent death of some kind. Likewise, it investigates whether children may have died through neglect or malice on the part of the parents. Where the deceased can be shown to have been murdered, or to have drowned, or been asphyxiated, it takes the necessary steps.

Each day a list of deaths is ... published in the *Wiener Zeitung* [cf. section 101]; for each person listed the information includes name, rank, the district of the city, house number and terminal illness. Since the population of the suburbs greatly outnumbers that of the city, and since the hospitals are located in the suburbs and most of the poor and needy reside there, it is natural that deaths occurring in the suburbs are always far more numerous than in the city. Generally, the number of deaths on any one day ranges from seven to a maximum of thirty-six.

The most avid readers of the lists of deaths are those with rich aunts, uncles or other relatives with whom they are not on good terms and therefore do not visit personally. These impatient souls peruse the black lists for months on end; eventually they find the right name and are immediately reconciled, then they go and collect their share of ducats and wish the deceased everlasting life.

55   Burials

An old and misconceived practice was the burial of the dead in churches and cemeteries in the middle of populous cities: Pour honorer les morts, on tue les vivans ['They kill the living to honour the dead'].

Actually, such places must have exuded fumes which could only be extremely unhealthy for the mourners, especially for large crowds in the warm season. Moreover, the pride of the rich and the pious folly of zealous Christians in particular had turned the whole affair into a point of honour and salvation. Some wanted to perpetuate their memory after their deaths by means of handsome gravestones; others thought that lying in consecrated ground near a church, sometimes with a little candle or lamp, and being sprinkled with holy water could not fail to hasten their arrival in heaven.

A healthy respect for the laws of nature finally, if extremely slowly, overcame the old beliefs. The burial places were transferred outside the city to more spacious and airy suburban locations. But ten thousand corpses each year still continued to create a disgusting amount of putrefaction among several hundred thousand of the living, and in 1784 something took place which should have happened long before. Several cemeteries were established beyond the *Linie*, in open fields, so that the bodies of all who died in Vienna could be brought there, except for deceased members of the Imperial family, whose bodies are placed in the crypt of the Capuchin Monastery in the Neumarkt, and of wealthy vassals, who generally have their dead removed to family vaults on their estates in Austria, Bohemia, Moravia, Hungary, and so on.

Moreover, there is nothing to stop anybody from being speeded to paradise with the bells of the whole of Vienna and its suburbs, if he considers it good for his soul; and he can order as many masses and requiems as he thinks necessary for his salvation. But in the evening the black-shrouded hearse comes and places him next to the poor worker for whom no paternoster was said.

It is well known that wood is very costly in Vienna, and the ten thousand coffins required for the dead each year use up large amounts of that commodity, which rots in the earth to no one's advantage. In order to conserve wood and to speed the decomposition of the dead, the Emperor ordered at the end of 1784 that every corpse should be sewn inside a linen sack and thus lowered into the ground.

No decree aroused such general displeasure as did this one. The resident Greeks first protested against it, saying that it was contrary to their rite. In Bohemia, Moravia, etc., people even considered emigrating. Some foreign manufacturers, who were considering settling in the Austrian states, stipulated as a condition of their immigration that they be allowed to be buried in coffins. This general dissatisfaction finally persuaded H.M. to accede to these prejudices, and to allow burials to take place in accordance with former practices.... [An Imperial decree along these lines, issued early in January 1785, is quoted *in extenso*.]

[They enjoy a short life-expectancy and sprout like poisonous mushrooms.]...Between April 1784 and April 1785 I counted about twenty-two new periodical publications, none of which survived a full year. Indeed, some survived for only four weeks,

56
Periodical
Publications

others closed after a week. [There follows a long list of titles, some religious, some secular.]

This literary mortality is seldom to be blamed on the public. Among these recent periodicals I know of only a couple which, from the standpoint of the quality of their content, deserved a better reception. The germ of their decay is almost always to be found in their form and content.

[Pezzl singles out some periodicals which he considers have a better chance of survival, but he considers it a forlorn hope that the kind of high-class periodicals which the best literary intellects could produce if they wanted to will ever appear in Vienna.]

57
Animal-baiting

If I wanted to excuse animal-baiting, I could perhaps find reasons and examples in its favour. But this I will not do, for it is and remains a wild, barbaric spectacle unworthy of a civilized nation.

On Saturdays a man in elegant hunting costume, a hunting knife [hanger] at his side, rides through the city and every suburb. Two men march in front beating drums, and behind his horse are three or four fellows all dressed in yellow leather and with faces like [American] Indian scalpers, who hand out, to left and right, leaflets as full of absurd nonsense as if they had been written in the Insane Tower [of the General Hospital; see section 53].

On Sundays, very early in the morning, a black-and-yellow flag is raised on the pole in the middle of the baiting amphitheatre, and the idiotic placards are stuck up at every street corner. The yellow scalpers rush round all the streets and, dressed in their murder uniforms, attend holy mass in the churches. At two o'clock in the afternoon the guard parades at the baiting place; a swarm of drummers and pipers from the regiments stationed in the barracks takes up position on the balcony of the amphitheatre where, at three o'clock, the din of Turkish music starts up.

After three o'clock, a dense mass of the curious throng through the Stubentor, cross the Customs Bridge and leave by the Theresa Gate. An hour later, many hackney-carriages arrive, some with four members of a bourgeois family, some with porters or artisans with their girl-friends. Half an hour later, many a gilt-trimmed carriage pulls up, bringing some noble or semi-noble creatures to attend the animal-baiting.

As soon as you are outside the city walls you hear the martial music, and by the time you are no more than about 300 paces away, you are deafened and shocked by the furious barking of a hundred angry dogs. When you reach the entrance to the baiting arena your nostrils are assailed by the stench...

You reach the wooden circus by small rickety stairways. The audience consists of several thousand people of every sex, age and rank....

A gate opens. The Baiting Master, now also dressed in yellow leather, leaps into the arena, cracks his whip, and in an instant the music and noise ceases. Everyone waits expectantly in silence. Another crack of the whip! An enraged ox crashes through another gate; the Baiting Master retires.

In the beginning a few useless dogs are let loose, just to annoy the beast and make it more furious. Finally, some veterans from the dog kennels arrive and the ox greets them with its horns close to the ground, pointing towards them; but as a result of this its ears are left vulnerable. They attack from both sides and hold it firmly by the ears. At the moment of this heroic deed, trumpets and drums are sounded, accompanied by stamping and applause by the crowd; with a wave from the Master the valiant dogs and the conquered ox are led out of the arena.

The same pattern is now repeated with bears, stags, wolves and wild boars. At present there are also a lion, a lioness, a hyena and a leopard among the animals; they seem to be kept constantly in a somewhat drugged state with opium, for their bravery is not the greatest. The climax is usually provided by a bear, which, despite the fireworks going off all round, catches his prey and consumes it.

[Pezzl, full of anger and sarcasm at this animal-baiting, suggests that it be forbidden.]

[Similar to section 14: the details listed by Pezzl have been omitted here.

Pezzl notes that, in addition to all the provisions brought into the city from outside, 'beer is also brewed in three houses within the *Linie*. Altogether, some 400,000 *Eimer* (kegs) are consumed. The figures given earlier (in section 14) are thus very wrong.']

58
Consumption in Vienna from 1 November 1784 to the end of October 1785

125

59
Inconveniences

[Quotations of criticisms of other large cities from antiquity to the present. Explanation of the bad air in Vienna – stables, sewers, tanneries, and so on. The water in Vienna is bad, except for that in the Schwarzenberg Palace and the Capuchin Monastery in the Neuer Markt. The many carriages – an indispensable convenience for the wealthy – can be a great nuisance. When parked, they block the entrances to houses; when in motion, they are a danger to pedestrians. Throughout the colder months the already narrow streets are further impeded by piles of wood used as fuel for the many domestic stoves. In the warmer months, when people want to go out to the gardens in the suburbs, the narrow city gates – created as part of the fortifications – which allow only one carriage to pass through at a time, and the small side gates which allow only one person to pass at a time, have the effect of creating a great bottleneck. And once you are outside the gates, the ever-present dust is intolerable (see also section 3).

In society, the clothes to be worn at receptions etc. are costly and must conform to certain rules (see also p. 199 concerning composers), and furthermore much valuable time during the day has to be spent at the hairdresser's just for the sake of a brief evening engagement.]

60
Conveniences

[The advantages of living in the country – clean air, good water, no carriages blocking your entrance by day, a good night's sleep, no necessity for visiting, for wasting hours at the dressing table or at the tailor's, no flights of stairs to climb – are compared to the advantages of city life. The rich are surrounded by servants and others ready to provide every possible convenience, the poor can easily find work, as long as they are in good health, and the man of leisure has endless possibilities to amuse himself. No man of society would want to be anywhere else, distractions in Vienna being many and varied. The city is where Alexander Pope's axiom 'the proper study of mankind is man' may most easily find practical application in so many ways. Small-town life, however, is obnoxious.]

... The monarch of Vienna has no need to put his people into a good humour, all he has to do is to preserve it, for the Viennese possess innate good humour, just as sparrows are born to chirp. ...

In north Germany the common man is notable for being stubborn, insolent, capricious, cantankerous, ill-humoured and inclined to violence: his whole nervous system seems to be tightly stretched. ... The reasons for this are difficult to explain. Some put it down to the Protestant religion, with its dark-hued and heavy liturgy, that features too little sensuality for the populace. Others attribute it to the lower level of fertility of those lands, to the greater poverty and the resulting discontent of the population; or to the consumption of heavy foods and strong beer. Presumably all these are factors which contribute to the tendency among the populace in those parts to be quarrelsome and to behave in public places in a rather unfriendly fashion.

In Vienna the people are just the opposite. Their temperament is on the whole very much inclined to joy, openness and good humour. Of course, this virtue does not necessarily derive from considered principles, but is more often due to a happy disposition and a reasonably satisfactory standard of living, such as can be found even among the poorest people here. This basic temperament goes hand in hand with a considerable degree of unconcern and indolence, with a taste for luxury and a love of comfort. ...

If anyone has an accident in a public square or street, there is certain to be someone with a sympathetic heart among the bystanders who will hasten to his or her aid, ... keeping watch until the next-of-kin can be fetched or other sorts of assistance organized. If there is an accident involving horses, or if carriages have collided, passers-by willingly hasten to uncouple the horses and pull the carriages apart, freeing the street of obstructions so as to prevent an even worse accident and keep the traffic moving. Everyone lends a hand. ... The man-in-the-street, when faced with doing unpleasant tasks, tries to see the funny side of it all and does whatever is required to the accompaniment of his own and others' laughter, whereas in the same situation a north German would perhaps make grimaces, raging and cursing.

[The French dramatist Louis Sébastien] Mercier writes, 'You no longer find among Parisians that cheerful frame of mind which was typical sixty years ago, and which provided the stranger with such a pleasant reception.'

I fear that in a few generations, perhaps even thirty years from now, the same will be true of the population of Vienna. That former open, good-humoured innocence, which up till now has been such a conspicuous characteristic of nearly all classes, has already ceased to exist in some. The unconcern that you could (to the distaste of some foreigners) read in the faces of some classes of people has gradually disappeared, and in its place you can now discern uneasiness, anxiety, scheming, secret worries, *Sturm und Drang* [storm and stress]....

62
Enlightenment

The nonsensical clamourings from all quarters during the last decade (more or less) concerning the *word* 'Enlightenment' have almost made the *cause* itself an object of general ridicule. This is the work of, and can be blamed on a large number of petty intellects, adolescent minds who, thanks to the current general intoxication with reading, have picked up some principles of great men but have not understood sufficiently or digested properly what they have read....

Such infantile babblings must now, however, be allowed to deflect us from honouring and encouraging the real Enlightenment or from enlarging its horizons. It is true that for the majority of the public, even of the educated sort, the concept and limits of the term are not precisely understood. Many people think that the sole and complete aim of the Enlightenment is to achieve a thoroughly purged religion; and that to recognize the abuses of the Church, to rid ourselves of them, means to be enlightened.

I do not believe that to be the case. For me an enlightened man is one with a properly developed moral instinct, one who can derive satisfaction from an occupation which chance or the laws has given him, who acts correctly from conviction, who likes his work, who shows respect for the law, who is receptive to advice, who shows a love of order in his domestic and public life, who is moderate in his eating and drinking and looks after his health – and makes it a regular habit to do all these things; who is never tempted to live beyond his means; who strives constantly to improve those talents necessary to his destiny in society; who knows and practises the duties of a citizen, friend, husband and father; who realizes that in bourgeois society it is necessary, for the maintenance of the whole, to bear individual burdens and to sacrifice private advantages, and to tolerate these things without bitterness; who never unreasonably attacks the religion publicly supported by the state, and if he has acquired other convictions, keeps them to himself; and finally who enjoys his existence and possesses the knowledge to enjoy a comfortable, long and quiet life.

... Although this is only the opinion of one man and certainly cannot be applied to the generality of a city, and especially a city like Vienna, it will not be difficult to accept that there are individuals present here whose lives actually correspond to this outline.

Anyone who wants to enlighten a whole nation or a wide public must take two major steps: the first is to rid oneself of old, unworthy and damaging prejudices; the other is to accept truths and principles which are new and beneficial to him and which encourage his spirit to self-understanding and reflection, and which accustom him to distinguishing appearance from reality, non-essentials from essentials.

From this standpoint one must admit that the Viennese, considered as a whole, are still only taking their first step. Only recently have they begun gradually to rid themselves of ancient prejudices in respect of religion, economics and domestic matters. Their whole-hearted attachment to monks, devotions, brotherhoods, pilgrimages, etc. has markedly lessened. Their partiality for everything foreign, even if only in name, has greatly decreased.... They no longer believe ostentatious extravagance to be praiseworthy.... These and other similar matters are indisputable advances towards national enlightenment.

[The adaptable nature of the Viennese assists them in throwing off more quickly and effectively stupid prejudices and bad habits. The monarch can attack superstitions, clerical and secular, and except for a gew grumblers no one objects. The Viennese differ from the Brandenburgers who, faced with a revised hymn-book, wrote the old words over the new and swamped the authorities with petitions. When the Emperor ordered much more sweeping reforms in the Catholic Church – the Latin *credo* or *oremus* have long been absent from the new liturgy here – no one objected; on the contrary, his reforms were readily accepted.]

63	*Religion*	[These sections, which contain, for the most part, a repetition
64	*Devotions*	of sentiments expressed earlier on various occasions, have been omitted.]

| 65 | *Tolerance* | Among the twenty-four million inhabitants of the Austrian Crown Lands there are approximately |

Calvinists	926,000
Lutherans	304,000
Socinians	86,000

[footnote: also Unitarians, as they prefer to be known, tolerated only in Transylvania, where they have one Superintendent and 135 priests]

Jews	290,000
Greek Orthodox	2,916,000

A total, then, of 4,612,000 [*recte* 4,522,000] non-Catholics. Under [Maria] Theresa's government there were already more than four million, evidence of the fact that religious repression was by no means as severe as was claimed abroad, although despotic clergy of the dominant religion did on occasion actively harass members of the other religious groups . . . to a far greater extent than was the Empress's intention.

Finally came the well-known Edict of Toleration in 1781. There can be no doubt that the Emperor [Joseph II] was motivated by excellent principles: that one can be a good citizen of the state without adhering to the one or the other rite; that it is wrong to try to impose ideas on someone who cannot be convinced about their correctness; that the state itself is guilty of an unpardonable transgression if it persecutes peaceful, hard-working and decent subjects, excludes them from society or indeed expels them simply because of differences in their religious opinions and customs.

This Edict of Toleration was indeed most welcome in the German Crown Lands, also in Bohemia, Moravia and Galicia. Here, under the Empress's administration, the supremacy of Catholicism has been maintained so assiduously that the resident Protestants were forced to worship in secret, but as a result of the Edict they were permitted to hold their services openly and others allowed to join in their worship if they so wished. They were given churches, schools and pastors, and their newly established congregations number some 60,000. In Hungary, Transylvania etc. they were always in some measure masters of their rights and had greater religious freedom, but the Catholic clergy had nevertheless been able to ensure their gradual exclusion from all public offices and honours within the kingdom. Since the Edict, they have been promoted in accordance with their skills, and without regard for their religious beliefs. The Hungarian-Transylvanian Chancellery in Vienna and the Viceroy's Office in Ofen [Budapest] now include Calvinists and Lutherans among their vice-presidents, councillors and lesser officials.

For a long time there have been so many Jews in Bohemia, Moravia, Hungary and especially Galicia that, simply on the basis of their numbers, it was evident that they were tolerated. Through the Edict of Toleration their existence was even more assured and they were granted several new advantages [see section 118].

The members of the Greek Orthodox community [see also section 70] constitute the second-largest religious group; they have one archbishop, eight bishops and 5,857 popes or priests.

In Vienna, all these various religious groups co-exist peacefully side by side, and anyone from among them who finds it necessary to complain about intolerance must be a very insatiable person indeed; for the statutory requirement that, when the Catholic sacraments are carried by [in procession or to give someone the last rites – see section 69], non-Catholics are either to move to one side or to doff their hat, will surely not be regarded as unreasonable by anyone with an understanding of propriety and order.

[Pezzl notes that there has been criticism of the Edict in certain quarters abroad, citing some disturbances created by Bohemian and Carinthian peasants, as well as some inflammatory sermons by village priests and monks, who spoke out against these new orders. In a land where officially Catholicism had been the sole and undisputed religion for centuries, it was clear that some strong reactions to the sudden introduction of religious toleration were to be expected. The government has therefore taken the necessary steps to deal with any such disturbances.]

66 *Protestants*

The Lutheran community in Vienna consists of some 3,000 souls; the Calvinists – including the Swiss factory workers living in Penzing – of 700. Both their pastors are also Superintendents of the Diocese of Austria.

131

[The Protestants have every reason to be content with their existence in Vienna. They enjoy legal protection (set out in a paragraph of the criminal code), any disruption of their services being punishable in exactly the same way as would a disturbance created in the (Catholic) Cathedral.]

67   *Freedom of Confession*

[When someone rents an apartment in Vienna, his landlord presents him with the standard police registration form, which includes a question concerning his religious beliefs. The question must be answered ... but after this declaration has been made there are no further checks or investigations into the state of one's beliefs. .... In former times confession and taking communion at Easter were compulsory, and under Maria Theresa, all officials in government departments and all army officers had to sign a declaration certifying that they had fulfilled their Easter duties, on pain of losing their jobs. The same was required by landlords of all their tenants. These certificates were of course soon 'arranged'. Nowadays each person goes to confession when he or she feels the need.]

68   *Concerning Deism*

[Pezzl relates the unexpected appearance of a cult of Deists in a remote corner of Bohemia, which group was forcibly transferred to the border with Turkey (i.e. the Ottoman Empire), and discusses the reasons why the government decided not to allow them to exist officially.]

69   *Extreme Unction*

... In Vienna ... Extreme Unction is taken to the sick in a kind of public ceremony. The sacristan heads the procession, ringing his bell, followed by the priest in his vestments holding in front of him the Holy Sacraments in a ciborium; a few sextons accompany him bearing a sometimes not very clean baldachin. Behind them come the dying person's relatives and friends, and perhaps a pious idler or two. [Pezzl, as might be expected, disapproved of this custom, suggesting that the sacrament be administered at the bedside, with no public ceremonial, which is more appropriate to the Corpus Christi procession – see section 149.]

70   *Greeks*

[There are some 600 members of the Greek Orthodox Church in Vienna, some of whom are true Greeks, some Rascians or Serbians; almost the whole of the old Fleischmarkt (meat market) is occupied by them, and in that street they propose to build their own church as soon as possible. The local population has many books translated into ancient and modern Greek, which are printed here and sent to Greece; there is also a newspaper in modern Greek.]

The number of hackney-carriages is steadily increasing: at present – March 1787 – there are 616. It is worth noting that 600 coachmen with 1,200 horses are on duty daily, ready to earn their livelihood relying purely on chance [i.e. depending on demand], but maintain it easily. Each must pay an annual tax of 36 gulden, which goes to the Poorhouse.... The hackney-carriage business seems to be thriving, judging by the increase in their numbers [see section 13]. Indeed, some of the coaches and harnesses are fitted up with gilt, plush, lacquer, etc., which lends them an elegance that is not at all typical of Paris, Brussels or Strasbourg; were it not for the fact that they display their official numbers on the back, you could mistake many such carriages for those regularly used by the aristocracy.

71 Hackney-carriages, Coaches for Hire

There are no officially fixed fares; each is agreed on the spot. I think this system is better than if a fixed rate were levied; with the latter one would either receive worse service or, in order to be driven well, pay more than the fare. [Pezzl advises clients to choose a young rather than an old driver.]

To travel from one end of town to the other, for example from the Castle to the Customs House, usually costs 10 kreuzer; from the city to a suburb 15 kr. (but only in fine weather; when it rains the price goes up). In some parts the hackney-carriages are more expensive than in others, e.g. those in the Landstraße suburb generally charge more than those in Mariahilf, and vehicles stationed at the Imperial Riding School charge more than those on the Kohlmarkt. A pleasure ride in an open carriage, a phaeton, is dearer than one in an ordinary hackney-carriage.

There are some 300 city carriages available for hire. They are not numbered and come in all kinds of shapes, and can be as elegant as a state coach, if such is required. For an etiquette visit a hackney-carriage is inappropriate; instead a hired carriage must be employed (it being considered more suitable). One pays 3 gulden per day for such a carriage with two horses, or 60 gulden for a whole month (not including a tip for the driver).

Many people hire such a carriage for a trip to the country. I would advise them to use a hackney-carriage for preference, because the drivers of hired carriages treat their steeds so gently that you never get anywhere.

[Private persons are beginning to cut down on the number of carriages and horses they own; as a result, some families now hire carriages to make visits, attend the theatre, go to church or driver in the Prater.]

72
The Bastions

[Description of the roughly circular fortifications, called the Bastei, on which you can circumnavigate the city on foot in about an hour. A description, hour by hour, of the daily activity associated with this favourite promenade, used by the Viennese all year round. Since the details duplicate in many respects section 27, they have been omitted here.]

73
Museum of
Natural History

[Description of a series of rooms in the Castle devoted to specimens for a natural history collection, including minerals etc., particularly renowned for its comprehensive range of precious stones.]

74
Sleigh Rides

In old Vienna, where there were still many magnificent public spectacles, the grand sleigh rides were one of the most fashionable of winter pastimes. Under Empress [Maria] Theresa the court gave them often and, following that example, the great and rich vassals did likewise. It was a delightful amusement. Since the snow rarely lasted long in the main streets of Vienna, because of the throng of people and horses, and since it was through these very streets that the train of sleighs moved, on the days appointed for such events several thousand cartloads of snow had to be brought into town from the Esplanade in order to provide a usable track. Apart from the new sleigh costumes worn by the ladies and gentlemen, the runners, grooms and horses also sported new outfits. The horses were hung with silver sleigh bells and the sleighs decked out with silver ornaments which, if they were to be worthy of the occupants, often cost 15,000 to 20,000 gulden.

Emperor Joseph considers that this entertainment is disproportionately expensive, and during his reign [since 1780] no court sleigh rides have been given. During the very snowy winter of 1783–4, the nobility suddenly rediscovered the joys of sleigh rides. Those given by the court always took place during the day, the others in the evening; the former were always the most extravagant, the latter having a romantic and rather magical air. A squad of torch-bearers on horseback led the way, closely followed by a sleigh with trumpets and drums; then a train of twenty or thirty sleighs of the nobility, each preceded by two postillions with torches, and with a runner on either side, the uniforms changing colour amid all the light, with everything illuminated by a myriad of gold and silver reflections. At the end of the procession came a huge sleigh carrying musicians, who added to the tumult of the horses adorned with sleigh bells by playing martial music.

The ladies' places are determined by drawing lots. They sit, attractively wrapped in Siberian furs, on the sleighs, each with a gentleman behind her; the latter, his Russian muff hanging at his side, guiding the horse, which is used to the noise, with silken reins and a light touch....

The procession makes its way through the noblest streets and squares. People throng to see the beautiful ladies on their sleighs...Sparks from the torches dance around their heads, the raw north wind blows around their bosoms and necks; but they don't mind: they are there for all to admire, the object of many a secret longing and sigh. This makes up for any physical discomforts.

Finally, the procession halts in front of the house of the princely host. The carriages are ready and waiting, the guests board them quickly and are driven home to change clothes before returning to a grand supper at which they dance, joke and laugh, whiling away the hours until daybreak at the celebration ball.

75 *Street Cleaners*

The cleaning of Vienna's streets is entrusted to a company on contract, and it in turn employs honest daily workers and also convicted criminals who have been sentenced to public penance, for which the company pays a fee to the police. These men are fettered hand and foot, clothed in rough brown garments, and grouped every day into two or three gangs – each of about twenty men – guarded by members of the police militia, and in this fashion are taken to work.

In the reign of the Empress [Maria Theresa], criminals of some rank and name were, when the penalty was particularly severe, locked up in some fortress for life. In those days, the possibility that in Vienna a court councillor or a cavalier might be made to mix with common criminals in doing public penance was not considered. Emperor Joseph gave criminal justice a new form.... He abolished the distinctions between classes in criminal affairs. He created the street-cleaning gangs and decreed that vassals of the highest rank as well as the worst common criminals should serve in them together. At first the appearance of these people was an altogether astonishing sight for the Viennese. Half the city's population thronged to witness the dreadful sight when the first such gentleman – his head shaven, broom in hand and with chains rattling – appeared on the street. Since then we have become more accustomed to seeing street-cleaning barons, court councillors, counts, etc., and the public today treats the matter with a kind of indifference, just as the criminals themselves go unconcernedly about the streets.

When he has served his time, the prisoner returns to his normal life, his good name restored. Recently there was a case of a man who one day laid aside his broom and on the next opened a coffee-house. The circumstances ensured that he had customers immediately.

Some people have felt that the idea of using criminals to sweep the streets is wrong, since this work, which could be done by other decent folk, has, in their opinion, been brought into disrepute. This is a wrong conclusion: it is not the work that is degrading, no work is; but when a criminal is sentenced to public penance, it is his chains, the insignia of his shame and his punishment, which disgrace him, not the work itself.

At the beginning, when this punishment was first introduced, shameless hussies were also taken from their houses of detention, a broom was put into their hand, and they were forced to clean the streets. This procedure gave rise to sundry indecencies; subsequently they were left at home and for the most part given the task, itself more appropriate and more useful, of doing the laundry for the General Hospital....

76 Italian and German Opera

There is nothing more boring than a play which lasts too long.... Vienna has had its share of all varieties: French plays, Italian plays, Italian operas, the grand ballets by Noverre, German opera, etc.... At the beginning one risked being half-crushed in one's eagerness to attend a new piece. After a few years the house was deserted. Finally, they concentrated for a while on German national theatre, but one soon got bored by the monotony of that, too, and in 1783 the Emperor, who knew the insatiable curiosity of his faithful Viennese [subjects], restored to them an Italian opera company, which is still the leading entertainment. . . .

The pieces which have received the most general applause are (in order of overall success) as follows:

Il barbiere di Seviglia [Giovanni Paisiello]
Fra i due litiganti il terzo gode [Giuseppe Sarti]
La grotta di Trofonio [Antonio Salieri]
Il rè Teodoro in Venezia [Paisiello]
Una cosa rara, os[s]ia bellezza ed onestà
[Vincente Martin y Soler]

These are delightful comic operas; everyone has grown weary of serious operas, as can easily be imagined. The *Barber* contains some very popular light tunes, and is welcome from time to time on account of its gossipy intrigue. – Recently, *Fra i due litiganti* etc. had an unbroken run of thirty-seven performances. – The *Grotta di Trofonio* ran for some thirty nights. – *Il rè Teodoro* for 43. – The *Cosa rara*, because its run was brought to an end by the arrival of Lent, only some fifteen times. But this was the piece that virtually took the town by storm; at every performance 300 to 400 people had to be turned away from the doors. . .

Since these works have been performed, one can never enter any fashionable house or society without hearing a duet, a trio, a finale from one of the above operas being sung or rendered on the keyboard. Even shopkeepers and cellar-hands whistle arias from the *Barber* and *Cosa rara* wherever you go. . . . The opera singers are sought after and indeed well paid. [Stefano] Mandini and [Francesco] Benucci are the two drollest opera comedians one can imagine. The star idol among the leading comic opera singers up to now has been [the soprano Anna or 'Nancy'] Storace, of Italian origin but born in London. She earned over 1,000 ducats p.a. One must in all honesty admit that she sings excellently, but she does not possess an attractive figure: a small, dumpy creature, without a single physical feminine grace, except for a pair of large – though not very compelling – eyes.

Storace left recently [in the spring of 1787] for England. She will be replaced by [Anna] Morichelli.

Since a large part of the public does not understand Italian, and as it was felt that they should be entertained with opera, a German troupe has been newly established, and usually performs in the Kärnterthortheater. Its budget is far smaller than that of the Italian Opera, hence it has less accomplished singers and is generally inferior to it. *Der Doktor und der Apotheker*, a farce which Ditters set to music, has been the only outstanding production.

77
Spinsters of
a Certain Age

Their number is great and their situation very unpleasant. Those of the second and third class are the worst affected. Men employed in government service – and there are several thousand of them – make such slow progress in their careers... that they reach the age of forty before they are in a position to be able to afford to marry.... Many an official keeps a regular mistress – and both go grey waiting....

Whereas married women lead a free and easy life, that of the old maids is by contrast constrained and boring,... and in fact their conversation is rather dry. A genuine innocent, so called (in the old sense of the word), is unfortunately more of a liability than an asset in the fashionable social circles we know today. People prefer to chat with married ladies.... The girls are well aware of the advantages enjoyed by married women, and that is why they are so anxious to join their ranks.

Many eligible young men avoid those houses where there are spinsters of a certain age without a lover, for if they visit too frequently their presence may well be taken for a declaration of love, and after a while the fathers and mothers tend to tackle the young men in private and insist on knowing what their intentions are.

78   Imperial
Library

[Description of this library, which still survives; of the great hall, where Mozart gave concerts for the Imperial Librarian, Baron Gottfried van Swieten. The architect was Fischer von Erlach, the frescoes by Daniel Gran. The personnel consists of the librarian, the director, two custodians, five scribes and four amanuenses. No open flame is ever allowed in the library, to avoid the risk of fire. Among the treasures is a substantial collection of *incunabula* numbering over 6,000 items. Describes other rare items. The library is intended for public use; the reading room is open in the winter months from 9 to 12, in the summer from 8 to 12 o'clock; access to the main library is allowed only when accompanied by an official, because the books are unprotected and many an otherwise honest person has been known to succumb to temptation.]

[Description of the famous palace built 1717–24 by Prince Eugene of Savoy, who used it as a summer residence. The building, on the south-eastern side of the city, is now (1787) used as a picture gallery, open to the public on Mondays, Wednesday and Fridays, and Pezzl deplores the practice of bringing children into the galleries. The formal gardens enjoy an excellent panoramic view of Vienna, but lack large trees to provide shade; consequently they are less frequented during the day, but are regularly visited in the evenings by the *beau monde*.]

79 *The Belvedere*

The fixed-price menu (*table d'hôte*), common in various provinces within and outside Germany, is virtually unknown in Vienna. [Advantages and disadvantages described; the former include fixed prices and eating in company, the latter include restricted hours and the presence of ill-mannered people who uncere- moniously grab the best items.]

80 *Traiteurs (Caterers)*

Anyone in Vienna who lacks his own table visits a tavern or goes to a *traiteur*. In the taverns here, customers are served at separate tables at any hour of the day, with as much or as little food as they require; each item has a fixed price, which one can ascertain before ordering. The other customary way of eating out is at a *traiteur* or caterer. These establishments only exist in the city proper, and are not very numerous, perhaps about thirty in all. Meals are provided at any chosen time between 10:30 a.m. and 2:30 p.m. The prices vary greatly, depending on what you eat. The top price for lunch is usually 1 gulden without a drink, the lowest $4\frac{1}{2}$ kreuzer – an enormous difference. Between these two extremes you can have lunch for a whole range of prices – 5 kreuzer, 8 kr., 10 kr., 12 kr., 15 kr., 24 kr., 30 kr., 45 kr., or 48 kr.

The customers vary as greatly as the prices, and include people from nearly every walk of life [enumerated]. . . . Estab- lishments providing meals at 10 kr. to 18 kr. are the busiest, . . . catering for officials, students, clerics, language teachers, the servants of merchants, lackeys, coachmen, etc. They swarm in from 12 or 12:30 o'clock . . . for example, at the Blue Bottle on the Stock-im-Eisen-Platz, in two average-sized dining rooms, up to 250 people are served each day in a three- hour period. The meal costing 8 kreuzer includes four dishes: soup, beef in gravy, vegetables with potatoes or noodles, roast or preserves. The portions are so substantial that only a glutton could fail to be satisfied. Every guest is served each dish on his own individual pewter plate. On each table there is a loaf of bread for each guest to cut as he desires, and likewise water is served in a pewter jug to be passed around. Beer or wine can be ordered at extra cost. Liveried servants make up the majority of the customers at these tables.

The 10-kreuzer meal consists of roughly the same food, but is served in a separate room, where every guest has a napkin, an individual white roll and his own drinking glass. The clientele is of a better class – artists, clerics, government officials...

There is a curious habit prevalent among the lackeys here, not only in the *traiteurs* but in beer-houses and other public places. You are sitting in one dining room of a *traiteur* and all of a sudden you become aware of the company in the other room. Only the most distinguished names are to be heard there – Li[e]chtenstein, Kaunitz, Esterházy, Dietrichstein, Pálffy, Harrach, Starhemberg, Zinzendorf, Kinsky, Hatzfeld, Kolowrat, Colloredo, etc. You imagine yourself to be in the antechamber of a room where members of the top aristocracy are holding a meeting. You open the door, and what do you see but a room full of lackeys, runners, hunters, coachmen, hussars, etc. wearing the colourful liveries of those great houses. These wags have made it a habit, instead of using their own names, to address each other by the names of their masters.

81   *Carnival*

That is the name in general use among the Viennese for what used to be called Shrovetide or Shrove Tuesday. For the Viennese – those old declared friends of everything pleasing to heart and mind – this is a major religious festival. The first question asked of one as the time for Carnival approaches is: How will you be spending Carnival?... Have you been out dancing? The man of quiet habits, a thinker or intellectual, is slightly embarrassed by all these questions, by all the invitations to private balls, picnics, music, and so forth.

The main activity is dancing and everything associated with it. The Carnival [season] begins on 7 January and lasts until Ash Wednesday.... On every street corner there are invitations in white, or red, blue and yellow, announcing in the largest type...: 'Today there is music in the such and such rooms', 'music with trumpets and drums', 'music by candlelight', etc.

The most distinguished place of entertainment is the Redou-tensaal [or Redoutensäle, there being both a small and a large hall; see section 93], and in the city the only other ballroom is in the Mehlgrube [on the Neuer Markt, where Mozart gave subscription concerts], for people feel there is a greater need to use available space for apartments rather than for large empty dance halls. The ballrooms are all in the suburbs; the entrance fee is usually 20 kreuzer, but the payment also covers the cost of food and drink.

Ambassadors and various other great lords give balls in their own houses for the nobility of the first rank. The middle classes, councillors, bankers, etc. . . . copy that idea. Picnics are given at 2 gulden per person. Private balls are given in *traiteurs*, private houses, taverns. House officers of the great palaces give their own balls with their wives, daughters, governesses, lady's maids, milliners, etc. They are often glittering affairs, and on these occasions you can see many a lady's maid adorned with the diamonds of her mistress. Ordinary people flock to any place sporting a wine bottle and a cymbalo [Hungarian or Gypsy instrument, played with little hammers]; they ape the great as best they can. In 1785 the amateurs of the suburb Neu-Lerchenfeld gave their own balls with an entrance fee of 5 kreuzer. Except in the Redoutensäle, wearing a mask is completely forbidden.

Carnival is a dangerous time. Many a virgin has lost her innocence and many a matron her virtue at this time. How could it be otherwise when, in those lovers' hours, flushed with wine and dancing, a couple find themselves alone in a closed carriage going home and, having arrived there, the cavalier escorts his lady to her bedchamber . . . while her strict father, her vigilant mother or her jealous husband . . . is otherwise engaged in pleasure . . .

Money-lenders, pawnbrokers and usurers never have it better than during Carnival. Watches, buckles, boxes, rings, clothes, letters of credit – all sprout wings. There is no better time than this to acquire fine furniture cheaply. Pawnbrokers' establishments are not big enough. Jews cannot raise enough ready cash, I.O.U. letters are signed promising double the amount of the loan in repayment, salaries are in hock for the next three months. . . .

Enough! The dance is over, smash the flutes. 'Strewing a little ash on heads makes the raving Christians come to their senses', says the Turkish spy. On the morning of Ash Wednesday one

82 *Lent*

141

leaves the dance floor and goes straight to church, receives ashes on one's head and then goes home to sleep it off.

Lent, which so little suits our present-day political or religious mores, is gradually beginning to be taken less seriously.... In the old days, Lent was strictly observed: in every restaurant a printed order was hung up, announcing that the owner would have to pay a fine of 10 thalers if he served meat to known Catholics on fast-days. Nowadays, that is generally dispensed with; ... you can observe this in the reduced prices for food which are fixed during this period. An honest fishmonger told me that, in each of the last three or four years, his sales of fish have been down by 20,000 gulden compared with the same period in previous years. This is partly because of the dispensations, partly because of the public's changed attitudes and partly because so many monasteries have been secularized....

Just as meat was forbidden during Lent in the old days, so also ... were the theatres closed. Now, this too has been changed. Last year [1786], plays were performed here during Lent for the first time, and in 1787 theatres in the provinces were also allowed to remain open.

83   *Census for the Year 1786*

84   *Consumption during the Year 1786*

[Both sections omitted: for similar lists, see sections 12 and 14.]

PART FOUR: 1787

This king of European rivers, which at Donaueschingen can be crossed with one pace and at Semlin [Zemun in Croatia] can accommodate a ship armed with thirty cannon, is one of enormous advantage to the Austrian states and to Vienna in particular. Together with the court, it has been the principal reason for the extraordinary expansion of this city; it will forever be the most powerful factor in ensuring the continuation of Vienna as the residence of the Austrian monarchs.

85 *The River Danube*

Each year some 1,500 vessels arrive in Vienna [sailing down] the Danube. The largest of these weighs about 2,000 hundredweight, the smallest is the kind of little tub used by peasant lads to carry a few pounds of fruit. None of these boats makes the return journey; either they are broken up in Vienna to yield wood for other purposes or for use as fuel, or they continue downstream to the Hungarian provinces. This is also the reason why Danube ships are not built to last.

The cargoes of these vessels consist of fruit, cattle, salt, building materials, food, merchandise, wine, vegetables, wood, etc. – everything one could ever think of – and of course they bring people, including recruits and troops which require rapid transport... to the capital... At the point where the river reaches the city it divides into many channels, some larger, some smaller, and these create pleasant islands covered with trees, bushes and grass, giving the surroundings of Vienna an attractive appearance. One disadvantage, an important one, is that frequently when the winter is severe all these arms freeze over, with the result that in spring, when the water coming downstream meets this immovable mass of ice, the Danube overflows and floods the suburbs situated along the river bank, destroys dams and bridges, severs communications with Bohemia and Moravia, and even causes damage in the city. This can also happen when the snow in the mountains... melts in early summer... causing the river level to rise. As a result of this happening two years ago, the [suburb of] Leopoldstadt was flooded four times in one summer.

For many years people have made theoretical and practical attempts to find some way of moving river traffic upstream... but this has proved impracticable, not because of lack of intelligence or industry...but because it is physically almost impossible. The river drops too steeply to be overcome by mechanical means or by wind: between the Kahlenberg and the city alone there is a fall of one foot, and passing through Hungary the fall is even more pronounced and hence the current even stronger. To wish to sail from Semlin to Linz would be tantamount to sailing up a mountainside....

86   *Literature*

Until Maria Theresa's reign one hardly knew what literature was in Vienna. A theological compendium, a commentary on the Pandects [digest of Roman law], a prayer-book were virtually the only topics with which our very badly equipped printers occupied themselves. Then light shone in the darkness: true medical science arose, and with it the related sciences of chemistry, botany, natural history, physics, mineralogy, etc., for the development of which the rich, hidden natural resources of the Austrian Crown Lands invited exploitation.

Somewhat later, [Joseph von] Sonnenfels, [Johan Michael] Denis, [Carl] Mastalier, [Thomas Philipp von] Gebler awakened in us a love of the liberal arts. One began to read German; the theatre was purged; some periodical writings taught, by means of seriousness and satire, the first principles of morality, knowledge of mankind, practical philosophy of life. With these ideas came the realization that our public education was inadequate, our jurisprudence pedantic, our theology dull....

[Maria] Theresa, who did so much that was of lasting benefit for her realm, supported the more serious sciences with Imperial bounty, laying perhaps too much emphasis on the most serious subject of all – theology; if no large number of great masters in those fields of human knowledge appeared, it was not for lack of support. She could not, on the other hand, find much sympathy for the liberal arts, popular literature,... [Censorship paralyzed literature in Vienna, where instead of studying Voltaire and Lessing, people would read *Swiss Family Robinson*.]

With the advent of the present government [of Joseph II], all these critical attitudes were abandoned. Censorship [applied to reading] was relaxed and freedom to publish granted to writers at home. Among the more serious fields of study, history, medicine, surgery, mineralogy, botany, chemistry and mathematics were cultivated especially.

In the field of the liberal arts, poetry has proved to be foremost in terms of the number and quality of writers. Much is written for the theatre, but mostly rather mediocre stuff. Very little good fiction has appeared so far. One of the faults of Viennese writers is that they pay too little attention to literary novelty. There is no organization here to keep the public informed of new and interesting publications or developments in the field of the sciences. Books which are very good but have not yet made a widespread impression on the German-speaking public, or contain nothing of special local interest, often remain unknown to the Viennese for years, sometimes totally so....

[Pezzl discusses literature in German-speaking countries, points out the predominant position of north German writers. Joseph II recently gave 100 ducats to the writer of a book about Hungarian geography; and a prize of 100 ducats has been offered for the best treatise on the history of the Christian Church. Pezzl suggests that royal patronage of literature would be of immense practical value.]

[The difference between scholars and writers: the former can be excellent without having published anything. A complete list of writers is not possible within the limitations of this publication, but a few may be singled out who have flourished not only here in Vienna, but abroad as well: Alxinger, Blumauer, Born, Denis, Eckhel, Haschka, Hunczowsky, Jacquin, Ingenhouß, Mastalier, Schmidt, Sonnenfels, Stoll (footnote: 'I have just learned that he has died ... He was my doctor, my friend. May his spirit live on through his pupils.').]

87 Writers

[A much expanded version of section 56. The enormous quantity of these pamphlets owes its existence to Joseph II's decree of 1781, allowing freedom of the press in the Austrian Crown Lands. By the end of August 1782 over one thousand pamphlets had appeared, notwithstanding the fact that all had to be read and passed by the censor. In order to speed up the checking process, a new proposal was made in May 1784: every writer was to deposit 6 ducats with his manuscript, the money to be forfeited if the censor did not permit publication of the work submitted. It was, however, realized that this procedure would prove to be impractical, hence the censors were given freedom to mark any unsuitable manuscript with the words 'Typum non meretur', with the result that it never saw the light of day. In 1784, the numbers of the pamphlets began to decline sharply, and by 1785 the situation had reverted to normal.]

88 Writers of Pamphlets

89   *Clerics*   In 1787 the *Wiener Almanach für Geistliche* ['Vienna Almanac for Clerics'] gave the following statistics for Austria:

Catholics

Archbishops and bishops.................................	57
Prebendaries	898
Parish priests in the German and Hungarian Crown Lands...	15,136
Monasteries..	1,074
Nunneries...	376

Greek Catholics

Archbishops and bishops.................................	7

Greek Orthodox

Archbishops and bishops.................................	9
Priests..	5,857

Lutherans

Superintendents and pastors	568

Calvinists

Superintendents and pastors	1,800

Unitarians

Superintendents and pastors	136

[for further statistics, see section 65]

Including the clerics of the Netherlands and Lombardy, the total number is about 86,000. Today the clerics in Vienna (as in the Austrian territories as a whole) ... consist of three parts:

The first follows the present system promulgated by the court, encourages Enlightenment, discourages superstition and ignorance, seeks to free itself from papal ideas, and preaches morality and practical religion. The number of such clerics is not great, but is growing daily....

The second group consists of the diehard conservatives and is still the most numerous, particularly in country areas and in the remote provinces. They walk in darkness....

The third part consists of the waverers, time-servers and hypocrites... The waverers really cannot make up their minds as to whether they favour the old or the new system... The time-servers... foresee an uncertain future and seek to hold the middle ground between the court faction and the conservatives... The hypocrites inwardly retain strong support for the old system while making an outward show of backing the new...

As is well known, the leader of the Catholic hierarchy here is Christoph Migazzi, Cardinal, Archbishop, etc. He comes from a Tyrolean family and was a page in the retinue of Cardinal Lamberg, the favourite of Emperor Charles VI. He arrived in Vienna as a young and well-liked abbé, made many and powerful friends, because *auditor rotae* in Rome, ambassador in Spain, coadjutor in Mechelen, Archbishop of Vienna, and administrator of the see of Waizen [Vácz], which appointment, however, he lost on 1 July 1785. The pamphleteers have been after him lately. They seem to be seeking revenge for the difficulties which His Eminence formerly – under the previous administration – created for good books and for readers by his terrible severity, aimed at even the most distinguished of men, unmoved by the fact that other and very different times might have been coming [and did].

[This reform movement within the Church, which created such chaos again at the beginning of the (18th) century in France, has arrived in Vienna; Jansenists are powerful and organized, but there is hardly any future here for their dark philosophies. Their only merit today is their untiring and courageous opposition to their longstanding enemies, the Jesuits.]

90   *Jansenists*

[Their importance in Vienna: the secrets of the entire fashionable world pass through their hands. Usually the lady's maid is the confidante of her mistress, especially if the latter is still fairly young, but other ladies treat these servants with indifference and even torment them wickedly, especially in matters of jealousy. In such case there is an early parting of the ways.]

91   *Ladies' Maids*

...Viennese ladies' maids lead a comfortable life. They take care of their mistresses' personal affairs and help look after their wardobes, and that is about the extent of their duties. Any time left over is theirs, to flirt with their lovers and to devote themselves to adorning their minds and their bodies. Indeed, some of them are possessed of taste, wit and grace; some are well-read and even have a knowledge of philosophy; they can quote Wieland and Blumauer from memory and read Voltaire, Petrarch and Pope in their original tongues. Altogether they are generally better educated and bred than most of the

147

young Fräuleins because their freer life-style allows them more experience of people and situations, leading to greater refinement.

So long as they are young and beautiful, they are idolized and spoiled, usually by young cavaliers who have staked a claim to the charms of the playful child, and indeed often cultivate the society of the lady only in order to be near her servant. When these girls reach thirty or so, they become more sociable and affable. Since many of them have secret connections with one of the great houses, care is taken to ensure that, before their charms fade, they are married off to an equerry, ... a major-domo, an estates manager ... who, in turn, is himself in many cases associated with the same great house. If it seems opportune to marry her off more quickly, some similar position is found for her on one of the estates of the nobility.

92
Chambermaids

In the great houses the lady is served by her lady's maid, and she in turn is served by the chambermaid. In less grand situations the chambermaid occupies the same position as the lady's maid in a palace. There is a large army of chambermaids, at least 4,000 of them, I believe. They are young, pretty, plump and lively creatures – flirtatious, spoiled teases.... They skip through life without really knowing what it is all about.... Viennese chambermaids are adept at making coffee and chocolate, warming a shirt, waxing a table, making a bed, ironing a scarf. They keep themselves very neatly attired, display taste in choosing their clothes, and are generally seen in the characteristic style of dress they have espoused, which is distinguished by a Bohemian bonnet and a pretty, short apron. When the entire world of feminine fashion adopted bustles ... only housemaids had the good sense not to spoil their pretty figures by having recourse to rolls of material to puff them up on both sides. They understood their advantages better and flattered their behinds. (Footnote: 'Why should the familiar term in everyday use in Paris – as in *culs de Paris, faux cul*, etc. – not also be allowed in German?')

They earn between 25 and 40 gulden p.a., just enough to pay for their shoes and hair-powder. This notwithstanding, they go about on Sunday dressed in silk, with gold earrings and large silver buckles, attending church, or strolling in the Prater, or attending a play. Guess where they have their capital assets?

The previous government of the Empress, so preoccupied with the Sixth Commandment ['Thou shalt not commit adultery'], considered these chambermaids a subject of the greatest importance. As everyone knows, they are genuinely decent girls living in genuinely decent houses: so if young gentlemen went to visit Frau von X or Widow von Y socially, the police couldn't very well go as far as to enquire whether a young gentleman knocked by mistake on the door of the chambermaid. It was a different matter, however, with less honest girls, whose presence in any room and at any time was a risky business. But now, when the government, very wisely, is less strict about investigating secret pleasures, the chambermaid's value has greatly decreased, and, with a few exceptions, they have returned to the circle to which they belong – as mistresses of huntsmen, runners, lackeys, house-hussars and especially the salesmen in shops selling silks and underwear. Since they have to go there to fetch items of clothing for their mistresses, lengths of material, ribbons, laces, etc. also come their way. These shop attendants may, as a reward, come on Sundays to take the charming girl out in a hackney-carriage for a drive in the country and – like Yorick [in Sterne's *Sentimental Journey*] – fasten her shoe-buckles.

[There was in 1781 a great controversy about these girls in the public press, started by Johann Rautenstrauch, a Viennese journalist. The whole of gallant Vienna took part and twenty pamphleteers wrote in defence of the good girls.] It is a curious fact that, at the very same time as the quills were being sharpened to defend the chambermaids in Vienna, in Berlin they were doing the same for an old hymn-book [see above, p. 129]. What makes more sense, viewed in the cold light of day, to defend a few thousand nice girls, or to worry about a collection of silly hymns?

93
Redoutensaal Activities

These are the principal amusements for the *beau monde* on Shrove Tuesday [during Carnival; see section 81]. In one wing of the Imperial Castle are two enormous rooms, dedicated to Comus and Bacchus. From 7 January to the morning of Ash Wednesday they are open, at first once a week, then twice a week, and throughout the three final days of Carnival. One alights at an iron gate, passes through the ranks of fifty moustached grenadiers, who with their bearskin hats and bayonets terrify any shy girl as, with palpitating heart, she enters the famous Redout for the first time on the arm of her lover. When you have pressed through this entrance hall and climbed a flight of stairs, all of a sudden you are in the great magical room. The light from many thousands of wax candles reflected in the great crystal chandeliers and from the pyramid-like candelabras arranged in symmetrical rows dazzles the eye; one's ears are enchanted and captivated by fanfares of trumpets and drums, intermingled with the softer tone of a hundred musical instruments; instinctively the youthful foot joins in one of the delightful dances... The entertainment begins at ten in the evening and goes on until six in the morning.

The Redout balls were more crowded at the time when they were first instituted, but dances and picnics in private houses have eaten away at the attendance in recent years.... Nevertheless the court balls are glittering enough, especially in the final weeks. If only a thousand people attend, it feels too lonely; 1,500 dancers make a nice Redout, and with that number there is still enough room to dance. With 2,000 there is no longer room to dance properly, and in the last few days, when there may be up to 3,000 pleasure seekers, it is a real squeeze. The orchestra plays its minuets and German dances in vain, for there isn't room to take three proper steps; everybody is jammed together, making a great awkward mass of people for whom only a slow wave-like motion is possible.

Formerly people used to wear remarkable and sometimes very costly masks,... but such finery has gone completely out of fashion, the masks being considered too heavy an expense for the short time they are used; and most of those attending today wear domino and Venetian capes. Ladies often come dressed in their usual finery. No one who does not have a special reason to remain unrecognized wears a mask over his face. Many attend in their ordinary clothes and simply attach a mask to their hat, in order to conform with the rule that everyone be masked, at least as a token gesture.

[The Redout's profits are given to the poor. The entrance fee is 2 gulden per person. Refreshments and food, at fixed prices, are available in the adjoining room.]

94
Girls for
Amusement

There are hardly fifteen women or girls whose lovers keep a coach and horses for them; of these not five drive around as known mistresses of great gentlemen – really a small number compared to conditions in other great cities.

There is a much greater number who are kept in some style by their wealthy lovers, but who are mostly incarcerated in their own homes; they are never seen in public with their lover, and cost them 2,000 to 3,000 gulden annually. Even greater is the number of those kept by less wealthy gentlemen – girls who live together in twos or threes at the house of some kind-hearted matron, and who cost their lovers 500 to 600 gulden, but who, if a sudden opportunity to earn a few ducats presents itself, will occasionally be unfaithful to them for a quarter of an hour.

All these kept girls are passed from hand to hand. After a time, either their lover has had enough of them, or another comes along with promises of several more ducats each year and, as often happens, is given preference.

There is a fourth class of girls who are supported by no one man, but equally are not available to just anybody; they have certain regular good friends who visit them in rotation.

After these comes another bevy consisting of those who, quite decently and sometimes nicely dressed, stroll about in the busiest streets at noon or in the evening. If they see someone who looks as if he might have a gulden in his pocket, they willingly take him home with them.

The final group...are those brutal whores who haunt the beer-houses of the suburbs, get drunk on mugs of beer and then lie in wild thrashings with soldiers, coachmen and rough manual workers. [Pezzl repeats that the girls of easy virtue are much better behaved and less persistent than those in Paris or Berlin; but connoisseurs complain that they are not really refined enough in the tricks of their trade, their apartments not comfortable and they do very little to amuse their clients.]

But how could it be otherwise? Under the previous government these poor creatures were severely persecuted, and not enough time has elapsed for this branch of the luxury trade to have reached any degree of perfection.

[The transition from girls for amusement to the subject of venereal disease is an easy one. Pezzl quotes a history of the subject by Hensler, in which the author disagrees with those who maintain that these ailments were first imported from the West Indies and America, and claims that they were endemic in Europe but known by other names. Whatever the origin, Vienna is just as susceptible to venereal diseases as anywhere else, especially among the upper classes.]

96
Should one set up Brothels?

[Several pamphleteers suggested some months ago that brothels ought to be introduced, and the government began to give the matter serious consideration. Expert opinions were procured from the police and the Faculty of Medicine, but no decision has been taken. Pezzl is against the introduction of brothels. The advantages of regulated whorehouses are supposed to be that they would be under medical supervision, hence there would be less chances of spreading venereal disease. If it were only girls of ill-repute who were affected, this method might be successful; but what about women of other classes who catch the disease? Their number is not unimpressive, they will infect the cavaliers who, in turn, will pass the disease on to the prostitutes. But Pezzl's main objection to officially approved brothels is that they would constitute a serious blow to civil liberties. In order to restrict the possibility of infection to legitimate houses of prostitution, a constant battle would have to be waged against unauthorized houses and individuals. Spies, denunciations, chastity commissions (as in Maria Theresa's time) and house searches would become prevalent, and would be a far more unpleasant experience for the majority of the public than is the presence of venereal disease in a few. It would be better for the police to insist that prostitutes visit a doctor every eight or ten days; any in need of treatment would be sent to hospital and those in good health would be given a certificate showing the date of their last visit, which could be produced if a client wanted proof.]

97   *College of Surgeons*

[Description of the handsome building, which still exists, on the Währingerstraße; with its 250 students in their distinctive uniform, the whole institution is organized on the lines of a military academy, independent and autonomous. Founded by Emperor Joseph II, it is known as the Josephinium. The course of studies lasts two years, and practical experience is provided through the close association of the college with the military hospital. The director is Johann Alexander von Brambilla, who was earlier responsible for the creation of its organization and statutes.]

98   *The Papal Nunciature*

On the Hof stands a stately building on the façade of which are three coats-of-arms. This is the palace of the Papal Nuncio. [Here the affairs of the Vatican are handled and the primacy of Rome maintained. Description of the various activities, especially the Church's opposition to Enlightenment policies, by actively working for suppression of the Press, persecution of liberal thinkers, etc.]

The Emperor has declared the Papal Nuncio to be a simple political ambassador, on a par with ambassadors from other courts, who should administer the secular affairs of his sovereign and no longer concern himself with religious affairs [in Austria]. The Nuncio took cognizance of this declaration, but – incredible as it may sound – he continues to perform a public act not listed in any known list of ambassadorial privileges: whenever he goes to attend the court in an official capacity, he dispenses blessings in the streets; I myself received one in most humble contrition last New Year's Day. This is about the same as if the Russian or Swedish ambassador were to give a public sermon to their fellow believers.... [Pezzl notes with relish that Joseph II had felt himself obliged to give Nuncio Zondadari in Brussels, 'who was not a very diligent messenger of peace and evangelical humility' three days' notice to leave the Netherlands.]

Clothes maketh man, and tailors maketh clothes, hence they are of prime importance in any state. [Discourse on the position of tailors.]

99 Tailors

Herr de Lucca maintains that there are over 3,000 master tailors in Vienna, a figure I consider rather exaggerated; for if Vienna and its suburbs contain something over 6,000 houses, by his reckoning every second house would have to contain one and one-twelfth master tailors – and anyone can tell at a glance that that is not the case. Counting masters, assistants and apprentices engaged in this profession, there might be 3,000 in all. Some make only men's, some only women's clothing, some, Hungarian costume. Some tailors in Vienna have introduced a curious practice, which as far as I know does not exist in any other city: they have price lists of all their wares printed, just as elsewhere a butcher might display his prices for meat or an innkeeper the price of wine; such fixed-price tailors include Otto, Karl, Krallitschek, etc.

Since these price lists are such a rarity, I include some short extracts...[The price list quoted overleaf gives details for tailored clothes supplied by Herr Adam Karl, whose premises are on the Haarmarkt.]

gulden
(fl.)

A complete suit of men's clothing, the cloth at 8 fl., lined with double-milled material, and with buttons covered in the same material.. 42

The same with the cloth at 6 fl. or in blended fabric $\frac{7}{8}$ [ell] wide at 2 fl. 30 kr. 35

The same $\frac{7}{8}$ [ell] wide in cloth at 4 fl. 28

The same in blended fabric 2 ells wide at 3 fl. 23

Jacket and Knee-Breeches, or Jacket and Waistcoat

Of cloth at 8 fl., lined with double-milled material....... 32

Of cloth at 6 fl., or $\frac{7}{8}$ [ell] wide blended fabric at 2 fl. 30 kr. 26

Of $\frac{7}{8}$ [ell] wide cloth at 4 fl. 23

Of blended fabric 2 ells wide at 3 fl. 17

Greatcoats

Of cloth at 6 fl. lined with double-milled material........ 28

Of worsted cloth at 6 fl... 36

Of cloth at 4 fl. 24

Waistcoats and Knee-Breeches

Of heavy silk material at 3 fl. 30 kr. the ell 18

Of medium-heavy material 13

Of woven, triple-milled linen 8

Of Manchester [cotton] for summer 15

Of medium-weight material 10

Summer Clothes

Plain man's suit of fine camlot lined with taffeta.......... 38

Of fine Harawin at 2 fl.. 28

Of triple weave at 28 groschen 26

Of half-silk camlot... 25

Of plain fustian, with canvas lining 13

Liveries

A complete livery in cloth at 2 fl. 30 kr. 20

The same in cloth at 1 fl. 30 kr..................................... 15

Anyone who supplies the cloth and lining pays 6 fl. for the work. Very tall or fat men pay a supplement....

The Pole Koltschitzky, who served as interpreter with the Austrian-Oriental Trading Company in Turkey, was equally proficient in the Turkish language and in the preparation of Turkish coffee; during the siege of 1683 he performed valuable services for the Viennese as a spy and courier. After the Turks had been expelled, the Emperor bade him ask a favour (as was then the custom) as a reward for loyal service; and Koltschitzky requested permission to open a public coffee-house. It was the first of its kind anywhere in Europe, ... although the first coffee had arrived from the Levant at Marseilles in 1644 and had been drunk in private houses. ... There are now some seventy of these institutions in Vienna and its suburbs, and so far there are no signs of any reduction in their numbers. Coffee-houses are now, as is well known, one of the indispensable ornaments of any large city ... vital for idlers to while away the time, for bachelors of modest means to enjoy a quick breakfast, ... and for poor souls to keep warm in winter.

100
Coffee-houses

Since its beginnings, the institution has considerably broadened in scope, and serves not only coffee but chocolate, punch, lemonade, almond milk, egg-flip, rosoglio [something like maraschino], ices, etc. – all of them unheard of even by name in Germany a few hundred years ago. Now one studies, plays cards, chats, sleeps, does business, talks politics, reads the newspapers, and so on in coffee-houses; in some, people are also beginning to smoke tobacco.

In Vienna, the best-known houses are Milano, Taroni, Kramer, Dukati, the one on the Neuer Markt, that next to the main Customs House, and Hugelmann's, near the Leopoldstädter Bridge. They are nicely furnished, the service is good and they are very popular. The usual game ... is billiards, for which usually two or three tables are provided; if well attended, they can bring in 12 gulden a day....

In Vienna the taste for coffee-drinking has even spread to the journeymen and market-women, and that is why in all the suburbs until noon there are wooden stalls where a drinking bowl and a little crescent roll can be purchased by any passer-by for 1 kreuzer: except that it is not real coffee, but roasted barley sweetened with syrup ... for these people, however, this is – at 1 kreuzer – the best and cheapest breakfast they can obtain. Such a coffee-stall can make a profit of 33 kreuzer on a good day.

101
Newspapers

[A discussion of the uses and virtues of newspapers. Pezzl maintains, wrongly, that no country in Europe has as many and such a wide variety of newspapers catering for all interests as does Germany in all its separate parts (Austria included). He believes sixty to be no exaggeration.]

Vienna has its political newspaper [*Wiener Zeitung*], with a kind of advertiser [*Intelligenzblatt*], which appears twice a week and costs 12 gulden [yearly]. Although it is in no sense a court newspaper, it is subjected nonetheless to rigorous censorship. The proprietor pays some 9,000 gulden p.a. for the privilege.

In addition, there are several newspaper-like political publications, a financial journal, one from the Church, a *Gazette de Vienne*, a *Gaz[z]etta di Vienna*, *Ephemerides Vindobonenses* (a Latin paper), a Hungarian paper, a *Compilation complette*. . . . Vienna has no literary periodical [of its own].

The other most widely read newspapers are those from Brünn, Erlangen, Hamburg, Frankfurt, Augsburg, Regensburg, the French paper from Cologne, Leiden, *Courrier du Bas-Rhin*, the Italian paper from Florence [*Gazzetta Toscana*], the *London Chronicle*, *Das politische Journal* and *Die allgemeine Literaturzeitung* [published in Jena from 1785].

For the last two years foreign newspapers have been reprinted here: it was a worthy idea of a Frenchman, who was granted the privilege of reprinting the . . . *Leidner Zeitung*, as a result of which he now lives comfortably at the expense of [the editor] Herr Stefan Luzac. Since it is doubtless very pleasant . . . to be able to live at the expense of foreign newspaper-writers, the industrious Frenchman rapidly found imitators, who, however, were not so successful. . . . So apart from the *Leidner*, the original edition of which may not be imported, the only other paper currently reprinted is that from Erlangen. . . . Three publications reprinting extracts from foreign-language papers in German translation are sold.

For the past several months . . . a *Schwarze Zeitung* ['black paper'] has been published twice weekly. It lists deaths on the front page, and includes details of accidents and biographies of suicides [an idea which Pezzl disapproves of, since he thinks it serves to impress the idea in the minds of the lower classes. The reports are written in Viennese dialect and the suicides are all famous men; the paper is printed in such a way that individual numbers, instead of being thrown away like any other newspaper, can be kept and later bound to make a regular book.]

Vienna has two handwritten papers, one in German [*Der heimliche Botschafter*, literally 'The Secret Ambassador', only one incomplete set of which for most years still exists] and one in French: the German one is dry, lacks style and is badly written; the French one, somewhat more tolerable, is written by the ex-Jesuit F.—— and even attempts to be witty, ... and succeeds as long as he sticks to political gossip. However, he lapses into Jesuitical practices, criticizes new books, attempts to defame their authors, inveighs against freedom of thought and the spread of deism, etc. ... These papers also appear twice a week and are circulated from hand to hand; an annual subscription costs 6 ducats. Very few people know who the writers are.

    The content of these papers is daily news and city gossip. Important things appear cheek by jowl with trifles: the decrees of the monarch next to those of the latest fashions ... in short, anything that happens at court, in the city, in the army, deaths, marriages, love affairs of the famous. ... On the whole, these papers contain one-third truth and two-thirds trash and lies. ... Yet they are distributed all over the Austrian provinces and sent to foreign courts by diplomatic representatives, etc., and their content is gleefully taken up and reprinted by papers in Hamburg, Frankfurt, Cologne, ... and so on. That is one of the explanations for so much of the rubbish that is written about Vienna. ...

102
*Handwritten
News Sheets*

In centuries past, ... when a little bad Latin and some theology were considered the height of human knowledge and the public education system seemed to have no other aim than to teach boys to become priests, the education of the fair sex was as good as non-existent. Since girls could not become priests, why bother to educate them? Even after boys' public education was put on a more serious footing, they still forgot the girls'. ... Not until recently was the importance of education for girls taken seriously ... with the result that in some places in Germany schools were founded for them; now at last the matter is being seen as a genuine need. ...

    Joseph II has now [1787] instituted a Boarding School for Girls which fulfils the same function as a schoolmaster seminary does for men, viz. a public state institute for the training of female teachers. This institute, which at present houses twenty-four girls between the ages of seven and fourteen, is the brainchild of the Emperor. The girls spend eight years in the

103
*Boarding
School for
Girls*

boarding school and are then destined to become teachers in public girls' schools. While here, they are taught religion, calligraphy and grammar, arithmetic, drawing, philosophy, natural history, geography, history, essay-writing, German and French languages, and the other usual female accomplishments....

The institute is housed in a wing of the Ursuline Sisters' convent, but has no connection whatever with the nuns. The girls are neatly but very simply dressed. The monarch has given them for their recreation a garden in the suburbs, where they play games and exercise. Madame Luzac is in overall charge. Admission to the institute is at the Emperor's personal choice and discretion.... On the first Sunday of every month, the institute is open to anyone wishing to acquaint himself with its organization.

104
The Prater

The name of this pleasure garden derives presumably from the Spanish 'Prado', corrupted into 'Prater' by the Viennese populace.... It is a wood inhabited by deer, pheasants and wild boar, and is the favourite place of recreation for the Viennese. You enter it from an alley of chestnut trees in the suburb of Jägerzeil and find yourself in a wide semicircle, from which five alleys fan out to the woods and gardens. In the central part are a number of taverns, summer-houses, tables, bowling alleys, a merry-go-round and other games providing opportunities for exercise....

...On holidays, the Prater is very crowded and has an altogether picturesque appearance – hundreds of carriages passing to and fro along the alleys; under the trees are tables with roast chicken and bottles of wine; all around there are games, music, the cries of children, the sound of happy laughing people,... some wandering in the shade, some playing dice, some lying on the ground, some further away, friends or lovers strolling arm in arm amid the shrubbery....

Next to the central alley on the left is the fireworks area: the scaffolding for the biggest displays remains in place all year round.... The fireworks displays are the Prater's best attractions. The entrance fee is 20 kr., which means that the common people cannot afford it and only the better-off come.... The spectacle usually lasts forty-five minutes,... and if the weather is good, Herr Stuwer, the fireworks' director, usually takes in 5,000 or 6,000 gulden [the attendance being *c.* 15,000 or more].

At the south-eastern end of the Prater, hard by an arm of the Danube, is the Lusthaus, a round, free-standing pavilion with three galleries on the outside affording pretty views. This Lusthaus is open to the public all year [and still exists today].... On fine summery days, and especially in the spring before the nobility depart for their summer residences, this Lusthaus is heavily frequented, and the whole road leading to it crowded with people, carriages and horses. To combat the troublesome dust..., wells were installed along this avenue last year, and from them the convicts sentenced to sweep the streets draw water and sprinkle it on the roadway.

It is a very pleasant experience to sit in a coffee-house at the Leopoldstädter Bridge on a fine Sunday evening and watch, as... the train of carriages rolls slowly back into town... sometimes over 1,200 of them in a period of 1½ hours....

The Prater used to be, in the era of Emperors Charles VI and Francis Stephen, reserved for the court and the nobility. The present Emperor, however, has opened it to the public.

[A short philosophical discourse which has been omitted.]   105   *Egoism*

This craze is now all the rage among Vienna's fashionable society. It began during the American War of Independence, and it was then that people began generally to learn English so as to be able to read the newspapers; in this fashion they became more familiar with the English and their habits. There have always been young Britons visiting here; under the present government their numbers have increased, with accompanying evidence of their style of dress, their silliness and their pleasures. The quest to imitate them has grown apace.

106
Anglomania

The results of this anglomania are to be seen in people reading and speaking English, round hats, large greatcoats of rough material, full neckerchiefs, dark frock-coats with high collars, boots and spurs at all times. A slovenly, heavy gait, large branch-like clubs instead of walking sticks, a kind of rusticity in attitude and in manners, cadogans [knot of hair at the back of the head], punch, jockeys, whisky, racing, etc.

For ladies it means a liking for horse-riding, tea, hats, *anglaises* [a dance], speaking English and reading books, and a general preference for any male, young or old, handsome or hideous, who lives anywhere between the Isle of Wight and the Orkneys.

[Pezzl concludes by saying that some silly Viennese men seem to regard themselves as English if they hold a glass of punch in one hand and a gnarled stick in the other; nor does he approve of Viennese girls who start a love affair with any Englishman who happens to be passing through. There have been too many impostors, young men who claim to be the sons of peers, who appear drunk at the distinguished dinner tables and want to practise the art of boxing on journeymen or cabmen. The Viennese have become more careful, more wary of welcoming with open arms anyone who comes from England.]

107 *Criticisms of Preachers*

[This section has been omitted.]

108 *Fashions*

'In matters of fashion Vienna generally follows the Parisian trends. There are ladies and fashion designers here who regularly have mannequin figures and sketches sent from France. It is rare for our fashion designers to create anything original, and when they do, it does not win the degree of approval accorded to a Parisian model.

'Altogether, however, one has to admit that fashions here are not constantly changing, nor are they elevated to the pinnacle of importance we hear they assume in Paris. There are in fact not very many ladies here in Vienna who consider it necessary to follow every new fashion without delay. Most seem to react rather slowly. I think fashions change at least four times in Paris before they change once here; many Parisian creations never reach here at all. It has to be something very pretty and comfortable before the style is generally adopted by the elevant world of Vienna, but once adopted, it lasts three-quarters of a year longer than in France....'

So states the *Journal des Luxus und der Moden*, the authoritative work on the subject for all who worship the goddess Fashion. The *Journal* is right....

Nowadays men usually dress in the English manner. Perhaps the neatness, comfort and solidity of an English suit accords better with our German national character than do the altogether too frivolous trifles of the French. The ladies, however, still preserve a greater dependence on the French capital and its designs, and that is why Vienna's two leading fashion designers...go in person at least once a year to Paris, to see for themselves whatever new developments have taken place and to bring back the latest [designs] for their Viennese clients. The scale of the demand here...is reflected by the number of accredited milliners in Vienna and its suburbs – 665.

109 Churches

[There are some thirty fewer churches and chapels in Vienna than six years ago. Under Joseph II, interiors have been simplified and many of the tasteless devotional articles removed. The former practice of celebrating several masses simultaneously at different altars in the same church has been altered, resulting in less distraction and confusion for worshippers. Wigs and coats have been removed from statues; popular German hymns have replaced those *opera buffa*-like choruses which were turned into a Sanctus. Pezzl considers all this a great improvement.]

110 Baths

[Pezzl reminds his readers that Vienna is a very dusty city, with a heavy atmosphere most of the time, and that the Viennese should take more baths than they do. Formerly, bathing in the Danube was banned on grounds of morals and safety. The half-dozen public baths provided are too few for a city the size of of Vienna and too expensive; the cheapest price, 17 kreuzer, is about what an ordinary worker earns in a day, hence he cannot afford to bathe. The government should promote bathing by providing free facilities for children of poor families and by encouraging doctors and priests in the country to persuade the people of its merits.]

111 Academy of Arts

[A description of this institution, founded in 1705, in the reign of Joseph I.]

112 Jewel Room

[A description of the famous Schatzkammer, in the Imperial Castle, where the Austrian crown jewels and other outstanding treasures, including the so-called Florentine Diamond, etc., are on display. Pezzl recommends a personal visit.]

113 Veterinary School and Animal Hospital

[A description of this institution, supported by Joseph II, which became fully active in 1777.]

114 New Year's Eve

[This holiday has become the one which the Viennese celebrate most avidly. It is the great family holiday and the occasion for making visits; it is a holiday for all classes, when good wishes are exchanged. In social terms, it was then much more important than Christmas – primarily a religious festival.]

PART FIVE: 1788

115
The Turkish War

After a fifty-year truce, Austria has recently begun fresh hostilities with the Ottoman Empire. On 9 February 1788 the Austrian declaration of war was made formally known to the Divan in Istanbul, the Pasha of Belgrade and the various Turkish border officials in Bosnia, Serbia, Wallachia, Moldavia, etc.; next day fighting broke out in several places. The whole of Europe has turned its attention to this spectacle, in which parts of Asia and Africa are also involved.

Vienna more than anywhere else is closely involved in this affair. The activities of the Austrian army, and its fate, on the Turkish borders, are the leading topics of interest among the public.... The motives for the present war are similar to those which prevailed in 1737. The Turkish attack on Russia required the latter's staunch ally [Austria] to raise its sword once again against the Pforte. We can only hope that these efforts will be crowned with more success and honour than was the case fifty years ago.

Austria has every reason to feel optimistic about the outcome of the present Turkish War; ... compared to the situation fifty years ago, its military strength has been transformed – the army has large numbers of picked men who are excellently equipped, its generals are experienced, and its artillery enormous and well supplied with full magazines. The state's finances are flourishing, and there exists a superfluity of all the necessities for waging war; but most important, the whole of this war machine is led by the monarch in person, who is to no small extent discerning and active, who knows when to apply severity and kindness, who will dismiss those who fail in their duties and punish the intriguers, the cowards; who will reward the steadfast, the loyal and the brave.

One must, however, take account of the fact that the Turks are in no sense an enemy to be despised. They have a high opinion of themselves, their patriotism, fanaticism, greed for money, lend them a high degree of personal courage. Considered individually, they may be counted the equals of soldiers of any army. They also have the advantage of an inexhaustible supply of manpower which their despotic rulers can draw on from

162

Asia and Africa; on account of their modest and poor nutrition the cost of feeding them is only about half of what our troops require.

It is to be presumed that superior strategy and good artillery, which habitually decide the outcome of wars nowadays and in which the Turkish armies are particularly wanting, will be decisive here as well, and will prevail over wild and disorderly fighting. . . .

One less pleasant aspect of the Turkish War is that the size of a loaf of bread in Vienna has been reduced by more than half, and that [conversely] items of food have become dearer in exactly the same ratio, because all supplies from Hungary have been stopped.

The court has not yet levied an extraordinary war tax. The government would be doubly pleased if it could effect all those conquests in the east without having to impose new taxes; it seems reasonable to hope that this will be the result, for considering the present state of the armies and relations with other allied powers, the war cannot possibly last very long. [In the event, hostilities dragged on for nearly two years; see also section 143, 'Victory Celebrations'.]

[Description of Vienna's harbour and Customs House on the Danube; here produce is delivered and passengers arrive on vessels sailing downstream. The Mozart family arrived here in October 1762 – see p. 9.]

116
Das Schänzl

[Operations of the Vienna City Bank (Wiener Stadt-Bank), whose bonds yield 3 to $3\frac{1}{2}\%$ and are used in peacetime in lieu of cash in many Austrian territories, including the Netherlands. After the costly Seven Years' War (1756–63), the rate of interest was reduced from 5% to 4%, and for many years new deposits have been subject to an upper limit of $3\frac{1}{2}\%$. Workings of the Stadt-Bank-Amt (City Bank Office) in the Singerstraße, and the Hof-Kupfer-Amt (Court Copper Office), where bonds are also issued at $3\frac{1}{2}\%$, though increased to 4% since the outbreak of the Turkish War. The Exchange is open from 11 to 1 o'clock and in the afternoons from 3 to 5 o'clock; its offices are in the Kohlmarkt at the 'Little Green Barrel' on the first (U.S. second) floor. Details of its operations.]

117 *Banking Businesses and the Exchange*

118 *The Jews*   [In Vienna the Jewish community consists of about 550 persons, mostly engaged in money-lending, their activities being centred on the Judengasse and the Preßgasse. An enormous contrast exists between the poor, unkempt Polish Jews and the rich families in Vienna, among which the best known are the Arnsteins, Wetzlars (Mozart's friends), Hönigs, etc. The Jews have no synagogue in Vienna, but they are free to worship when and how they choose in their own homes. Any Jew wanting to marry here must prove assets of 10,000 gulden. Anyone wanting to settle must provide the police with evidence of means. Foreign Jews who come to visit the various fairs receive a permit to stay for six weeks only; once it has expired, they must re-apply for a further six-week period. In order to integrate this 'exotic' race into the way of life and thought-processes of the brave German nation, the Jews have been ordered to adopt certain German family names; they are to write all their bills, synagogue books, court records, contracts, letters of credit and indeed all public documents, in the German language and using German (i.e. Roman) script. Their schools in the Austrian Crown Lands have been placed on the same footing as German state schools, and German must be taught there. In Galicia (Poland) they have been permitted to acquire property on favourable terms, and have been given other inducements to accustom them to agriculture and tilling the soil. In a footnote Pezzl quotes the *Wiener Zeitung* of 21 May 1788, where it is reported that Galician Jews are – like other citizens – to be subject to conscription for military service, from which they were previously exempt.]

119 *Convents*   [Following a long diatribe against convents and the reasons why girls are often forced into taking the veil, Pezzl continues:]

In Austria one had had enough of this race of human beings and their supposed profession. The present government has suppressed all convents that concern themselves only with choral singing. Only two kinds of religious orders were retained: on the one hand, those whose sisters maintain infirmaries for needy women, and on the other, those which provide instruction for girls.

Vienna has only three remaining convents: the Elizabeths on the Landstraße, who run a hospital, ... an admirable example in these times of great economic stress [Turkish War], the Ursulines in the city educate bourgeois girls; and the Salesian

164

Sisters on the Rennweg run a boarding school for daughters of the nobility. Although these institutions have their good sides and justify their continued existence, it is well known that education at the hands of nuns is always distorted... Many an honest husband has had reason to regret the impressions and habits instilled in his wife's mind when she was attending a convent school....

Foreigners here and we abroad have found German, and particularly Viennese cuisine to be the best, the most nourishing and also the most substantial. The English content themselves with roast beef, the French with roast mutton and a few little meat pies, the Italians with seafood fried in oil and their stracchino cheese [a soft cow's-milk cheese from Lombardy]. But the Viennese love a whole range of dishes, from woodcock to pigeon, from trout to tunny-fish; his table must be provided with choice morsels of every kind of poultry and all the fish in the sea. His soups are nourishing and tasty; the frequency and number of gout-sufferers here proves the point.

120 *Wines*

A good wine is a necessary adjunct to his table.... The patriotically minded drinker prefers the products of his own country to wines from France and Italy. The hills all around Vienna – Grinzing, Nußdorf, Bisamberg, Brunn and Gumpolds-kirchen – supply wines which become increasingly costly as they age... When aged, they can be compared without embarrassment to Rhine wines. Doctors prescribe wine for the aged, and for those with stomach troubles, and seldom to no effect.

It is said that the Germans, and especially the Austrians, are heavy drinkers.... This is a somewhat exaggerated claim today. The German eats more and better than his neighbour, hence he drinks more....

Class differences also account for the differences in the wine people drink.... The nobility of the first rank... bitterly regret the ban on the importation of wines from abroad. Only rarely does one see Spanish wines, Burgundy or champagne on their tables. An import duty of 60% and having to furnish the name of the family wanting to bring wines in from abroad have brought about this scarcity.

Their place has been taken by Hungarian wines.... The ladies have developed a taste for Tokay wines, but they are served hardly anywhere except at court and in a few great houses.... This is the best wine for weak nerves and stomach cramps, its fire being tempered by its sweetness.... Even the Russian court has a vineyard near Tokay in Hungary, guarded day and night by a garrison of thirty men and an officer....

It would be amazing if the production of wines did not attract swindlers. Therefore I advise you not to touch any Tokay wine unless it comes from one of the Hungarian estates. The wine-dealers have found ways of making it from dried berries and syrup....

Besides Hungarian wines, some sweet wines from Friuli, Istria, Lombardy and Tuscany [all Austrian lands] are drunk. With the spread of Anglomania [see section 106], punch has become extremely popular; instead of rum or arrack [*Raké*], one often prepares it using a good Hungarian slivovitz [plum brandy]; even young women now give punch parties....

The best wines from the monarchy are to be had in the cellars of monasteries that have not yet been dissolved; the Benedictines at Melk, the Augustinian Canons of Klosterneuburg, the Barnabites of St Michael etc. are wine-dealers. Hungarian wines are best purchased from Himmly in the Trattner House and Hammer at the 'Red Hedgehog', Friulian and Italian from the spice-dealer Patuzzi at the 'White Rose' and Kappler at the 'Camel'.

In the most famous restaurants only mediocre wines are served, the most expensive being worth barely half the price. The owner wants to recoup the costs of his kitchen by selling wine and often resorts to diluting and colouring his drinks.

121 *St Stephen's Cathedral* [A short description of the famous Gothic building where Mozart and Constanze Weber were married on 4 August 1782.]

122 *Garrison* The garrison at Vienna usually consists of two battalions of grenadiers, six battalions of fusiliers, one artillery regiment, one cavalry regiment, the four royal life guards [cf. section 30], the corps of engineers, the gunnery corps, the corps of transport and the medical corps. The War Ministry with its staff of about 700 is responsible for all uniformed personnel.... Unlike German cities,... where military parades take place every day,... there is hardly room for such a public spectacle in Vienna, with its throng of people, carriages and goods.... At one time the guard was paraded on the bastion adjacent to the Castle, later on the Esplanade, but no longer.... For some of the divisions on guard duty it was about three-quarters of an

hour's march from their barracks to the Castle, and the parade itself detained them even longer.

At present a company of grenadiers with standards and regimental band marches through the Castle gate at 11 a.m. each day and occupies the Castle guardroom, outside which stand two cannon [see also section 127]. A corps of fusiliers marches to take up guard duty at the War Ministry, where four cannon are in place. In German cities soldiers are often a pest, begging, stealing and ... molesting the population. This is not the case in Vienna, where very few soldiers are to be seen, especially in the city itself, except for those on duty – proof that the populace is very well-ordered here and of a situation that deserves to be imitated everywhere. Unpleasant punishments for breaches of military discipline, such as running the gauntlet, which take place in the main streets of other cities, are here carried out in private in the courtyard of the barracks. ...

The garrison of Vienna seems to be present only for parade duties. ... For nearly a year now the city gates have been without guards, and this situation will presumably continue for the duration of the Turkish War. ...

This amusement park is for Vienna more or less what the [Jardin des] Tuileries is for Paris. It lies just to the north of the city at the end of the Leopoldstadt ... and laid out in alleys, rather like the Prater. ... It is ... rectangular in shape ... and bounded on the north side by an arm of the Danube ... the entrance is at the south-eastern corner and above the gate is a sign [erected by Joseph II] which reads: 'This place of recreation is dedicated to the people by one who appreciates them'. All numbered vehicles, i.e. hackney-carriages, must stop outside the gate and only the carriages of the gentry, or others that may be considered as such, are allowed to enter the great courtyard. Here there are four alleys and a pavilion containing two large halls for eating and dancing, a billiard room and a few other rooms. ... After passing through the building, you will see to the right the very simple domicile of the Emperor, with a small flower-garden. ... When he is in residence, the Emperor often mingles with the public, in the company of ministers, generals or ladies. To provide an added pleasure for himself and for those who visit the Augarten early in the morning, he purchases a large number of nightingales each year and has them released in the garden. ...

123
The Augarten

124   *Lackeys*   The total number of domestic servants in Vienna has been estimated to be about 40,000,...which includes some 6,000 lackeys. This description embraces not just ordinary footmen, but heyducks, runners, huntsmen, personal hussars, uhlans, jockeys, blackamoors, etc. One could perhaps add all porters, coachmen, grooms, postillions, outriders, etc., since they also wear livery. They might increase the total figure by rather more than 2,000.

Footmen are the most numerous category....In the best houses tall, strongly built fellows are sought after as lackeys. To distinguish them from the servants of middle-class households, they are provided with a heavy livery trimmed with velvet and silk and made, as is the general custom, in colours matching those of the house's coat-of-arms. They earn 16 fl. a month. In less grand houses the livery is generally not as heavy, and lackeys from houses further down the social scale can be recognized by their grey livery with coloured collar. Their earnings work out at 7 fl. monthly.

Heyducks have almost entirely gone out of fashion. Only a few elderly ladies still retain them to accompany them to church. Runners are numerous. They are employed in the main for delivering letters and messages in town, and at night to run ahead of the carriage with a torch. Huntsmen or musket-loaders are just for show, to have a man on one's carriage in fancy green livery with wide silver stripes, horn slung over the shoulders and a pretty hunting knife at his belt; most of them never fire a shot from one year to the next. The personal hussars arrived here with Hungarian families, but are now to be found in most German noble houses as well, riding out with the young gentlemen....The Polish costumes of the Uhlan regiments found favour...and were copied for servants who ride either on horseback or on the coach. The many Englishmen staying here brought their grooms with them, and the Viennese have imitated them. Such a jockey is a young man in short riding waistcoat, his hair cut short all round, and wearing a round hat, a broad band around his body, and boots. They ride with their masters, stand on carriages and serve at table....Some ladies and gentlemen with a taste for the exotic employ a blackamoor, clad in an East-Indian fashion, to perform footman's duties [Prince Esterházy's entourage at the time included one such]. There are very few of these.

Lackeys are as a general rule a shameless race. The finer the house, the more arrogant the servants are likely to be. Tavern-keepers who want to keep their ballrooms respectable always include in their announcements the warning 'Liveried servants not admitted'. But what happens? The elegant lackey keeps a second set of clothes. As soon as he has taken his master or mistress home from an evening party, he discards his fancy livery coat, dons a modish frock-coat and an English hat and, with feigned aristocratic demeanour, proudly enters the hall. If as a bonus he can chat a little in French, he may act the part of the young cavalier to such perfection that he turns many a bourgeois girl's head by paying her compliments.

[Because of the need to deal with the Ottoman authorities, the Austrian government required the services of loyal subjects capable of speaking Turkish, Armenian and other such 'oriental' languages, and to this end the Oriental Academy was founded in Maria Theresa's time, following the example of the one established in Paris in the reign of Louis XIV. Graduates were sent especially to Istanbul, where they entered the embassy and began to conduct business with the Pforte. A revised and improved edition of Meninski's dictionary (Turkish-Persian-Arabic-Italian-Latin) is being issued by this academy in four volumes and will be unique of its kind.]

125
The Oriental Academy

Being an old city, Vienna does not have many large squares, ... but one is the Hof, ... the biggest of them all, almost literally square and surrounded by impressive houses, with a monument in bronze and two fountains. Here, on Easter Day 1782, from the balcony of the church on this square, Pope Pius VI gave his blessing to the faithful of Austria.... [see ill. 15].

126   *Squares*

The Neuer Markt, also fairly large, is rectangular in shape, and is graced by a fountain and a fine bronze group sculpture by [Raphael] Donner. The Hoher Markt, also quite spacious and rectangular, has a stone monument and two fountains.... Here, hard by the city's Palace of Justice, the courts' punishments (though not executions) are carried out in public. The Graben, smaller than those already mentioned, is really little more than a long, wide street, though embellished with the Trinity Pillar and two fountains. The Josephsplatz, with the Imperial Library, and the Burgplatz or Castle Square are likewise not very large....

The Graben is for Vienna what the [Piazza] San Marco is for Venice, and is never deserted, whatever the time of day. Anyone with half an hour to spare or who wants some exercise walks up and down the Graben a few times. ... In the summer months the whole of one side of the square is occupied by chairs, and here one can order ices or other refreshments from the two coffee-houses close by. The constant general activity in this square is like a magnet for the city's girls of easy virtue, who are known as 'Graben nymphs' ... (Footnote: There exists a 'Pocket Book of Graben Nymphs' [*Taschenbuch für Graben-nymphen*], a delightful little thing which describes their charms and way of life in a comical and witty fashion.)

127
Castle Guard

[A description of the personnel of the Castle guard, and their duties; see also section 122. The number of guardsmen has been reduced since Maria Theresa's time, when the streets were lined all the way from the *Linie* to Schönbrunn during the summer while the court was in residence there, and when the officers enjoyed a number of special dining privileges. The Emperor has now cut down on expenses, especially the number of kitchens and kitchen staff, and the Castle guard officers receive a daily allowance and the soldiers from corporal downwards a pound of beef and a portion of wine and bread, meat being replaced on fast days by a double ration of bread and wine.]

128
Orphanage

[Girls who have given birth secretly in the lying-in wing of the General Hospital (see above, section 53) can place their children in the orphanage for 24, 12 or 6 fl., depending on whether they occupied a first-, second- or third-class room in the hospital. Each receives a specially marked memorandum which enables her to remove her child if she so wishes. The child's Christian name is registered, but status and family name remain the mother's secret. Abandoned children are also sent here, a payment of 12 fl. being made by the local authorities of the district where the child was found. Many children are sent into the country, some are given to artisan families in the suburbs, where they grow up to be useful citizens.]

129
Women of the Market Stalls

[A description of these shameless creatures, the roughest and nastiest breed of the female sex, whose stalls clutter the already narrow Viennese streets all year round. They sell every conceivable kind of cheap produce and clothing. They mob any farmer who tries to sell his produce to the public and force him to sell to them for whatever they are prepared to pay.]

It is said that the Parisian fishwives are mistresses of the art of swearing. I wonder if the Viennese market-women would not win a catcalling contest with them. With only the slightest provocation, they will let rip with a stream of expletives. Such a creature is a living encyclopaedia of every term of abuse in the Austrian provinces. [There is also another kind of market-women – the almond-candy sellers, who are to be found on every street corner, in public squares and in amusement parks. It is said that their confections are often made from adulterated sugar, flour and other impure ingredients – unsuited to the delicate stomachs of children, for whom they are usually purchased.]

... The military Order of Theresa holds its annual celebration on the first Sunday after St Theresa's Day [15 October]. The Order was created on 18 June 1757, following the victory at the Battle of Kollin [in the Seven Years' War]; the heroes were immediately rewarded for their deeds, the insignia of the Order being presented while their bleeding wounds were still fresh. It is an Order awarded to those who perform acts of conspicuous bravery in war.... Anyone who makes a valuable contribution ... to military affairs in peacetime or who is an outstanding state official is eligible for the Order of St Stephen, and several generals have been honoured in this way.... The procession of newly honoured generals and staff officers, followed by His Majesty, who is flanked by the Field Marshals Hadik, Lascy and Laudon, on their way to the church, makes an inspiring sight....

The Order of St Stephen and that of the Golden Fleece are celebrated on the first Sunday after the Feast of SS. Emeric and Andrew [5 November].... The celebrations of the orders and New Year's Day are now the only feasts held at [Joseph II's] court with the same pomp as under his predecessor.... His Majesty's table is set with the magnificent gold service made for Emperor Francis Stephen and surrounded by the captains of the noble guard. The Gentleman of the Bedchamber who happens to be on duty acts as the royal carver. The noble guards form a complete circle around the whole, which also includes the table of the knights grand cross, who are waited on by uniformed officers of the Imperial court. The Chancellor

130
*Celebrations
of Orders of
Chivalry*

of the Order of St Stephen is always the current holder of the post of Hungarian Court Chancellor, and during the celebrations court duties are performed only by the Hungarian Noble Guard.

The fourth Order – that of Elisabeth – has no special feast day and is less well known. It is awarded to former officers who have given long and faithful service. With it, as with the Order of Theresa, go certain pecuniary benefits. It was founded by Empress Elisabeth and revived by Maria Theresa, and the number of its knights never exceeds twenty.

The Sternkreuz Order is our only one for ladies. Ladies-in-waiting and other wives of members of the nobility of the first rank receive it from the Grand Mistress, who at present is the Grand Duchess of Tuscany [Maria Luisa, later Empress, consort of Leopold II].

131
The University

[Some German universities are established with an eye to attracting foreign students, whose fees increase the fortune of the often modest town in which the university happens to be. This is not the case with either the University of Vienna or other Austrian universities, which were and are organized to teach the students of the Crown Lands. Vienna University was formerly in the hands of the Jesuits. There follows a description of the institution and a list of some of the famous teachers of the day. The annual fees are very modest – for the philosophy course 18 fl., for law and medicine 30 fl.]

132   *Monks*

[Extraordinary changes have taken place here in the space of only twenty years, accelerated by the present government. In 1770 there were 1,572 monasteries and 591 convents in the Austrian monarchy; in 1773 Jesuit institutions were closed, 139 in all, and from 1780 to the middle of 1786 under the present government 413 monasteries and 211 nunneries have been dissolved. Since then the monasteries of the Pauline Order in Hungary and many others have been closed, so that the combined total of monks and nuns in 1770 – 64,890 – has since been reduced to about 27,000. It is forbidden for any of these monasteries to accept novices; Pezzl presumes – wrongly – that this will gradually lead to their complete extinction. Only the Hospitallers (Barmherzige Brüder) have found favour with the present administration, and are permitted to take in new members, since they serve humanity.]

[It is not only the great courts of Europe which send ambassadors, chargés d'affaires, consuls, etc. to Vienna; the smaller principalities, cities, counties and so on also have their agents here. The agents fall into two groups; *Reichs-Agenten* (agents of the German *Reich*) and *Hof-Agenten* (court agents), the latter subdivided into several branches such as the Austro-Bohemian Court Agency, the Hungarian-Transylvanian Court Agency (later separated), the Netherlands Agency and the Lombardy Agency. Some are universal agencies, i.e. for the court agencies of all the provinces.

There follows a brief description of the intelligence-gathering activities of the great embassies, etc., and of the agencies. There is a substantial number of these agents, who seem to flourish; some have annual budgets of 9,000 or 10,000 gulden, maintain equipages and hold receptions, give concerts etc., employ secretaries and half-a-dozen scribes. The so-called War Agents are the representatives of regiments stationed in the provinces; they attend the Court War Council and are kept busy submitting petitions and requests, however trifling, to the military authorities here.]

133
Ambassadors,
Agents of
Government

[A short history of printing in Vienna. Forty years ago this activity was a monopoly of the Jesuits. Later, newly established printers were poorly equipped and their production consisted largely of prayer-books, school books, legal documents and news sheets, and paper was of poor quality. In 1781 the general publication of pamphlets was permitted (see section 88) and many printers came into existence, with the result that there are now twenty publishers in Vienna with about 118 presses at work. Trattner alone has thirty-one, and can offer normal Turkish letters; he prints many school books, calendars and court documents. Kurzbeck has fifteen presses; he prints oriental books, while Baumeister prints books in Greek, both ancient and modern. Gay prints French, and Schmidt, Wappler and Weimar are among the best of the remaining printers. In general, books printed in Vienna lack beauty and are neither well designed nor free of errors; most publishers do not even employ house proofreaders, hence printers' errors are legion. Kurzbeck has recently acquired some nice Roman typefaces (rather than Gothic), which are gradually gaining ground. Mansfeld now offers both Gothic and Roman type, the latter being as attractive as any used abroad; a corresponding

134 *Printers*

improvement in the quality of paper and printing ink would soon raise standards to the level of those found elsewhere.]

135
Book Trade

[Formerly severely hampered by strict censorship regulations, making it well-nigh impossible to import even a far from suspect book. Much has changed under the present administration. Freedom of the Press has given great encouragement to the book trade, in which notable names are Rudolph Gräffer & Co. (who issued Haydn's piano sonatas in 1774), Krauß, Kurzbeck, Wappler (a fellow Mason in Mozart's lodge), Stahel, Hörling, Mößle. They trade ideas and publication rights with the northern booksellers at the Leipzig fair. Trattner markets his own publications covering a wide range of topics, both within the country and in the provinces. Hartel was the leading printer of pamphlets, but has gone over to less ephemeral works. Wucherer has made a name for himself by printing publications sharply critical of the monarch and the government. Gay deals only in French books. There are also antiquarian booksellers, foremost among whom is August Gräffer.

The north-German book trade is at pains to subvert that of south Germany, for years overshadowed by the products of Leipzig etc.]

136
The Art Trade

[The best-known art dealer is Artaria & Co. on the Kohlmarkt, where the firm has a delightful shop stocked with the finest engravings from every available source. It keeps an excellent selection of the latest British coloured engravings, also caricatures and satirical works printed in London which are calculated to make even the most serious-minded of men roar with laughter. Artaria has commissioned engravings of works of art in the royal collection, as well as a series of views of the city of Vienna and its surroundings; these views include the main squares, walks, the most striking aspects of Schönbrunn Palace and its gardens, all very realistically depicted and beautifully executed; there are already forty-seven folios in existence and they are intended to provide useful and attractive views of Vienna that are of especial interest to foreigners.]

Apart from the art dealers, ... special mention must be made of [Hieronymus] Löschenkohl. Just as in certain places there are occasional poets, so Löschenkohl is, I would venture, the occasional artist of Vienna. Without exception, every notable event in Vienna is recorded and on show at his shop a few days thereafter in a coloured representation. One of his first successful prints was 'Therese's Last Hour' [1781], of which he sold 7,000 at 2 fl. each. Since then he has recorded every important event: the arrival of the Russian Tsarevich [1781], the arrival of the Pope [1782], ... and so on. At the moment, the Turkish War is an inexhaustible source for his talents. Apart from all these subjects, he also prepares silhouettes, miniature portraits and calendars with many and various subjects [see section 138].

[A short eulogy of Prince Liechtenstein as an art collector and connoisseur (the contents of this famous picture gallery are now in Vaduz, capital of the Principality of Liechtenstein).]

137 Li[e]chtenstein Gallery

[Lists several such calendars, including the so-called *Hof-Schematismus*, which provides, for anyone having business in Vienna, invaluable lists naming every member of the Imperial court administration – even down to the lowliest furnace stoker – complete with rank, title, office and salary; in addition, all diplomatic representatives accredited to the Habsburg court are listed (with their addresses in the city), as also are Austrian diplomats posted to foreign courts. Gerold on the Dominikaner-platz publishes it at 3 fl.

138 Calendars

During the past few years there has appeared a *Wienerischer Taschenkalender* ('Vienna pocket calendar'), at once useful and entertaining, along the lines of the social calendars of Gotha, Göttingen, etc. The *Damen-Kalender* ('Calendar for Ladies'), also a new arrival, contains notes on fashion and is a pretty plaything for girls and young women. For the last couple of years Trattner has been putting out an 'Almanac for Clerics', a very useful publication (see also section 89). Löschenkohl has issued a so-called 'National Calendar', containing silhouette portraits of Austrian savants and artists – including, in 1786, Haydn, Mozart and Salieri; and his 'Theatre Calendar' includes all the members of the German National Theatre Company.]

[Under Maria Theresa, pensions had been distributed with unlimited largesse, and her successor Joseph II was obliged to introduce some order into the granting of pensions.] There is no entitlement to a pension unless the subject has given at least ten years' service. After ten years a person whose services are no longer required receives one-third of his salary; after twenty-five years, half; after thirty years, two-thirds; after forty years,

139 Pensions

full salary. For widows and orphans, graduated pensions do not apply, the amount being based on the office held by the deceased; a court councillor's widow, or a general's, receives 600 fl. annual pension, but in order to qualify for such a pension, she must have been married to her late husband for at least four years. Curiously, university professors and other teachers, together with their families, formerly did not qualify for a pension. It was only a short time ago that the Emperor brought all other state employees into the pension scheme, extended very recently to include the actors of the National Theatre.

[The situation is different for army officers: a subaltern who wishes to marry must either produce a capital sum as security for a pension to be paid to his widow, or the wife must sign a declaration waiving any claim to a pension. However, during the current Turkish War, the Emperor made an exception, whereby 'the families of all officers remaining in the field should be eligible to receive pensions, even in those cases where the wives have signed a waiver'.

Following the example of the court, noble families have also been generous in paying pensions to old retainers and their families, though less so now than in former times.]

140 *Debtors' Prison*

Every year at least half a million [gulden] are, I believe, lost in Vienna through bad debts, be they public bankruptcies on the grand scale or the smallest of sums owed by private individuals. . . . For that reason it is very difficult to raise money, and it is getting more difficult all the time. . . .

If you wish to force your debtor to pay, he can – following the presentation of documentary proof and formal legal proceedings – be committed to the debtors' prison of the police department. The plaintiff must furnish the debtor with 4 gulden *per diem* for his keep. This prison is otherwise quite a tolerable place, and is organized in the British fashion: there are two or three prisoners in each room, and they are provided with beds, light and some furniture. For two hours in the morning and two in the afternoon they can move about, visit each other, and amuse themselves, men and women alike; during these hours they can also receive visits from friends, . . . play cards with them, and so on. They are allowed to receive better food from the prison *traiteur*, or nicely cooked dishes brought in from outside, if they can find some kind soul to pay for them; and they may receive linen, clothes, etc. If a debtor has been in prison for a full year without finding the means to repay his creditors, they are obliged to let him be released; however, they retain the right to sue the debtor for restitution, should he come into a fortune again. However, the same creditors cannot have him committed to prison again ... If he has repaid his creditors and then incurs fresh debts, he can be incarcerated once again.

141
'Der Kasperl'
[Harlequin]

[This is the theatrical name for a harlequin or a Punch and Judy show, used to refer to any popular entertainment put on in the various suburban theatres.

'Is the playbill for the Kasperl there yet?' asks the goverment worker as he enters his office. 'We'll see you over there, today they're performing *Cosa Rara* ... ' (see section 76). Kasperl is the kind of entertainment offered by the Marinelli Troupe in the Leopoldstadt Theatre; Marinelli knows the taste of his public and astutely entrusts the presentation of Kasperl to an actor named La Roche. The repertoire caters for those who can barely understand or appreciate the plays performed in the National Theatre (Burgtheater). Marinelli has Italian operas translated into German, and chooses the right pieces for his troupe and his public; he has nice scenery and costumes, and a good orchestra. There is a new piece almost every week, but, apart from a few sentimental plays, he has never dared to stage anything serious. He often plays to full houses, even after twenty-five performances of the same piece.

In the princely Starhemberg Freihaus is the Theater auf der Wieden, now leased by Johann Friedl, the writer (and predecessor of Emanuel Schikaneder, who took over the theatre soon afterwards). This theatre is now regularly visited because it is new. Various groups of strolling players arrive during market hours and play in wooden buildings erected for them on the main squares. 'You have better take some tobacco with you, or you will not be able to stand the smell of the lamps, of spilled beer and garlic sausages' in the midst of the crowd. The action on stage includes some very rough play, and vulgar exchanges frequently occur between the public and the actors.]

142
The River Wien

[The tributary of the Danube from which Vienna takes its name (or vice versa?) was finally dredged in 1787, the banks also being raised and stabilized to prevent it overflowing. This had previously been a regular occurrence, resulting in extensive flood damage; see also section 85.]

PART SIX: 1790

143
Victory
Celebrations

...In 1788 Emperor Joseph II went to war with the Pforte in a better state of preparation... than could be claimed for any previous campaign in history [see section 115]. Although the two wings of the army registered some victories in Croatia and Moldavia,... the main part of the troops, after having taken Sabacz, took up defensive positions, with the result that in the first campaign the Viennese were not treated to any victory celebrations.

In the following year, matters changed considerably... and on 1 August Prince Koburg won a victory at Foczan which was worthy of being celebrated, and was; on 22 September in Wallachia he was again victorious, this time over the Grand Vizier himself. On 1 October, an officer who had witnessed and fought in the battle arrived with the news, entering the city with much pomp, accompanied by four-and-twenty postillions sounding their posthorns; and that Sunday a Te Deum was sung in the Church on the Hof and a salute of 36 cannon was fired on the ramparts.

At 7 o'clock on 12 October, General Kleebeck, drawn by panting horses, arrived with the news that Belgrade had been taken. Now began a victory celebration lasting three days.... Within a few hours... the news had spread... and masses of people jammed the streets and squares,... as they had done for the arrival of Pope Pius VI [in 1782]...

On 14 October, a grand Te Deum was performed in St Stephen's Cathedral, attended by the Emperor, who rode there in full dress, escorted by his entire official retinue and by the noble guards. Every window and side street en route was crowded with spectators, and when he arrived in the Kohlmarkt, a hundred thousand hands applauded, and in the Graben he was greeted with deafening cheers. A cavalry regiment paraded before the church and a battalion of grenadiers with green battle insignia on their caps fired a triple salvo during the singing of the Te Deum. With each salvo of the grenadiers, fifty cannon all around the city walls thundered out the victory signal....

In the evening entrance to the theatres was free, and as

night fell there began a spectacle I shall remember with pleasure all my life. The night was fine, dry and clear, the air mild. Within an hour the whole of Vienna was lit up from the first-floor windows to the attics. On palaces and in the great squares . . . likenesses of [the generals] Laudon and Koburg were displayed, with weapons of all kinds, trophies and inscriptions, all illuminated by lamps and torches. Some of the great houses handed out free wine and beer; from others money was thrown among the crowd. . . . The celebrations continued all night long: at 6 o'clock in the morning bands of musicians were still wending their way through the most crowded streets.

[On 6 January 1788, the nuptials of Archduke Ferdinand and Princess Elisabeth of Württemberg were celebrated publicly. Entrance to all theatres was free (in the Burgtheater, Antonio Salieri's *Axur, Rè d'Ormus* was performed), and a grand ball was given in the Redoutensaal, for which 4,500 free tickets were distributed.]

144 *Court Celebrations*

[A list of the highest appointments, the holders of which were the equivalent of modern cabinet ministers, responsible for affairs of state within the Holy Roman Empire.]

145 *Positions at Court*

[A philosophical discourse on foreigners residing in Vienna, whether for reasons of business or pleasure, and travellers from abroad passing through.]

146 *Foreigners*

. . . Parties are given by all classes, from the nobility of the first rank down to well-to-do middle-class people [see also section 20]. In winter they usually begin at 7 o'clock, in summer at 8 o'clock, and continue until about 10. In some houses they are given three times a week, in others twice, once, or perhaps only once every two weeks, but only in a very few houses are they given every day. They vary greatly: at some, everybody must gamble, at others you may gamble if you wish; at some there is music; at others there is dancing; at others, people simply spend the evening in friendly conversation. Readings were also attempted, though without success. . . . Except for parties given by the upper nobility, where proof of rank is required, those attending all the others come from every kind of back-ground. . . . These parties are very pleasant and useful occasions for foreigners, but care must be taken not to attend those held

147 *Parties*

only for gamblers. They are a good way of getting to know a great many people quite well, for the Viennese are very open-hearted in society. On the first occasion the visitor must simply secure an invitation through an existing acquaintance; thereafter he is always welcome and as a result will gain entrée to other houses.

148
Conversation

[A brief philosophical treatise on the art of conversation in society.]

149
Corpus Christi Procession

[In former days, public religious processions took place almost every week in Vienna, but they were curtailed in Maria Theresa's time. Emperor Joseph has forbidden all such processions except the one held on the Feast of Corpus Christi (the Thursday following Trinity Sunday). For any foreigner who is here for only a short visit, this procession, if the weather allows, is worth seeing.]

The municipal guilds and similar groups assemble very early in the morning, but the actual procession does not begin until 9 o'clock. It starts at St Stephen's Cathedral, wending its way across the Stock-im-Eisen-Platz to the Graben, Kohlmarkt, Herrengasse, Strauchgäßchen, across the Hof, the Judenplatz, the Wipplinger Straße, the Hoher Markt, the Bischofgasse, finally returning to the Cathedral. The four Gospels are read in turn: (1) at the column on the Graben; (2) next to St Michael's Church; (3) at the column on the Hof; (4) at the column on the Hoher Markt. Window places overlooking all four spots are avidly sought after on this occasion. Wooden stands are set up along the entire route, ... which is lined on both sides of the street by a grenadier battalion, and the way is strewn with grass and flowers. If the Emperor is in Vienna, the procession is magnificent. First come the city artillery, then the ecclesiastics from the four remaining monasteries and all the parish churches, then the entire court household, University officials, Cathedral canons, chamberlains, privy councillors, and knights of the Order of St Stephen, of the military Order of Theresa and of the Order of the Golden Fleece. The *venerabile* [host] is carried by the Archbishop, who is immediately in front of the Emperor and leading members of the reigning house, followed by the ladies. They are escorted by members of the German Guard and the German Noble Guard, dismounted. Next come the mounted Hungarian and Galician Noble Guards and, at the end of the procession, a company of grenadiers playing martial music [a wind band]. Throughout the whole ceremony, you hear the majestic tolling of bells from all the churches, and there is vocal and instrumental music. The conclusion is marked by a triple salute fired by a grenadier battalion posted in the Graben. [Pezzl notes that the religious aspect of the ceremonial staged in the city is overshadowed by the secular; most people come to see the court, the ladies and the guards.] The following Sunday, every parish in the suburbs holds a local procession within its own boundaries.

[An outline of the new criminal laws, replacing the old laws promulgated in Maria Theresa's reign; the new Josephinian codex, edited by Herr (Franz Georg) von Kees, court councillor of the High Court, was published on 13 January 1787.] The death penalty is abolished except for offences tried under martial law (hanging being the only method of execution allowed). Other punishments are the irons, imprisonment and public work, first- or second-degree imprisonment alone, and flogging . . . as well as the pillory. [Various degrees of punishment to fit crimes of every sort are set out in detail.] Sentences involving flogging are limited to 100 strokes at any one time. On being convicted, a criminal forfeits all his personal income; for the duration of his prison term, his family is to be provided with enough money to live on, the rest of his income going to the criminal fund. When set free, the ex-criminal has all his (her) property rights restored. Being stripped of any title applies only to the convicted person, not to his family. The penalty for *lèse-majesté* is the total forfeiture of property and a prison sentence in the second degree, never of less than 30 years' duration, and may also include public branding. The same applies to high treason. Prisoners in irons are clapped in a dungeon and their fetters attached so as to permit only essential movements of their limbs. Prisoners of this kind are to be flogged once a year as a public example. In cases of insurrection, the leaders are to forfeit all their property and to be executed. Suicides are to be buried by the hangman, in so far as they die instantly or without confession. If the suicide results from fear of a deserved punishment for a criminal act, the body is to be exposed on the gallows. If suicide is attempted but unsuccessful, the perpetrator is to be imprisoned until he/she may be expected (by means of re-education) to show regret and improvement.

150
Criminal Laws

Punishments for political offences may include flogging, the pillory, imprisonment, public work in irons, dismissal from a specific post. Fines may be imposed only as a penalty for playing forbidden games (gambling). Floggings are to be carried out at all times in public. At any one time a man may receive not more than 50 strokes of a hazel-rod, women not more than 30 strokes of a leather thong or horsewhip, and these only on the buttocks. In this context the word 'political' is used in reference to quack doctors, swindlers, and all manner of misdemeanours, civil and religious.

Pezzl sets out his own views about the advantages and disadvantages of the laws. He considers that it might be bad for public morals to witness public whippings and flogging. Arguments about the death penalty, nearly but not quite abolished. Pezzl concludes with a plea that finding the right balance between crime and punishment – the avowed aim of the laws – depends on the introduction of uniformity throughout the nation in matters of culture, sense of honour, education and life-style.]

151 *Marriages* [Pezzl criticizes the fashion in which the 'happy marriage' is portrayed in the theatre – a romantic concept which in no way reflects daily life today. In our grandparents' time a man was expected to achieve happiness by taking a wife, any wife; now we are more circumspect.]

152 *Lemonade Stalls* These are an invention of recent times. They are tents put up in public squares in summer months; they serve lemonade, almond milk, ices of all kinds, etc.... Around these tents are placed a number of chairs. On warm summer nights the *beau monde* frequents these refreshment tents in droves.

....A glass of lemonade costs 7 kreuzer, a glass of almond milk 10; ices, which cost between 12 and 30 kreuzer per bowl,...are made in many different flavours – tangerine, lemon, sour cherry, strawberry, blackcurrant, sweet cherry, pineapple, almond, vanilla, chocolate, etc. In warm weather it is pleasant to eat ices, but only in moderation, if you want to avoid gripes which are painful and which even prove fatal on occasion. For the past few years, the proprietors of these lemonade stalls have provided the additional attraction of *Harmonie* [wind band] music,...a most pleasant accompaniment to the soft breeze of a balmy, moonlit summer night. If the weather is fine, this entertainment lasts until around midnight.

An Italian idea, imported into Germany. There are several of them, in various houses, and they are a cross between a tavern, a *traiteur* and a coffee-house, providing amusement for the nobility and gentry, foreigner, officers, etc. – in short, for anyone with education and good manners.

153   *Casinos*

They open at 8 a.m. and remain open all day and in the evening as long as there are people present. Breakfast is served, and *table d'hôte* lunch and dinner are served at fixed times and at a fixed price. To help pass the time, newspapers, musical instruments and music itself are provided, as well as permitted games of every sort. In the colder months a ball is given every week. Private balls and parties can be held by prior arrangement – also musical events, picnics, card parties, dinners, etc. – since all the necessary facilities and comforts are available.

[A description of those in Vienna – the Imperial Arsenal in the Renngasse and the municipal arsenal on the Hof – and of those in the provinces.]

154   *Arsenals*

One of the sights of Vienna, ... it consists of a tree-trunk some 7 feet high, its surface covered with iron nails so closely packed that the wood cannot be seen. It is attached by means of iron hoops and a lock to a house in the square which derives its name from it – the Stock-im-Eisen-Platz [Square of the Iron Tree-trunk] ... Legend has it that a locksmith's apprentice once promised his master that, if he could be granted his freedom at once, he would make a lock that no master would be able to open. The master agreed to this. The apprentice sold his soul to the Devil, who helped him construct the lock, the key to which the young man threw into the Danube. After presenting the lock, he gained his freedom but was immediately dragged down into hell by the Devil. Afterwards, every apprentice locksmith would hammer a nail into the tree-trunk in remembrance of his visit. As this is no longer possible, they just gaze at it for a while and ponder the intricacies of the Devil's lock.

155   *The Stock-im-Eisen*

In former times there was also ... a hole in the wall of the corridor in the Minorite [Franciscan] Monastery, through which the Devil had led away a blasphemer. The worthy friars walled it up frequently, but in the night Satan would tear it open again. Recently the Minorites were obliged to leave their monastery; before departing, they had the hole filled, and this time the Devil left it untouched – proof that he has a greater fear of laymen than he does of monks.

156
*Goods Produced
at Home*

When, some years ago, the Emperor forbade the importation of all non-essential foreign foods or those that could equally be produced at home, tailors, merchants and members of the public objected. Many people claimed that the Austrian state could not manage without foreign goods.

His Majesty's persistence has temporarily reduced his critics to silence and has disproved claims put forward by others. When this edict was published, all merchants had to place their foreign goods in a special warehouse and, because no new stocks were allowed in, its contents were soon exhausted....

It is forbidden for Austrians to emigrate; why should the currency be treated differently? Except for spices, medical supplies and cotton, Austria does not – on the whole – have any real need for most foreign products. In the early years of [Maria] Theresa's reign, a similar system was established. Factories were erected in our country. Under the pretext or in the mistaken view that imports would provide a healthy source of emulation and rivalry, foreign goods were once again allowed into the country; but it happened too soon. Naturally, the new Austrian factories were unable to compete with the long-established products from abroad, hence they closed down. Now, thirty years later, the same project is being attempted; let us hope the same mistake will not be repeated.

The city of Vienna alone now has over one hundred works and manufactories of all kinds, most of them established since the new edict banning imports came into force. Some were put up too quickly, without the necessary technical knowledge...and soon failed; on top of this, the present [Turkish] War has reduced the market and forced up prices of daily essentials. But these are only the symptoms of an industry in its infancy, and we shall soon see [i.e. after the war is over] what was soundly based and what was not....

157
Improvements

[Changes and improvements in the structure and outward appearance of Vienna. The mere expansion of a capital city, with many new suburbs, is regarded as a good thing, also the cultivation and laying-out of the Esplanade under Joseph II, the increased amount of lighting in public places, replacement of dark Gothic houses and old monasteries with modern buildings, roomier and with more light. The streets are no longer covered with filth and mud, but are regularly cleaned. The use of large paving stones has made conditions for pedestrians much more comfortable in the city streets. The wretched wooden passage from the Castle to the church of the Augustines has been removed, no longer darkening the charming little Josephsplatz and spoiling the view of the Imperial Library. After listing other improvements already made, Pezzl notes that there is much scope for further work, but that one should not make unreasonable demands.]

[Pezzl criticizes the appearance and lack of comfort and cleanliness of Viennese inns, which, in a capital city, make a very poor impression on visitors from abroad.]

158 *Inns*

[A description of the Botanic Garden in the suburb of Rennweg, beyond the Belvedere (used by university students); the garden in the Währingergasse (used for the teaching of medicine); and the nursery at the Palace of Schönbrunn, where many beautiful and interesting trees and plants are raised.]

159 *Botanic Gardens*

[Pezzl discusses the seasons and the weather, expressing a personal preference for winter in the city.]

160 *The Four Seasons*

[Pezzl contrasts the traditional view of life in the country, characterized by hard work, with the luxuries of life in the city, where some people are so wealthy that by the age of thirty they are world-weary and incapable of enjoying life.]

161 *Children of Fortune*

[Discussses the various subjects taught in different kinds of school in Vienna.]

162 *Schools*

[Auctions are held very frequently in Vienna, and serve a very useful purpose. Household furnishings, clothing, etc. can all be purchased at quite reasonable prices. In addition, plots of land, houses, gardens, equipages, furniture, books, paintings and wines can all be acquired at auction.]

163 *Auctions*

[A description of the collections; formerly combined, the ancient and modern sections have since 1774 been under the control of separate curators, even though still housed in the same place

164 *Collections of Antiquities and Coins*

in the Imperial Castle. The collection of antiquities consists of carved gems (cameos) and ancient medals. The collection of modern coins and medals includes at least 32,000 gold or silver pieces, and the numbers grow daily. Both collections are recommended viewing for all connoisseurs and visitors with refined tastes.]

165 *Sundry Remarks*

For an unmarried man, the cost of food and drink here represents about half of his annual living expenses; for a lower-class family, about one third; for the upper classes, one fifth or one sixth.

***

A private individual generally lives in a completely free and easy way in Vienna today, not subject to any constraints.

***

On formal social occasions one never speaks openly, and never about matters of importance. It is known that walls have ears. Only a person newly arrived from the provinces or someone with no worldly knowledge would bring up such subjects and embarrass others present. The customary topics of conversation are the newspapers, theatre and fashion, spiced with a little city gossip.

***

The arts are much more appreciated and better supported than the sciences here in Vienna. A painter, a sculptor, an engraver, a musician, etc., possesses a certain cachet in society, where he is respected and welcomed, especially in the great houses. A simple scholar, an author, a man of letters, is accepted only with some equivocation, and his title is seldom mentioned without a hint of scorn. Hence, over the years, Vienna has produced many important artists, but hardly any writers of distinction. Now, galleries, art collections and operas are of course very pretty things, but they are concerned only with the imagination, and do not improve the intellect. Surrounded on all sides by works of art, a people can still live in an intellectual vacuum, as for example in Italy. That is why Vienna, for all its beautiful features, lags so far behind Berlin, Hamburg, Brunswick, Leipzig and even the larger cities of Catholic [i.e. southern] Germany in matters of knowledge and enlightenment. In this respect, Schmidt's *Geschichte der Deutschen*, Montesquieu's *Esprit des lois*, Gibbon's *Decline and Fall of the Roman Empire* are of more value to the public than a *Resurrection* by Raphael, a

Cupid by Titian, a *Casting out of Devils* by Rubens, or Correggio's *Holy Night*, and indeed all the operas of [Nicola] Piccinni, [Giovanni] Paisiello and [Vincente] Martin [y Soler].

***

The society of soldiers and clerics is not much sought after in Vienna. – Why should that be?

***

Children are being brought up much more sensibly than in the past. They take a great deal of exercise, their baths are colder, they are more comfortably dressed. . . .

***

The cabriolet [chaise] has come into fashion recently.

***

One sees many ladies aged fifty or more who are painted and powdered. Some do so out of a ridiculous sense of vanity, but many out of necessity – they have worn make-up since their youth, and it has so ruined their complexions that if they did not continue wearing it, their repellent appearance would resemble a skull.

***

Spending 2 ducats on taking a drive is less shocking to the Viennese than paying 30 kreuzer for a book.

***

Anyone who dresses well and lives a life of luxury can obtain credit ten times more easily than someone who dresses quietly and leads a retiring life: no one asks how the former can afford to live in style.

***

The Viennese are very quiet in public streets. Even when a hundred people are crossing a square, almost all you will hear is the sound of their footsteps.

***

. . . Ladies in full finery are much less attractive than they are in négligé.

***

. . . A newly arrived visitor from the provinces is immediately recognizable by his gait, his bearing, his clothes and his manners, all of which betray him in an instant.

***

Formerly people took a keen interest in the court and every aspect of it. Now that the public has been deprived of any display of luxury, people are very indifferent about its doings.

166 *Old and New Vienna*

In the last ten years, and particularly so in the last twenty, Vienna has changed enormously. The changes include physical as well as moral ones, and concern both the city and its inhabitants – the city's size and architectural style, manners, attitudes, pleasures, life-style, dress, education, speech, religion, pomp.... The average Viennese of 1790 bears little resemblance to the Viennese of 1770 or even of 1780.... Not all of these changes are for the better. Here are some examples:

Old Vienna	*New Vienna*
Youths inexperienced in the delights of love; they become fathers rather late and as old men they still retain youthful fire.	Youths trained in Cupid's school, fathers at eighteen and worn out at thirty.
Mothers with a sense of economy, faithful, nurse their own children, rather superstitious but pious.	Mothers who gamble, flirt, give their children to wet-nurses, emancipated but without principles, or pious and hence equally superstitious.
An honest German character; a handshake instead of a contract; a man keeps his word; general kindness of heart.	Politics and deviousness; signature, seal, letters of credit; a gentleman's word rarely to be trusted; egoism everywhere.
Food – cheap and easily affordable.	Food – daily more expensive, lack of money.
The nobility – great, generous and still wealthy.	The nobility – economical, often miserly, for the most part deeply in debt.
The poor cared for even without a Poorhouse.	Poorhouse, but the poor are not really well cared for.
Few tacticians and many good generals.	Many tacticians and fewer great leaders.
The voice of truth heard reluctantly, and punished	The voice of truth apparently heard gladly, but not heeded.

Old Vienna	*New Vienna*
Wealthy citizens, proud to be bourgeois, and with no aristocratic pretensions.	A lot of ennobled bourgeois, rich but not always gentlemen.
Casual talk about the most important affairs of state.	A ridiculous secrecy surrounding the most unimportant matters.
Spies – in wartime and against the enemy.	Spies – in peacetime and against the state's own employees and subjects.
A bad police, but good large loaves of bread.	A good police, yet a shortage of bread, while flour is allowed for use in almond confections, unwholesome baked goods and hair-powder.
Reward according to services rendered.	Reward according to number of years' service.
The state body politic sick from constipation.	The state body politic becoming sick from too many purges.
Pardons – a pleasant prerogative of the great.	Strict fairness for all.
The turnpikes maintained at state expense – and excellently.	The turnpikes leased out – and miserably kept.
The Jews persecuted and despised, contrary to Christian teaching.	The Jews encouraged, and sometimes given preference over Christians.
Thieves and murderers – hanged, broken on the wheel, beheaded; the death penalty.	The death penalty abolished – thieves and murderers now only flogged, or condemned to a slow death [from exhaustion, towing ships on the Danube].

189

Old Vienna	New Vienna
Lottery – imported into Austria by Italian guile but only leased out and considered a pest by any true statesman.	Lottery allowed to continue simply to fill the state's coffers – still considered a plague by true patriots, but protected by financial schemers and regarded as a good source of income for the state.

167 *History and Topography*

[In which Pezzl lists some recently published histories of Vienna and deals with them critically, and then discusses topographies which have appeared shortly before 1790, as well as a map of the city and its surroundings (1783) and the nearly 50 views of Vienna issued as engravings by Artaria & Co. (see also section 136.).]

168 *Vienna's Surroundings*

... The castles in the neighbourhood of Vienna are fewer in number and less luxurious than one might expect near such a capital city, ... and the reason for this is simple: the great and rich vassals of the Austrian monarchy have their own lucrative estates – with splendid castles and gardens – in the provinces, particularly in Hungary, Bohemia, Moravia, etc., and there they spend the summer months. Hence they do not spend money on building new country houses near the city.

Pride of place in the city's neighbourhood goes to Schönbrunn, formerly the regular summer residence of Maria Theresa, but so far not lived in at all by the present Emperor. The palace, though fairly luxurious, is in a rather mannered style. The gardens are open to the public all year round. ... I prefer it to any other garden in Vienna, for it has ... shady walks, fine marble statues, obelisks, [imitation] ruins, artificial fountains, and a menagerie, where the chief attraction was once the elephant, which has not been replaced since it died in October 1784 of a throat infection. ...

Laxenburg is three hours' drive from the city. The two roads leading to it, from Schönbrunn and from the city, are planted with avenues of horse chestnut trees. In the days when the court lived a life of luxury, it was quite a glittering and crowded place. The Imperial Castle is simply designed; hard by are gardens and a large, well-maintained park. The court is usually in residence there for a while in the spring and enjoys the pleasures of heron-hawking. For many years during peacetime, 12,000 to 14,000 men were camped each August outside the park, in the neighbourhood of the village of Minkendorf; they would hold manoeuvres in the nearby countryside over a period of several days.

The Imperial pleasure seat Schloß Hetzendorf is of less importance and very seldom in use.

Privately owned country houses include those at Dornbach, with the castle and park of Count Lascy; at Erla, with the castle and park of Prince Starhemberg; the country seat of Count Cobenzl on the slopes of the Kahlenberg; and, most notably, the country seat of Prince Galitzin [near Dornbach]. All these country houses have parks in the English style, with grottoes, pavilions, waterfalls, exotic birds, fish, etc. In order to be able to visit any of them informally, one needs to obtain the owner's permission.

...One of the most magnificent views of the city may be had from the Kahlenberg, an hour's ride from town and also overlooking the Danube. [A description follows.] Frequently in summer whole caravans wend their way from Vienna to the Kahlenberg, where they enjoy the fresh country air for a few days.

The observant reader will have realized my intentions from the very beginning: I wanted to write neither a dry, precise topography nor to give a complete, comprehensive description of the greatest, ... richest city in Germany. To my knowledge there is no other city which has had so much ridiculous rubbish written about it as has Vienna in this century.... Apart from a few unsatisfactory descriptions, no book has yet been published which gives a philosophical and moral survey of Vienna for the unbiased German public. The present sketch is neither complete nor is it perfect: to write such a book is beyond my powers. That task must be left to my successor.

169
Conclusion

VI
Mozart's stay in Vienna, 1781–91, and its ramifications

M OZART'S FORTUNES in the decade during which much of his time was spent in Vienna follow something of a *crescendo*, reaching a high point with *Le nozze di Figaro* in 1786, followed by a *decrescendo*. At the beginning, all his dreams seemed to be coming true; in 1782 he married, though only with his father's grudging assent, Constanze Weber, with whom he was passionately in love. The visit Wolfgang made to Salzburg in 1783, to introduce Constanze to his father and sister, was not a success. Musically, however, his career was flourishing and his subscription concerts in Vienna were not only artistically successful but also financially rewarding. By the time Leopold Mozart came to visit Wolfgang and his family in 1785, he was able to report home that Wolfgang's large and expensive apartment was a hive of happy activity. The family entertained and were entertained widely. In 1784 Wolfgang had become a Freemason and now persuaded his father to join the Craft, which had attracted many brilliant men. Next year Mozart composed *Le nozze di Figaro*, which was relatively successful in Vienna following its first performance at the Court Opera on 1 May, especially so when it was performed in Prague early in 1787. Although the visit Wolfgang and Constanze made to Prague in January 1787 was enormously profitable and paved the way for a commission to compose his second opera written in collaboration with Lorenzo da Ponte, *Don Giovanni*, Mozart's everyday extravagance meant that he was living beyond his means and it was with relief, therefore, that he learned of Emperor Joseph II's decision to confer upon him the modest title of Court Chamber Musician (*Kammer-musicus*), with a 'middle-of-the-road' annual salary of 800 gulden. During the last five years of his life, Mozart continued to sink further into debt; but even more curious, his subscription concerts began to go out of fashion as the desire of the Viennese to hear him performing his own piano concertos waned. Mozart's public concerts in the capital dwindled into nothing. His financial situation became the more alarming because of his wife's constant illnesses, aggravated by successive pregnancies (a total of six, with only two sons surviving infancy); she was obliged to take the cure several times at Baden, which proved very expensive. In the end,

Mozart's situation became desperate, and when he died on 5 December 1791, he left considerable debts (see p. 199) and was buried in a suburban cemetery in an unmarked grave.

Mozart's ignominious end has provoked many outspoken reactions, and many writers have blamed not just the circumstances of his death, but the city in which he was living. One of the most powerful statements is the description at the end of Wolfgang Hildesheimer's biography:[1]

> Thus died Mozart, perhaps the greatest genius in recorded human history. We feel no qualms in using the sentimental cliché. This is the exemplary coincidence of reality with its overused notation. His was not an unusually premature death, it is true, but he was on the threshold of the years that are usually called 'the prime of life'. Impoverished, broken (our examination obliges us to retain this cliché, too), he 'leaned his head against the wall' (a dubious recollection of the factotum Joseph Deiner, whose presence has not been verified) and left his world, which, to the end, consisted only of his city, the scene of his futile efforts. It had scorned what he offered, quashed his aspirations, and rejected his applications. And yet in an inexplicable way he had remained true to it, no doubt bound by debts and miserable obligations. Here and there the city remembered him, but then again failed to appreciate him; it favoured inferior musicians, who surpassed him. His operas ran in Berlin and Hamburg, Frankfurt and Mannheim; Hungary and Holland offered him honorary awards; but he never knew about them. True to the rules of tragedy, the rescue came too late....
>
> In all likelihood, the caesura of his death did not even disturb Mozart's most intimate circle, and no one suspected, on December 6, 1791, when the fragile, burned-out body was lowered into a shabby grave, that the mortal remains of an inconceivably great mind were being laid to rest – an unearned gift to humanity, nature's unique, unmatched and probably unmatchable work of art.

Why, then, did Mozart choose to remain in this city which had, effectively, rejected him? What other options were available to him? As it happened, at least two major proposals had been made to lure him to different European capitals. The first of these was that he should travel to London.

Many years earlier, in 1764–5, the young Mozart had been to London, but by the time he began to turn his attention once again to the British capital, his successes there as a child prodigy had been largely forgotten. The idea for the trip was prompted by Wolfgang's friends from England in the Vienna Opera – the soprano Nancy

Storace (the first Susanna in *Figaro*), her brother Stephen (a successful composer, who learned many useful tricks-of-the-trade from Wolfgang), and the Irish-born tenor Michael Kelly (who, as well as singing in the first performance of *Figaro*, became a close friend). It is not known if Wolfgang was intimate with Nancy Storace but (as we shall see) they seem to have been in correspondence after she left Vienna and returned to England; and for her farewell benefit concert on 23 February 1787 he wrote the *Scena con Rondo* 'Ch'io mi scordi di te' (K.505) with an obbligato piano part to be played by himself. It had been decided that the Storaces and Kelly would return to England together with Thomas Attwood, who had been studying with Mozart. On 17 November 1786, Leopold wrote to his daughter, now married and living in St Gilgen, that Wolfgang had wanted to go to England with Constanze, leaving their two sons in the care of Leopold in Salzburg. Wolfgang had somehow learned that his father had taken little Leopold (Nannerl's son) into his own house – 'something I never wrote to him', Leopold told his daughter in a letter dated 17 November 1786, 'so he or perhaps his wife conceived that great idea. That wouldn't be bad at all, they can quietly travel, they could die, could stay in England, then I could run after them with the children . . . Basta! . . .'. That Mozart really was planning such a trip can be surmised from a notice published in a Prague newspaper, 'The famous Compositeur Hr. Mozart intends to travel to London next spring, where the most flattering offers have been made. He will pass through Paris *en route*.'[2] On 2 March 1787, Leopold Mozart again wrote to his daughter, explaining that 'Wolfgang will have his pupil [Attwood] make some firm arrangements in London, i.e. a contract to write an opera, or a subscription concert . . . Since I wrote telling him in a fatherly way that he won't earn anything if he goes there in the summer, and will arrive there at the wrong time, and that he must have at least 2,000 f. in his pocket to undertake this trip . . . he will have lost heart.'[3]

There matters rested until 1790, when a new and serious attempt was made to persuade Mozart to travel to London for a concert season. This development has been the subject of an important article by Curtis Price published in 1989.[4] His researches have revealed that the King's Theatre at the Pantheon in Oxford Street, one of two rival opera houses (the other being the Haymarket Theatre with Sir John Gallini as its director), had in 1789 been placed under the directorship of an idealistic though inexperienced young Irishman named Robert Bray O'Reilly. The Pantheon evidently had an inner organization

much like that of a typical Italian house, with box subscriptions and ticket sales used to cover day-to-day expenses, while the salaries of top performers and other major outgoings were guaranteed by princes or great nobles. The music department was divided into *seria* and *buffa* casts, with a separate ballet troupe which, ironically, had the largest proportion of the total budget. In other respects, too, the Pantheon was simply a satellite of Italy, drawing its repertoire and performers from a common fund upon which Naples, Bologna, Florence, Venice and a dozen other centres also depended.[5]

O'Reilly, who was untrained musically, hired as his assistant manager Luigi Borghi, a violinist later acquainted with Haydn; the two men entertained dreams of staging an entirely different kind of opera, not seen for many years in the British capital. The team set out to hire singers and dancers on the Continent. At this point there enters on the scene the Prince of Wales (later George IV), who was to be Haydn's patron after 1791.

The Prince of Wales put immense pressure on O'Reilly to appoint Nancy Storace as *prima buffa*. Why the future King George IV should have taken such a keen interest in Mozart's first Susanna is not entirely clear, but a special relationship emerges from O'Reilly's letters. La Storace stood at a crossroads in her career. The days of glory at the Burgtheater lay behind her, and the slight edge which had always caught on her voice had now turned to harshness. Appearances at the Haymarket before the fire and at the little Haymarket thereafter had been reasonably successful, but neither she nor her brother Stephen – with two Viennese *opere buffe* in his portfolio, one of them to a libretto by Da Ponte – had found stardom in Italian opera in London.

Their equivocal position cannot be attributed to cabals of the sort that ruined the Burgtheater. The sometimes partisan Gallini had commissioned Stephen to acquire scores for the King's Theatre at Vienna in 1786 and later gave him several opportunities to compose, while Nancy was always treated deferentially by the Italian circle in London. There may well have existed an unscrupulous coffee-house lobby which Casanova warned Da Ponte to avoid, but it was too diffuse, too overshadowed by the lawyers of the rich and powerful to have significantly influenced the Storace careers.

In mid-September 1790, when O'Reilly and Borghi began to negotiate with a proud and obstinate Nancy Storace, she was flush with the recent success of her performance in Stephen's comic opera *The Haunted Tower*, and was doubtless already committed to appearing in her brother's next major English work, *The Siege of Belgrade*, which was scheduled for performance at Drury Lane in 1791. In a letter dated 16 September addressed to Borghi, O'Reilly expresses irritation over the singer's prevarication concerning her draft Pantheon contract. At this stage the Prince of Wales offered to arbitrate, as is evident from a letter dated 9 October 1790 from O'Reilly to William Sheldon, a solicitor who headed the board of trustees of the Haymarket Theatre and had 'effective control over Italian opera in London for more than two decades'.[6] In this letter the manager reveals that Storace was holding out for the freedom to perform elsewhere besides the Pantheon, a privilege not granted even to the great castrato Gaetano Pacchierotti. O'Reilly notes that the Prince of Wales

> begged of me to engage Storace & sd if I did he would oblige me in return – I told him of her offers to me & that she would not bind herself for 50 Nights, & also mentd my having wrote abroad – His answer was that he would make her engage on My terms & added that *it was better for me to have a performer of whose merit I was sure than Trust to a new Singer of whom I could not know the success here. – & particularly at this moment* ...
>
> This Morning he sent for me again and asked me if I had Determined as to Storace – I begged a little time to consult with my friends but assured H.R.H. I would do everything in my power to arrange with her – & he sent for Storace & with a vast deal of Good Humour said he would shew me the best way to know a good singer ...[7]

This hastily arranged morning audition suggests that Storace was already waiting at the Prince's residence, Carlton House, when O'Reilly arrived and thus may have conspired with the Prince in an attempt to force O'Reilly into accepting her terms. Nothing came of the Prince of Wales's manoeuvrings, however, for on 17 September O'Reilly had already engaged Anna Casentini as *prima buffa*. Having engaged the principal singers and dancers required for the forthcoming season, O'Reilly and Borghi 'turned next to finding a house composer for the Pantheon'. On 26 October O'Reilly wrote in his best schoolboy French a letter to 'Monsieur Mozart Célèbre Compositeur de Musique à Vienne', prefacing his proposal with the statement that he has heard of Mozart's desire to come to London through 'a person attached to H.R.H. the Prince of Wales'. He then proposes that if Mozart could make himself available by the end of December and remain until the end of June 1791, he would receive £300. Mozart would be expected to compose two operas, but he would be free to write for rival organizations such as the Professional Concert.[8]

Curtis Price goes on to suggest that the confidant of the Prince of Wales

> can now be identified as Nancy Storace, who was probably in correspondence with Mozart in 1790. A plausible reason for the invitation thus emerges from O'Reilly's letter to Sheldon of 9 October, in which the manager reviews the singer's main demands... The absence of any correspondence from Mozart [to O'Reilly] in the Bedford Opera Papers does not necessarily mean that he failed to respond, since very few letters addressed to O'Reilly, besides office copies from Sheldon, survive. One can only speculate why Mozart did not accept the invitation: commitments in Vienna, or was it the prospect of direct competition with the far more famous Haydn in a foreign city?... Mozart may have done the honourable thing by not accepting O'Reilly's invitation, but a likelier explanation is that he simply waited too long to respond.

The letter from O'Reilly reached Mozart in Vienna after his return from the coronation service for Leopold II as Holy Roman Emperor in Frankfurt-am-Main; and a few weeks thereafter the London-based impresario Johann Peter Salomon arrived in person in Vienna to try to engage both Haydn and Mozart for his regular concert series at the Hanover Square Rooms. Can Salomon have been aware of O'Reilly's proposal? The Professional Concert, an organization for which under O'Reilly's terms Mozart would have been allowed to compose, was Salomon's main rival in the quest to obtain the best musical talent for their respective series.

There must have been very pressing reasons for Mozart to have resisted offers to travel to London in the late autumn of 1790. Somehow rivalry between Mozart and Haydn (or rather the lack of it) does not seem entirely plausible as an obstacle. In the sources, Salomon's offer was such that Haydn (who was immediately available and free to travel) was to leave at once and Mozart was to follow the next year.[9] I consider that, by December 1790, Mozart may already have been verbally committed to composing a German-language opera – *Die Zauberflöte* – for Schikaneder's suburban theatre, and moreover he may have considered that it was not an appropriate time to absent himself from Imperial-Royal service, just when a new Emperor (Leopold II, who had succeeded Joseph II in February), was feeling his way into the seat of power. After all, Mozart's efforts in Frankfurt, and later in Munich, intended to draw Leopold's attention to his Court Chamber Musician, had met with a singular lack of success. Perhaps it would have been very foolhardy indeed to disappear to London for six months at this crucial period early in the reign of the new Emperor. By contrast, Haydn was assured of a handsome pension from the late Prince Nicolaus I Esterházy, in whose service he had been since 1762, and he had permission from Nicolaus' successor, Prince Anton Esterházy, to leave for England (though as subsequent events turned out, Haydn overstayed his leave and soon found himself in difficulties with Prince Anton).

The reasons why in 1789 Mozart had not taken up the offer of Frederick William II of Prussia to come to his court in Berlin are equally unsure. The history of this offer is recorded in the biography of Mozart by Georg Nikolaus Nissen (1761–1826), who had married the composer's widow in 1809; the work was published in 1828 at Constanze's own expense, hence the account may be taken to bear the stamp of her approval. Mozart was offered a handsome salary – 3,000 thaler – by the King, yet he refused to give the matter serious consideration.[10]

I believe that Mozart had very valid and indeed thoroughly compelling reasons for wishing to stay in Vienna. He did not want to risk placing in jeopardy his appointment with the Imperial court, which provided him with a steady source of income, even if the sum was not princely. But there were also artistic factors: the Court Opera was one of the best in Europe, its company including virtuoso Italian singers. The orchestra too, on which Mozart had earlier relied for his subscription concerts, was without question one of the very best, and certainly unique in the skills of its woodwind and horn players. Church music in Vienna was of the highest standard anywhere in Catholic Europe, boasting two major centres, St Stephen's Cathedral and the Hofmusikkapelle (or the Imperial and Royal Court Chapel), as well as many other churches which once again – now that Leopold II had become Emperor and allowed orchestral forces in the churches which had been banned or severely curtailed under his predecessor Joseph II – maintained first-rate musical organizations. However, the overriding element in Mozart's decision to remain in Vienna was the fact that he had been promised, and would in due course have received, the position of Cathedral Chapel Master (Domkapellmeister) at St Stephen's when the incumbent – the aging Leopold Hofmann – retired or died in fact, Hofmann lived on until 1793. Had he survived, Mozart could have been expected to receive the substantial salary of 2,000 gulden plus emoluments in kind (firewood, candles, etc.).[11] It was a position to conjure with. At the time of his death, Leopold Hofmann was one of the richest composers in Vienna at any time in the half-century 1790–1840. Julia Moore has demonstrated this graphically in tabulated comparisons of the estates of Salieri (died 1825), Hofmann, Haydn (died 1809), Mozart, Beethoven (died 1827) and Schubert (died 1828), together with that of the dramatist Ferdinand Raimund (1790–1836).[12] The extreme differences in the net estates, after the respective totals have been converted to 1793 values, are startling. In descending order of wealth, the list is as follows:

	Net estate (gulden)
Salieri	20,352
Hofmann	18,522
Haydn	10,281
Raimund	8,514
Beethoven	5,811
Schubert	−132
Mozart	−826

A further table lists in detail the items of clothing owned by five of the same group of composers in the 1790s, the comparative values are again instructive, being in descending order:

Composer	Value (gulden)	Date
Hofmann	363	1793
Salieri	56	1795
Mozart	55	1791
Schubert	30	1795
Beethoven	24	1795

Julia Moore notes that 'highly detailed descriptions were provided for single items of Mozart's, Hofmann's and Salieri's clothing, and most items were valued individually, whereas neither Beethoven's nor Schubert's clothing was described in detail'.[13] The reason for this is that the first three were Court composers, who by virtue of their positions required costly and elaborate dress for official ceremonies, whereas Beethoven and Schubert were freelance composers and dressed more simply and less expensively. In those days 'Most Viennese had far less clothing than any of these composers, and indeed there were many who owned only a single change of clothing, while others died with their entire wardrobe on their back', continues Julia Moore.

Mozart knew, certainly, of Salieri's comfortable financial position, and he must have been aware that Hofmann was a wealthy man. Mozart obviously considered that he too could expect to attain that kind of status once the coveted position of Cathedral Chapel Master had been conferred upon him. Mozart also placed high hopes on the prospect of avoiding the intrigues of Salieri's Court Opera by going to the suburbs and composing German-language operas, and in that hope he was not disappointed: his new German opera, *Die Zauberflöte*, first performed at the Theater auf der Wieden in 1791, was to become the biggest single success of his life, going on to conquer the whole of German-speaking Europe in the years following the composer's death. Certainly, had Mozart survived, his collaboration with Schikaneder would not have ended there.

Finally, one must add a truism: Vienna was an intensely *musical* city, where people of every class and rank in society, from Emperor to chambermaid, were regularly involved in some sort of music-making or listening. The same could certainly not be said of Berlin or London, from where Mozart had received concrete offers; whereas post-Revolutionary Paris, in 1791, presented other problems.

Vienna simply held Mozart because in the final analysis he preferred that city to any of the other possibilities available to him. Those who dislike Vienna – and there are many – may not understand how he could have turned down the offers from London and Berlin. But for all those for whom Vienna is still a magical name and a place of enthralling fascination, it is easy to appreciate why Mozart chose to give this enchanting (if occasionally faithless) city his undivided love and devotion in the final years of his short life.

Notes on the text

========≈∞◊◊◊◊○◊◊◊◊∞========

I The First Journey (1762)

1 Stein was later (1800) to be the birth-
place of Ludwig, Ritter von Köchel,
immortalized as the author of the
standard catalogue of Mozart's works.
2 Many years later, in 1791, Mozart
was commissioned at short notice to
compose an Italian opera – *La clemenza
di Tito* – for performance in Prague as
part of the celebrations associated with
Leopold's coronation there as King of
Bohemia. Leopold had succeeded to
the Imperial and royal titles on the
death of his brother Joseph II in February 1790.
3 Landon, *Haydn: Chronicle and Works*,
vol. I, pp. 367ff., 555–9.
4 A modern facsimile edition, ed. J.H.
Eibl, was published in Kassel in 1974.
5 Niemetschek biography: 2nd edition,
Prague, 1808; facsimile, ed. Peter
Krause, Leipzig, 1978; English translation by Helen Mautner, London,
1956.
6 Mozart, *Briefe*, I, pp. 49f.
7 Deutsch, *Dokumente*: Addenda, p. 3.
8 Mozart, *Briefe*, I, pp. 50ff.
9 Niemetschek, op. cit., pp. 8ff.
10 The episode in which Emperor Francis
Stephen asked Wolfgang to cover the
keys is mentioned in a letter of 1792
written by the composer's sister
(Deutsch, *Dokumente*, pp. 398ff.), and
this account provided the basis for
the story as told in the Schlichtegroll
biography.
11 *AMZ* I (1799), pp. 855f.
12 Deutsch, *Dokumente*: Addenda, p. 4.
13 Mozart, *Briefe*, I. pp. 53ff.
14 Op. cit., pp. 55ff.
15 Op. cit., pp. 58ff.
16 Deutsch, *Dokumente*, pp. 19f.; Mozart,
Briefe, I, pp. 60f.
17 Mozart, *Briefe*, I, pp. 62f.
18 Op. cit., pp. 63ff.
19 Op. cit., pp. 65ff.

II The Second Journey (1767–8)

1 Deutsch, *Dokumente*: Addenda, p. 11.
2 Mozart, *Briefe*, I, p. 238.
3 Op. cit., pp. 239f.
4 Op. cit., p. 240.
5 Op. cit., pp. 240ff.
6 Op. cit., pp. 242–4; Deutsch, *Dokumente*: Addenda, p. 11.
7 Mozart, *Briefe*, I, pp. 244ff.
8 Op. cit., pp. 248ff.
9 Op. cit., pp. 251f.
10 Op. cit., pp. 253f.
11 Op. cit., pp. 254–8.
12 She proposed to Kaunitz that he
should 'mettre cette honnête famille
sous l'ombre de vos ailes'. Deutsch,
Dokumente, pp. 73f. See also Landon,
Mozart, The Golden Years, pp. 80, 108,
127, etc.
13 Mozart, *Briefe*, I. pp. 260f.
14 For Galitzin, see Landon, *Mozart, The
Golden Years*, pp. 111ff.
15 Letter of 11 May: Mozart, *Briefe*,
I, pp. 264ff.
16 Letter of 29 June: op. cit., p. 269.
17 Op. cit., pp. 269ff.
18 Op. cit., pp. 275ff.
19 The text of *Bastien und Bastienne* was
a translation by Friedrich Wilhelm
Weiskern of Jean-Jacques Rousseau's
Le Devin du village (1752).
20 Op. cit., pp. 284ff.
21 Report in *Wienerisches Diarium*:
Deutsch, *Dokumente*, p. 78.
22 Mozart, *Briefe*,
I, pp. 285ff. (14 December 1768).
23 Melk visit: Deutsch, *Dokumente*, p. 78.

III The Third Journey (1773)

1 Deutsch, *Dokumente*, p. 124
2 Mozart, *Briefe*, I, pp. 483–5 (21 July
1773).
3 Op. cit., pp. 485–7 (12 August 1773).
In a P.S. there is a note by Gottlieb
Stephanie, Jr., which reads: 'Land-

straße the 12th. M: Stephanie Junior and his beautiful wife send their compliments.' He would write the word-book of *Die Entführung aus dem Serail* for Mozart in 1781 and 1782.

4 Mozart, *Briefe*, I, p. 488.
5 Op. cit., pp. 489–91 (last sentence).
6 Op. cit., pp. 494–6.
7 Deutsch, *Dokumente*, p. 131.
8 See Landon, *Haydn: Chronicle and Works*, vol. II, p. 185. *Preßburger Zeitung* report, December 1773: 'die wohl harmonisierende Musik des mit verschiedenen Instrumenten stark besetzten Orchesters'.

IV *Mozart and the 'Sturm und Drang' School*

1 Bernard Rywosch, *Beiträge zur Entwicklung in Joseph Haydns Symphonik* (dissertation), Turbenthal 1934, p. 65.
2 Mellers, *The Sonata Principle from* c. *1750*, London 1957, p. 22; reprinted in Alec Harman and Wilfrid Mellers, *Man and his Music*, London 1962, Part III, pp. 600f.
3 For a sensitive appreciation of this visionary work, see Laszlo Somfai's introduction to the beautiful facsimile edition, Budapest 1959.
4 H. C. Robbins Landon, 'La crise Romantique dans la musique Autrichienne vers 1770. Quelques précurseurs inconnus de la Symphonie en sol mineur (KV 183) de Mozart', *Les influences étrangères dans l'oeuvre de W. A. Mozart*, Colloquium, 10–13 October 1956, La Sorbonne, Paris, pp. 27–47.
5 *Mozart, His Character, His Work*, London 1946, p. 225.
6 Op. cit., p. 39; reprinted 1962 (see note 2 above), p. 609.

V *Mozart and Vienna in the 1780s*

1 For a fuller account see Landon, *Mozart, The Golden Years*.

VI *Mozart's stay in Vienna, 1781–91, and its ramifications*

1 Wolfgang Hildesheimer, *Mozart*, London 1983, p. 366.
2 Landon, *Mozart, The Golden Years*, pp. 184f., 187. Letter of 17 November: Mozart, *Briefe*, III, 606. Prague

report: Deutsch, *Dokumente*, 248.
3 Mozart, *Briefe*, IV, 28f.
4 'Italian Opera and Arson in Late Eighteenth-Century London', *Journal of the American Musicological Society*, XLII/1 (1989), pp. 55ff.
5 Price, op. cit., p. 61.
6 Price, op. cit., p. 58.
7 Price, op. cit., pp. 66f. O'Reilly's letter of 9 October 1790 is in the Bedford Opera Papers (5.D.9), an extensive collection of material including the artistic and managerial records of the King's Theatre, 1790–2, and private legal papers of the New Haymarket opera house; the collection is owned by the Marquess of Tavistock and the Trustees of the Bedford Estates. Both the Duke of Bedford and the Prince of Wales were prime movers in the building of the Haymarket Theatre, burnt out in 1789.
8 The letter from O'Reilly reads:

Monsieur!
Par une personne attachée à S.A.R. le prince de Galles j'apprends votre dessein de faire un voyage en Angleterre, et comme je souhaite de connoître personellement des gens à talents, et que je suis actuellement en état de contribuer à leurs avantages, je vous offre Monsieur la place de Compositeurs ont eus [*sic*] en Angleterre. Si vous êtes donc en état de Vous trouver á Londres envers la fine du mois de Decembre prochain 1790 pour y rester jusqu'à la fin de Juin 1791 et dans cet espace de tems de composer au moins deux Operas ou sérieux ou comiques, selon la choix de la Direction, je vous offre trois cents livres Sterling avec l'avantage d'écrire pour le concert de la profession ou toute autre salle de concert a l'exclusion seulement des autres Théatres. Si cette proposition peut vous etre agréable et vous êtes en état de l'accepter faites moi la grâce de me donner une résponse à vue, et cette lettre vous servira pour un Contract.

Jai l'honneur d'être Monsieur Votre très humble Serviteur Rob. May [*sic*] O'Reilly

Ayez la bonté de diriger au Panthéon à Londres.

[English translation of O'Reilly's letter:]

'By someone attached to H.R.H. the Prince of Wales, I learn of your desire to undertake a trip to England, and since I like to know talented people personally, and since I am in a position to contribute to their advantages, I offer you, Sir, the place that [word or words missing] composers have had in England. If therefore you are in condition to reach London by the end of next December 1790 to remain here until June 1791, and in that space of time to compose two operas, either *serie* or *buffe*, according to the directors' choice, I offer you three hundred Pounds Sterling with the additional advantage of composing for the Professional Concert or any other concert organization except for other theatres. If this proposition appears agreeable to you and you are able to accept it, please do me the honour of a reply at your earliest convenience, and this letter will serve as a contract.

I have the honour to be, Sir your very humble servant Rob. May [*sic*] O'Reilly.'

Price, op. cit., pp. 68f. The letter to Mozart in Deutsch, *Dokumente*, 332. Curtis Price notes that this letter, the original of which has not been traced, was first published by Nottebohm (1880, pp. 67–8), and suggests that the misreading of O'Reilly's middle name (Bray) confirms that the letter was written by O'Reilly himself, for elsewhere his handwriting reveals a 'Br' formation that is virtually indistinguishable from his capital 'M'.

9 Landon, *Haydn: Chronicle and Works*, vol. III *passim*; also *1791*, pp. 18f.
10 Nissen, 535f.; see also Landon, *Mozart, The Golden Years*, p. 207.
11 See Landon, *1791*, Chapter V.
12 Julia Moore: 'Mozart in the Market-Place', *Journal of the Royal Musical Association*, vol. 114/1 (1989), pp. 18ff.
13 Op. cit., p. 37.

Abbreviations of Bibliographical Sources

AMZ
Allgemeine Musikalische Zeitung, Leipzig, 1798 *et seq.*

Deutsch, *Dokumente*
Mozart: die Dokumente seines Lebens, ed. Otto Erich Deutsch, Kassel etc., 1961. Vol. II: Addenda und Corrigenda, ed. J. H. Eibl, Kassel etc., 1978.

Köchel
The edition of the Köchel catalogue to which reference is made is, unless stated otherwise: Ludwig, Ritter von Köchel, *Chronologisch-Thematisches Verzeichnis sämtlicher Tonwerke Wolfgang Amadé Mozarts . . .*, 8th ed., Wiesbaden, 1983. In the text the 'old' (i.e. customary) Köchel numbers are given; in the index the latest revised numbers are also given in parentheses where appropriate.

Landon, *Haydn: Chronicle and Works*
H. C. Robbins Landon, *Haydn: Chronicle and Works* (5 vols.), London and Bloomington, Ind.:
  I *Haydn: The Early Years, 1732–1765* (1980);
  II *Haydn at Eszterháza, 1766–1790* (1978);
  III *Haydn in England, 1791–1795* (1976);
  IV *Haydn: the Years of 'The Creation', 1796–1800* (1977);
  V *Haydn: the Late Years, 1801–1809* (1977).

Landon, *Masons*
H.C. Robbins Landon, *Mozart and the Masons. New Light on the Lodge 'Crowned Hope'*, London and New York, 1982.

Landon, *Mozart, The Golden Years*
H.C. Robbins Landon, *Mozart, The Golden Years, 1781–1791*, London and New York, 1989.

Landon, *1791*
H.C. Robbins Landon, *1791: Mozart's Last Year*, London and New York, 1988.

Mozart, *Briefe*
Mozart: Briefe und Aufzeichnungen, ed. Wilhelm A. Bauer and Otto Erich Deutsch. Letters: 4 vols., Kassel etc., 1962–3. Commentary (ed. Joseph Heinz Eibl): 2 vols., Kassel etc., 1971. Indexes (ed. Eibl): 1 vol., Kassel etc., 1975.

Nissen
Georg Nikolaus Nissen, *Biographie W.A. Mozarts nach Originalbriefen*, Leipzig, 1828; facsimile reprint Hildesheim, 1972.

Pezzl
Johann Pezzl, *Skizze von Wien*, 6 *Hefte* published in 2 vols., Vienna 1786–90 (new edition, in revised order, Graz 1923).

Select Bibliography

General

BRAUNBEHRENS, Volkmar, *Mozart in Vienna 1781–1791*, New York, 1989, and London, 1990 (English translation by Timothy Bell from the original German, *Mozart in Wien*, Munich, 1986).

BRION, Marcel, *Daily Life in The Vienna of Mozart and Schubert* (translated from the French), London, 1961.

FEKETE, Johann, Graf, *Wien im Jahre 1787*, Vienna etc., 1921.

Guide du voyageur à Vienne. Description et Précis historique de cette capitale, Artaria & Co., Vienna, 1803 (a charming and important early guide).

LANDON, H.C. Robbins, *Mozart, The Golden Years, 1781–1791*, London and New York, 1989;

———, *1791. Mozart's Last Year*, London and New York, 1988.

Österreich zur Zeit Kaiser Josephs II. (exhibition catalogue), Melk, 1980 (includes important essays, together with illustrations of documents, objects and portraits).

Biographies, correspondence

ANDERSON, Emily (trans. and ed.), *The Letters of Mozart and his Family*, London, 1938; 2nd revised edition (ed. A. H. King and M. Carolan), London, 1966; 3rd revised edition (ed. S. Sadie and F. Smart), London, 1985.

ARNETH, A. von (ed.), *Briefe der Kaiserin Maria Theresia an ihre Kinder und Freunde* (4 vols.), Vienna, 1881 (the standard edition of the Empress's letters).

———, *Marie Antoinette, Joseph II. und Leopold II. – Ihr Briefwechsel*, Leipzig, 1866 (the essential correspondence).

BEALES, Derek, *Joseph II* (2 vols.): vol. I: *In the Shadow of Maria Theresa 1741–1780*, Cambridge, 1987; vol. II forthcoming.

BEER, A., and J. VON FIEDLER (eds.), *Joseph II. und Graf Ludwig Cobenzl. Ihr Briefwechsel* (2 vols.; Fontes Rerum Austriacum, vols. LIII, LIV), Vienna, 1901 (mostly in French, covering politics, culture and daily affairs – essential background to a knowledge and understanding of Joseph II and his attitudes).

Briefe von Joseph den Zweyten..., Leipzig, 1821.

MITROFANOV, Paul von, *Joseph II. Seine politische und kulturelle Tätigkeit*, Vienna/Leipzig, 1910 (the standard biography of Joseph II, still not superseded).

WANDRUSKA, Adam, *Leopold II.* (2 vols.), Vienna, 1965 (the standard work).

Index

To the brave men and women in the fire service

Contents

Maps

Foreword

By RCFD Deputy Chief Mike Bell

They say prayer changes things. I believe it. What happened, or *didn't* happen, in Rancho Cucamonga on the night of October 25, 2003, is hard to explain any other way. Certainly, good planning, years of training, and courageous firefighting contributed to the success we experienced in Rancho, but it does not tell the whole story.

The truth is, brave firefighters fought just as hard to save lives and homes in San Bernardino, Devore, Lytle Creek, Lake Arrowhead, Scripps Ranch, San Diego County, Claremont, San Antonio Heights, and other nameless places throughout the two-week firestorm of 2003. But something special occurred in Rancho Cucamonga and it defies logic.

As the story you are about to read explains, despite plans and agreements made in advance of the fire's attack in Rancho Cucamonga, we were caught off guard. Promises were broken and homes were lost. We quickly recovered and prevented further destruction, but our best-laid plans were of little use that day. Bruised and battered, we humbly retreated back to the drawing board hoping for a better tomorrow.

With more than seven miles of urban/wildland interface, unburned for thirty years, laced with homes tucked in and out of hilly terrain, Rancho was a sitting duck. Having responded to calls for nearly two decades in the community, anytime the winds blew I was concerned about what would happen if flames, instead of just leaves, were pushed through the city. Over the years I had seen several smaller versions of the Grand Prix. Dozens of wind-driven roof fires, field fires, and eucalyptus windrow fires brought a scare but were always tamed before they could grow to conflagration status. The ten-thousand-acre Texas Fire in 1988, a three-hundred-acre blaze caused by ninety-mile-per-hour winds toppling two giant powerline towers in Etiwanda in 1996, and the westerly-driven twelve-hundred-acre Etiwanda Fire in 1992 were all the proof and experience we needed to be convinced that the "Big One" would someday make them each pale in comparison.

Even then, none of us could actually imagine the ferocity and relentlessness that would be unleashed upon our city during that October 2003 weekend. Friday the twenty-fourth was a teaser. The fire jumped us, made us mad, and we fought back, mostly winning, but nevertheless we were startled by our vulnerability. Once things simmered down, we regrouped, made new plans, and resolutely drew a line in the hills past which no fire would survive, we hoped. As we puffed our chests, pushed back our chairs, and began to shake hands in a precongratulatory way, one in our midst softly put forth what I am convinced was the single most important element of our plan. A prayer.

And why not? The leadership of this organization had often prayed together for wisdom, guidance, and strength to carry out the public safety mission entrusted to us by the community. Staff meetings and conference rooms, however, are serene, sterile, and mundane environments, perfect settings for heady words, lofty notions, and even occasional reverential corporate introspection. We prayed often in those settings, and I believe the combination of those prayers and the combined faith of those leaders has resulted in a rare and blessed fire organization. Funny, then, how in the middle of the firefighting battle of our lives, a true fight to save the city, we would almost neglect invoking the help of Almighty God into the midst of this most desperate of situations. I'll never forget the collective look on the sleepless, fire- and weather-beaten faces of men I had lived and worked with for so long after we each whispered, "Amen," and lifted our bowed heads. Victory would come, we were certain, but only after we marched through a living hell.

This account of the events surrounding the Grand Prix Fire records several moments of apparent indecision, lack of coordination, and even frontline disagreements. These are not uncommon on multijurisdictional incidents. We train during the winter and build relationships through the years to minimize much of this inevitable confusion. Our goal is to work together for the common good. None of us can go it alone on the Big One; this we know in advance. Thus we submit to an organizational system called incident command and trust it will work to bring together the pieces and mold them into a cohesive unit working from the same sheet of music toward the accomplishment of common objectives. In the case of the Grand Prix, it worked but it wasn't pretty. Nor could it be. The combination of multiple large-scale fires, unprecedented fire behavior, and thousands upon thousands of homes and lives at stake made for a "perfect storm" of influences that all aligned into a chaotic situation ripe for Monday-morning quarterbacks and naysayers to look back in hindsight and take potshots at those who were in the midst of the fray. That too is inevitable and perhaps unavoidable given human nature.

Much can and will be learned from this and the other fires that burned in the fall of 2003 in Southern California. Suffice it to say, as one who was on the line from start to finish, I saw and participated in decisions that were at times questionable and other times brilliant. I watched fireground leaders yield to others they barely knew in order to do the right thing. At times, emotional, gut-wrenching decisions were made, people balked, but their professional, disciplined response was the norm rather than the exception. Local, state, and federal firefighters, each with missions that at times oppose one another, put those differences aside for the greater good and in most cases learned to value and respect each other more than ever before as they often stood side by side in the face of smoke and flames the likes of which few of them had ever encountered in all their collective experience. At the end of the Grand Prix Fire, many more homes and lives were saved than lost. Firefighter injuries were a fraction of what they might have been without such cooperation. These are the true measures of success, especially for such an unbelievable event as this.

The book captures just a glimpse of the overall story that unfolded in the fall of 2003 in Southern California. It could focus on any one of a dozen episodes of heroism, sacrifice, victory, and defeat. In this treatise, the spotlight shines for a moment on Rancho Cucamonga. Naturally, the emphasis is placed on the frontline battle, where flames and fire hoses met. I fought fire with some of the bravest and finest firefighters anywhere in the world, men and women who stood their ground when their community needed them the most. Many are never mentioned in this book: Pat Proulx, Ivan Rojer, Eric Noreen, Sam Spagnolo, Tim Fejeran, Rob Elwell, Mike Ploung, Mike Redmond, Allen Lee, Mike Jerkins, Jeff Roeder, Jay Davenport, Jim Townsend, Mike Post, Don Cloughesy, Augie Barreda, Steve Kilmer, Dave Cruz, Art Andres, Dave Larkin, Tom O'Brien, and so many others. A true "Band of Brothers" knitted together forever through the forge of this shared experience.

I must add here, however, that, as in most notable achievements, behind the efforts of the firefighters was a vast array of support that enabled them to put up the fight they did. There are too many to note them all, but a few are representative of the whole. Rancho Cucamonga Fire Department (RCFD) battalion chief (now fire chief) Peter Bryan organized the city's emergency operations center (EOC). This facility was staffed around the clock starting early Friday. From this effort logistical support was provided for the operation in Rancho Cucamonga. Evacuations, shelter, communications, media information, and disaster assistance were coordinated through the EOC even weeks after the fire had passed. The facility was staffed by rank-and-file city employees as well as managers and elected officials. It was a true team effort by professional public servants who each went above and beyond the call of duty to perform new jobs at odd hours even as some of their own homes and families were affected by the fire. For Chief Bryan, who no doubt would have loved to be on the line, stayed back and did the harder, less glorious thing, but his and the rest of the EOC's unsung efforts had a profound effect on the successful outcome of this incident.

RCFD captain Dan Holloway, who volunteered to drive me around throughout Black Saturday, provided invaluable knowledge and assistance during the entire episode. We do not normally have drivers for chief officers in the RCFD. It's a luxury to be sure, but on this night it was a necessity and Dan was outstanding. At one point during the night, his family evacuated from their home, and he spotted his wife, Amy, standing on a corner just out of the evacuation area. It was quite an emotional scene as he took a moment to embrace her, provide assurance and comfort, then wave good-bye and drive back into harm's way.

The members of the Alta Loma Riding Club, a local equestrian group, took it upon themselves during the year prior to get the training necessary to participate within the incident command system and provide large-animal evacuation services. This group worked tirelessly to move more than four hundred horses out of the threatened area, not once but twice, as the primary evacuation center itself became shrouded in wind-driven smoke and ash. It was quite remarkable that these folks actually had the training to do what they did. It is a testament to their vision and community spirit and has served as a model for similar groups nationwide.

The cooperation, understanding, and outpouring of support from the general population of the city of Rancho Cucamonga during these trying days was unbelievable. The out-of-town fire crews who were staged at Los Osos High School could hardly believe the treatment afforded them. Hot showers, endless food, gourmet coffee, cots, and quiet rest areas all served to help them *want* to stay in Rancho, which kept them closer to where they would eventually be needed than the main base in Glen Helen ten miles to the east. This effort often continued into the field, where homeowners and neighbors would bring food and drink to the firefighters protecting their homes. The gratitude and appreciation expressed by the citizens after the fire was very moving to our organization, especially since more than half of our members live in the community as well as work there.

Finally, I must mention my wife, Diane. Countless nights through the years she has mumbled a soft "be careful" as I rolled out of bed to attend to an emergency in the community. For twenty years, she would walk me to the door and say a prayer, hoping to see me in one piece twenty-four hours later. Three times she was at my side in the hospital after job-related surgeries. On this night, with flames raging just a mile north of our home, she too was pressed into service. Welcoming into our home no fewer than nine very frightened teenage girls, friends of my daughter's who had been evacuated from their homes, she was a rock during a very difficult time. She's a firefighter's dream and I dedicate my portion of this story to her. And it is to God in heaven in whom I personally trust and believe that I give all the glory and credit too for any success that I was fortunate to have had the blessed opportunity to have witnessed during these wildly exciting and harrowing days.

Acknowledgments

A very special thanks goes out to RCFD firefighters Mike Bell and Mike Costello for risking their necks on the frontlines of the Grand Prix, opening their fire station to me, guiding me through the hills and across the front country of Rancho Cucamonga, and spending countless hours gathering photos and editing. I would like to thank Frank Scatoni and Greg Dinkin for being such wonderful friends and agents. I would also like to thank the countless men and women from municipal fire departments and wildland firefighting agencies who spent so many hours talking with me in person and over the phone, including the Lassen Hotshots, the Fulton Hotshots, and the Rancho Cucamonga Fire Department. Firefighters are a rare breed indeed. Last but not least, I would like to thank Stephen S. Power, my editor at Wiley, for believing in this book. Without his exceptional guidance, editing, and support, this book could not have been written.

THE INITIAL ATTACK

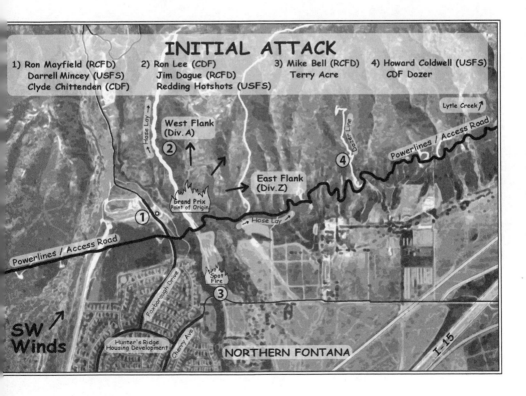

INITIAL ATTACK

1) Ron Mayfield (RCFD)
Darrell Mincey (USFS)
Clyde Chittenden (CDF)

2) Ron Lee (CDF)
Jim Dague (RCFD)
Redding Hotshots (USFS)

3) Mike Bell (RCFD)
Terry Acre

4) Howard Coldwell (USFS)
CDF Dozer

Lytle Creek

Hose Lay

West Flank
(Div. A)

Dozer Line

Powerlines / Access Road

East Flank
(Div. Z)

Grand Prix
Point of Origin

Hose Lay

Powerlines / Access Road

Spot
Fire

Foxborough Drive

SW
Winds

Hunter's Ridge
Housing Development

Cherry Ave

NORTHERN FONTANA

I-15

1

A Bird's-Eye View

"It appears as though we have a couple of wildfires," the pilot announced over the intercom as he began the descent into Ontario International Airport. "One on the horizon off to our left, and one in the foothills on our right."

Sitting in a window seat on the right side of the commercial airplane, Rancho Cucamonga fire chief Dennis Michael squinted as he looked out upon the bright afternoon of Tuesday, October 21, 2003—a day that would be remembered as the beginning of the most devastating fire siege in California's history.

With a clear view of the round peaks and steep canyons of the San Bernardino Mountains, a sixty-mile range running east and west between the Mojave Desert to the north and the heavily populated San Bernardino Valley to the south, Michael subconsciously searched for the world-famous resort communities of Lake Arrowhead, Crestline, and Running Springs nestled among the ponderosa pine and Douglas fir trees on the mountaintop. The quaint little towns served as weekend getaways for millions, but after a severe five-year drought, a massive infestation of bark beetles, and a hundred years of effective fire suppression by the fire service, the forest that engulfed the prominent neighborhoods had been turned into a powder keg. An estimated twenty million

3

dead trees littered the San Bernardino National Forest, putting the area's various firefighting agencies on edge all summer.

Unable to spot a smoke column in the high country, Michael pressed his head against the glass and panned his eyes thousands of feet down the steep, south-facing slopes to where the timber gave way to an unruly mesh of brush along the foothills. Encroaching up into this brush he could see the northernmost reaches of the valley communities of Alta Loma, Cucamonga, and Etiwanda—the three of which had incorporated in 1977 to form the city of Rancho Cucamonga. Thankfully, Michael saw no sign of a wildfire in the foothills. The last thing he needed after a two-week vacation with his wife was to find a blaze creeping up on Rancho Cucamonga's back door, threatening his city.

Waiting for the pilot to change course so he could catch a glimpse of the fire, Michael studied the grid of streets below. Back when he'd been hired as a grunt fireman in 1976, Rancho Cucamonga's main north-south arteries had led up to citrus groves and vineyards that sprouted from the soil along the foothills. But as he was promoted up the ranks, through fire engineer, fire captain, and battalion chief, finally becoming chief of the entire department in 1984, the root structures of the citrus groves and vineyards had been replaced by the cement foundations of

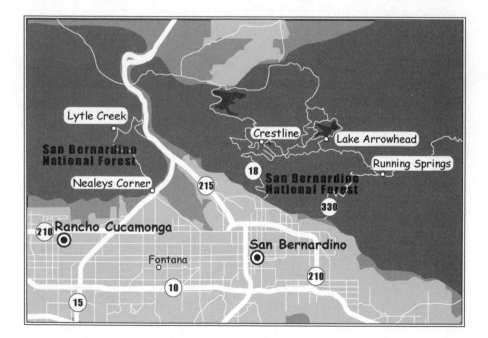

housing tracts and mini-mansions. Expansion was healthy for the city, but the direction in which it had expanded made Michael's job ever more difficult. Gazing downward, he could see the nearly perfect row of houses that marched to the east and west across the foothills. The residents who lived along this northern row could sip coffee on their back porches while watching wild animals traverse the slopes leading up to the San Bernardino National Forest, yet when they wanted the hustle and bustle of the city they only had to drive a few minutes south. These residences, along with the ones built smack-dab in the middle of the urban/wildland interface farther up the mountainside, were considered dream homes to those who lived in them, but to Michael they were a disaster waiting to happen.

During Michael's two decades as chief of the Rancho Cucamonga Fire Protection District, the homes in the northern part of the city had been the number one target hazard in the community. To prepare his department to combat wildfire, he sent many of his officers and firefighters to classes being offered by the U.S. Forest Service. They used the opportunity to strike up relationships with battalion chiefs in the Forest Service and the California Department of Forestry (CDF) in an attempt to break down the barriers that had for so long existed between their agencies. Back in the early seventies, such a feat would not have been easily accomplished. Boundaries had been drawn firmly in the ground, and seldom did firefighters from different departments communicate with one another on the fire line, often resulting in confusion and a mismanagement of resources. But with hundreds of homes in the Rancho Cucamonga Fire Protection District located in the urban/wildland interface, and with fires in the foothills only getting larger and fiercer due to years of fire suppression, Michael needed all the help he could get. Stubborn pride was not something his city could afford.

Luckily, maintaining bonds with the wildland agencies came easier in Rancho than in most cities, simply because they always trod in each other's backyards. When a fire broke out along the foothills, all three agencies routinely turned up. The Rancho Cucamonga Fire Department (RCFD) had the responsibility of guarding a sliver of grassland that skirted along the northern edge of the city. Just north of that boundary began a long, narrow strip of land known as a State Responsibility Area (SRA), in which CDF watched over the vegetation while RCFD protected any improvements such as structures and utility equipment.

CDF then turned the wildland responsibility over to the U.S. Forest Service at the boundary of the San Bernardino National Forest, which started low in the mountains and carried up to the top of the 8,900-foot Cucamonga Peak towering over Rancho Cucamonga. In a different time, it wouldn't have been uncommon for agencies arriving on scene to back off if a fire wasn't burning in their jurisdiction, but after ten years of communication and interaction, the commanders from the different agencies now knew each other's faces and what to expect from one another, which eliminated much of the tail-sniffing that could occur out on the fire line.

Michael truly believed that his department's willingness to mesh with the wildland agencies would save their community in the years to come. There had, however, been skeptics of the bonds his department had forged. To someone who didn't worry about the homes stranded out in the dry sea of vegetation in the foothills each and every night, it might appear as though the RCFD had gotten the short end of the stick in the mutual aid agreement because most fires occured outside of their jurisdiction. After all, fire had a natural tendency to climb uphill. In fact, it traveled uphill seventeen times faster than it did along flat ground. In addition, the foothills typically received onshore winds out of the southwest. So if a fire broke out north of the city, both the topography and the wind typically pushed the flames up and away, across the SRA and then up into the San Bernardino National Forest, leaving Rancho Cucamonga unscathed in the flatlands.

But history had proved that just because a fire abandoned the foothills for higher elevations didn't mean that it wouldn't come back down in the subsequent days. The Myers Fire of 1970, the Summit Fire of 1980, and the Texas Fire of 1988 each started down along the foothills and then climbed upslope toward the higher elevations. The fires would have remained there, brewing around the forest until extinguished, but the arrival of Southern California's infamous Santa Ana winds, dry winds that come off the high desert usually between Labor Day and Thanksgiving, had drastically changed their course. With fifty- to seventy-mile-per-hour winds pumping out of the northeast, the three fires had clawed their way back downslope, across the foothills, and then out into the flatlands, throwing hundred-foot flame lengths overtop of the firefighters who had emerged to battle them. From the satellite photos Michael had reviewed, the path of the three fires resembled an

EKG, moving up and down the mountain under the competing winds, nuking everything in their path until all the fuel along the foothills had been consumed or the northeast winds abated.

Numerous fires had burned deep into the once unpopulated foothills of northern Rancho Cucamonga, and if such a fire were to be relived, as Michael was certain would be the case, the city would not get off as easily as before. Despite the lessons taught by history, an overwhelming amount of development had moved into the burn zones of the three fires. For over a decade now Michael's department had worked side by side with CDF and the Forest Service to protect those homes, and together they had become masters at suppressing the majority of wildfires in the foothills during initial attack, but after they had hit every blaze hard with aircraft, hose lays, and hand crews, the chaparral along the front country had grown thick and unstable. It stretched for miles and miles without any breaks. Michael had ensured that each new home in the urban/wildland interface was built to retard flame, the outside walls plastered with stucco and the roofs covered with tile, but for those who had witnessed the ferocity of the Texas Fire when it laid siege to the foothills, there was little doubt that when the next big fire broke under Santa Ana winds, homes would be lost.

Rancho Cucamonga could not escape the fact that in the near future Mother Nature would collect the debt owed her; this Michael knew for sure. He just hoped it wouldn't happen on his watch.

As his flight made its final approach into Ontario International, Michael finally caught sight of the wildfire the pilot had pointed out. It brewed in the chaparral one mile east of Rancho Cucamonga, just above the neighboring city of Fontana. He'd been a little worried when he'd heard the words "fire" and "foothills" mentioned in the same sentence, but now that tension began to fade. It was 4 P.M., and judging by the size of the smoke column, the fire had probably been burning for an hour and a half. Both the Forest Service and CDF had most likely been hitting it since shortly after it started. With the drought and the millions of dead trees up on the mountaintop, neither agency waited to confirm the authenticity of a fire before sending out resources. When a call came in to dispatch of a possible smoke column, they got aircraft, engines, and hand crews rolling to the scene. On more than one occasion this summer, an armada of firefighting personnel and equipment had descended upon a group of campers roasting burgers at a late-afternoon barbecue.

There was not much to worry about. As usual, the winds blew out of the southwest, pushing the fire away from the valley toward the SRA. For the rest of the afternoon, aircraft would pound the various flanks of the fire with water and retardant. In the evening the temperature would drop and the relative humidity would rise, slowing the fire's upward advance. It would give hand crews from the Forest Service and CDF time to cut line around the fire, box it in. When Michael arrived at headquarters the following morning, he would undoubtedly hear stories from his management-level firefighters like Ron Mayfield, Mike Bell, Jim Dague, Mike Costello, and Dave Berry, all of whom were probably helping out with the brush fire at this very moment, even though the fire had little chance of affecting their city. They'd crack jokes about how they'd helped defeat a wildfire while he'd sipped a beverage in a plane thousands of feet above.

Michael breathed a sigh of relief, but a little tension remained knotted in the back of his neck. The one thing he had learned over his long career fighting fire was never to take a blaze lightly, no matter how inconsequential it might seem. The area in which the fire currently burned had been the breeding ground of many devastating fires in the past, including the Summit Fire of 1980, but those former monsters had all shared a secret ingredient—the Santa Ana winds. Although Michael hadn't studied the weather data since before he left on his vacation, he could see an inversion layer holding the smoke close to the ground, suggesting that the northeast wind would not peek its head around the corner anytime soon. It was certainly Santa Ana season, but the majority of wind-driven fires they had experienced in the past had occurred in November and December. He told himself to relax, that everything would be fine, but something about the brightness of the afternoon continued to irk him.

"Welcome home, honey," said his wife as she fastened her seat belt.

Michael smiled, a part of him enjoying the mild dose of adrenaline coursing through his veins as he looked down upon the fire. It would be hard to step down from the helm of the Rancho Cucamonga Fire Protection District, but his decision had already been made. In September he had announced to the city that this would be his last year. It had been a good ride, filled with many victories and just a few regrets. But regrets made in the line of firefighting were the kind that you carried with you for a lifetime. The deep, lasting wounds rarely had to do with the loss of homes or property—those could be replaced. Even the most gung-ho firefighters eventually realize that it is impossible to save every structure. No firefighter, however, came to work prepared to deal with the loss of life. The city's last fire death, which had occurred ten months earlier, involved an eleven-year-old girl trapped in a home over on Malachite. The house was well involved with fire when Rancho crews arrived, and despite an aggressive attack that left one firefighter injured, they couldn't reach her in time to save her life. Michael could still remember the look on his men's faces when he arrived on scene. The incident had cut deep into the organization, and he never wanted to experience such tragedy again.

When he'd announced his retirement, he had told his wife that the one thing he wished for more than anything was to be able to make it through this final season without a major incident that stirred up controversy and made him feel as though he had failed his community at the tail end of his watch. He'd begun the year on edge, but after months passing without a disaster unfolding, he started to feel as though his wish might be granted after all.

"I guess it's back to reality," he said to his wife as the plane touched down.

"Is the fire going to be a problem?"

"I don't foresee it being a big problem for Rancho," he said, shaking his head uneasily. In his mind, however, he knew that if forces couldn't get the fire boxed up in the next twenty-four hours, the entire area could be in danger. "Let's just pray that it's not going to be."

2

Point of Origin

At 2:13 P.M. on October 21, 2003, the U.S. Forest Service, the California Department of Forestry, the San Bernardino County Fire Department, and the Rancho Cucamonga Fire Department began receiving
reports of a grass fire in Area 37A, a long, narrow section of foothills
above northeastern Rancho Cucamonga and northern Fontana. The various dispatch centers contacted stations throughout the area and ordered
them to respond. Within seconds, troops began to roll.

Forest Service captain Bud Berger, based out of Station 37 in eastern Rancho Cucamonga, saw the smoke the minute his engine hit pavement, and he raced with his crew toward the top of the Hunter's Ridge
housing development, which reached precariously out into the grasslands. He'd navigated Engine 37, a 4 × 4 monster of a truck that carried
hand tools, hose, and a surplus of water, down the streets above Fontana
dozens of times to reach Hose Lay Hill, a brutally steep ridge close to
the fire's current location that his department used for exercise and
drills. But today the commute took longer than normal. Dozens of
bystanders clogged the streets, both in their cars and on foot, turning the
drive into an obstacle course that took ten minutes to complete.

Still, Berger was the first to arrive on scene. He parked his engine by
a massive water tank at the top of Foxborough Drive, the northernmost
street in the subdivision. After spending a few moments surveying the

fire, which currently worked hungrily toward the toe of the mountains in the grasslands off to his left, he contacted Forest Service dispatch. He informed them that the fire was roughly two acres, moving at a moderate rate of speed to the northeast under southwest winds. As a captain, he had the authority to bump the fire from a first alarm up to a second, which would increase the amount of resources being sent, but he didn't feel the need to do so. Judging by the resources the various agencies had sent to initially attack fires all summer, a fleet of engines and hand crews was most certainly heading his way, ready to leap into action the moment they arrived. He did, however, advise that aircraft should be sent. Ordering helicopters and airtankers outright was out of the question, simply because the fire currently burned on the SRA. Aircraft was costly, and the agency that placed the order was expected to foot the bill. Until the fire began edging in on the forest boundary, it was CDF's responsibility to get machines buzzing overhead. CDF would also be responsible for sectioning the different flanks of the fire into divisions and assigning incoming resources to them.

Berger didn't plan to wait around for such organization to occur. During his thirty years with the Forest Service in the San Bernardino area, he'd fought dozens of fires in this exact location, most notably the Texas Fire of 1988. The hillside faced the south and received a large amount of sun, making the vegetation naturally dry and flammable. An occasional fire was necessary to clean out the dead and dying brush, but with so many homes having edged out into the urban/wildland interface, the fire service had swooped on each and every fire the moment it started, contributing to the dense and combustible chaparral now clinging to the mountainside. On a day such as today, with the temperature in the nineties and the relative humidity down to 8 percent, they had to be swift in their attack. The fire yearned to reach the hillside where it could get firmly established and gain both ground and speed. If that happened, they very well might have another Texas Fire on their hands. Berger studied the weather reports nearly every morning, and this morning he had seen high pressure building, which meant that the north winds could be lurking just around the corner.

Time was of the essence, and Berger wasted none of it. Once he had talked with dispatch, he spent a few moments studying the fire behavior and the terrain. This was the part he loved most about firefighting, the reason why he'd turned down numerous promotions over the years. Sitting on the sidelines and directing an armada of resources was not his cup of tea. He thrived off the fight, being out in the thick of it with his crew. And they needed him. With many of the old-school captains retiring, the Forest Service had filled a good portion of the low-level leadership roles with inexperienced kids. They were too young and gung-ho to realize that sometimes the overhead sending them on missions made mistakes, that their leaders had been removed from the fire line for so long that they'd forgotten what is doable and what's not, which often steered crews into precarious situations. Some of the kids today would boldly attack two-hundred-foot flame lengths simply because they didn't want to say no to the overhead.

Berger, on the other hand, had no problem refusing orders if he thought they would jeopardize the safety of his crew. Such had been the case on a recent fire over on the Angeles National Forest in Los Angeles County. The battalion chiefs responsible for formulating a game plan couldn't agree on a damn thing, leading to an organizational breakdown on the fire line. Berger had told them that if they didn't come up with something soon, he would pull his crews out. The battalion chiefs informed him that he couldn't do that, and Berger had responded with a firm "Watch me."

The decision hadn't awarded him any bonus points, but it was better than having regrets. Berger had seen many good firefighters die in the line of duty over the years, and blazes like Colorado's 1994 South Canyon Fire, which claimed the lives of fourteen firefighters, had kept him awake many nights. On a recent vacation he had actually traveled to Storm King Mountain in Colorado and visited the hillside where the fourteen lost their lives. He tried to put himself in their shoes, imagine what it had been like running from a wall of flame. The temperatures had been in the nineties, the crew wore heavy packs, and in places the slopes they had to climb were quite steep. They were confused and exhausted, and then the hot gases shooting uphill had hit their backs, robbing them of any rational thought.

Those fourteen men and women had made the ultimate sacrifice, as had dozens of others over the years. Their memory was carried on in books and documentaries and in the mind of every firefighter who stepped out onto the line, but Berger wanted to do more, so he had helped to create the Forest Service Honor Guard. Dressed up in class A–type uniforms, for the past ten years the honor guard had served as pallbearers and ushers at the funerals of firefighters who had fallen. It gave Berger a sense of satisfaction, but it also brought him closer to the harsh realities of his profession.

Now, at the tail end of his career, safety still sat at the top of Berger's list. And the safest way to fight fire was to hit it hard and fast before it got established, which was just what he planned to do with the two-acre brush fire off to his left.

It took him less than five minutes from the time he arrived to contact dispatch, absorb his surroundings, and then leap into action. He had his crew snatch up packs of coiled hose, and then they strung line off the large water tank on their engine. They could head in two different directions from the fire's point of origin just off to the left of Foxborough Drive—up the western flank of the fire toward the base of the mountain, or directly to the east along the fire's bottom edge.

For Berger, it wasn't a debate. Protecting life and property always came before vegetation, and right now the western flank, being pushed back into itself by the southwest winds, threatened nothing but the overly dense chaparral. But south of the fire sat a scatter of homes. If the winds shifted direction or an eddy formed out of the canyons, those homes could be in jeopardy. They wouldn't be hard to protect. A power-line access road shot to the east and west between the homes and the fire. They could follow that road with the hose lay, beating the fire back if it pressed down on them. That would help them achieve their second goal—reaching the eastern flank of the fire, which had the largest potential for growth under the southwest winds. Once they got out in front of the eastern flank, they could hook north along one of the many ridges leading up the mountains. By that time, dozers, hotshot crews, aircraft, and additional engines would have arrived. With helicopters and air-tankers cooling the eastern flank, dozers could cut a fuel break straight up the ridge in front of the advancing face. Hand crews and hose lays would follow right behind them, widening the line and pushing back the flame with water to keep it from jumping. If all went well, they could have this thing boxed in by nightfall.

With the game plan firm in everyone's mind, Berger and his crew strung line down the powerline access road, turning their hose on any flame that attempted to head south toward the homes. In the heat of battle, Berger lost track of time. It wasn't until ten or fifteen minutes later that he realized something wasn't right. Where was all his backup? All summer long each of the agencies had responded to fires with lightning speed and heavy artillery. By now, engines and hand crews should have been filing in behind him to help. He pushed the thought away, reckoning that perhaps less time had passed than he actually thought.

When another five minutes went by and still he hadn't gotten the backup he'd been expecting, Berger looked up from his work and to the north. The fire had pushed well out ahead of them to the east. He'd been confident that they could catch the eastern flank, but now he wasn't sure. If this fire got away from them, hundreds of homes in the area could be in jeopardy in the days to come. The people who lived in those homes were his relatives and coworkers and friends. Unlike the majority of wildland firefighters who traveled the nation to fight their battles on ground far away from the nearest home, he had been charged with protecting the community in which he worked and lived.

Berger needed reinforcements, and he needed them now. Frustrated, he looked to the south, hoping to see the smoke-filled air shimmering with red and blue lights. That's when he caught sight of the spot fire three hundred yards below the main body of fire.

3

The Spot Fire

Rancho Cucamonga fire marshal Mike Bell saw the spot fire fan to life not a hundred feet away, and it put him in an awkward position; he was alone in his Explorer without any water or sufficient hand tools to beat out the growing flame.

Fifteen minutes prior, he'd been sitting at his desk in Fire District Headquarters, located in Rancho Cucamonga's city hall. As he sifted through the files of a current fire investigation, his radio crackled with beeps and voices at his side, allowing him to subconsciously track his fellow municipal firemen traversing the city from vehicle accident to heart attack. He found the background noise soothing, but when he heard that a grass fire had been reported in northeast Rancho Cucamonga, he immediately dropped his pen, leapt to his feet, and jogged out of city hall.

Even before he made it down the front steps, he saw the smoke column billowing in the distance. From the looks of it, the fire burned in the county area above Fontana, not a part of Rancho's jurisdiction, but he hopped in his Explorer and sped across town nonetheless. When he made it to Cherry Avenue, the main street cutting north through the Hunter's Ridge housing development, he communicated with RCFD battalion chief Ron Mayfield, who had just arrived on scene with RCFD captain Jim Dague. Although the fire burned in a neighboring

15

jurisdiction, Mayfield and Dague had come to the same conclusion as Bell—this incident would require everything en route and then some.

Mayfield and Dague led the normal resource response for a fire in or near Rancho's high-fire-hazard area, with equipment that included two engines, a water tender, and the brush engine Rancho had acquired from the Forest Service under their mutual aid agreement. Instead of remaining on Cherry Avenue, which came to a dead end just south of the fire, they had hung a left on Bridlepath Drive, and then an immediate right on Foxborough, which carried them a few hundred yards north to the water tank where Bud Berger had parked his engine. Their goal was to stop the fire from working up the mountain toward the forest, and the only way they could accomplish that was to keep the flames from getting established in the chamise, scrub oak, and tall, dry grass in the drainages.

Knowing plenty of resources would converge on the fire's point of origin, Bell decided against following Mayfield and Dague up to the top of Foxborough Drive. Instead he decided to do some scouting on the east side of the fire, which would give him a better idea of what they had to tackle. Besides, he didn't want to get pulled into the chaos that would surely ensue at the incident command post (ICP) up by the water tank. In the nineteen years that he had been with the department, the Forest Service, CDF, San Bernardino County Fire, and Rancho Fire had all responded to fires in the foothills, simply because when a fire broke out they never knew who it belonged to until they actually arrived on scene. They had learned to work together quite well, but it was always a little bit of a madhouse trying to decide who would take control of the blaze. In this case, it looked like CDF had the most at stake. In the next few minutes, a battalion chief from CDF would arrive and assume the role of incident commander (IC). He would assign divisions to the various flanks, order additional resources, and deploy the resources currently on hand. With four different agencies converging on the fire, it was not an easy task. In order for the incident command system to work, everyone had to be willing to follow the IC's game plan rather than their own instincts. If a bunch of freelancing occurred, the fire would not only have a greater opportunity to escape the initial attack, but the lives of firefighters could also be put in jeopardy.

Since Bell hadn't been ordered for the initial attack, arriving at the top of Foxborough in his Explorer might only confuse matters with so many different agencies on scene. He remained in communication with

Mayfield, who helped to organize the incident, and proceeded to the end of Cherry Avenue. With the majority of troops positioning themselves at the fire's point of origin a quarter mile to the northwest of him, traveling below the fire would give him a different vantage point. If he saw something that the others didn't, he could contact them by radio. If nothing arose, he could pull the camera from his glove compartment and snap photos for his album back home.

He didn't get a chance to pull out his camera. Where Cherry came to an end, he'd hoped to continue farther east below the fire on a dirt road, but a wooden barricade, a locked gate, and a vehicle blocked his path. The obstacles could pose a problem down the road. If the fire grew, as it appeared it would, incoming resources would need as many access points as possible to the fire's various flanks. With the dirt extension off of Cherry leading up toward the foothills, he needed to get it cleared.

After climbing out into the smoky air, he found the owner of the vehicle a little ways down the dirt road watching the fire. Bell convinced him to park in a better location, and then snapped the lock on the gate with a pair of bolt cutters. A Southern California Edison crew happened to be close by, and Bell helped them tear down the wooden barricade blocking the road.

While heading back to his vehicle, Bell heard an explosion to the immediate north and spun around. A quarter mile south of the main body of fire, directly below a set of powerlines that linked the homes around Cherry Avenue with the massive east-west powerlines up near the base of the mountain, smoke started rising off the ground. Sparks still sprinkled from a transformer ten feet above, and Bell shortly deduced what had happened. All the smoke in the air had caused a surge in the main powerlines up above, which in turn sent a massive jolt down the smaller lines, causing the transformer to rupture.

This was not good. Bell's first instinct was to rush up there and stomp the fire out, but in the few seconds it took him to figure out what had happened, the spot fire had already consumed ten square feet. With the heat of the afternoon, the southwest winds, and the low relative humidity, the spot fire could become a major problem in just a matter of minutes—a much bigger problem than he could handle with the heel of his boot and a shovel. If the fire gathered steam, it would push in a northeast direction toward the southern flank of the main fire, threatening the homes on Cherry Avenue, as well as Bud Berger and his crew.

He contacted Rancho's Chief Mayfield, who was currently working with the overhead from CDF and the Forest Service to get a unified command going over by the water tank, and informed him of the spot fire. Mayfield, who had worked on the fire line for the past twenty years with Bell, said, "Do whatever you have to do to handle the situation."

Without an engine or a crew, Bell couldn't get much done on his own. While he tried to figure out a game plan, he saw several engines bypass the turnoff to Foxborough Drive and continue toward him on Cherry Avenue. It was a great stroke of luck. The incoming engines must have seen the smoke from the spot fire and thought that it was actually the main body of fire. Rising smoke could be deceptive, and so could the network of winding streets that led up toward the foot of the mountains. Such confusion happened often in the foothills, especially with engine crews that weren't based in the immediate area.

Before Bell could flag them down, however, the drivers realized that they had taken a wrong turn. They were actually supposed to head up toward the water tank, where they would get assigned to help Bud Berger with the hose lay along the southern flank. The engines slowed, and then Bell watched as they pulled a U-turn and headed back the way they came.

With the spot fire already having consumed half an acre, Bell jumped in his Explorer and raced after them. It would have been nice to contact them by radio, but the different agencies converging on the fire were still operating on their own frequencies. Once the CDF incident commander arrived, those issues would get worked out, but for the time being Bell had to do things the old-fashioned way.

Honking his horn and flashing his lights, Bell managed to snare the attention of CDF captain Terry Acre, who was in command of Engine 3581. Bell informed him of the spot fire and the possible ramifications if it got firmly established. Acre looked over his shoulder and immediately saw Bell's point. The bulk of firefighters up above were trying to keep the main body north of the powerlines, and this didn't fit in with their plan of attack. The last thing they needed was another fire creeping up behind them from the south, so Acre turned his engine around and led the charge back down Cherry.

Bell felt confident that Acre's crew could handle the spot fire on their own, but the moment their red CDF engine headed back down Cherry Avenue, the captains piloting three incoming green Forest Service engines filed in behind it, perhaps thinking Acre was heading to the main body. This was both good and bad. It meant that the spot fire would most certainly get handled, but it also meant that Bud Berger and his crew, which desperately needed reinforcements on the southern flank, would have to make do on their own for a little while longer.

This worried Bell, so he headed slightly north along the dirt extension off Cherry to see the progress of the fire's eastern flank. He worked past Acre's crew, which busily doused the spot fire with a hose attached to the water tank on their engine, and then another hundred yards to the north.

From his current location, Bell saw Bud Berger's crew coming toward him, trying to catch up with the eastern flank. Another engine crew had joined Berger, Rancho Medic Engine 173, but it didn't come close to fulfilling his needs. Bell could also see Terry Acre working the spot fire down below, which had grown to two acres. Bell had been fairly confident upon arriving that they could catch the fire, but now he began to have his doubts. They needed to get divisions assigned and establish some organization, both of which seemed to be taking longer than normal. The western flank would be called Division A, and the eastern flank, where Bell now stood, would be called Division Z. If the fire grew against all their efforts, they would use the letters between A and Z to create new divisions. Bell had been on fires where all the letters in the alphabet had been used up and they had started assigning double letters, but he certainly hoped that wouldn't be the case with this fire, not in these foothills during Santa Ana season.

It was a frustrating few moments for Bell, especially since he was so accustomed to fighting fire in homes and apartment buildings. He didn't like seeing fires spread; no firefighter does. On the structure fires his department handled, they normally established an incident command the moment they arrived. Then they got in and got it done, always with that time frame in the back of their mind. But fighting wildfire was more complicated. To choose an incident commander on a blaze out in the foothills, the responding agencies had to first discern whose jurisdiction the fire most affected. Once that got figured out, the designated incident commander would throw a map on the hood of his truck and have a group meeting with the various agency representatives to figure out who would pay for what. This depended upon their predictions of how big the fire would grow and who it would most severely affect in the hours to come. This was especially important when talking about aircraft, which came at a hefty hourly price tag. Wildland agencies understood that letting a fire spread as they worked out these important details was just part of the game.

Knowing this didn't ease Bell's anxiety. With Bud Berger struggling with the south flank, and Terry Acre working to extinguish the spot fire down below, Bell was in a perfect position to assume leadership of Division Z, which would entail developing a game plan and assigning resources into the area. "It is almost like you are in class and you want to raise your hand and say, 'Give me Division Z, I will handle this side for you. There is nobody else in here,'" Bell later said. "But I didn't do that. They [the ICP] knew I was there, there's no point in being obnoxious about it. I just hung out and observed the situation until things could shake out."

Although Bell was more than qualified to handle the task, he was not put in charge of Division Z. The reason for this, he suspected, was that he had never before worked on a fire with Clyde Chittenden, the CDF battalion chief who had arrived and assumed command. Chittenden didn't know what Bell was capable of, whether he would run with the ball or drop it. What Chittenden needed now was friendly faces, people he knew he could count on, so when he heard that Terry Acre was on the eastern flank handling the spot fire, he gave him Division Z, even though Acre wasn't currently in the best position to handle it. It was testament to just how important developing working relationships with the overhead of the other agencies had become.

Having done all he could, Bell kept an eye on Berger and his struggle to keep up with the eastern flank of the fire. Being a fire marshal, Bell instinctively pondered how the fire had started. It could have been anything—a spark from a motorcycle, kids playing with matches, a construction issue. Powerlines ran through the area, and perhaps one of them had given off a spark. Arson would be suspected in the days to come, but Bell knew it would be difficult to prove.

In addition to pondering how the fire started, Bell also thought about a half dozen communities in the area that had sprawled out into the urban/wildland interface. He had spent a fair amount of time meeting with families who had built their lives in this high-fire-hazard area, discussing ways to prep their home to reduce their vulnerability. In the process, he had learned their names and life stories. He considered many of them dear friends. The majority of them had one thing in common: after struggling to build a home in an area that they thought was suitable to raise children, they were dreadfully afraid of losing it all in a matter of just a few hours. Such thoughts didn't rule their lives, but a part of Bell's job was to ensure that those fears were always in the back of their minds. The moment history was forgotten tended to be the moment the past repeated itself. If this fire got away, they were looking at one magnificent battle ahead of them. Homes that had been properly prepped would most likely survive, and those that hadn't might not. He prayed that the men and women who had anchored into the urban/wildland interface wouldn't have to abandon their dream homes in the days to come, but in his mind he prepared for the worst-case scenario.

Approximately fifteen minutes after he arrived on scene, Bell started to grow very concerned that the fire might escape the initial attack. Things appeared to be going south in a hurry, but then he saw Howard Coldwell, a Forest Service dozer operator, appear from the smoke on his eighteen-ton machine to lend a hand. Bell was glad to see him, and he was sure Berger felt the same. Berger's hose lay had been outrun by the eastern flank, and a dozer could help him catch up. Dozer operators tended to be gung-ho firefighters, and they often saved the day. Bell hoped that would be the case today. The fire had spread to more than twenty acres, and it was expanding fast.

4

A Charge up the Hill

At about 2:20 P.M., Howard Coldwell watched Engine 3519 and its crew pull out from his U.S. Forest Service station in Devore Heights, located just a few miles east of Fontana, and head to the grass fire burning in Area 37A. Being a heavy-fire-equipment operator, Coldwell wasn't on the first alarm dispatch plan, but that didn't stop him from bending the rules and dispatching himself and his massive bulldozer a few minutes after Engine 3519. The Forest Service overhead tended to wait just a little too long to call in the dozers on the second alarm, and Coldwell's response time was considerably longer than that of engines or hand crews. Maneuvering eighteen tons of steel down residential streets wasn't easy. If he headed down the wrong street and had to make a U-turn with his trailer, mailboxes and parked cars became victims. With all of San Bernardino County yearning to burn, Coldwell figured no one would mind if he got a few minutes' head start.

His map remained in the glove compartment. During his twenty-six years with the Forest Service, Coldwell had fought numerous fires in the foothills. He had beaten back flames consuming the brush above Rancho Cucamonga on foot and as part of an engine crew, but nothing compared to battling a blaze in a dozer. He could crawl up inclines engines could not, and tear through dense vegetation that would take hand crews hours to clear. The fire, smoke, action, and danger of being out on the front line had worked into his blood, just as it did with all firefighters, but the rush of battling flame while mounted on an iron horse was indescribable. While hand crews were required to back away from four-foot flame lengths, and engines from eight-foot flame lengths, dozer operators such as Coldwell pretty much relied upon their own instincts as to when to retreat.

Despite the general consensus that dozer operators were one part gung-ho and two parts crazy, safety had always been Coldwell's number one concern. Often working far ahead of the main body of troops, he faced the constant threat of being overrun by flame. Fire-protective glass and heat shields surrounded his cab, but they could only repel so much heat. If a fire pressed in on him, Coldwell's life depended upon the width of the line he had carved into the vegetation. The wider his line, the less direct impingement the flame would have on his dozer. When working an overly volatile fire, he had no qualms about scraping a huge path through the woods to ensure his survival. But with environmental concerns becoming more and more of an issue, the size of Coldwell's lifelines had fallen under scrutiny.

A dozer in action on the Grand Prix.

Three years before, on a blaze in Idaho, due to environmental restrictions, the overhead had wanted Coldwell to head into a forest of sixty-foot lodgepole pines and blaze a path no wider than the blade of his dozer. The fire burned under an inversion layer, which kept all the heat and flame brewing close to the earth. Coldwell knew that once the inversion layer lifted, the fire would get rushed with oxygen and things would go to hell in a handbasket. Fearing for his safety, he had planned to refuse the assignment, but instead he came back with a stipulation. He told them, "Okay, I'll put in your one blade, but I get to cut safety zones where and when I need them."

Those in charge of the fire agreed, but they weren't the slightest bit happy when Coldwell carved out a football field every five hundred feet. It might have seemed vindictive, but Coldwell's precautions were justified when the inversion layer broke just minutes after he decided to pull his crew and equipment out of the forest. The entire mountain blew up, including the football fields he had carved for his protection.

The environmentalists who worried about saving all the "three-spine wooly flowers, four-legged rats, and all that kind of stuff" frustrated Coldwell. Fighting for regulations that required dozer operators to dig lines one blade wide seemed ridiculous, especially if the fire jumped that line due to its being too narrow and claimed sixty thousand acres of prime country. Coldwell knew that he put a lot of scars on the earth with his dozer, but unless his safety was jeopardized, he tried to be as light on the land as possible. He avoided riparian habitats, marshes, and meadows. And after the fire had been extinguished, the Forest Service often went back into the area to pull back all the topsoil. Firefighters loved a healthy, unscathed forest more than anyone, but the factors everyone should concern themselves with first and foremost were making sure that a small fire didn't turn into a big one and that everyone walked away with their lives.

Despite hairy situations in the past, Coldwell felt confident that everything would go smoothly on the fire currently burning in the foothills above Fontana. He planned to hit the fire hard, as did his swamper, the second firefighter on his two-man team. A part of his swamper's job was to scout the terrain on foot to ensure Coldwell didn't head over a ridge and then drop off the edge of a cliff. His swamper also looked out for spot fires or wind shifts. Basically, he kept an eye on the big picture while Coldwell had his head down in his work. Together they could work with speed, especially when supported by the aircraft, which were certain to arrive that afternoon. With firefighters and resources from four agencies already getting busy in the foothills, the fire shouldn't be all that hard to contain.

As he exited Interstate 15 into the Rancho Cucamonga area ten minutes after leaving the station, Coldwell got the official word to respond to the fire. He surprised everyone by arriving on scene a few minutes later, well ahead of the other resources ordered on second alarm.

From the top of Foxborough Drive, Coldwell could see the fire burning in the chaparral to the northeast. The majority of firefighters had just begun to flank it from its point of origin, and they needed all the help they could get. With the eastern flank being most active due to the southwest winds, Coldwell felt that his best option was to jump out in front of it, drop his shovel, and then carve a fuel break straight up the hillside. As long as aircraft arrived in the immediate future, he felt he'd have enough time to put in a solid fuel break. Just as he had predicted, it was most definitely doable.

Coldwell studied the lay of the land, searching for a good ridge to head up. If he picked one that was too steep, he wouldn't get up the mountain. And if he picked one too close to the eastern flank of the fire, he would get overrun before completing his line. He contacted operations to see if they had a particular ridge in mind, but when he talked with the overhead, there was still some confusion as to who the fire belonged to, which meant a firm leader hadn't yet been designated. They told him, "Pick a ridge," which was fine by Coldwell. He didn't concern himself too much with the politics. While they tried to sort out their issues, he would be out there implementing initial suppression tactics.

After unloading the trailer, Coldwell and his swamper walked the dozer along the fire's bottom edge. They stopped for a moment to visit with Bud Berger and his crew, who had fallen far behind the eastern flank, and then continued ahead. Coldwell found a ridge several hundred yards east of the advancing flame and then dropped his shovel and began to cut a line to the north, chewing through the dense brush. If the fire pressed in on him, aircraft would douse the flames to slow it down. Hopefully he would have enough time to carve a path to the top of the ridge—a path that Berger and his crew could protect with a hose lay in the hours to come.

Five to ten minutes into his upward climb, however, a Forest Service battalion chief who was watching Coldwell's progress from the top of

Foxborough contacted him by radio and said, "Pull out, it's getting too hot." Coldwell didn't argue. The battalion chief was in a position to see what the fire was doing. It was moving fast now, and the last thing he wanted was to get burned over.

He backed down the line he had already dug, pushed farther to the east, and then dropped his shovel and got out. Despite his best efforts he didn't make it to the top. The fire was well established in the big brush sprouting from the drainages off the mountain. Looking to the east, the northern tip of the flank actually beat him to the top of the ridge. With a wall directly to the north, Coldwell couldn't continue. Frustrated, he backed down.

Determined to catch the eastern flank, he moved four more ridges to the east, accompanied by a CDF dozer that had arrived. Heading up would be a risky venture. Approximately thirty minutes had passed since Coldwell had arrived on scene, and he hadn't seen a single aircraft in the sky—no helicopters or airtankers, not a single drop of water or retardant to cool the front of the fire as it raced toward him. And the new slope he had picked was steep. In the manual, he wasn't supposed to attempt a grade greater than 45 percent. In places on the ridge before him it was 50–60 percent, easy. He'd gone up greater over the years, up to 70 percent grade, but it all depended on the dirt, whether he could get a good bladeful to stabilize his machine. What made this ridge particularly difficult was its width. It was no more than fifty feet wide, and he would need all of it.

If Coldwell had been responsible for leading engine crews or hand crews up the hillside, he probably wouldn't have gone for it. But as of right now, the CDF dozer operator and himself were the only two this far out in front of the eastern flank. Knowing he could make a swift escape if necessary, Coldwell decided to charge. After all, it couldn't be much longer before aircraft arrived and started their drops.

Putting his beast into first gear, Coldwell headed uphill. Once he reached a 50 percent grade in the slope, however, he stopped moving. His dozer didn't have enough steam to climb the hill and punch line at the same time. He did the only thing he could—headed back down to the last flat spot he'd gone over. Instead of abandoning his mission, he remained midslope on the flatter terrain and spent several moments cutting a circular safety zone that he could head into if shit hit the fan. Once it was complete, he made another run uphill, only this time he did it with his blade raised. After struggling up the 50 percent grade, he reached another relatively flat spot. He used the location to pull a deft U-turn, and then he dropped his blade and cut line downhill into the safety zone he had carved. He did this over and over, connecting a solid line between the various safety zones he'd made on the flatter spots of the hill.

Because the width of the ridge prevented him from carving the football field–sized safety zones that he liked, Coldwell had left his swamper down at the bottom. If fire came tearing up to his line, anyone out in the open would get torched. Coldwell suspected that he too would feel some heat, even behind the protective glass of his cab, but he felt confident that he'd made his safety zones large enough to ride it out.

He knew he was pushing the envelope, but that was what dozer operators did. They put themselves in precarious situations and got the job done. If either his swamper or a battalion chief stationed back at the water tank informed him that the fire was making a run, he wouldn't hesitate to head south. Until then, he would charge up the mountain.

A few minutes into his project, things weren't looking good. A helicopter turned up and began making sporadic water drops on the fire's edge, but it certainly wasn't what Coldwell had anticipated. The fire was moving now, and it was going to beat him to the top of the ridge. He radioed division and requested more air support, and they said, "We're working on it." Expecting it to arrive any moment, he continued on up. As he built his series of safety zones high up on the ridge, the fire continued to edge closer. He called division again and told them that if he didn't get some air support he would lose it. Once again, they were working on it.

A few seconds later, Coldwell's swamper came over the airwaves and informed him of the fire's location. It had reached the drainage between the ridge he was working on and the ridge to the immediate west. Instantly Coldwell knew what that meant—the fire was getting ready to make a massive push uphill to his location. He informed division for a third time that they needed aircraft to keep from losing it. They were still working on it.

Less than five minutes later, Coldwell contacted division for a fourth time. This time, however, he only said three words—"We lost it."

Down below, Bud Berger, Mike Bell, and Terry Acre, who had come up from the spot fire to assume control of Division Z, all had their eyes on Coldwell. One minute he was racing down the slope toward his safety zone, and the next minute he was engulfed by a sixty-foot wall of flame. The second it happened, a terrible image surfaced in the mind of Mike Bell. Several years prior, he had spent a night in a hospital burn ward to have surgery on some minor injuries he'd received on a fire. A CDF dozer operator lay in the room next to him, burns covering the majority of his body.

With Coldwell completely gone from sight, Bell was bombarded with ghastly memories of that night long ago. He prayed that Coldwell's predicament only looked bad from his vantage point, but that didn't seem to be the case. The topography, fuel, weather, fuel moisture, and aspect of the slope were all in alignment for this fire to explode. And now that it had gotten established in the drainage, it had done just that, putting Coldwell's life in danger.

According to Coldwell, it wasn't as bad as it looked. Only seconds after he'd been informed that the fire was heading up toward him, he had slapped his dozer into third gear, which he generally reserved for moments when he needed to get the hell out of Dodge, and trucked downhill, topping the eighteen tons of steel out at fifteen miles per hour. The CDF dozer operator had been working on widening and improving the line Coldwell cut earlier, so he was already positioned in the nearest safety zone.

"You're cut off," Coldwell's fellow dozer operator shouted over the radio, trying to warn him.

It was a true statement. In order to reach the safety zone, Coldwell had to plow blind through a tower of flame. He had a gauge that measured the outside temperature, but he was too busy navigating through his orange surroundings and listening to radio traffic for any important information to look at it. But the temperature outside was hot enough to catch his work pack, which was strapped to the back of the dozer, on fire, melt the CAT stickers on the side of his ride, and bubble his outside running lights. He began to feel the radiant heat inside the cab, so he dropped a cloth shield that covered the right window. The hardest thing to deal with was the smoke. The cab wasn't airtight, and it quickly grew foggy inside.

While he made the dangerous journey down to his safety zone, a helicopter circled overhead, ready to drop a bucket of water to aid his escape. Before the pilot could do this, however, a surveillance plane much higher up called the drop off. With Coldwell completely engulfed in flame, it was impossible to tell his exact location along the ridge. If the water drop landed directly on his dozer, it could shatter the glass surrounding his cab. Then there would be nothing between Coldwell and the flame.

Although it seemed like an eternity to everyone below, Coldwell joined the CDF dozer operator in the safety zone in a matter of minutes. Flames pushed around them, searing the sides of their dozers and melting anything that wasn't metal except for the safety glass around their cabs. Both of them watched the fire jump their line and continue running to the east.

While Coldwell rode out the storm, Terry Acre climbed into Mike Bell's Explorer, and together they contacted Coldwell on the radio. Even though they wouldn't be able to help, they felt they needed to hear Coldwell's voice. Both of them were surprised when Coldwell spoke without a trace of fear. Submerged in an orange sea, he actually said everything was fine, that he would be back in action once the fire passed.

It wasn't bravado. When the bulk of the flames had pushed over them, Coldwell and the CDF dozer operator came down off the ridge and attempted to head farther to the east to find another ridge. Despite what they had gone through, both of them were still determined to cut off the eastern flank of the fire. A few minutes into their search, however, Coldwell got a call from operations. They wanted him to come back to the west and meet them at a chicken ranch south of the blaze. This didn't make sense to Coldwell; the fire was going the other way, how was he expected to catch it? He didn't pay attention to the first few requests, but on the third transmission the voice on the other end began to lose patience. They wanted him down there now to talk.

Coldwell knew what that meant. They wanted to interview him, conduct a critical debriefing, and "all that other human relations crap." For him, it had just been another hard day at the office. All he wanted to do was get back into the fight, but that could very well put his job on the line. So he ended up turning his dozer around and tying in with a safety officer, who took pictures of his bubbled lights and melted stickers. Coldwell responded to the process with a "You've got to be kidding."

Eventually Coldwell's Forest Service battalion chief, Darrell Mincey, who was working in unified command with the CDF, came to his rescue. He said, "Howard, are you good to go?"

"I'm good to go."

"Okay, we're going to write it up as some aggressive firefighting, no burnover. Go!"

Coldwell headed back into the race, but by this time Terry Acre, now in charge of Division Z, didn't feel comfortable trying to cut off the eastern flank. When Coldwell had headed up that last ridge, Acre had his doubts. An engine crew had actually wanted to follow Coldwell up and put in a hose lay, but Acre had held them back. It had been a good call. No one out in the open could have withstood such a surge of heat.

In Acre's mind, the moment the fire had gotten established in the drainage and made a run at the dozers, they had lost it. Not wanting to put anyone at risk, he pulled everyone off the hill. Once the troops were repositioned safely below the fire, Acre jumped into Mike Bell's Explorer. Together they traveled several miles east on the powerline access road, and then veered several miles to the north along another dirt road that led up into the mountains. Acre wanted to get a bird's-eye view of the fire, and he didn't see anything he liked. It moved too quickly and erratically for them to try and stop it anytime soon. A much better approach, he felt, would be to set fires of their own down along the powerline access road, which wrapped around the base of the mountain. The fire they started would get pulled up to the main fire. After that, the fire would have a very hard time spreading below the powerlines and attacking homes. This action would cause the fire to get much larger than anyone had hoped, but Acre felt it was the best plan of attack, especially when considering the safety of all the men and women out on the line.

The decision came as a disappointment to Bud Berger and Coldwell, both of whom wanted to get this thing tied off in the next few hours, but neither of them argued with Acre over his decision. Acre was currently in charge of Division Z, and his actions were well justified. In the Forest Service, firefighters were required to retire at the age of fifty-seven. For years they had lost experience faster than they could replace it, and the number of fatalities had risen accordingly. Because of tragedies like Colorado's 1994 South Canyon Fire, which claimed the lives of fourteen firefighters, there had been more reluctance to issue a "grab the bull by the horns" kind of attack. With inexperienced firefighters out on the line, it was much safer to back off and go indirect. Coldwell felt that sometimes management could be a little too gun-shy, but it was better than sending troops into precarious situations and having them get burned over.

Besides, by the time Acre made the decision to back off and go indirect, the fire had already been allowed to expand much farther than Coldwell had expected. He felt the whole co-op issue, trying to figure out who would pay for what, had hindered some of the good old-fashioned firefighting. But then what did he know, submersed in his own piece of the pie? He knew he had no idea what it was like to deal with political issues such as those. It was easy to armchair quarterback, but the truth of the matter was that every firefighter was forced to make split-second decisions. And just like anything in life, some are going to be the right ones, and some are going to be the wrong ones. So far, Coldwell had never seen a fire that didn't go out. Sometimes that just happened later rather than sooner.

5

Struggle up the West Flank

Shortly after Howard Coldwell joined the fight on the eastern flank, the firefighters over on the western side of the fire ran into their own share of problems.

Rancho Cucamonga's Battalion Chief Ron Mayfield, Captain Jim Dague, and Captain Phil Loncar arrived at the water tank at the top of Foxborough approximately ten minutes after the first alarm dispatch with six firefighters staffing a municipal engine, plus the surplus brush engine Rancho had acquired from the Forest Service several years earlier. Mayfield, who had two decades' experience fighting fire in the foothills, had a pretty good idea of what the fire would do and how they needed to combat it, so instead of heading down one of the flanks, he opted to remain at the top of Foxborough Drive, wait for the battalion chiefs from CDF, San Bernardino County, and the Forest Service to arrive, and then help with establishing an overall game plan.

Dague and Loncar jumped into action. The fire currently burned on the SRA, but because the CDF overhead hadn't yet turned up, they got their assignments from Steve Goldschmidt, a patrolman from the Forest Service. It was decided that Loncar and his crew from Medic Engine 173 would assist Bud Berger on the east flank, and Dague, commanding Brush Engine 176, would help with a hose lay being put up the west flank. If all went well, the two would reunite in the near future on the north side after boxing in the fire.

Dague got his crew rolling, but they didn't have to travel far. Where Foxborough ended, a dirt road began. It shot straight to the north up the mountainside, the western flank burning to its immediate right. A few hundred yards down the dirt extension, Dague found Forest Service Engine 32 and a San Bernardino County engine. Dague had a quick face-to-face with Ken Munsey, a captain with San Bernardino County, and they put their heads together to work out a plan of attack. Two ridges came off the mountains on their side of the fire, one directly above them and one slightly to the east. The fire still burned in the flats, but before too long it would reach the drainage between the two ridges. Once it got into the dense brush, it would shoot upslope toward the forest.

To keep that from happening, Dague and Munsey agreed to connect with Forest Service Engine 32's hose line and continue it along the fire's western edge in the flats, chase the fire up the ridge directly above them, and then work out into the drainage to hopefully meet Bud Berger coming from the east. To support them, aircraft would paint the brush at the top of the two ridges with water and retardant to cool down the flames. Between the two measures, it should buy them enough time to get some hand crews in there to cut a fuel break around the west and north flanks.

Attaching hose to the water tank on Engine 32, the crews dropped down into the brush on the east side of the dirt road. They beat back the flame with water as they worked their way north toward the ridge. As the hose became fully extended, one of Dague's men came running up carrying another hundred-foot section of hose wound up in a doughnut. He clamped the end of the charged hose, bled out the pressure, attached the new section, and then recharged the hose so they could continue their progress toward the ridge. The brush that hadn't burned was thick, in places several feet over their heads, so instead of trying to beat their way through it, they worked over the brush that had already burned, just a few feet inside the "black."

Along the flats they made good progress, attacking twenty-five-foot flame lengths not ten feet away. It looked like they might beat the fire up the hill. But when they reached the toe of the mountain, things slowed down. They only had to climb three hundred feet to reach the top of the first ridge, but the slope was a 70 percent grade. The ground was a mixture of soft soil and loose rock, so with every three feet they took upward, they'd slide two feet back down. A hand crew blazed past them to help clear a path for the hose lay, but they still inched along. They watched as the fire hit the drainage below them to the east. In a matter of minutes, it shot right past them, eliminating their chance of meeting up with Bud Berger on the north side of the blaze in the near future.

Dague didn't like how things were panning out. At this point in time, a decisive plan on how to attack this fire should already have been established. That, however, didn't seem to be the case. First off, a single tactical channel for all the agencies to use hadn't been set up. With the Forest Service and Rancho Cucamonga operating on different frequencies, they had to be standing right next to each other in order to communicate. In addition to that, the west flank of the fire still hadn't been classified as Division A, which meant that an incident commander hadn't been designated to take control of the incoming resources. The first unit to arrive on scene usually handled these issues, and Dague couldn't figure out why it hadn't been done. As of right now, everyone was still freelancing, doing what they thought best. That had worked fine in the first few minutes, but pretty soon it would be a mess. They needed to get organized so they could get up the hill and catch this thing.

With over a dozen firefighters struggling to get up the ridge, Dague approached Munsey and said, "You need to call your chief and see if we can get a division here. Either you or me can handle it, I don't care, but we need a little organization."

Munsey couldn't agree more, and after radioing to his superiors down below, he assumed control of Division A for the time being.

With one leader, things began to operate more smoothly, but before they could reach the top of the ridge, which would give them a vantage point to see how far up the mountain the fire had climbed past them, they were informed by their lookouts down below that the fire had jumped their hose lay. They had strung their line a few feet inside the black, assuming that the fire would continue to push to the east under the southwest wind. But that hadn't been the case. It had somehow gotten into the unburned brush to the left of their hose lay down in the flats, and now the fire raced upward through the fresh fuel. With the fire's edge having moved twenty yards farther to the west, all the firefighters working up the ridge were in danger.

Trying to flee through the brush to the west would most likely result in tragedy, so they only had one real option. The troops working on the hose lay took a few steps to the east, into the charred brush of the drainage. A few minutes later, the spot fire blew by them on its journey up the ridge. Dague watched the hand crew that had forged ahead do the same, and the last of them scrambling into the black "had thirty-foot flames licking over their backs."

It was a tense few moments, but after the majority of heat had passed, the hand crew worked their way back down to Dague. Continuing to head uphill from this location was no longer an option, not with the fire now burning to their left. Although it pained them to do so, they were forced to head back down to the flats, move farther to the west to get around the spot fire, beat back the new flames, and then begin their upward climb once again. While they did this, the main body of fire continued to push up the drainage between the two ridges, hungrily racing toward the higher elevations.

Down by the water tank at the top of Foxborough Drive, Rancho's Chief Mayfield wasn't having much better luck. While waiting for the CDF and Forest Service battalion chiefs to arrive, he had studied the chaparral clinging to the hillside. Some patches hadn't burned since the Myers Fire in 1970, and others hadn't burned in over a hundred years. The manzanita bushes had grown to the size of trees, and underneath them sprouted plenty of flashy fuels. They needed to get on this one quick, but he didn't foresee that being a problem. The various fire agencies in the area had worked quite well together for years in the foothills. A part of what made them so effective was that the overhead from the different agencies all knew each other.

That, however, wasn't the case this afternoon. Shortly after Mayfield had arrived, Forest Service battalion chief Darrell Mincey turned up, and then eventually CDF battalion chief Clyde Chittenden. Mayfield hadn't worked with either one of them, so they didn't bring him into the picture right away. Mayfield gave them a few minutes to work out jurisdictional matters, but it was a frustrating few minutes. "I have sat and watched a fire go while people were like, 'It's yours, it's mine' over the years," said Mayfield later, "but that is a discussion that has to take place because someone is going to flip the bill."

Knowing they needed to get the ball rolling, Mayfield eventually approached them. "The fire is going to sweep to the east along the base of the mountains toward Lytle Creek, and the houses down below the southern flank are going to be in jeopardy before too long," he said. "It is also going to make a push up into the canyons."

Mincey and Chittenden listened, but they didn't seem to take heed. In their minds, it seemed, Mayfield was a municipal firefighter, not a brush expert like the firefighters who made up the Forest Service and CDF. Mayfield bowed out with a simple, "I'm here if you need me," and then he proceeded to release some of his troops so they could return to their duties in Rancho. He was brought into the equation a short while later when the fire lived true to his predictions. The overhead handling the incident finally acknowledged his capability and put him in charge of structure protection, but by then Mayfield had his doubts about being able to catch the blaze at all. On this one, he knew they would be in it for the long haul.

6

At Least a Couple Thousand Acres

The Redding Hotshots joined Jim Dague's push up the western flank not long after the fire had made its jump into the brush west of the hose lay. Like many hotshot crews, Redding had been brought down from Northern California due to the fear of a terrible fire breaking out on the mountaintop. While most of the additional crews ordered under severity spent their days clearing dead trees from alongside the roads in the mountains, Redding had been tasked with removing the brush from around communications towers located at the top of San Sevaine Canyon, which was less than a mile west of where the fire broke.

Upon arriving at the top of Foxborough Drive at the tail end of the first wave of troops, Robert Holt, superintendent of the twenty-man crew, had been given the opportunity to take charge of Division A but turned it down. Under normal circumstances, Holt wouldn't have hesitated. But with it being so late in the season, the majority of his overhead had already knocked off, including one of his captains and both of his squad leaders. And every crew member still toughing it out, including Holt, was pretty banged up. In a two-week period earlier in the summer, they had fought six different fires in Montana. It had been a giant mess. Because so many fires had broken at once, the Forest Service had run out of resources and began ordering contract crews. When it became evident that the contract crews couldn't do the job that needed to get done, Holt's crew got called in to clean up the mess. It had run them ragged, and the project work they had been conducting for the last ten days hadn't been a walk in the park. The communication towers were at the very top of the mountain, and each morning they had to beat through wasp-infested fields of poison oak to reach them. Every crew member had been stung multiple times and had scratched their bodies raw.

Despite their sorry state, they wasted no time climbing out of their crew buggies, arming themselves with their hand tools, and heading up the western flank hose lay to reach Dague and the rest of the firefighters on the line. Hotshot crews were the elite firefighters of the U.S. Forest Service. They were used to spending weeks out on the fire line, pushing their bodies and minds to the limit, so the hike up the ridge went quickly. After a brief face-to-face with the leaders, Holt and his gang pushed out ahead, clearing a path for the engine crews that would soon follow. While they worked, two helicopters arrived and dropped water on the ridge up above, cooling the advancing flame. It wasn't phenomenal air support, but after eighteen years fighting fire on a hotshot crew, Holt had a strong feeling that in addition to the hand line his crew put in, it would be enough to bring the western flank under control in the coming hours. Then one of the helicopters just stopped showing up. "I remember a green-, black-, and -white ship, and then a red-and-white ship—both Type I or Type II," said Holt. "And then all of a sudden one of those got out of rotation. That was right in the beginning, the first part of initial attack."

Holt wondered in the back of his mind where it had gone, and even more importantly, what its absence might do to Division A. He kept his crew advancing upward, one foot in the black. Eventually he decided to work out in front of his crew to develop a game plan, maybe see if he could get some folks up to the front to catch the hotspots. "Obviously that didn't work out because we had lost our air support," said Holt. "It was really broken topography, and I thought that if the fire got established, if we didn't catch it in the first couple of hours, it was going to go to at least a couple of thousand acres."

CDF captain Ron Lee felt the same. With the fire still burning on the SRA, he had taken the Division A leadership role off Munsey's hands the moment he arrived. Fifteen minutes or so into the second ascent up the ridge, he decided to climb up past the Redding Hotshots and scout out the situation. He hoped that they might still be able to catch the head of the fire, but the moment he reached the top of the ridge, gaining a view of the next several ridges stepping up the mountain, he realized that that was wishful thinking. The fire had already pushed several thousand feet beyond where he now stood. It had turned into a monster. "When it got into that canyon and went to the top, you could have put the whole world on it and you weren't going to stop it," said Lee. "So that part was impressive, as far as I couldn't believe it had burned that far that quickly."

To have any chance at all of catching the fire, they would need air support—and lots of it.

7

Broke Bucket

Corporal Stewart had flown helicopters for sixteen years. Over that time, he'd chased car thieves down freeways, transported search-and-rescue teams into remote canyons, hovered over houses under surveillance, rushed heart attack victims to the hospital, deployed dive teams over lakes, and used his powerful spotlight to illuminate hundreds of criminals being pursued by law enforcement agents. As a part of the San Bernardino County Sheriff Department's Helicopter Program, Stewart had gone on just about every mission imaginable. This afternoon he was fighting fire.

At 2:38 P.M., roughly twenty minutes after first-alarm resources had been dispatched, he spotted the fire from behind the controls of 305, a medium-sized helicopter classified as Type II. The journey had only taken a few minutes. His department had a contract with CDF, so during peak fire months, 305, which was actually owned by both the Sheriff's Department and CDF, was based out of Prado Fire Camp, located in Chino, fifteen miles southwest of the incident. The fire was still in the grasslands at the base of the mountains above Fontana, just a couple of acres. Although Stewart wasn't an expert at judging fire behavior, he felt they should be able to pick it up by the end of the day, most certainly by the following morning.

Guiding his bird forward, Stewart flickered his eyes across the sky. This was the scariest part of fighting fire, being the first helicopter in on the initial attack. Plans were usually still being formulated down below as to where they wanted him to go. While he hovered in limbo, waiting for orders, he had to watch out for other arriving helicopters that worked at the same elevation, as well as airtankers that swooped in just above with their heavy loads of retardant. Eventually Air Attack 12, a fixed-wing surveillance plane, would begin circling high overhead, directing all the air traffic, but in the first few minutes of a blaze confusion tended to be the norm. Tying to focus on all the movement in the sky and on the ground could be taxing to say the least.

Directly behind him, accompanying him on the ride, were nine fire-fighters. Eight of them were inmates, hired directly out of state prisons by CDF and paid a few dollars a day. Their experience fighting wildfire varied. Some had been in the program for two months, others for two years. Generally speaking, they didn't have the same gung-ho attitude as the men and women in the Forest Service or on CDF engine crews, simply because they hadn't dreamt their whole life about fighting fire. The moment their sentence was up, the last place they wanted to be was on a fire line.

But the ninth firefighter among them, a CDF captain, possessed initiative. His job was to slide open the cargo doors once Stewart found a safe place to land out in front of the fire, order his crew out, and then begin constructing a fuel break. Stewart kept in contact with the captain on an air-to-ground frequency, and if things got hairy for the crew down below, Stewart could swoop in and slow the fire's advance with a bucket drop.

With the crew gearing up in the back, Stewart piloted his craft nearer to the foothills and studied the lay of the land below. Getting out ahead of this particular fire would be tricky. The wind blew out of the south-west at ten to fifteen knots. The manual stated he could fly in wind up to thirty knots, but the wind speed wasn't the problem. The southwest winds were pushing a dense cloud of smoke up the hillside, making it nearly impossible to see the exact location of the fire front. In order to find it, Stewart would have to head into the smoke, which required a good deal of skill and experience. In addition to having to maintain his bearings with little or no visual reference, he also had to ensure that his engine, which ran off a mixture of fuel and air, didn't suffocate and flame out. The danger of flying in smoke was one of the reasons why he'd had to spend three years flying on night and mountain missions before he had been allowed to enter this area of piloting.

Stewart took a deep breath as he mentally prepared himself for the fight. By the time he made it over the fire, he got his orders—support the west flank. A few minutes later, at 2:41 P.M., he contacted Clyde Chittenden, the CDF battalion chief, who was still driving to the fire. Stewart told him that after he put the crew down, he would bucket up his ship. He also added, "If we can get the tankers in here quickly, we might have a chance."

Because of the amount of smoke being pushed up the drainage between the two ridges on the west flank, Stewart touched down near where Ron Lee and Jim Dague were putting in the hose lay up on the hillside. The moment Stewart landed, the inmate helitack crew slipped out the cargo doors and attached the Bambi Bucket to the bottom of the helicopter. As the crew members sped off toward the hillside to help with the hose lay, Stewart lifted off again and headed to the south, searching for a water source. It could be a lake, a golf course pond—any body of water that he could maneuver safety into. Although scooping water was supposedly the safest procedure during a firefight, that wasn't always the case. Earlier in the summer on the Picture Fire in Arizona, a disgruntled rancher had opened fire on a collection bucket as it reached down into his pond. Apparently, it had been an act of revenge: the rancher claimed that on a fire the previous year the fire service had stolen two thousand dollars' worth of his water.

Stewart found a pond close by, and he scooped 324 gallons of water into his bucket, which dangled from a steel cable twenty-five feet below. As he headed back to the fire, he could feel the three thousand pounds of added weight strapped to his belly. The heavy load wasn't much of a burden when fighting grass fires in the flatlands, but up in the foothills things got more complicated. To reach a fire front on a hillside, Stewart sometimes had to fly upslope, drop his water, and then do a quick turn-around so he didn't crash into the hillside. Other times he had to come downhill at the fire, drop his load, and then dive toward the flats. While performing both of these maneuvers, he had to be conscious of the heavy bucket below, which constantly swung underneath him and pulled his bird one way and another. He also had to keep his airspeed as fast as possible, especially in box canyons. If his bucket malfunctioned and he couldn't make the drop, the added weight might hinder him from getting out of there.

All these factors were on Stewart's mind as he approached the western flank with a full bucket. Less than five minutes had passed since he'd dropped off the crew, but the fire had already pushed farther up the drainage. Down below, he could see a number of crews working the fire's edges. Stewart knew that as much as the general public liked to see aircraft over a fire, it was the ground troops that always brought a blaze under control. Aircraft was an effective tool to slow and cool the front of the fire, but if there weren't men on the ground to actually cut a line around the blaze, it was only a matter of time before the fire evaporated the water and burned through the retardant. This was especially true after a fire had escaped the initial attack. As the fire grew, bucket drops would become less and less effective. They mattered most during the first hour, right at the beginning of the initial attack. Luckily, Stewart had made good time to this fire. He still had the power to keep it small, to buy some time for additional ground crews to arrive and dig their fuel breaks.

Swooping down on the west flank, Stewart hit the button to jettison his water on the fire's head, but nothing happened. He could still feel the three thousand pounds below tugging at his craft. He pulled up, circled around, and then came in on another run and tried again. Still nothing.

After the third attempt, Stewart realized he would not be fighting fire anytime soon. He contacted pilot Ray Sauceda, who circled high overhead in the surveillance plane, and said, "My bucket is malfunctioning. I need to go get it fixed."

Thankfully, Stewart was within ten minutes' flight time from his main facility at Rialto Airport. If all went well, he would be back in the fight in half an hour or less. But it was a critical thirty minutes. Other than Air Attack 12 up above, which could only scout the fire and relay commands, no other aircraft were on scene. That meant that Ron Lee, Jim Dague, the Redding Hotshots, and the CDF inmate helitack crew on the western flank in Division A, as well as Bud Berger, Terry Acre, and the two dozers over on the eastern flank in Division Z, had no support from above.

If a substantial number of aircraft didn't arrive soon, it looked more and more like they would lose this thing. Stewart felt the stress close in, as did the men and women working several miles to the east at the San Bernardino CDF Emergency Command Center, the unified ordering point for the blaze.

8

Aircraft

At 2:13 P.M., Rod Delgado, a floor supervisor at the CDF Emergency Command Center, received a transmission over the intercom from Ontario Fire, which handled the majority of 911 fire calls in the foothills. There were reports of a small grass fire just northeast of Highland and Etiwanda avenues in Rancho Cucamonga. Having worked for San Bernardino CDF since 1981, Delgado knew from the cross streets that the fire was still several miles south of the State Responsibility Area (SRA), but because of the mutual aid agreements CDF had with both the Forest Service and San Bernardino County Fire, he got a CDF battalion chief and two CDF engines rolling toward the fire to assist County Fire just two minutes later. He sent Captain Terry Acre with Engine 3581 out of Devore, and Captain Ron Lee with Engine 3577 out of Chino. Both would arrive a considerable amount of time before CDF battalion chief Clyde Chittenden, who was coming from San Bernardino CDF headquarters, a twenty-minute drive blazing at Code 3. At this point, Chittenden's transit time wasn't a major concern, simply because everyone thought the blaze was on county land.

Less than a minute after getting the engines rolling, however, San Bernardino County Fire contacted Delgado over the intercom, which linked the CDF Command Center with nearly a dozen fire offices in Southern California, to ask if CDF had resources heading to the fire burning up near the Hunter's Ridge area. The Hunter's Ridge housing development was nowhere near Highland and Etiwanda. It was several miles north, pressing in on the SRA. Uncertain if this was the same fire as the first report or if a second fire had broken, Delgado got prepared to issue a full wildland response, which included a surveillance plane, two airtankers, and a helicopter.

Once he got the cross streets of the new report, which were Shetland and Grand Prix, Delgado entered the location of the fire into the Multi-Incident Resource Processing System (MIRPS), a computer program used by both CDF and the Forest Service to order aircraft. In the later stages of a fire, Delgado had to send his MIRPS aircraft requests to the Southern Operations Center (SouthOps), a clearinghouse of all firefighting aircraft in Southern California, and they would search the various air bases to fill the order. During the initial attack, however, Delgado had permission to bypass SouthOps and send the aircraft requests directly to local bases to cut down on time. And with the entire area eager to burn, time was of the essence.

Having monitored the whereabouts of local aircraft over the course of the afternoon, Delgado suspected that the nearby San Bernardino Air Tanker Base would be able to fulfill his order for the two airtankers, and Prado Fire Camp in Chino would be able to fulfill his order for the helicopter. If that were the case, the ground troops should have plenty of air support right from the get-go. But before Delgado could send the MIRPS aircraft request to the two local bases, he needed to punch the name of the incident into the computer to eliminate any confusion. Generally the first arriving unit named the fire, but Delgado didn't want to wait for that. He pressed a button on the intercom, which placed him through to both the Forest Service and the county. "Can we name this thing the Grand Prix?" he asked them. "Will that work for you?"

"It will work for us," they both responded.

As Delgado worked out the orders for aircraft, a chief from the county arrived to the fire burning above the Hunter's Ridge housing development ten minutes after the first call had come in, and he put the fire at about two to three acres. Needing to know if CDF planned to run the incident, the county batallion chief contacted his superiors, and in turn his superiors contacted Delgado at CDF headquarters.

"Yes, CDF will take it," Delgado answered, and then got Helicopter 305, a number of engines, and a transit dozer moving toward the fire. In addition to this, he also ordered up hand crews over the telephone. He had a feeling that this was not going to be an easy job; in fact, he felt that it was going to be a "significant fire."

Forest Service battalion chief Darrell Mincey thought the same thing. Coming from his station in Lytle Creek just to the east, he'd made good time, pulling up to the water tank at the top of Foxborough shortly after the forces from Rancho Cucamonga. The fire was clearly burning on the SRA, which meant that it belonged to CDF. But Clyde Chittenden, the CDF battalion chief who had been ordered by Delgado, was still in transit to the fire, and it would be some time before he arrived. In many parts of the state, the leadership role would normally be left vacant until the battalion chief from the most affected agency turned up, but that was not how they functioned in San Bernardino. With the jurisdictions of the two agencies so closely intertwined, battalion chiefs from both sides had a spoken understanding that they would assume the leadership role until their counterparts could get there and take over. This is exactly what Mincey did, so instead of searching for a specific problem or fire front that needed attending, he looked at the fire as a whole and figured out what needed to be done. The fire was between five and ten acres now, spreading rapidly. His game plan was to try and protect the houses being threatened along the southern flank, and then catch the northeastern expansion of the fire at about forty acres. But in order to rope it in before it got established in the ugly country up in the forest, they "needed a lot more resources than what we had coming."

Out of professional courtesy, Mincey hopped on the radio and contacted CDF battalion chief Clyde Chittenden, who was trying his best to get there in a hurry to take control. Mincey said he was going to order the Redding and Del Rosa Forest Service hotshot crews, which happened to be doing project work in the area. There was also some talk about transitioning the central ordering point from CDF to the Forest Service. Mincey knew that if they couldn't catch it on the SRA, which was a high probability, then it would soon be a Forest Service problem. It only seemed fitting then that the Forest Service become the central ordering point. If that happened, the responsibility of placing the aircraft orders would be out of Delgado's hands. But "everybody sounded like they wanted to keep it SRA, so all right," said Mincey. "We didn't want to get into a contest with them about it. You want it, you got it."

Shortly after contacting Chittenden, at 2:27 P.M., Mincey contacted

Delgado at the CDF Command Center to discuss aircraft. In addition to sending out airtankers and a helicopter, the Forest Service also sent out a helitanker to initially attack fires. CDF did not, the main reason being price. The birds cost nearly seven thousand dollars an hour. But with the fire being in the hands of the Forest Service until Chittenden arrived, Mincey told Delgado, "Because of the threat to the forest, we would like to order a helitanker," noting that the Forest Service would foot the bill.

Five minutes later, the Forest Service told Delgado over the intercom that the helitanker would most likely be 794, coming from their tanker base in San Bernardino. Then, just a short while later, Delgado heard the Forest Service contact their tanker base just to make sure that they could fill the order. They could not. Just four minutes prior, the Roblar 2 Fire, which had broken at noon near Camp Pendleton in San Diego County, requested two additional airtankers and a helitanker, and with structures being threatened, they got what they asked for. So instead of getting the airtankers stationed close by at San Bernardino Air Tanker Base, the Grand Prix would get airtankers 151 and 152, which were stationed at Fox Field in Lancaster, fifty miles northwest of the fire in the high desert of Los Angeles County. These two airtankers, however, wouldn't take off from Fox Field until 3:05 P.M., and they wouldn't arrive at the Grand Prix until 3:25 P.M., over an hour after it had started.

This came as a great disappointment to those working at San Bernardino Air Tanker Base. Tom Inocencio, an assistant air tanker base manager in charge that day, felt someone had dropped the ball. If those running the Grand Prix had placed the order for aircraft directly to San Bernardino Air Tanker Base just a little bit sooner, the two airtankers and helitanker stationed there could have made at least a couple of drops on the Grand Prix before getting diverted to the Roblar 2 Fire.

"It just didn't fit in with anything they did all year," said Inocencio. "Anytime there was smoke on the hillside, we had a full aircraft response. Somebody held off on this one, and I don't know whether it was the county or state or whatever. The fact that they probably just didn't understand the jurisdiction, something like that. But the fact is that aircraft didn't get ordered in a timely manner. With two airtankers and a helitanker sitting here, it would have been the thing to do. We had them sitting here for fifteen minutes. [The pilots] knew they were going to go to the Grand Prix Fire. All common sense dictated that that was where they were going to go. And then I had to give them their orders that they were going to Camp Pendleton, and they couldn't believe it. They were just sitting here staring at me. A good initial attack would have knocked that fire down probably at twenty acres at the most. . . .The IC [incident commander] didn't get on scene right away. The IC was coming en route from another area, and he was talking during the initial stages of this. He was still up in the Cajon Pass somewhere."

﹁Delgado could understand their frustrations. He had spent a few of his younger years on a Forest Service helishot crew, getting dropped into remote wilderness by helicopter to battle the front of a blaze. He knew what it was like to sit in staging at the incident command post, waiting to be sent into action while the overhead made their decisions. But stationed in the command center through which all resources for the Grand Prix were ordered, Delgado got to see the bigger picture. The fact of the matter was that there were other fires burning, drawing resources. The Roblar 2 Fire had structures threatened, and he could only imagine the ramifications if aircraft heading to that fire were diverted to the Grand Prix, and then homes burned up in San Diego County. In his mind, one or two water drops on the Grand Prix wouldn't have changed much. "I don't think anything on the initial attack fell through the cracks," said Delgado. "It was just a matter of circumstance at the time aircraft was being ordered."

At this point, it became obvious to Delgado that the Grand Prix would go extra innings. But things could have been worse. Although they didn't get the helitanker or the two airtankers from San Bernardino Air Tanker Base, they did get a surveillance plane, which was due to arrive over the fire soon, as well as Helicopter 305 out of Prado Fire Camp. The county called over the intercom to say they were responding with a dozer, a brush engine, a medic engine, a water tender, and a battalion. With ground troops starting to file in, Southern California Edison advised Delgado to remind everyone not to stand near or under the transmission line towers due to arcing.

Things picked up quickly. At 2:35 P.M., CDF captain Terry Acre arrived with Engine 3581 and got pulled over to the spot fire below the main body of fire by Rancho's Mike Bell. A few minutes later, Corporal Stewart arrived on scene with Helicopter 305 and informed CDF battalion chief Clyde Chittenden, who was still en route to the fire, that he was going to set his inmate crew down and bucket up his ship. He also added in the same transmission, "If we get the airtankers in here quickly, we might have a chance on this one ridge," referring to the western flank where Jim Dague and Ron Lee were now at work. The fire was currently being placed at forty acres, spreading rapidly. It would be on the forest "momentarily."

Ten minutes later, Delgado heard a familiar voice over the command channel, pilot Ray Sauceda in Air Attack 12, the surveillance plane. Sauceda's job was to fly over the fire, make contact with the incident commander, verbalize to the commander what he saw from the sky, and then make a recommendation for what he thought they would need in the way of aircraft. Once firefighting aircraft started arriving, Sauceda would monitor the whereabouts of the planes and tell the pilots where and when to make their drops. In order to do his job he needed all the facts, so shortly after arriving at the Grand Prix, Sauceda wanted to know what aircraft he could expect in the near future. Delgado told him, "Tanker 151, Tanker 152, Helicopter 305, and yourself."

"What happened to 794?" Sauceda asked. "He started out this way, and then he returned back. Did he get canceled?"

This threw Delgado for a loop. Sauceda was referring to Helitanker 794, which had supposedly been sitting at San Bernardino Air Tanker Base when the Grand Prix broke. It was the same helitanker the Forest Service had wanted to send, but four minutes prior to their placing their order, it had been diverted to the Roblar 2 Fire. Later on, after all the chaos died down, Delgado figured out what most likely had happened. After being in the department for twenty-three years, he knew how hard it was for pilots to remain at their bases when a fire burned close by. The pilot had most likely seen the smoke and thought, "There are all of these other fires going on, and I'm the only helitanker in town. I know I'm going to get sent to this thing, so I'm not going to wait until the bell." The pilot had most likely followed Ray Sauceda in Air Attack 12 toward the fire on his own initiative, but then got ordered for the Roblar 2 Fire before he got there. This led to even more frustration among those stationed back at San Bernardino Air Tanker Base. "The helitanker had a load of water, and it was told to return back to San Bernardino," said Tom Inocencio. "They didn't even get to drop their load of water on the fire. They had to drop it off here before they landed."

Brushing off the strange disappearance of Helitanker 794, Sauceda circled above the fire in his surveillance plane. Once he had a good grasp of the situation below him, he contacted CDF battalion chief Clyde

Chittenden via radio and suggested ordering two additional airtankers beyond the two that were supposedly going to arrive any moment.

"Okay, Ray, you've got a better look than I do," responded Chittenden, who had now arrived and was in the process of taking over the role of incident commander. "I'm going to get face-to-face with Darrell Mincey right now. It sounds like it is still on the SRA. Right now does it look like it is going to run into the forest?"

"Well, if we don't stop it now, it'll get out in the forest," said Sauceda, gazing down on the fire from high above. "Right now the forward uphill rate of spread has slowed somewhat. It has gotten to a little flat spot on top, Clyde. It is just starting to heat up on the westerly side, the left flank, and it is all pretty steep in there. I think if we had some good turnarounds—we could sure use about four airtankers total. We should be able to hold it fairly close if we get them quickly. We've got 151 and 152 reportedly assigned out of Fox, and I'm going to give you about seventy or eighty acres at this time." What Sauceda did not know, however, was that airtankers 151 and 152 were not even airborne. They wouldn't arrive to the Grand Prix until 3:25 P.M., more than thirty minutes after this transmission.

Before the two could end their conversation, things got worse. Saucedo was informed that Helicopter 305, the only firefighting aircraft on scene, had to return to its base due to a bucket malfunction. To compensate, Sauceda advised Chittenden to order two more helicopters for the fire. Delgado had been listening to their transmission back at CDF headquarters, and he informed Chittenden, who was now in control of the fire, that he'd shoot the order down to SouthOps to be filled.

Things were quickly falling apart. Just a few minutes before three o'clock, CDF captain Terry Acre, working to contain the spot fire below the main body, contacted Chittenden to tell him that the fire was burning around the powerlines. Chittenden, who had arrived to a fire already well established because of his travel time, needed to get some organization going in a hurry. More than thirty minutes had passed since the fire broke, and still divisions hadn't been assigned.

"You're Division Z," Chittenden told Acre.

Whether Acre was in a good spot to handle Division Z was a matter of debate, but the fact that leadership roles were getting delegated came as a huge relief to Rancho's Mike Bell on the eastern flank and Rancho's Jim Dague on the western flank.

It happened not a moment too soon. At about this time, pilot Ray Sauceda, still circling over the fire in Air Attack 12, could see that things were really starting to pick up. He informed Chittenden that the fire now had two heads. One pushed to the northeast, and the other pushed up into the drainage between the two ridges coming off the mountain on the western flank. The fire had grown to a hundred and fifty acres, spreading rapidly. He also told Clyde that airtankers 151 and 152 still hadn't arrived.

"Okay, confirming that you do not have airtankers on scene yet," Chittenden responded.

"Nothing on Z, just 305 with a broke bucket," said Sauceda. Down below, he could see Howard Coldwell trying to cut off the eastern flank of the fire in his dozer. If they didn't get aircraft in there to support him soon, he would get overrun.

Back in the CDF Command Center, Delgado felt the pressure. Aircraft was in short supply due to the Roblar 2 Fire. Sauceda, circling high over the fire, understood what the Grand Prix needed in the way of aircraft to bring it under control—and yet he wasn't getting it. Delgado knew it had to be frustrating, and he informed Sauceda via radio that he was still trying to get an estimated time of arrival for airtankers 151 and 152.

"Yes, I understand that," returned Sauceda.

Delgado took a deep breath and crossed his fingers that things would soon pan out in the way of aircraft. And from the sound of the transmissions he heard, the troops on the ground needed all the help they could get. Then, only a few minutes after Sauceda had put the fire at around a hundred and fifty acres, he put it at between two hundred and fifty and three hundred acres, with the potential to go to a couple of thousand. Sauceda also told Chittenden, "I see we are going to need at least three more airtankers."

"That is in addition to the order we just placed a little bit ago?" Chittenden responded.

"Yep. I'm not going to say we are going to get them, but if we have them, that is what we need."

Chittenden placed the order with Delgado, who in turn placed the information into MIRPS, hoping that SouthOps could do some maneuvering and get them the planes. Before he could finish punching the request into the computer, however, Delgado's attention was pulled back to the intercom. A CDF dozer transport had arrived on scene and contacted Clyde Chittenden for orders. Chittenden, however, already had his hands full. "I'm going to have to hold you off—we have a spot here threatening crews," he said, referring to the group of firefighters trying to put the hose lay up the west flank. "They just had to run into the black. Stand by, just try to get to the north end of Foxborough."

Working in the command center, Delgado didn't get to hear the normal radio traffic occurring out on the fire line. As a result, he wouldn't know until later that night that the men on the western flank were all right. The thought of firefighters having been burned over made him sick, and he wanted to run out there and help any way he could. But he knew he could best serve everyone out on the line by making sure things ran smoothly at the central ordering point. The Grand Prix had grown so large that they were now getting reports of fires in Crestline up on the mountaintop. All the residents living in the high country were absolutely panicked about a fire tearing through all the dead timber in the San Bernardino National Forest, and rightfully so. But every time residents in the higher elevations saw smoke, they assumed that the forest around them was on fire. The phones out in the main command center went crazy, and they had to answer each call, even though Delgado was quite certain the majority of reports had to do with drift smoke off the Grand Prix. But anywhere there was smoke there could also be hot ash, and with the forest being overly volatile, you could never play it too safe. Checking up on every report, however, would inevitably draw more resources away from the Grand Prix.

Pilot Ray Sauceda continued to put in new orders for aircraft, and Delgado continued to punch the information into MIRPS and send it to SouthOps. Then, at around 3:30 P.M., aircraft began arriving. Helitanker 790, which was inbound for the Grand Prix, suffered a mechanical problem and had to land at San Bernardino Air Tanker Base, but airtankers 151 and 152 had finally reached the fire. They dropped their loads of retardant, but despite their efforts, the blaze turned into a beast fifteen minutes later. "I'm going to give you about fifteen hundred, working on two thousand," Sauceda said about the acreage.

Over the next half hour, firefighting aircraft continued to arrive. By 4 P.M., there were three helicopters and four airtankers being directed by Sauceda. More were on the way, but many of them would get diverted. At 4:11 P.M., Delgado heard from SouthOps that the Pass Fire had started in Reche Canyon fifteen miles east of the Grand Prix in the hills on the border of San Bernardino and Riverside counties. They were going to divert two airtankers to handle it.

Delgado continued to work with Air Attack 12, the incident commander, and SouthOps to get the Grand Prix the aircraft it needed, and until aircraft were bedded down at dark, twenty-three different helicopters and airtankers would be ordered for the Grand Prix. It wasn't enough, however, to bring the little fire that had turned into a big one under control. "You can speculate what the difference would have been if aircraft would have been available to get right on the fire," said Delgado. But hindsight is 20/20, so no one will ever really know.

9

Trouble on the Horizon

As firefighting aircraft returned to their bases for the night, ground troops continued to fight the Grand Prix. On the western flank, the game plan remained the same. Jim Dague and Ron Lee worked to get the hose lay farther up the mountain, dousing the blackened edge of the fire to ensure hot embers didn't ignite the unburned fuel on their left. They sent arriving Forest Service hotshot crews several thousand feet up ahead with the mission of cutting as much line as possible straight up the mountain, hoping that once night hit and fire activity settled down, the crews would be able to veer their fuel break to the east and cut off the head of the blaze near the top of the mountain.

The race was on to punch line upslope on the western flank, but the Redding Hotshots were not in good shape. They had seventeen men and women on what was supposed to be a twenty-man crew. And four of those seventeen were in such bad shape from nonstop firefighting all summer that they had been bedded down shortly after the Grand Prix started. Luckily, they had plenty of help. First the Del Rosa Hotshots, a local crew based in the foothills of San Bernardino just to the east, turned up, and then the Dalton Hotshots. Later that afternoon, they were also joined by the Lassen Hotshots, who had been brought down from Northern California to do project work up in the mountains. But having fought fire all over the western states the last couple of months, Lassen wasn't in much better shape than Redding.

Despite the general fatigue of all the hotshot crews along the western flank, each crew member kept his head down and worked with speed. The lead sawyer from each team worked in front of the line, hacking away at the brush with his spinning chain. Behind him came a group of ground pounders with a variety of handheld tools. Some chopped at roots with Pulaskis, tools that resembled a hoe, only with a sharper edge. Others dug up stubborn rocks with picks. By the time the last man in line passed through an area, a four-foot-wide line was cut through the brush, scraped down to the mineral soil.

After three hours pushing their line uphill, trying to box in the fire, the crews got hung up. The western flank had climbed over the ridge they were working on and gotten established in a deep canyon to the west. Before they could continue up the mountain, they first had to head down into the canyon and cut line around the fire, but the superintendents of the hotshot crews didn't feel comfortable doing this. Temperatures soared down in the canyon, making it unsafe. The hotshot crews could only wait it out, so they took off their packs, set down their tools, laid out their space blankets, and stretched out on the blackened soil to get some rest. Rest, however, came hard with a raging wildfire nearby. Many times through the night the fire would flare up, and the crews would awaken to hundred-foot flame lengths shooting up into the night air.

"We knew at that point that this was no longer going to be a cakewalk," said Lassen crew member Brian Anderson. "Shit was hitting the fan down there—it was time to go to work."

The firefighters on the eastern flank stayed more active during the night. The fire continued to push to the northeast under the southwest winds, moving along the base of the mountains as well as up the slopes. Before too long, the section of the eastern flank racing along the foothills would reach the nearby community of Devore. And once the northern flank of the fire reached the top of the mountain, it would start to head downhill toward the community of Lytle Creek on the other side.

The Forest Service's Bud Berger, the first to arrive on the blaze, continued to be in favor of heading farther east along the powerline access road and finding another ridge coming off the mountains. "I would have taken a hose lay off that front-country truck trail," he said. "I would have gotten a few engines and started a hose lay up one of those ridges and flanked it. But I wasn't making the calls. That is the way we have always done it. When [the Forest Service is] in charge, we try to flank the fire out and pinch it off the best we can. . . . For a little bit there, the flames were kind of intense, but as the evening came on they kind of died down. There could have been some good work done there. At least try to keep it up on the hill and not expand it any further to the east. . . . At that point in time, I knew that the winds weren't far off. Even though it looked like everything was going good, you had to think about what was coming."

CDF captain Terry Acre, who had taken charge of Division Z, continued to see it differently. After the two dozers got burned over, he didn't want to take any chances sending crews up the ridges. Not with the wind blowing in every direction. "There is a canyon influence there," said Acre. "You've got up-canyon winds because of the temperature, and down-canyon winds because of the topography. . . . When they brush each other, they just expand, shoot winds everywhere. That is what caused the erratic fire behavior."

After taking his trip to the top of the mountain and getting a look at the fire as a whole, Acre devised a plan that would not only keep crews safe, but hopefully rope the fire in before morning. The powerline access road ran east along the base of the mountain, and then cut north into the mouth of Cajon Canyon. All they had to do to put the fire in check was to start lighting their own fires on the side of the road pointing toward the mountain. They would burn along it across the foothills to the east, and then do the same across the foothills to the north. Their fire would head uphill toward the main body of fire, and when the two converged, both would lay down. "So it was just a matter of getting around that hill, firing it up, and letting it catch the other fire," said Acre. "That would have been the end of it. The only reason that it came down below us after the fact was on the end around Lytle Creek they were trying to fire in the morning. We told them that the winds were going to come up, don't do any firing. But a hotshot crew decided they had a little time frame to jump in there and do it, but the winds changed all of a sudden and pushed it back down. It burned from the north back down to the south—everything we were trying to cover."

They didn't have much luck halting the northern flank either. Dozer operator Howard Coldwell got sent up San Sevaine Road, a dirt trail that shot straight up the hillside off Foxborough Drive and then near the top of the mountain veered toward Lytle Creek in the east. His job was to widen the trail as much as possible so when the fire eventually reached the top, it wouldn't be able to cross. "The fire wasn't slowing down at all," said Coldwell. "It was just romping and stomping. Putting in a dozer line was one thing, but are you going to get aircraft on it, are you going to get a hand crew out there to do some backfiring? Are you going to have an engine out there with a hose lay? Usually it is a combination of all the stops."

Forest Service battalion chief Darrell Mincey, who had gone into unified command with Clyde Chittenden from CDF, didn't feel safe giving Coldwell the kind of backup he needed. "I knew we would have to start sending stuff up to San Sevaine Road; that was the only place we were going to catch this," he said. "We tried to get dozers and crews up there, but another thing we had to factor in was fire behavior because it was more or less a midslope road. I couldn't really commit a bunch of stuff up there because there was basically no way out."

As a result of the topography, vegetation, and weather, the Grand Prix expanded at a rapid rate throughout the night. This, however, didn't come as much of a surprise to those in charge. The incident commanders knew late in the afternoon that this would be a big fire. At around 4 P.M., Darrell Mincey ordered a Type II Forest Service incident management team, which would develop a game plan and manage the fire in the days to come. At 6 P.M., Clyde Chittenden made calls to the county to secure Glen Helen Park, located at the base of the mountains just a few miles east of the fire, as well as all the portable trailers the incident management team would need to run the incident.

Then, at 11 P.M., both Mincey and Chittenden traveled to the Sycamore Station less than a half mile off the fire line and briefed the incident management team on all the recent developments. They had hoped to box the fire in during the night, but as of yet they weren't having much luck.

The incident management team decided that Chittenden would continue to run the fire for the duration of the night so they could get set up. Already trailers had arrived to Glen Helen Park, the fire camp coming together. By this point, everyone had become aware of the Santa Ana wind predictions, so the race was on. "It was still burning extreme at five in the morning," said Mincey. "Normally at five in the morning you pretty much got a good handle on it—we didn't have a very good handle on it. And so, as soon as the Santa Ana winds kicked in, I knew we were going to have trouble."

As midnight rolled around, Mike Bell, who had served as Terry Acre's driver on Division Z after reporting the spot fire, headed over to the incident command post that had been established at the corner of Lytle Creek Road and Duncan Canyon, an area known by the locals as Nealeys Corner. He dropped Acre off, took one last look at the fire burning in the distance, and then headed home. The fight was now in the hands of the wildland agencies, and they seemed confident that they could catch up with it by the end of the following day. Bell knew it would be a fight, but he felt they could attain their goal. He had no idea that in a little more than forty-eight hours he would be engaged in the battle of a lifetime to save the city in which he worked and lived.

THE EXPANDED ATTACK

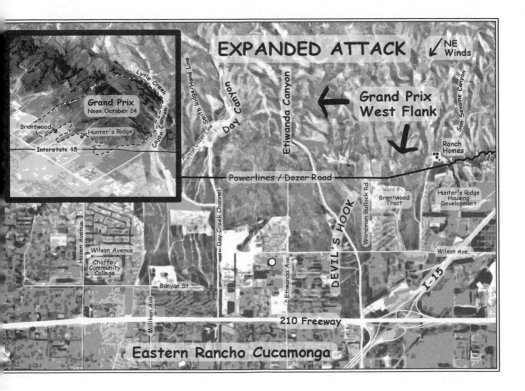

10

The Big Picture

In the early-morning hours of Wednesday, October 22, Mike Dietrich stood at the top of Foxborough Drive, gazing up at the Grand Prix burning in the foothills as if it were an equation that needed to be solved. He factored in the fuel conditions of the overly dense chaparral, the winds out of the southwest, the low relative humidity, the rugged terrain, the warm temperatures, and the threat to structures and property, which included the scattered homes at the base of the mountain just below the fire, the community of Lytle Creek to the northeast, and the high-voltage powerlines marching along the foothills, providing the L.A. basin with 25 percent of its power. More than six hundred firefighters were currently at work on the hillside, but from the looks of things, it would take a whole lot more in the days to come.

The conditions were just right to turn a small, two-acre fire into a massive blaze, but it could have been prevented. For years the foothills had screamed for fuel management. The fire service could have thinned out the brush or issued a series of controlled burns during low fire season. Back in the late seventies and early eighties, the various wildland agencies were still learning how to conduct prescribed burns, which had led to Michigan's Mack Lake Fire of 1980, a controlled burn that escaped and ended up claiming ten thousand acres and the lives of several people.

The fire service had almost lost prescribed burning as a tool, but Dietrich and several others had developed a formal plan and clear objectives, and had trained the appropriate people. They had turned the guesswork into a science, and over the past twenty years they'd issued hundreds of successful burns across the United States in an attempt to bring back a healthy, natural environment to grasslands and forests. But in recent years, as hundreds of thousands of families moved out into the urban/wildland interface, fuel treatment had become increasingly more difficult to conduct. Homeowners and environmental agencies threw up miles of red tape, and by the time the Forest Service received the green light to treat a designated hazard area, it was often too late.

"Firefighting is expensive when you are in the emergency mode," said Dietrich. "One, two, three thousand dollars an acre. You could treat fuels for five hundred dollars an acre, so there is a trade-off there. It seems like we are willing to pay for it after the fires occur in the wildland/urban interface."

Standing in the foothills above Rancho Cucamonga the morning after the Grand Prix started, however, the last thing on Dietrich's mind was fuel treatment. As the commander of the Forest Service incident management team now in control of the Grand Prix, it was his job to find a way to bring the blaze under control.

His primary concern was stopping the northeast front from heading over the mountains and down toward the community of Lytle Creek, so he had helicopters pounding the fire's edge with water and retardant. He got dozers up on the mountain scraping fuel breaks. He put hotshot crews in the locations where the dozers couldn't reach, connecting the fuel breaks by hand. And then, to protect the structures along the southern flank, he positioned dozens of engines along the powerline access road to beat back the flames with their hose lays.

It was a direct attack, the most favorable way to fight fire. If they could continue hitting the blaze directly along its edges, Dietrich's team estimated that the fire would grow to two thousand acres, take seven days to contain, eleven days to control, and the suppression costs would amount to $3.82 million. But if the fire behavior became too erratic, he would have to pull his troops back and resituate them along ridges in the distance to build contingency lines. In that case, the fire would most likely grow to fifteen thousand acres, take twelve days to contain, fifteen days to control, and cost $5.85 million. Judging by what Dietrich saw up on the mountainside, it would most likely be a combination of both, splitting the difference between the two costs.

No matter what happened, it would be a major incident, involving almost a hundred hand crews, dozens of water tenders and engines, and a fleet of aircraft. The incident commander role was a large one. Dietrich had to manage all the resources as they came in, make decisions on appropriate strategy and tactics, and communicate with the public, elected officials, and forest administrators. He had to watch that his troops didn't get trapped in canyons or veer too close to the powerlines, which had a tendency to arc and snap under severe heat and smoke. On the environmental side, he had to ensure that the campaign had a minimal impact on riparian areas, and that firefighters kept an eye out for the arroyo toad, the mountain yellow-legged frog, the California red-legged frog, spotted owls, kangaroo rats, California gnatcatchers, and willow flycatchers.

In addition to all of this, Dietrich also had to deal with the media, keeping them up to speed on the fire's developments. CDF public information officer Bill Peters had been assigned to the command team to help with this because it could be such a time-consuming chore. On one hand, the media could be very beneficial at a fire, broadcasting various road closures and evacuation plans to the public. On the other hand, they could quickly bog down the incident command team with requests for interviews and reports, which took the team's focus away from fighting the fire. Although such information was relatively easy and quick to provide, the hours began to add up as the fire attracted more attention. What really threw a monkey wrench into the operations of the incident command team, however, was when the media and public perceived something had gone wrong.

Such was the case with the Grand Prix relatively early on. The media and general public wanted to know why the initial attack on the blaze had failed. Because the front lines were largely off-limits to nonfirefighting personnel, few got to see firefighters digging line and risking their lives to bring the fire under control. In this case, the public could only look to the sky. Aircraft became the topic of conversation—why streams of water and retardant hadn't dropped from big buckets in the first few hours to bring the fire down.

"Aircraft is a tool, and it is only one of the firefighting tools that we have," said Bill Peters. "They are not the end-all, be-all. Otherwise, if they were all that people wished they were, then we would launch the aircraft and everyone else would stay home. But it doesn't work that way. Everyone is just so bought into the notion that if only we had helicopters we could have saved it. You can't win a war with aircraft; we learned that in Bosnia. Somebody has to be on the ground. Somebody has to turn the dirt and put the fire out."

To keep such matters from burdening the fight, the incident command team was broken down into five divisions: command, operations, planning, logistics, and finance/administration. While a designated public information officer in the command staff focused on media inquiries and any other issues that should arise, Dietrich worked with operations, which handled the frontline battle. So far on the morning of the twenty-second, they were making progress on the east and north flanks, but the western flank continued to be a problem. No structures were currently threatened on that side of the fire, but it had gotten established down in some hairy canyons and ravines, which had stopped the upward progression of hotshot crews the night before. Dietrich's team needed to find a way to pick up the left flank before it started pushing farther to the west, into San Sevaine Canyon and across the foothills above Rancho Cucamonga.

Jim Topoleski, a division supervisor working for operations, was on top of it. Unlike Dietrich, he didn't work for the U.S. Forest Service. Topoleski was a municipal firefighter from the city of Redlands and spent the majority of the year fighting structure fires. With the urban/wildland interface problem now affecting everyone, the Forest Service had opened their doors to local and state agencies, allowing concerned firefighters such as Topoleski to join the Forest Service incident management teams and not only fight the big ones, but also acquire wildfire tactics to help protect their jurisdictions back home. Over the past several years, every time Dietrich's team got ordered for a blaze, Topoleski had been in the heat of battle.

When he learned on the morning of the twenty-second that he would be taking over Division A, the western flank, Topoleski knew that some tricky firefighting lay ahead. The night before, when Darrell Mincey and Clyde Chittenden briefed their team at the Sycamore Station, Mincey had said, "We've got to do something here on this west flank, because when the winds shift, you're going to end up with a big problem."

Topoleski soon understood Mincey's concerns. After parking his vehicle at the top of Foxborough, he hiked the hose lay Jim Dague had helped put in the previous afternoon. It was well supported; dozens of firefighters had spread out along the lower portion of the hill, making sure the fire didn't jump the line as it had done the previous day. But once he got higher up, reaching the location where the Redding and Lassen hotshots had been forced to bed down the night before, he saw the problem. The fire had gotten established down in a ravine. With no aircraft support and limited resources, it had been impossible to safely send crews down there under the cover of darkness.

It still seemed risky in the light of day, but with the fire continuing to push up the mountain north of the drainage, they needed to get past this obstacle. Knowing every minute counted, Topoleski immediately got some dozers up on the ridge to blaze a road. Hopefully by the following morning the road would be wide enough to get some engines up into the area. With that going, he then radioed the pilot of the surveillance plane circling high overhead, pointing out his current location by holding a small mirror in the sun. Once the pilot spotted him, Topoleski inquired about the fire behavior in the general vicinity. The surveillance plane pilot not only had a perfect view of the fire as a whole, but being in a fixed-wing aircraft, he could also feel any updrafts or mixing air currents, both of which led to increased fire behavior. He said he saw or felt nothing out of the ordinary, so Topoleski ordered helicopter drops into the drainage. Before he sent hand crews down in there, he wanted the ravine to be like mud.

With some of the heat having been removed from the drainage, Topoleski sent in the hand crews. They worked down to the bottom, where they cut out the hotspots, and then until well in the afternoon they cut line up the north side of the drainage. But as evening approached, Topoleski had to pull them out. Aircraft didn't fly at night, and it was just too risky having men down in there without support. Right now the fire smoldered in the ravine, but it was only a matter of time before the embers evaporated the water and burned through the retardant, and the entire drainage could unexpectedly flare back up in a matter of seconds.

When the night crew took over his division, which extended from the base of the mountain all the way up to the top of the drainage, Topoleski had cut a good amount of line, but he still didn't feel it would hold up against the northeast winds. The newly formed Division B, which picked up at the top of the drainage and carried up the mountain, was even worse off. Throughout the afternoon, it had gotten hotter and hotter up there. Over the radio, Topoleski could hear Air Attack coordinating helicopter drops just north of the drainage, but the fire refused to lie down. They needed to connect a solid fuel break from the bottom of the mountain in Division A, through the difficult ravine, and then to the top of the mountain in Division B. If they couldn't get that continuous line put in, the arrival of the Santa Ana winds would push the fire between any gaps in their line and then shove it farther to the west. Then they would have serious problems.

11

Serious Problems

"We might have a serious problem on our hands," pretty much summed up Mike Dietrich's thoughts on the evening of Wednesday, October 22. His incident management team had just received a weather report that stated in bold letters: MODERATE TO STRONG NORTH-EAST TO EAST WINDS EXPECTED TO DEVELOP THURSDAY AND LAST WELL INTO THE WEEKEND.

Familiar with both the Texas and Myers fires, Dietrich knew what the Santa Ana winds could do with a blaze. If they kicked up in the next couple of days, they could push the Grand Prix west across the foothills, and then send a wall of fire tearing down into the flats toward the homes in northern Rancho Cucamonga. As a matter of fact, the Grand Prix could rip right through Rancho and head into Upland, San Antonio Heights, and then clear into L.A. County. He'd been formulating a contingency plan to deal with such a scenario since morning, and now it was time get the ball rolling.

He would keep resources battling the blaze up on the mountain, but he would also send several dozers down into the foothills to construct an east-west fuel break just north of the long row of houses above Rancho Cucamonga. "That was just in case we weren't able to pick up the fire up above," said Dietrich. "So we had essentially two strategies going, two tactics that we were implementing. One was fighting the fire, trying to pick it up and contain it, and then at the same time we were looking at the contingency plan, which was to take the fire around the foothills and possibly into L.A. We established trigger points. If the fire crossed the main ridge system of Day Canyon, then we would be full blown into the implementation of the contingency plan. You always have your first plan, but then you also have to say, 'What am I going to do if it doesn't work, what are my trigger points, and what resources will I need if it should cross those trigger points?'"

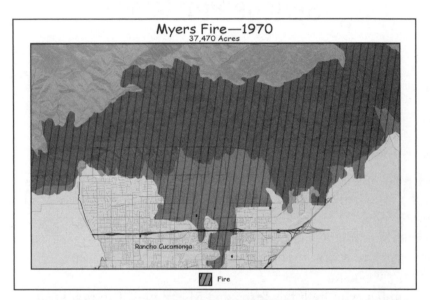

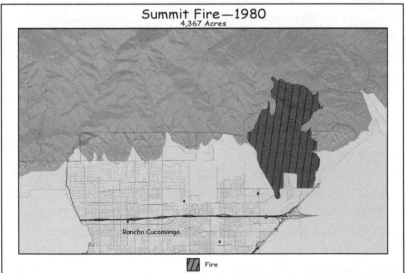

To make sure that the contingency plan went smoothly if implemented, Dietrich brought the city of Rancho Cucamonga into unified command. From this point out, the city's fire chief, Dennis Michael, would be a part of the process, expressing his concerns and working in conjunction with the wildland agencies to save his city.

Michael was glad to be on the team. He got together with the city manager and some other key city officials. They had a unique opportunity in that they knew the fire was coming their way, so they used the

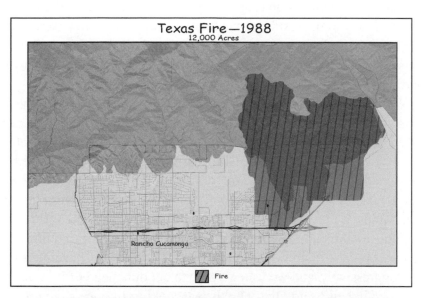

Texas Fire—1988
12,000 Acres

Rancho Cucamonga

Fire

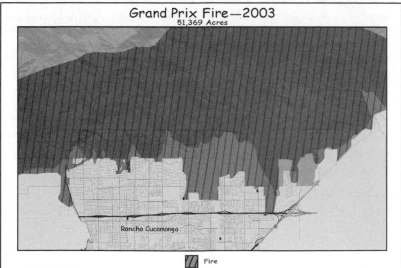

Grand Prix Fire—2003
51,369 Acres

Rancho Cucamonga

Fire

two-day jump to notify residents along the urban/wildland interface. Once Channel 3 started broadcasting warnings, Michael prepared for the influx of municipal engines that would help defend his city. Forest Service and CDF crews were all based out in Glen Helen Park to the east, but Michael wanted his troops to be stationed closer to the battle. During the course of Wednesday night, he turned the parking lot of Los Osos High School, located at the north end of Milliken near the urban/wildland interface, into a staging area. Dozens of businesses and hundreds of residents soon dropped by with coffee, food, and emotional support. Many of the residents had tears in their eyes—they were counting on the firefighters to save their homes and all the history they had wrapped up in them. They thanked the men and women who would shortly risk their lives in an attempt to save the community.

While Michael put the finishing touches on his staging area the following morning, across town Dietrich stepped into a portable trailer parked in the middle of Glen Helen Park for one of the many meetings he had each day. Overnight, the Grand Prix had grown to thirty-five hundred acres, pushing upslope to the northeast, and then downhill toward Lytle Creek, prompting the evacuation of four hundred homes in that area. Almost a thousand personnel from hand crews and engines were on scene, establishing anchor points near threatened communities, trying to keep the fire up on the mountain. "The fire was burning a little more aggressively, and we weren't able to get out ahead of it as quickly as we had hoped," said Dietrich. "It was looking like we were going to have to implement plan B. That's when we began to think about the fire moving across Rancho Cucamonga."

When Michael heard the news, he busied himself with the logistics of what they needed to do and when. It was all that he could do to stifle his concern. Two days prior, looking down on the small fire in the foothills from the commercial airplane, he never would have guessed that the Grand Prix would grow into such a beast. He'd made a wish not eight months before to finish this last year without a major incident that might make him feel as though he'd failed his city at the end of his career.

Michael prayed for all the firefighters out on the line, and he prayed that everyone would have the courage to stop the fire from destroying his city.

12

Backing Away

When Division A supervisor Jim Topoleski came out to the fire line on the morning of Thursday, October 23, he had high hopes for the western flank. His mission was to get one continual fuel break cut from the bottom of the mountain up to the top before the northeast winds arrived.

The bottom half of the fuel break was coming along fine. Dozer operators had finished carving a road up the first several ridges during the night, which would allow Topoleski to position engine crews on the bottom portion of the mountain who could beat back the flames when the winds flipped directions. But having engine crews halt the bottom edge of the fire wouldn't do much good if the Grand Prix crossed to the west directly above them. If Topoleski could only get a similar line punched all the way to the top, they would have a much better chance at stopping the fire from heading west toward Rancho Cucamonga. It would be a fight, no doubt about it. While meeting with the Division B supervisor at the morning briefing, Topoleski had been told to expect much stronger winds than the initial predictions, up to sixty or seventy miles per hour.

At the top of Foxborough Drive, Topoleski slipped his truck into four-wheel drive and drove up the dirt trail the dozers had just completed. He wanted to test it out, see if it was something brush engines could ascend. He made it all the way up the ridge to the nasty drainage without a hitch, but that's when he saw the problem with his game plan.

Above the drainage, the fire had somehow backed over the ridge they were trying to protect and worked down into the massive San Sevaine Canyon just to the west. It was ugly country down in there, full of thick chaparral. The fire had gotten well established, and with the winds expected to surface the following afternoon, Topoleski knew they would never get it cut out in time. Just to be certain, he contacted the Air Attack pilot and told him to fly over the canyon and get a bird's-eye view. A few moments later, the pilot said, "There is no way we will get that done today; we need to think of something different."

With his original game plan blown out of the water, there wasn't much else they could do to box the fire in. The entire west flank fuel break had been lost.

Topoleski came down the mountain and met up with the troops assigned to help him, which included the Fulton and Big Bear hotshots and a CDF strike team of engines. Big Bear superintendent Jimmy Avila and Fulton superintendent Ron Bollier were ready to have their crews cut line straight up the mountain. The CDF strike team had already picked out the spot on the west flank fuel break where they would burrow in and defend against the advancing flame. Topoleski liked to see such enthusiasm, but he couldn't risk sending them in.

"The plan of going direct is no longer good," he told them. "We aren't going to be able to reestablish our line before the Santa Ana winds surface. I'm sorry, but we have to back off."

It was a great disappointment for the engine crew. They headed up the mountain a few minutes later, but instead of bunkering in as they had planned, they broke down the hose lay that had been two days in the making, leaving the fuel break abandoned. The hotshot crews were more optimistic. Spending the majority of their days working solo out in the forest, they had gotten used to fires jumping their line. Although they had spent two days cutting line up the ridge, now that a direct attack was no longer possible, options for an indirect attack began to open up.

Bollier and Avila, the two hotshot superintendents, trained their eyes on the mountainside, as did Topoleski. Starting on San Sevaine Canyon, they slowly panned to the west, across Henderson Canyon, East Etiwanda Canyon, the massive Day Canyon, and then Smith Canyon just north of Rancho Cucamonga. Topoleski's eyes stopped on the west side of Smith Canyon, on Smith Ridge. It stretched from south to north about a mile west from their current location, which would give them some time to put in "indirect line with dozers, support that with aircraft, and then try to fire the whole thing off before the Grand Prix got there."

Jumping ahead of the fire and prepping Smith Ridge seemed doable, but Topoleski had fought wildfire long enough to realize that no ridge was as easy as it appeared from a distance. First off, it was steep. He didn't think dozers would be able to ascend the nearly vertical incline, but then he saw a jagged line running from the base of the mountain up to the top of Smith Ridge. It looked like a dozer line from a previous fire, and Avila confirmed that it was. On a fire in the distant past, dozers had attempted to cut line up Smith Ridge, but the incline had been too steep, so they had headed around the mountain and then come down the ridge instead. Mimicking their actions would have been great, but Topoleski didn't think they could manage it. The most accessible route to the top of Smith Ridge was on the San Sevaine Truck Trail, a dirt road that ran from east to west across the top of the mountain. The eastern portion of the truck trail was currently engulfed in flame, so that was out of the question. They could head up into Cucamonga Canyon far to the west, just above the city of San Antonio Heights, and then get on the western portion of the San Sevaine Truck Trail and head east toward Smith Ridge. Topoleski didn't know if the dirt road was traversable on that end, but it was worth a try.

Since Avila was stationed in the area and knew the canyons better than anyone, Topoleski sent him and the rest of the Big Bear crew up into the mountains to scout out the western portion of the truck trail, to see if it was something dozers could maneuver across to reach the ridge.

As Big Bear headed off, Topoleski turned to Fulton superintendent Ron Bollier and his crew. Topoleski would have loved to catch the fire on Smith Ridge, but he had to prepare everyone for the worst-case scenario.

"It looks like we are going to be out here tomorrow morning, chasing this thing as it runs through the flats," Topoleski told Fulton. "So let's get out ahead of this thing, size up what we need to do for structure protection. Let's see what we actually have out here so we're not going to be running around completely blind."

Bollier agreed, and both Topoleski and the Fulton Hotshots drove around the front country in eastern Rancho Cucamonga. Topoleski took pictures of the houses at risk, jotting down their exact locations using

GPS. Bollier studied the terrain, making predictions as to how the fire would come down and when. Once they had a good feel for the eastern reaches of Rancho Cucamonga, which were largely uninhabited, they continued west toward the long row of homes in the western portion of the city. They started at Haven Avenue, the first north-south artery leading up to the urban/wildland interface on the west side of town. As they scratched at-risk addresses in their notebooks, their hearts grew heavier by the moment. Every home in the area, whether it was a mini-mansion or a part of a housing tract, was heavily individualized. They saw toys scattered across lawns and beautiful gardens that had taken decades to grow. They saw Halloween pumpkins sitting on porches and imagined the children who had carved them returning home to a pile of ash. In the next couple of days, people's lives would be forever changed. An entire community could get wiped off the map.

Big Bear superintendent Jimmy Avila returned about five hours after he'd gone scouting. He had some bad news. He'd tried hiking the western portion of the truck trail, but it was completely washed out. And where it wasn't washed out, massive boulders blocked the way. So the plan of getting dozers up to the top of Smith Ridge quickly fell apart, another devastating blow. When the Santa Ana winds arrived, there would be no defense to keep the blaze from pushing west across all the ridges and then tearing down into the flats.

Topoleski and Fulton continued to travel the front country, developing a strategy to combat the storm when it arrived, but as the afternoon progressed, the supervisor of the eastern flank began calling for reinforcements. With the winds still blowing out of the southwest, the eastern flank had overrun the containment lines and pushed down toward the community of Lytle Creek. Around 3 P.M., the Fulton and Big Bear hotshots prepared to head around to the other side of the mountain to help out. Before Rob Bollier left the foothills above Rancho Cucamonga, however, he took one last look at the front country. Dozer operators worked to get line cut along the powerlines at the base of the mountains, but the contingency plan would take some time to complete due to rough terrain. There was no question in Bollier's mind—in less than twenty-four hours the area would be crawling with firefighters engaged in the fight of their life.

13

Structure Protection

While Topoleski and the Fulton Hotshots scouted the foothills above Rancho, Mike Rohde, a battalion chief from Orange County Fire, ran into Incident Commander Mike Dietrich in Glen Helen Park. The two stopped to talk, and before the conversation was over, Dietrich asked Rohde if he would assume the role of branch director on the Grand Prix.

Currently, the operations section of the incident management team was combating the fire up on the mountain as well as guarding the endangered homes in Lytle Creek. This had been the best way to handle the fire up to this point, simply because both aspects fell under one command structure. If the northeast winds surfaced the following afternoon, however, the communities of Rancho Cucamonga, San Antonio Heights, Upland, and Claremont would also be at risk. There would be no way that operations could adequately fight the fire and protect the communities at the same time. At that point, Dietrich's incident command team would continue to combat the Grand Prix as it came off the mountains into the flats, and the branch director would break away and start a separate command structure to protect the forty thousand threatened homes.

It was a large responsibility, but Rohde felt up to the task. His first assignment was to take a look at all the communities at risk, prioritize the threatened structures in each community, develop a plan to protect those structures, and then, if he felt inspired to, present his plan to the various local fire departments. Those were the traditional steps a branch director would take, but with the winds expected to surface in just twenty-four hours, Rohde opted to throw them right out the window. Having started in these foothills with CDF thirty years prior, he understood that the local firefighters knew how to defend their turf better than anyone. It didn't make sense to tell them how to fight fire in their own jurisdiction. If the Grand Prix came down into the foothills with half the ferocity everyone expected, then it would be impossible for him to be everywhere at once, and something would slip through his fingers. To keep that from happening, he decided that each of the fire departments of the communities at risk would not only get to draw up their own structure protection plans, which would be added into his overall plan, but they would also get to elect a deputy branch director who would be by his side, helping him make the hard decisions as the fire pushed through their particular community.

When Rancho Cucamonga batallion chief Ron Mayfield heard this news on the morning of the twenty-third, he was overjoyed. As of right now, city planners expected Rancho to lose between sixty and a hundred homes. Such might have been the case if they'd placed Rancho in the hands of strike team leaders from out of the area, but now that Rohde had allowed the Rancho Cucamonga Fire Department to come up with its own plan, Mayfield felt confident that that number could be significantly reduced. Everyone in his department had trained for such a fire for years. They knew the exact locations of all the threatened homes, water tanks, and powerlines, and they knew how to defend them. This knowledge came from fighting and learning from the Texas, Myers, and Summit fires in the past. Sure, there would be firefighters from around the state who weren't familiar with how fire acted in the front country, but in his plan Mayfield would make sure that each of the strike teams would be led and organized by one of his men.

When the Santa Ana winds kicked up the following afternoon, the fire would come down into the eastern portion of the city, just as the other fires had before. The first homes at risk would be on Wardman Bullock Road, a north-south street leading up to the base of the mountains along the eastern corner of their jurisdiction. At the very top of that street sat six ranch houses, nestled into the brush of the foothills. Most of them had been built before the building codes were improved, so they would be hard to protect. Farther south on Wardman Bullock Road sat the Brentwood housing tract, a nearly perfect square of almost a hundred homes sitting smack-dab in the middle of the grasslands. All those homes were of newer construction, but they would still need looking after. These two groups of homes, the little one up near the foothills and the bigger one down below, would get hit hard in the first hour, so Mayfield assigned the division to Jim Dague, one of his best wildland firefighters. To eliminate any confusion as to the area this division encompassed, Mayfield named it the Brentwood structure group after the main housing tract. That way, when incoming resources arrived to Los Osos High School in the west, all they had to do was look at a map to know where to go. Once they got there, Dague would show them exactly where to position their engines and hoses.

Once the fire had passed Wardman Bullock Road, most wildland firefighters would expect the blaze to keep pushing west along the base of the foothills, but that was not what the fire would do, and Mayfield knew it. There was a narrow brush field that separated Wardman Bullock in the east from Etiwanda Avenue in the west, and that brush field went all the way down to the 210 freeway. Rancho Cucamonga firemen had named it the Devil's Hook. After the Grand Prix had crossed Wardman Bullock, it would turn sharply to the south and make a run down to the freeway. There were homes in the area that needed protecting, so to cover the area, he made two divisions. Mike Bell would protect the area east of Etiwanda and south of Wilson, and Dave Berry would cover the area north of Wilson.

To ensure that the whole process went over without a hitch, Mayfield would become the deputy branch director for Rancho Cucamonga and ride along with Rohde as the fire moved through Rancho. Together they would make all the hard decisions, such as when to pull forces out of an area. Mayfield hoped it wouldn't come to that, but firefighter safety was his number one concern. And there was much to be concerned about. In less than twenty-four hours, hundreds of firefighters would be spread out along the urban/wildland interface. The troops from the wildland side would be out in the brush performing perimeter control. Their job was to keep the fire from reaching the houses, and they would be using wildland tactics in an attempt to do that, which meant constructing fuel breaks with dozers and conducting burn operations. Then, backed right up against the houses, there would be the municipal firefighters, ready to defend the city if the fire got past perimeter control. They were not accustomed to seeing a hundred-foot wall of flame tearing toward them, and they were especially not accustomed to firefighters starting fires of their own. There would be some varying opinions as to what methods to employ and when between municipal and wildland firefighters, Mayfield knew, but it was his job to ensure that everyone worked together. Communication was the key to avoiding disaster.

With that in mind, Mayfield sat down with Rohde and worked out the details for setting the plan in motion. They didn't want the strike teams sitting out there all night waiting for the fire to arrive, but they also didn't want to get them in there too late. Because Rohde was responsible for overall structure protection, it was decided that he would notify Mayfield the moment the winds shifted so he could get Rancho's troops in place.

14

Plan B

By the early afternoon of Thursday, October 23, Mike Dietrich had put plan B into full effect. Weather reports still predicted that strong Santa Ana winds would most likely arrive the following afternoon. He had dozers and hand crews constructing fuel breaks along the foothills, but they still needed to prepare the residents of Rancho Cucamonga for a potential wall of flame heading their way.

In the past, a considerable amount of chaos would most likely have ensued. The incident command team would have started contacting the local sheriff's department for evacuation plans, Cal Trans for road closures and escape routes, and a number of other agencies that were needed to evacuate a large group of people from the area. Each agency would have begun scrambling to develop a plan, not sure exactly what was being asked of them, not sure how their little piece fit into the big picture.

Fortunately, all of the major players had come together and worked out a plan months ahead of time. This was practically unheard of prior to an incident, but they'd had reason to break the norm. In November 2002, it dawned on the emergency agencies that with twenty million dead trees up on the mountaintop, they all faced a very serious problem. "CDF had responsibilities on the mountaintop, the Forest Service had responsibilities up there, and the County Fire Department had responsibilities up there," said CDF public information officer Bill Peters.

"Everyone was in their corner, trying to figure out how to deal with the responsibility with all these bugs killing all these trees. It was like, 'Okay, what is wrong with this picture?' So instead of three separate entities, we decided to build a bigger, more functional windmill. The chief officers got together and they conceptualized this group, the Mountain Area Safety Task Force, or MAST."

Right out of the gate, the talks didn't go very well, especially on a bureaucratic level. It was very clear in the beginning that to preplan for a mountaintop disaster, each agency would have to make compromises. In the different regional offices, they were quite content being agency-specific, saying, "That is not my job, that is county's job, that is some-one else's job." The firefighters who had all sat down at the table, however, felt they were on to something, and in order to progress they all put their personal reputations on the line. "There were actually a lot of skeptics with our organization," said Dietrich. "People are just inher-ently reluctant to embrace something that isn't their idea or hasn't been done before. We had to push, keep pushing, and people from the various agencies became friends from sitting through agonizing meetings. They put their hands around this animal, trying to figure out which part of the elephant they were touching."

The National Park Service and the California Department of Forestry working together to save homes.

Once everyone was on the same page, determined that the eighty thousand people on the mountaintop wouldn't lose their lives because of jurisdictional boundaries and red tape, they got to the meat and potatoes of the process. They set priorities in slow motion of how they were going to deal with the incident. They brought in people and agencies that had jurisdiction. They also brought in the sheriff's department, Cal Trans, the California Highway Patrol (CHP), the water districts, and the Red Cross. They sat down and developed an incident action plan for how they would deal with the priorities. The sheriff's department developed evacuation plans. Cal Trans identified what equipment they would need. CHP mobilized what frequency they would use to establish coordination with the sheriff's department. It came together quicker than anyone could have imagined, because they all knew which agency had which role.

With everything in place, they got a trial run when the Bridge Fire broke out three miles south of Lake Arrowhead on September 5, 2003. The initial attack incident commander reported the fire at five acres when he arrived, but five hours later, fueled by steep terrain and erratic winds, the blaze had consumed fifteen hundred acres. Twenty-four hand crews and sixty-five engines fought the fire on the ground. In the air, twenty firefighting aircraft swooped over the flames, dropping retardant and water. The various agencies involved hit the fire with everything they had, but by nine at night only 2 percent of the blaze had been contained. Given the fire's course, fifteen hundred homes in the mountains could have been destroyed in just a few hours.

There was no time to ponder how to evacuate the threatened communities, and fortunately they didn't have to. The MAST group stepped up to the plate, and in a few hours the sheriff's department evacuated more than a thousand people and got them resituated at Rim of the World High School. With the facility inadequate to hold that many people, the Red Cross quickly found an alternate location. Cal Trans got to work on road closures and evacuation routes. And the Forest Service incident command team in charge of the blaze planned a community meeting for the following day to keep residents informed. More than fifteen hundred people attended.

It had been a success because each agency had cast aside jurisdictional boundaries. They had forgotten the color of their uniforms and realized they all shared the same goal—to save people. If they had not had those plans laid down in dry ink, it would have been much more difficult to marshal resources, work collectively to get the evacuations done in a timely manner, and also just plain fight the fire. "We actually did the job we are supposed to do," said Peters. "It sounds kind of corny, but half the time each agency is doing their own thing because they are all on the taxpayer dollars, and all the elected officials are looking at them. The officials don't care what the other agencies do; they want to know that their money is being well spent. It was one of those things where any one of us could get steamrolled, and we all had to have a stake in it. We all had to be involved. And so we got rid of all the boundaries. I won't tell you that it was easy, and I'll tell you that periodically we still stub some toes. Every once in a while it is like walking around in the street with bare feet in the summertime. But no matter how thick the tensions grew, there was somebody around that was sober and said, 'You know, guys, remember what we are fighting for.'"

Mike Dietrich, who'd been instrumental in getting MAST off the ground, saw no reason why he couldn't implement all their preplanning efforts on the Grand Prix. Although the original plan was developed for the mountaintop communities, they could simply transfer the working model down to the foothills. So he threw the MAST plan into full-blown activation—fire response, staging, evacuations, everything.

In a matter of hours, all the players had begun working on their piece of the pie, preparing for a public meeting just a few hours later. To advertise the meeting, they had spots on radio and television. They even managed to get flyers to each child before they headed home after school.

Then on the evening of the twenty-third, just a few hours after putting MAST into effect, they held a community meeting in the gym of Rancho Cucamonga High School, and more than six hundred residents attended. Instead of the sheriff's department telling everyone to simply get out of their house and down the road, they gave detailed evacuation plans for the various parts of the community. It was the first time Peters had ever heard of a law enforcement agency presenting a traffic flow plan for evacuations. Their plan was to get the residents out as fast and safe as they could, while at the same time get the fire service into the area as quickly and safely as they could. To notify the public it was time to leave, they said they would head up and down the street with bullhorns and try to go door to door when possible.

When the meetings came to a close on the night of the twenty-third, both the community and the command team felt confident that they could get residents out of the area and the fire crews in to fight the advancing blaze. Weather forecasts predicted the winds to hit the following afternoon, and that would give them at least twelve hours to finish any last-minute preparations. When the fire came into the city limits, they would divert the flames around the northern end of town.

During the meeting, Rancho Cucamonga's Chief Mayfield went over his structure protection plan for the city again and again just to make sure he hadn't missed anything. He had three structure groups that would position themselves in the eastern part of their city, right there along the foothills. To alleviate any confusion as to which area those groups were to defend, he had assigned Jim Dague, Mike Bell, and Dave Berry, three of his most qualified men, to run those divisions. Because it made no sense to keep the strike teams out there all night, he had staged the majority of them at Los Osos High School. It was crucial that the moment the winds shifted that he wake them up and get them out there, but the only way he could do that was for someone to give him the heads-up. To ensure no mishaps occurred, he approached Mike Rohde after the meeting. "He told me personally, 'I will make sure you are notified,'" said Mayfield.

Feeling confident, Mayfield went back to Los Osos to see how his guys were holding up. Around 11 P.M., it looked like the fire was coming off the hill. Mayfield tried calling division to see what was going on up on the mountain, and they said they were busy, that they would get back to him. They didn't get back to him by 1 A.M., so he returned to Station 5 and lay down in his bunk with all his gear on. Ten minutes later he was sound asleep, worn out from three days of nonstop firefighting.

15

The First Assault

A few minutes after getting rousted from sleep at four o'clock on Friday morning, strike team leader Chris Cox led his five engines from Glen Helen Park into eastern Rancho Cucamonga. His orders were to reach the Brentwood housing development and protect homes, but getting there proved difficult. The Grand Prix had come down into the flats, inciting pandemonium.

Through all the smoke and ash and flame, Cox could see two of the homes at the top of Wardman Bullock Road engulfed in flame. If that wasn't bad enough, off to his left he could see a helicopter out in the grass field that would soon be surrounded by fire. He didn't know when it had touched down or why, but with flames threatening the helicopter, it looked like it had been shot down. As a matter of fact, the entire eastern portion of town looked like a war zone. Cox knew all the Rancho fire chiefs personally. They'd been preparing for this fire for more than a decade, yet there wasn't a single Rancho unit in sight. Although the northeast winds had surfaced a good ten hours ahead of schedule, the plan had been so airtight that they should have been able to deal with this new development. The sheriff's department was scrambling to maintain order, but the evacuation plan had completely fallen apart. Residents fled any way they could, clogging up the streets and making it hard for Cox to get his engines into the area.

"The evacuations were terribly done," said Cox. "The sheriff's department did everything it could do, but we were trying to move engines in at the same time people were trying to leave. . . . We kept telling people, especially the people who lived on streets a block away from the wildland areas, 'Don't leave, just stay in your house! If we need you out, we will come and bang on your doors.' . . . There were several people just running around, trying to throw stuff in their cars, and I told them to just go back inside. We call that sheltering in place. That seemed to work with a lot of people, but others wanted to see what was going on. It was five in the morning, so the first thing they did was open their garage doors and walk outside. That was my biggest fear, someone's garage catching on fire from the inside out. Garages are all open wood on the inside, and there are always piles of flammable stuff packed inside. And the winds were just howling, blowing embers into the garages. I don't know what the wind speeds were, but they were well over thirty miles per hour, perhaps even forty or fifty."

Someone had dropped the ball big-time, and Cox had a strong feeling it wasn't the Rancho Cucamonga Fire Department. If they had been notified of what was transpiring in the eastern portion of their city, they would have been out there in a heartbeat.

For whatever reason, the Grand Prix had gotten the jump on them. With flames tearing through brush out in the interface, Cox knew that their goal of diverting the fire around the northern end of the city had become impossible. His mind reeled: *It is going to go into Upland, it is going to go into Claremont, it is going to go into Mt. Baldy.* There just weren't enough resources to stop it. Right then, he knew that the ball game was on. The only thing that might stop the Grand Prix was the Williams Fire, which had burned a large portion of the chaparral in the foothills above Claremont the previous year. But there was a lot of land between eastern Rancho Cucamonga and Claremont. Without a doubt, Cox knew it was going to be one hell of a battle.

16

Behind the Power Curve

At four o'clock in the morning on Friday, October 24, Chief Ron Mayfield awoke to the scream of the station bell. Even before opening his eyes, he focused his attention on the radio crackling in the background. He expected to hear the voice of Branch Director Mike Rohde telling him that the winds had shifted and the Grand Prix was making its way down into the eastern portion of the city, but instead he heard a report of a structure fire in the western portion of town, totally unrelated to the Grand Prix.

Already dressed in his gear, Mayfield jumped into the truck with the rest of the assignment and they raced Code 3 through the darkness. Ten minutes later, after reaching the location of the supposed fire, they turned around. It had been a false alarm. While driving down Haven Avenue on the way back to the station, Mayfield looked to the east. From his current location, he could see the bright glow of the fire up on the mountain, but he could also see a bright glow coming from down in the foothills. *Holy crap*, he thought. *This thing is out in Etiwanda!*

He kept his cool because he knew that was impossible. Everyone had been very clear on the plan. The moment the winds shifted, the branch director would notify him. Mayfield would have plenty of time to organize his men and get the three structure groups he'd designed to protect that portion of the city into place. Just to be certain, he snatched up his radio and called dispatch, asking them the current location of the fire.

"We are getting ready to reinforce the back of Etiwanda," said the operator.

Mayfield felt a sinking sensation in his stomach, but the news only got worse. Less than a minute after he hung up with dispatch, Frank Sexton, a longtime friend from the Chino Valley Fire Department who had been out on the front line all night, called him on his cell phone.

"You better get out here," Sexton said. "This thing has already gone around Wardman Bullock Road and into Etiwanda."

"You're kidding me!"

"I know what your guys' plan was, and it didn't happen. You never got notified."

After grabbing some extra gear at the station, Mayfield blazed east along Banyan Street, and then north up Etiwanda Avenue, thinking the entire time, *I've got to get Berry out there, I've got to get Bell out there, I've got to get Dague out there. I've got to get going. We are behind the power curve.* Those individuals had been notified as planned and were making their way in at that very moment.

Halfway up Etiwanda Avenue, Mayfield could see just how far behind they were. A line of fire stretched all the way from the top of the front range of mountains down to the flats. It was the longest line of fire he had ever seen, and he had seen some long fire lines. But what drew his eyes more than the line of fire was the damage being inflicted upon his city. Just to the east of his current location, two of the six ranch houses nestled into the foothills at the top of Wardman Bullock Road were already engulfed in flame. Currently there were no resources up there, leading him to believe that nobody had defended those homes when the fire came through.

"CDF was in there," said Batallion Chief Mike Rohde later. "[Rancho] thought the only assets that were going to be in there were the structure protection groups, and in fact perimeter control people had put all their engines in there. So we were still cooperating between those two organizations, and I think [Rancho] felt if the pavement puffers didn't get in there, nobody got in there. That was not the case. There were plenty of wildland engines up in there, which were much more mobile and fitting for the terrain. . . . It was just that the fire behavior was so extreme when it came down in there, there was nothing that they could do to protect them."

Mayfield felt differently. They had been defending those homes for decades, and they knew just how to do it. And they would have proved that very thing if he had been notified as everyone had agreed upon. But they hadn't, and now homes had been lost. "That really ticked me off," said Mayfield. "We wouldn't have left them."

But the problem was bigger than the two burning homes; they had lost the initiative on the entire east side of town. Farther south on Wardman Bullock Road, the fire had already moved past the Brentwood housing tract. Mayfield didn't know if any resources were in there. The homes had been built to withstand fire, not a firestorm. In the plan they had all been covered, but that had become a moot point.

Mayfield contacted Jim Dague, who was supposed to be in charge of the Brentwood structure protection group. He told him to ignore the Brentwood housing tract and go down below and catch the fire as it made the Devil's Hook toward the 210 freeway. After he got off the radio with Dague, Mayfield contacted dispatch and had them put out an all-page for every engine in the city. He told them to empty all of Rancho's five stations. Then he contacted Ontario Fire and asked them to send two of their closest strike teams, totaling ten engines, which would go over to Dague.

With resources on the way, Mayfield hit the gas. At the top of Etiwanda Avenue, he ran into a strike team from L.A. County waiting for the blaze to come into the area from the east, but Mayfield knew it would be some time before that happened. As he had mentioned in his plan, the fire would veer to the south right there at Devil's Hook and make a run for the 210 freeway in the sliver of brush between Wardman Bullock and Etiwanda. There were homes in there that needed protecting, as well as the junior high school.

"I'm Rancho structure branch, and I need you down by the junior high," he said to the strike team leader, pointing toward the 210 freeway south of the Brentwood housing tract. "It is going to get hit hard, and so are a number of houses down there. I don't need you up here, I need you down there!"

"Wait a second," said the strike team leader. "I'm working with Division B."

"Listen, I know what I'm doing," Mayfield reasoned. "I've run this fire before. I'm going to go up and talk to Division B right now. Trust me, we have a plan. I'm taking over this area."

As Mayfield headed farther up the mountain in search of the Division B supervisor, Jim Dague chased the fire toward the 210 freeway. He couldn't believe what was happening. Currently Division B was trying to run both perimeter control and structure protection. They needed to get Mayfield's plan activated, and they needed to do it fast. "It was a madhouse," said Dague. "I was with the Brentwood structure group, but when I got out there, it had pretty much blown past the area in Brentwood. . . . We should have learned our lesson because the same thing happened in the Texas Fire. We left it up to somebody else to tell us, 'Here it comes,' so we could dump all of our resources. We should have learned from that to have one of our own people out there watching the fire."

Dague hooked up with the L.A. County strike team and they formulated a plan to protect the structures down near the freeway. By this time, Mayfield had made it to the Division B supervisor staked out up in the foothills north of Etiwanda Avenue.

"What the hell is going on?" Mayfield asked. "Why weren't we notified?"

"I thought you were," said the division sup.

"I'm Rancho Cucamonga structure protection branch, and we've got a plan all set up. Where is Mike Rohde, the branch director?"

The division supervisor didn't have the answers, and Mayfield pushed his wonder away; he had bigger things to deal with. Other than the Brentwood structure group falling apart, it looked like he could stick to the original plan. In order to do that, he contacted Mike Bell to take charge of his structure group.

Bell had arrived on scene a few minutes prior. After the community meeting the night before, he had gone up to Lytle Creek to help a friend protect his home. Just before he'd fallen asleep at two-thirty in the morning, there had been a slight breeze, nothing to be overly concerned about. If northeast winds began to surface, he would get a call so he could head out and set up. That call came at five-thirty, but it wasn't an early notice. It was one of his guys saying, "It is making its way into Rancho, get out here!"

As Bell stepped out of his friend's house in Lytle Creek, the winds had increased and the fire behavior had worsened. The units that had been protecting the house had pulled out—it had gotten that dicey that quick. The night before, Bell had given his friend a quick lesson in fire tactics, and now he was on his own. Bell needed to get back to Rancho to save his city.

As he raced into the eastern portion of Rancho Cucamonga, he was shocked to discover that the fire had been pushed down off the hill. All the weather info had claimed that the northeast winds wouldn't surface until Friday afternoon. At the neighborhood meeting the night before, Bell had told residents to start making preparations to evacuate, assuring them that if it came down to that, they would have plenty of notification. Now those promises were out the window. He watched the same residents who'd attended the meeting frantically fleeing their neighborhoods in the smoky darkness, and he could tell that homes in the foothills had already been lost. As horrible as he felt, there was no time for remorse—that would come later. Right now, he had work to do.

Bell found a strike team from out of town that had lost their way, so he steered them over to protect the homes in the Brentwood tract and along Wardman Bullock. Then he got a call from Chief Mayfield, who didn't have a clear view of the fire from his current location and was in desperate need of intel.

"Chief, this thing is going to blow past Banyan and make it to the freeway in no time," Bell told him. "We need to send units down East Avenue for structure protection."

Mayfield acknowledged the transmission, but Bell could hear in his voice that the suddenness of all this had rattled him. It rattled Bell. With fire shooting south and west through the flats, it rattled everyone out on the line.

As Bell traveled down Banyan Street, trying to figure out how they were going to keep fire out of all the homes, his hands suddenly tensed on the wheel and his foot stomped on the brakes. Not twenty feet in front of him, a wall of flame roared across the street on its journey south. It made Bell certain of one thing—if they didn't jump ahead of this thing and gain some control, things would get a lot worse.

When the wave of fire passed, Bell stepped on the gas, turned onto East Avenue, and headed toward his department's new fire station, which was still under construction. Several homes in the area sat along a dirt road lined with rows of old, explosive eucalyptus trees. The homes had been threatened and defended numerous times over the years, but he knew today it would be one heck of a fight.

He arrived just as a pissed-off fire front swept into the area. It would take a fight to save the homes, something he couldn't manage single-handedly. Luckily, he spotted one of the L.A. County strike teams Mayfield had pulled out of the foothills and sent down into the flats. They were stuck behind a locked gate, so Bell made his way down to them and took care of the barricade. Instantly the strike teams deployed among the homes in the area. In a matter of minutes, the battle came to them. One of the homes and the new fire station sustained damage, but it was minor compared to the destruction the massive flame lengths could have sowed. The important thing was that they all walked away with their lives and had saved all the homes.

Before too long Dague joined Bell on East Avenue. The two Rancho leaders had a quick face-to-face, briefed each other on critical developments, and then went their separate ways to continue orchestrating the attack. Dague moved to the north end of East Avenue, shoring up his defenses as units spread out to protect homes and the vulnerable junior high school campus. Bell moved south on East Avenue, trying get out ahead of the havoc the fire was wreaking on its descent toward the 210 freeway.

Such a goal proved difficult. The fire had already gotten around homes south of Banyan, so Bell deployed Rancho units into the area. He also sent one unit south of the freeway. The solid line of pavement proved to be a godsend in stopping the southward descent of the fire, but the Grand Prix trucked along with such force that it actually spotted over in several places.

Once satisfied that his men could keep the Grand Prix from digging into the city south of the 210, Bell repositioned at Etiwanda and Wilson as the fire made a spectacular broadside run at a newer tract of homes just to the north of him. Other than a single strike team of engines, the only barriers standing between the housing tract and the fire were a wide fuel break, a concrete-block wall, and fire-resistant construction. The area could have done well with serious reinforcements, but there were even more pressing matters to deal with. At the intersection of Etiwanda and Wilson sat Rancho's temporary Fire Station 176 and the Lloyd Michael Water Treatment Facility, both of which were threatened by fire.

If the Grand Prix got established on the site, water treatment buildings housing chlorine cylinders and other hazardous chemicals would soon catch fire and send a toxic cloud of smoke downwind. Then everyone would have a much bigger problem to contend with than just losing structures.

Bell summoned Rancho units to his location, and they arrived just in time to knock down several spot fires and a burning outbuilding before the flames could get established and do significant damage to the site. "Firefighters call this 'breaking the chain reaction' because it keeps the fire from getting a foothold and moving through ornamental vegetation and into the structures," said Bell. "Firefighters know that when flames are wind-driven, there is little chance of stopping them, so they work instead to move the flames around homes and buildings. This type of action was typical throughout the day as crews fought to prevent the fire from progressing into established developments."

As the threat to the Wilson/Etiwanda area subsided, the Rancho units regrouped. Bell conferred with Rancho captain Jim Curatalo, and after scraping together a number of units, they formed Rancho Task Force One. With Bell overseeing structure protection for his designated area, Curatalo took control of the task force, but that posed a bit of a dilemma. Riding along with him for the day was Jim Brulte, the highest-ranking Republican in California's state senate. Even though Brulte was the main ally of Arnold Schwarzenegger, who was currently taking office up in Sacramento after winning the wild recall election on October 7, the Rancho Cucamonga resident had come by to see how things were shaking out. Curatalo asked Bell if he wouldn't mind taking the senator in his Explorer, and Bell gladly agreed. How could he not?

While Bell, Dague, Dave Berry, and others focused on protecting homes, Mayfield continued to scout the entire front country. Instead of the fire being diverted around the north end of the city as they had planned, the fight had been taken out into the streets. The flame lengths stretched forty feet in height, reaching over two-story houses and across streets. They licked off eaves, which instantly burst into flame. They burned tiles, patio furniture, and bushes all along the back of the houses at the top of Etiwanda. Mayfield had already lost two homes this morning, and he refused to lose any more. He had units dashing this way and that, dousing all the fires before they could get going. He organized backfiring operations, moved around strike teams, and talked with everyone out on the line to make sure they were operating on the same page. He planned to take the high-paced action into the next day and the day after that, but fortunately he didn't have to. The northeast winds began to abate just before noon, slowing the fire to a crawl.

Jumping on the opportunity, Mayfield had strike teams flood out into the interface to fight fire side by side with the wildland guys working for perimeter control. Together they began corralling the fire with the intention of pushing it back up onto the hill. Unbelievably, the only houses lost as of yet were up at the top of Wardman Bullock Road, but Mayfield knew the worst was yet to come. He promised himself that from now on, the Grand Prix couldn't so much as hiccup without him knowing about it.

17

Buying Time

On the perimeter control side of the battle, it had been an all-out ground war. With the northeast winds pushing the majority of smoke back down to the ground, airtankers and helicopters hadn't been able to take off due to poor visibility. If they had tried to join the fight, they most likely would have crashed into a mountainside.

Jim Topoleski had joined forces with the Fulton Hotshots early in the morning, and together they executed some aggressive burning operations to save a water treatment plant and a number of structures, but what they had really been waiting for was an opportunity to stop the westward crawl of fire across the foothills altogether. The moment the northeast winds died down around noon, they got their chance.

Directly above the eastern portion of Rancho Cucamonga stood Day Canyon, a gaping wound in the mountainside capable of pushing large amounts of water down into the flats during heavy rains. To deal with the runoff, the county had built cement channels to catch the water and steer the flow south. The channels were between twelve and twenty feet wide and eight to ten feet deep. They wouldn't stop a Santa Ana-driven fire such as the Grand Prix on their own, but both Topoleski and Fulton superintendent Ron Bollier knew that if they burned off the chaparral on the east side of one of the channels, they might be able to create the kind of buffer that could halt, or at least slow, the Grand Prix's destructive advance.

A few minutes later, the Fulton Hotshots dropped fire to the ground on the east side of the channel, and they carried it all the way up into the mouth of Day Canyon. A Forest Service strike team followed behind them, mopping up the edges of the controlled burn to ensure no embers were left. As Fulton tied the burn off into a pile of rocks that had tumbled down over the years, Topoleski turned his focus to the north. Fulton had put in a nice buffer down in the flats, but that would do little to stop the main body of fire from creeping to the west high above. In order to protect the western portion of Rancho Cucamonga, he needed to keep the fire from crossing Day Canyon altogether, both down in the flats and at the higher elevations. Achieving such a goal was probably impossible, but they had to try.

As Topoleski worked out the details of how to create a fuel break along the ridge on the west side of Day Canyon, an ABC Channel 7 News van came into the area to film their progress. Topoleski knew the

A firefighter surveying the Grand Prix.

area wasn't safe. Although the winds now came out of the southwest, pushing the fire up the hillside, there were too many slight fluctuations for his comfort. He told the reporters to turn around, but they didn't listen. They headed into the canyon as Fulton was on the last leg of the operation. Then the north winds resurfaced. The main body of the Grand Prix blended with the fire Fulton had started, creating a massive wall of flame that swirled around and around in the mixing winds. In a matter of minutes, a six-hundred-foot tornado filled with fire lifted off the ground in the mouth of Day Canyon.

The taillights of the news van lit up, and then its tires spun in reverse. Fulton and the other crews in the area also bailed out, and from a distance everyone watched the class 5 tornado hover through the sky. At first it headed south, down toward the homes, but then it suddenly reversed direction and drove up into Day Canyon. Topoleski squinted in the wind, trying to see where it touched down. Smoke and ash poured into the area, and he became certain it had caught the western slopes of the canyon on fire. That was the worst possible news. Their whole goal with this latest operation was to keep the fire on the east side of the canyon. With that blown, there wasn't a workable ridge for miles and miles to put in a fuel break. The next one to the west was Cucamonga Canyon, but that was all the way on the other side of Rancho. As the fire made its way across the mountains under the northeast winds, it would send walls of flames right down into the long row of houses.

To avoid a disastrous outcome, their only defense now was to start lighting fires along the dozer line just north of the homes, starting at Haven Avenue. Under such winds the fire they put down could jump over into the homes, but it was better than having a hundred-foot wall of flame directly hit the community.

As Topoleski prepared for this final plan to protect the city of Rancho, a pilot came over the radio and said that he didn't think the fire whirl had touched down on the west side of Day Canyon. Topoleski asked if he was sure, and he was. That changed everything. Topoleski didn't want to fire along the powerline road, not under these winds. Not if he didn't have to. Instead he decided to have the crews under his command, which included the Arroyo Grande crew, the Fulton Hotshots, and the Redding Hotshots, dig a fuel break straight up the western ridge of Day Canyon. To make sure none of them got into a tight spot, Topoleski contacted the Air Attack pilot to enlist his support.

The Grand Prix coming down off the mountain.

"I'm not sure what you guys are trying to do," said the pilot.

"We know that we are not going to stop this," said Topoleski. "What we are trying to do is buy some time. What we would like you to do is support the crews as they cut a check-line up that canyon."

"Okay, I completely understand. I'll throw everything your way that I can afford."

Topoleski had no expectations that the meager fuel break would stop the fire, but hopefully it would slow it down, give the night shift an opportunity to come in and get their resources deployed. Once the fire got over that line, that's when they would fall back and burn the dozer line all the way west to Cucamonga Canyon.

The hotshot crews got to work, and before too long five helicopters turned up, dumping water over the entire ridge to cool it down. Despite the added help, it was backbreaking work. The terrain was nearly vertical, and knowing that time was of the essence, the hand crews pushed upward at a furious pace. A few hours into it, one of Bollier's guys asked him how high up they were going to cut line; they were already over a hundred feet above the valley floor. Bollier told him that they were going up to 2130. At first the crew member thought he was crazy, but then Bollier smiled. Hotshots go by the military clock, and he had been referring to time. They would get as far as they could, and then at 9:30 P.M. they would knock off for the day. Their goal was simple—get as much line punched up the ridge in hopes of slowing down the fire. That way, night shift could come and do whatever they wanted with that line instead of inheriting a "whole wad of shit."

In addition to this plan, Bollier also had another operation going on down below in the front country. He'd sent Val Linch, one of his captains, off with four dozer operators. Their job was to widen and improve the dozer line that had been put in along the powerlines down below. They were to begin directly beneath Day Canyon, and then carry it west along the base of the foothills. When they reached the mouth of Deer Canyon, which was right above Haven Avenue, they were to veer to the north and tie the line off in the catch basin over there. That way, when the night shift took over, all they had to do was come in and burn the entire north side of the dozer line. In Bollier's mind, it was a crucial operation. When the fire came down the following morning, it would head straight for Haven Avenue and begin tearing into the homes. If night shift burned off that chunk from Day Canyon all the way out to Deer Canyon, however, the fire would hit black and lie down. It didn't solve the problem of the fire crossing farther to the west up in the mountains, but it would give them a few more hours to fortify their defenses in the flats the following morning.

By ten o'clock that night, both projects were completed. They had put four thousand feet of hand line in along the western ridge of Day Canyon, and they had improved the dozer line all the way out to Haven. Despite the loss of the two homes at the top of Wardman Bullock, it had been a successful day. They had stopped the fire from heading past Day Canyon, both down in the flats and up in the mountains, just as they said they would. But in order to keep the successes coming, Bollier knew the night shift had to burn off the dozer line along the powerlines. Absolutely had to. If they didn't, the morning of October 25 could be ten times worse than anything they had seen today.

18

A Prayer

With both structure protection and perimeter control mopping up in eastern Rancho Cucamonga, Los Angeles County battalion chief John Tripp took a much-needed break. It had been a chaotic day. Working down in San Diego early in the morning, he had received a call from his wife. She told him that the Grand Prix was coming down off the mountain and heading straight for their home on the corner of East Avenue just south of the 210 freeway in Etiwanda. Tripp had rushed back to Rancho in his Crown Victoria staff vehicle, but by the time he arrived the Grand Prix had already bumped the freeway. Thankfully it had held the fire, and his neighborhood, while shaken, was intact.

Around noon he ran into Jim Dague, who was surprised to see him.

"I'm just here helping stabilize the neighborhood," Tripp said. "Nothing official."

They shook hands and both went back to the fight. A few hours later, around one in the afternoon, Tripp stepped inside his house to get some water and heard the phone ringing. It was Chief Ron Mayfield, another longtime friend, asking for his help. Other than the lag in the morning, the structure protection plan they had put together for Rancho had worked flawlessly. The only problem now was that the fire had gotten too big. With all of Rancho's chief officers having assumed control of structure groups in the eastern part of the city, they had no one left to coordinate the structure protection groups when the fire pushed into the western portion of town. They needed more officers who knew where all the homes were, how fire behaved in the front country, and the exact locations to position the strike teams.

Tripp realized that Mayfield wanted him to take a command position on the fire. It was a difficult request to grant, simply because it went against the ordering process. Normally Mayfield had to submit the request for more officers to Mike Rohde, the branch director. Rohde would then place the request with the incident management team, and the team would send the order on to SouthOps to be filled. But with everyone up the chain already having their hands full, the additional officers might have taken a great while to arrive. And when they did arrive, they would most likely be from out of the area. They would be just as lost as the strike team leaders as to how to best defend the structure groups.

Tripp had worked as part of an incident management team for years, and seldom had he seen a deputy branch director go outside the ordering process to fulfill his needs. The whole reasoning behind creating incident management teams was to eliminate freelancing. They needed everyone to follow the overall strategy of putting the fire out, not developing their own strategy. Mayfield, however, was not freelancing. He

Rancho Cucamonga firefighters developing a game plan on the afternoon of October 24.

was taking independent action, and Tripp knew there was a huge difference. Mayfield was still working under the overall strategy of the fire,
but he was getting his own reinforcements to execute his part of the
plan. It showed huge initiative on Rancho's part. They had developed a
plan to protect their city, and they were going to see it through.

Tripp contacted his boss and got approval to assume an overhead
position on the Grand Prix. Fifteen minutes later, he met Mayfield at Los
Osos High School, which by this time had become a full-blown staging
area, equipped with bathrooms and sleeping areas. They decided that
Tripp would take charge of the Haven structure group, which would be
the first structure group to get hit the following morning if the fire came
down off the hill. To prepare, Tripp went to the top of Haven and walked
the entire area to decide how many strike teams he would need to defend
it. While he did this, Jim Dague, Mike Bell, and the rest of the Rancho
overhead did the same in their structure groups.

In the evening they all gathered for a meeting at Rancho's Station
175 on Banyan, one block west of the Los Osos High staging area. They
developed their strategy and went over the plan of attack for the following day. Mayfield had broken the western portion of the city down into
six structure groups, each bearing the name of the major north-south
artery leading up to it. Heading from east to west, they would have
Haven structure group, Hermosa structure group, Archibald structure
group, Amethyst structure group, Carnelian structure group, and Sapphire structure group. The incoming resources would get assigned to a
group at Los Osos High School, and then all they had to do was look at
a map to know where to go.

Despite the simplicity of the structure group concept, it was quite
uncommon. Normally, all of Rancho Cucamonga, from Haven over to
the neighboring city of Upland, would have been classified as one division. But having fought fire along the foothills for more than two
decades, Mayfield knew that such a strategy in this fire would only create chaos. None of the engine crews arriving from out of town would
have known where to go or when. Huge gaps in the northern row of
homes would have been left unprotected, and residences would be lost
as a result. Mayfield realized that the only way to manage so many strike
teams and guard the entire row of homes in the western portion
of town was to have one of his men up at the top of each major artery
calling the shots. Mayfield was simply thinking outside the box to help

The Rancho Cucamonga staging area at Los Osos High School under attack from the Grand Prix.

protect his city, and he had no idea that months down the road his plan would get national attention from the firefighting community.

Once everyone had a clear picture of what was going to happen, Topoleski, who had decided to attend the meeting, stood up. He wanted to be certain Rancho troops knew exactly what would transpire on the wildland side of things while they were protecting structures. Municipal firefighters had a very different way of combat than the troops from both CDF and the Forest Service, and misunderstandings could not only endanger their mission, but also the lives of everyone out on the line. Communication was the key to success.

Topoleski told them how he had worked with hotshot crews to corral the fire back up onto the mountain, but they had no expectation of holding it. During the night, they would fire the dozer line Fulton had put in above Haven Avenue. That would hinder the fire from reaching the homes in the area early in the morning, but when the winds really kicked in and the fire reached the west side of Day Canyon, it was "going to roll down like crap through a Christmas goose." When that happened, they would fire the main containment line dozers had constructed near the powerlines all the way west to the mouth of Cucamonga Canyon. "I

wanted to make sure that they knew the plan, because structure protection would be busy doing structure protection, and perimeter control
would be busy doing perimeter control," said Topoleski. "And we probably weren't going to have a lot of interaction. But I had so much faith in
Rancho when I saw Dague, Mayfield, Mike Costello, and those guys. I
just had a sense that things were going to get taken care of. If they knew
what our plan was, I felt confident that they would know how to operate
inside that plan."

This was important information for John Tripp because for the next
twelve hours he would be the only chief officer from the structure protection side out on the front line. Mayfield, Bell, Dague, Dave Berry, and
Mike Costello, who had returned to home base after spending the last
several days on the Roblar 2 Fire as a part of an incident management
team, were exhausted and needed sleep. It was decided that Tripp, positioned at the top of Haven, would keep a close eye on the fire, and the
moment the winds shifted he would personally contact Mayfield so they
could all take their places. That way there wouldn't be any slipups as
there had been that morning.

Before heading their separate ways, everyone attending the meeting
gathered around the table and prayed. RCFD battalion chief Darrell Lut-
trull, who watched over the unaffected portions of the city while the
other officers had their hands full with the incident, prayed for safety, for
wisdom, and for the ability to make good decisions in the day to come.
It was local government, and they knew they weren't supposed to be sitting around a table praying, but they did. At that point, it was no longer
about the job; it was about their city and their family of firefighters who
would protect it. Over the years, they had been on hunting trips together
and celebrated one another's birthdays. Some of them went to the same
church. In many ways, they knew each other better than they knew their
own families. The prayer was their way to remind everyone in the room
that as long as they stuck together they would be just fine.

As the overhead from Rancho headed home, Tripp took his position
at the top of Haven. The winds had died and the fire brewed high up on
the mountain, but things could turn bad in an instant. For the first several thousand feet, the smoke column from the Grand Prix rose straight
up into the night air. Higher up, however, it made a sharp turn to the
southwest, which meant that the Santa Anas still blew, just not down
along the ground. The fire was currently fuel- and topography-driven,

but that could change at any moment if the northeast winds fell to a lower elevation.

Tripp stayed on his toes and worked with Gary Marshal, the night-shift branch director. They had six strike teams under their command to protect all of Rancho during the night, so they spread them out in each of the structure groups. Tripp spent his time going back and forth between them, seeing how they were doing and developing contingency plans. He wanted everyone to know what to do if the fire blew this way or that, designating different points of attack for each scenario. In between these little meetings, Tripp kept looking up the mountainside, monitoring the fire. But it just sat there like a snake waiting to spring.

While Tripp worked back and forth along the row of houses, he could see Ray Blackburn, who had taken control of Division B for the incident management team, working out by the base of the mountain. Out in the field Blackburn sat at the helm of the perimeter control chain of command just as Tripp sat at the helm of the structure protection chain of command. Although both their missions were to protect life and property, the tactics they employed were much different. Blackburn's objectives were to secure the perimeter and catch the fire as it came down off the mountain. The way he achieved that was by having his troops dig fuel breaks and conduct firing operations around structures. They worked with one foot in the black and one foot in the green, right along the fire's edge in an attempt to keep it from growing. Tripp, on the other hand, was not employing any offensive tactics. Structure protection was strictly in defensive mode—protect structures as the fire came at them.

Maintaining such clear objectives was often hard, especially with many municipal firefighters now versed in wildland tactics. In the early-morning hours, one of the strike teams under Tripp's command wanted to fire the dozer line Fulton had constructed the day before. Tripp wasn't against his troops conducting firing operations; it just had to be under the right conditions. Usually they could employ such tactics to protect a group of homes, but that wasn't the case here. The firing operation they wanted to conduct was a major campaign. Tripp had to tell them no. He didn't feel they had sufficient resources to do the firing operation safely; it should be handled by perimeter control. Perimeter control, however, also didn't feel comfortable firing the dozer line.

"You want the conditions to be just right, and the conditions were not right," said Tripp. "For a few hours there, the fire really laid down. Not to where you could put it out, but it just laid down up on the hill. In order to do burning, you need a fire that is pretty active, because what that does is it sucks in the fire you create. If you light fire without that kind of environment, it could make a bigger mess than what you wanted. That is a very critical point about firing—there is accountability to it. . . . You don't want to create fire that is going to either endanger people's lives or endanger property. That was exactly the reason why. The fire was hung up. The winds had lifted and gone to an upper loft. They weren't surface winds anymore."

Throughout the night there would be much debate about burning out the dozer line Fulton had constructed, but in the end everyone felt safer waiting until adequate resources arrived in the morning—waiting to see if the fire was in fact going to come down off the mountain. For a while there, both perimeter control and structure protection began to think that the fire was just going to sit up on the mountain for the rest of the day. That, however, wasn't the case. At four in the morning the northeast winds dropped down to the ground and the fire made a run just as it had the day before, only now it came down farther to the west.

Tripp contacted Rancho Cucamonga dispatch and told them what was transpiring. Dispatch contacted Mayfield, and then Mayfield notified his officers. In less than half an hour, the overhead from Rancho met at the staging area at Los Osos High School to gather up their resources.

While the Rancho troops set up their structure groups, Tripp studied the fire coming directly down toward Haven, the area he was tasked with defending. Now was definitely the right time to conduct a firing operation along Fulton's dozer line. They needed to find some way to halt the fire, otherwise it would crash right into Haven View Estates, a large housing tract located at the very top of Haven. But before troops could get out there and lay fire down on the ground, their window of opportunity closed. The brush north of the dozer line was thick, and although Tripp didn't know what was the percentage of live fuel moisture in the area, it was definitely beyond critical. It was beyond extreme. He knew that under these winds there was no way a firing operation would have held on the north side of the dozer line. The fire would have spotted over the dozer line and then the troops doing the firing would have fire on both sides of them without a clear escape route or safety zone. They had been working toward that firing operation for more than twenty-four hours, but it just wasn't going to happen. You could develop the best plans in the world, but it all came down to how the fire wanted to behave. Their only option was to back off.

This would come as a great disappointment to Fulton superintendent Ron Bollier. With the fire romping and stomping down the mountain, there was nothing to stop it from heading directly into the homes at the top of Haven Avenue. Without a doubt, it was going to be one hell of a day.

19

The Calm before the Storm

As John Tripp briefed firefighters arriving for day shift at the top of Haven Avenue, Mike Dietrich stepped out of his trailer in Glen Helen Park and met with a reporter from the *Today* show. Together they gazed up at the fire on the mountain.

"The fire looks pretty benign," the reporter commented.

Dietrich's eyes remained locked on the column of smoke now pushing to the southwest under Santa Ana winds. "Well," he said, "it's going to get a lot better."

BLACK SATURDAY

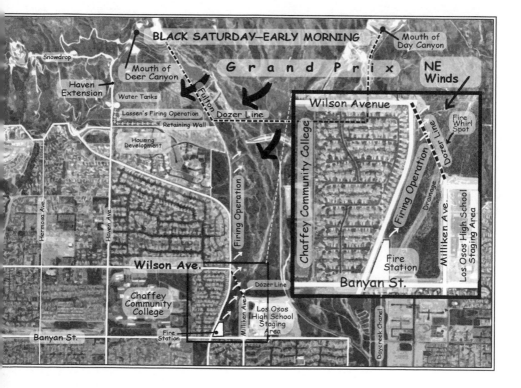

20

Hold 'Em Back

As Jim Topoleski drove into Rancho Cucamonga on the morning of Saturday, October 25, huge billows of smoke and ash washed off the mountains under the northeast winds. With the fire pushing westward, Division A had moved. Topoleski was now responsible for protecting an area that encompassed everything in the flats from Cherry Avenue, which was where the fire had started three days before, all the way west to Haven Avenue. It was imperative that he meet with Gerry Brewster, who had handled Division A throughout the night. Topoleski wanted to know everything that had happened in the past twelve hours so he wouldn't get caught with his pants down.

Driving north on Etiwanda Avenue, he snatched up his radio and tried to summon Brewster, but instead he got Randy Unkovich, the superintendent of the Dalton Hotshots, who had worked under Brewster all night. "I need to meet with you to give you the layout," Unkovich said. "We're getting hit with fire whirls."

Having experienced a fire whirl the day before, Topoleski knew exactly what he meant. They looked like class 5 tornadoes, only filled with fire and ash. Topoleski hit the gas, and in less than 5 minutes he had reached the Dalton crew camped out by the rock quarry plant in the mouth of Day Canyon. The winds howled between thirty-five and forty miles per hour, throwing fire everywhere. The moment Topoleski stepped out of his vehicle, another fire whirl lifted off in the north and sped toward him. He jumped back behind the wheel and quickly parked between two sand piles. The whirl of fire passed overtop of him and proceeded south.

Topoleski didn't like to see such extreme fire behavior, especially not at the beginning of his shift. He talked with Unkovich, and that's when he realized that the dozer line Fulton had put in the previous night from Day Canyon into the mouth of Deer Canyon hadn't been burned off. At first Topoleski wondered what had happened. Everyone had understood the plan; when the fire crossed Day Canyon, the night shift would fire the dozer line. That way the Grand Prix would run into charred vegetation instead of shooting into homes and charging down to the 210 freeway as it had the previous morning. It had been a critical operation.

Apparently, a few hotshot crews working night shift had wanted to conduct the burn, but the division supervisor held them off. Topoleski had worked as a night-shift division supervisor on many occasions, and he could buy off on what they had been thinking. Putting fire on the ground involved risk. If the firing operation got out of control and slopped over into the homes, the one responsible for issuing the burn would have been crucified.

The problem still remained, however. Instead of heading toward the Brentwood housing development on the east side of Etiwanda Avenue as it had the day before, the fire now pushed west of Etiwanda Avenue toward the homes on Wilson, a major east-west street north of the 210 freeway. It also headed toward the Rancho Cucamonga fire station on Banyan Street. If the fire got too far south, it would once again reach the freeway, taking out homes along the way. And if got too far west, it would reach Haven Avenue. From there, it would tear across the foothills, impacting the long row of homes that stretched all the way out to L.A. County. Burning Fulton's dozer line would have prevented all that, but there was no point thinking about that now.

They needed to do something. Topoleski had a list of resources assigned to him, which included the Big Bear Hotshots, the Fulton Hotshots, and a group of dozers, so he got on the radio and told everyone to meet at Chaffey Community College, located on the northwest corner of Haven Avenue and Wilson just a half mile south of the foothills.

The Grand Prix making a push at the Rancho Cucamonga staging area at Los Osos High School.

The Big Bear Hotshots were still in transit when Topoleski arrived, but the twenty members of the Fulton crew were ready for action. Before Topoleski sent anyone out, he needed to know what the fire was doing right at this moment, not half an hour ago, so he sent Fulton scouting to gather current intelligence. While the hotshots trekked across the foothills on foot, Topoleski took a step back and looked at the big picture. It was impossible to see every part of the fire, but he could see enough. Fire whirls lifted off and touched down, starting spot fires all across the interface. The Grand Prix also moved at incredible speeds. If it had been just a do-nothing little fire, he would have put fifty or sixty men right there along the fire line, but he couldn't put firefighters that close to 150- or 200-foot flame lengths, especially not with the wind in their faces. So he decided to stay away from it. In the fifties, they fought wildland fires with Levi's and cotton shirts, and Topoleski didn't know if they burned any more or any fewer people than they did today with all the crap that they wore. There was something to be said about using your skin as a thermometer. The safest way to fight fire was naked, because you're not going to get too close.

Topoleski didn't want his men out in the brush conducting firing operations and cutting line. In fact, the fire behavior was so erratic that he didn't even want the dozers out there, so he had all the dozer operators under his command just hold tight at Chaffey Community College on Haven Avenue. He planned to start an aggressive burning operation; it just wouldn't be the same one they had come up with the night before. The time to do that had passed them by. To work out the logistics, he went up to the top of Haven and met with John Forester, who had taken control of Division B for the day. Once they had devised the new firing operation, Topoleski contacted Fulton.

The plan was to have Bollier's crew go up to the top of Haven and begin firing at the mouth of Deer Canyon, carry it around the Haven View Estates housing development, which sat between the top of Haven Avenue and the grasslands to the east, and then directly south to Wilson just north of the college. As this occurred, they would start a second burn operation down south near Banyan. Because Big Bear still hadn't arrived, it would be done by the Horseshoe Meadows Hotshots, who had carried over from the night shift. They would burn off a triangle-shaped patch of brush that lay between Wilson and Banyan to protect Los Osos High School and Fire Station 175. With Fulton's operation heading south and Horseshoe's operation heading north, both crews would come together at Wilson, and then all the homes that faced the urban/wildland interface, from the top of Haven on east to Rochester, would no longer have brush right up against their back doors. It would be a tricky operation; the crews had to burn around corners, which was often hard to control. But at least they would be backed right up against the houses, not standing out in the middle of the brush. Following directly behind them would be strike teams assigned to John Tripp's Haven structure protection group. The engine crews' objective would be to douse the flames the hotshot crews laid down before they got out of hand. They wanted to create a buffer, not another problem.

The Horseshoe Hotshots understood what Topoleski wanted, and they started their portion of the operation down south. Twenty minutes or so into their project, the winds started to die down. The dozer operators camped out at the community college got antsy, so they started scouting around to see what they could do. After several minutes, they came up with a plan of their own that would save Horseshoe a great deal of trouble. By heading to the east end of Wilson where it dead-ended out

A firefighter on the Grand Prix.

in the middle of the brush, they could cut a diagonal line to the south-east, right to the top of Milliken. Once that was complete, a hand crew could come in and fire the east side of that line. The project would cut the Grand Prix off, keep it from reaching the triangle-shaped brush patch altogether. Horseshoe would no longer have to burn up against the homes between Wilson and Banyan.

"Dozer operators sometimes tend to do their own gig," said Topoleski. "Where they got their direction will be complete speculation between now and eternity. I don't want to sound like I am throwing it off on someone else, but it wasn't from me."

As the dozer operators cut their line, the Big Bear Hotshots arrived. Topoleski quickly informed Jimmy Avila, superintendent of the Big Bear crew, of the game plan, and then Avila brought his men down to relieve Horseshoe, which had worked all night. Topoleski expected them to continue with the original operation, so he focused his attention on the fire front. But Big Bear didn't continue with the original plan. On their way down, they ran into Division B from the night shift, and it was decided that Big Bear would go and fire the dozer line being put in between Wilson and Milliken. Topoleski would have advised against this. Despite the lull in the wind, everything he had seen this morning led him to believe that the fire could blow up at any moment. "We were holding the dozers at Chaffey College because they weren't working," said Topoleski. "No dozer lines were working. The only thing working out there was asphalt."

Big Bear didn't realize this, and they headed after the dozers with their drip torches. What happened next would cause that Saturday morning to hang over Topoleski's head like a black cloud.

21

The Wrong Foot

It looked like a good plan to Jimmy Avila, superintendent of the Big Bear Hotshots. A group of dozer operators had cut line from the top of Milliken up to Wilson, straight through the plot of brush separating the two. The entire distance, which was measured later on, was 1,064 feet. Avila figured if he got in there and burned on the east side of the line, it would halt the Grand Prix when it arrived. They would have brush on both sides of them while at work, so they had to be careful. If either the Grand Prix or their burn operation jumped over to the west side of the dozer line, they'd get pinched between two walls of flame. Because of the danger, Avila picked his ten best men and left the rest of the crew behind.

Armed with drip torches, they dropped a mixture of kerosene and gasoline into the brush on their right the moment they stepped off Milliken. After they had burned approximately two hundred feet toward Wilson, Avila noticed that embers wafting off the Grand Prix had started a spot fire on the west side of the dozer line just up ahead. Immediately he instructed his crew to stop firing. Currently they had two escape routes: they could head up the dozer line to Wilson eight hundred feet to the north, or they could head two hundred feet back down to Milliken. Neither option seemed all that appealing. If they headed north and the

119

spot fire picked up, they would get cut off. If they headed south and the fire they'd dropped on the ground flared up, they would take some serious heat.

The best option was to get the spot fire taken care of so they didn't need to worry about an escape. To do this, Avila flagged down a couple of nearby dozers and instructed them to contain the spot fire by cutting a line around it. The dozer operators managed this in a matter of minutes, but they couldn't put direct line around the fire due to the limited maneuverability of their dozers. There were still patches of unburned brush inside the circle the dozers had carved, and it would be quite easy for that brush to ignite and start yet another spot fire outside the circle. So Avila moved his crew into the black area burned by the spot fire and had them clean up the edges.

While the crew mopped up, Avila walked twenty-five feet up the dozer line toward Wilson to get a better look at the Grand Prix. He didn't like what he saw. For the past half hour there had been a lull in the wind, but now it started to regain its former ferocity. Off in the distance, he could see the fire behavior becoming erratic, throwing massive flames every which way. He snatched up his radio and contacted his crew. "It's time to get out of here," he said. "Let's go ahead and move out."

A few minutes later, three crew members moved past him, heading up the dozer line toward Wilson. As Avila turned back south to round up the rest of his crew, a massive fire whirl lifted off the Grand Prix and touched down to the east, starting a fire in a drainage that ran perpendicular to their dozer line. Avila hadn't noticed the drainage before—it was buried underneath a carpet of brush. Had he known about it, he wouldn't have brought the crew into the area. With the winds pumping out of the northeast, aligned perfectly with the drainage, fire would rocket out of there like a bullet from a shotgun, throwing flames in the face of anyone standing on the dozer line.

Avila needed to warn his crew back on the spot, but there was no time. The world instantly went black as the fire flared up, ran through the drainage, and then hit the dozer line not far from where the crew worked. "If you look at the pictures of it after the event, you can see the stubs outside the drainage are about five feet high," said Avila. "And then you look at the stubs that were in the drainage and they were all half an inch tall. So all the heat that was generated came out of the drainage."

In the confusion, it would have been easy for Avila to follow the three crew members making their way toward Wilson. That, however, was not the route that he took. With the majority of his crew still twenty-five feet to the south where the first spot fire had occurred, he turned and headed blind into the advancing fire. He didn't know if he could reach his men. The only thing he knew for certain was that his boys were in danger. "I couldn't see two or three feet," said Avila, "but I could definitely see the orange glow that was behind the area where the crew was at."

Despite being surrounded by flame, Avila reached his men without taking any heat. Instead of wrapped up in their shelters or screaming for their lives, he found them all huddled down close to the earth. The area was certainly hot, but the charred brush of the spot fire had actually served as a safety zone. The crew member who had been closest to the drainage when the fire flared up took some heat. He was pretty shaken, as they all were, but he didn't appear injured.

"Are you guys okay?" Avila shouted over the fire's hiss.

The crew members nodded their heads, more than happy to see him.

"You're in the black," Avila told them. "You're safe, don't worry. Is everyone here?"

Avila looked around, trying to discern faces through all the smoke and ash. He took into account the three crew members who had passed by him on their way toward Wilson, but there was still one missing. He double-checked, and a terrible fear built in his stomach as he realized his captain wasn't among them. Avila assumed that he had gone with the other three crew members toward Wilson, but as the leader of twenty men, assumptions were a luxury he couldn't afford.

Taking his radio and pressing it to his ear, Avila tried to contact his captain. No answer. He tried again a few seconds later, and still he got no response. He took one last look at his men to make sure they could all mentally cope with the situation, and then he moved out of the safety zone and headed north along the dozer line. The entire world around him burned. The smoke and ash were so thick that he had to keep his eyes pinned to the ground. If he veered off the dozer line, that would be the end.

After working his way twenty yards to the north, he came across a set of hand tools. They had been dropped by one of his crew members, and a chill crept up Avila's back. Those who landed positions on hotshot crews were considered the best of the best, trained to deal with hairy sit-uations. Hand tools were their weapons to fight fire, and the only time they discarded them was when their lives were in serious jeopardy.

Avila picked up his pace and tried once again to contact his captain, but he still got no answer. There was always that chance that one of his crew members had dropped his tools by accident, and then he couldn't find them due to all the smoke and dashing embers. That possibility, however, quickly evaporated when he came across another set of dis-carded tools. It became clear to him then that the three men who'd come down this dozer line just moments before had been forced to run for their lives. Avila's concern turned to dread, and he picked up his pace even more, not knowing if he would find his men or in what condition if he did.

It seemed like an eternity before he reached the end of the dozer line at Wilson. He pushed through the smoke, his heart racing as he searched for familiar faces. By the grace of God he found them a few seconds later. The three crew members who had worked past him earlier lay sprawled out on the pavement, coughing violently through the oxygen

Firefighters on the Grand Prix.

masks strapped to their faces. Avila ran to them, his eyes probing their bodies for major burns. They all suffered from smoke inhalation, but the fire seemed to have avoided direct contact with their skin. Avila experienced a brief moment of total and utter relief as he contacted a safety officer for an ambulance, but then his thoughts focused on his missing captain.

He prepared to head back down the dozer line to find him, but he didn't need to. He got his captain over the radio a few seconds later and learned that he had worked his way down the dozer line to Milliken when the fire flared up. It had gotten pretty heavy for him—he took some radiant heat and suffered some burns—but surprisingly he had made it through the chaos and reached the pavement they'd stepped off to begin the operation. Avila wasted no time getting him up with his other wounded men, and the four were rushed to the hospital.

The rest of the crew came down the dozer line a few minutes later, all of them badly shaken. They were given hotel rooms to clear their heads, and then a short while later they met with a professional counselor and went through a critical incident stress debriefing. As they talked about what had happened and why, word of their unfortunate experience traveled down the fire line, putting both municipal and wildland firefighters on edge. The day had only just begun, and already a crew had been burned over. As they looked at the massive flame lengths in the near distance, they wondered what the Grand Prix had in store for all of them.

22

Close Call

The Fulton Hotshots had their own problems to contend with. Under Topoleski's orders, Rob Bollier had taken his twenty-man hotshot crew up to the top of Haven Avenue early in the morning. When they got there, a massive C-shaped line of fire was marching up the mountainside, pushing to the southwest under Santa Ana winds. The top part of the C didn't pose an immediate threat to the community; it lay high up on the mountain, and the topography was such that the only way it could come down into the flats was out the mouth of Cucamonga Canyon miles to the west. They would definitely have to contend with it in the hours to come, but there were more pressing matters at hand.

The bottom part of the C had already come out the mouth of Deer Canyon, heading toward Haven View Estates right there at the top of Haven. Not twelve hours before, Bollier's crew had cut line from Day Canyon to Deer Canyon. Bollier had instructed the night shift to lay fire down on the north side of the east-west line. In his mind, the burn operation was instrumental in stopping the lower part of the fire from advancing into the city, which in turn would buy them some time to work out a game plan to deal with the top part of the fire later in the day. But to Bollier's surprise, the night shift hadn't conducted the firing operation. "It would have held the fire up on the hill," said Bollier, "and it is very probable that Big Bear would not have had their incident in the transition of the shifts."

Bollier wasn't sure what had happened during the night. The only thing he knew for sure was that his crew had just inherited a whole wad of shit. Just as he turned to his men to delegate tasks, the Lassen Hotshots showed up to relieve the Del Rosa Hotshots, who had worked in the area for the past twelve hours. In fact, Del Rosa had been struggling to conduct Fulton's burn operation since the northeast winds returned, but erratic fire behavior had forced them to back off.

Bollier had a face-to-face with John Bristow, Lassen's superintendent, and they discussed possible ways of stopping the fire's downward slide into the homes. Creating a fuel break before the Grand Prix slammed into Haven View Estates would be tough, but they both thought it was still manageable. Where Haven Avenue ended, a smaller one-track road began, shooting north through the brush toward the base of the mountain. Several hundred yards up the extension were a couple of city water tanks. If one of their crews started burning at those tanks and carried flame down the east side of the extension road all the way to the top of Haven Avenue, they would create a north-south fuel break that would catch the Grand Prix's western crawl below the foothills. That, however, wouldn't stop the Grand Prix's southern descent toward Haven View Estates. To solve that, the other crew could begin another firing operation along the cement retaining wall that separated the housing complex from the grasslands. They would start in the east and carry fire directly to the west along that wall, ending at the top of Haven. If all went well, the two firing operations would come together at the top of Haven, creating a massive L-shaped fuel break that would catch the lower portion of the Grand Prix like a glove.

The firing operations were only the beginning of what needed to get done to prep the front country. Bristow realized this, and he agreed to handle both firing operations so that Bollier and his crew could attend to other matters. With everything square in the back of their minds, the two hotshot superintendents parted ways.

"We have Santa Ana winds fifty to sixty miles per hour pushing downslope," Bristow told his crew a few moments later. "We're basically going to steer this fire around these homes, so let's get cracking."

The Lassen Hotshots broke into two ten-man modules. One module hiked several hundred feet up the extension off Haven and dropped kerosene and tossed flares out into the brush on the east side of the road. When they looked up from their work, they saw the Grand Prix barreling down on them from the north. It wasn't the most welcoming sight, but the module working along the retaining wall down below didn't have a much better environment. Hanging a hundred feet over their heads were 220 kv powerlines arcing in the smoke and showering them with sparks. And once the fire they laid on the ground got going, they got a nice little scare every so often as shotgun shells lost in the brush exploded at their feet.

As Lassen worked furiously to get the fuel break finished in time, branch director Mike Rohde took position just to the south. If the fire got past perimeter control, it would be his job to protect the homes. He kept his eyes locked to the north, and the moment Lassen's firing operations grew under the wind, he saw what the day had in store for them. He had fought fire since 1973, and these were the worst fire conditions he had ever witnessed. "We were seeing tornadoes of fire build," said Rohde. "As the fire came off the mountainside, it moved straight toward the community as a fire tornado. Even as the tornado diminished, the vortex, the spitting cloud, would continue for another three-quarters of a mile, tearing trees out of the ground. . . . So this was kind of a worst-case austere condition that I think you can face."

Watching over the Lassen Hotshots was Dennis King, one of the many safety officers on the Grand Prix. The fire was already romping and stomping, forcing crews on the line to get aggressive. His job was to keep a level head and pull those crews out when things got too hairy. The last thing he wanted was a burnover. But instead of being able to focus his attention on Lassen out in the brush, he spent the majority of his time fending off citizens who had homes up on Snowdrop and at the top of Haven. Many of them wanted to go home despite the danger, as if their presence would somehow stop Mother Nature's ruthless actions. They had worked a lifetime saving to build their dream homes here on the edge of the urban/wildland interface, and now they realized that their security could turn to a pile of ash in the blink of an eye. They were on the verge of panic. "There were people standing on the street corner in flip-flops and T-shirts," said King. "And I felt when they were out there in the brush over their heads, in the radical winds and fire behavior we were having—it wasn't the place for them to be. So I finally had to start threatening that we were going to get the sheriffs down to get them out of there."

As it turned out, Lassen didn't need King's watchful eyes. After three hours pushing the envelope, the team tied both of their firing operations together at the top of Haven. It wasn't a moment too soon. Less than half an hour later, the Grand Prix came tearing down into the area, searching for fuel that would carry it into the homes, but found none. At the top of Haven, all the homes had been saved—at least for the time being.

When Bollier received news of Lassen's victory, he felt a surge of relief. But it didn't last long. For the past three hours, he'd been engaged in his own race against the clock. The incident management team controlling the Grand Prix had been widening and improving the dirt path underneath the powerlines with dozers and hand crews for the past three days. It would do wonders to help protect the long row of homes along the interface, from Haven to the west end of the city, but there was a problem with the strategy. Not all the homes were below the powerlines. High up in the foothills, the one-lane extension off Haven Avenue veered to the west and became Snowdrop Street. It zigzagged about a mile to the west along the base of the mountain and then dropped south to connect with the top of Archibald, another of Rancho's major north-south arteries.

Snowdrop was basically a big loop meandering through the brush, and there were a dozen high-dollar homes sitting on both sides of the loop. Burning out the dozer line underneath the powerlines would do nothing to save them. As a matter of fact, any fire lit along the dozer line would most likely carry straight up into those homes. The residences that didn't get annihilated from the Grand Prix coming from the north would surely get taken out by the firing operation in the south.

Although Bollier knew saving those homes wouldn't be easy, he still had to try. He couldn't just let the Grand Prix run straight over them. After studying the terrain for a few moments, he pulled aside Val Linch, one of his captains, and instructed him to round up a group of dozers, take them to the very top of the extension off Haven Avenue, and have them cut line due west above all the homes on Snowdrop. Once a fuel break had been cut on the north side of all the homes, Linch was to direct the dozers south so they could tie their line into the existing dozer line near the powerlines. They were still sticking with the incident command team's strategy, which was to create an east-west dozer line above the majority of homes in northern Rancho. The only difference was that they would redirect a portion of that dozer line farther into the foothills to protect the residences along Snowdrop.

Linch enlisted the help of three other Fulton crew members, and they quickly headed up to Snowdrop Street. After spending a few minutes scouting out the rough terrain, figuring out the best way to cut line around the homes, they rounded up four dozer operators and got to work.

It was a good start, but Bollier knew that a simple dozer line would never stop the Grand Prix up on Snowdrop, which meandered through a thick expanse of ten-foot-tall brush. With the winds blowing up to sixty miles per hour, the fire would jump the dozer line in a matter of seconds and tear right through the homes. To keep that from happening, Bollier pulled aside Jake Cagle, the second captain in the crew. Cagle's job was to walk around every house on Snowdrop, find the ones buried deep in the brush, and develop a plan to burn around the endangered homes without turning them into ash in the process. Bollier knew that numerous city engines were positioned up in that area, but conducting firing operations was not their forte. Their job was to defend homes once the fire came at them. If Cagle could do some firing, get those houses prepped before the fire came, it would take a great burden off the strike teams. "I figured that we would try to hold the top line and do some structure protection," said Bollier. "In my mind, we had already written all those structures off. But we still had to try. That was all we could do, give it a shot, put dozer line in and around them."

With his two captains racing across the front country to accomplish their objectives, Bollier flagged down a helicopter pilot who had landed at the top of Haven. The fire stretched so far up the mountain not all of it could be seen, and Bollier wanted to know exactly what they had coming their way in the hours to come. The pilot agreed to give him a sightseeing tour, and once they got up into the air, Bollier saw the big picture. Lassen's firing had held the bottom part of the C, but now they had to deal with the top part, which headed west behind the first ridgeline toward Cucamonga Canyon. Once it got there, fire would shoot out the canyon's mouth and into the flats in the western portion of Rancho. They still had some time. The big push was to get the dozer line constructed above Snowdrop, widen the existing dozer line underneath the powerlines, and then burn off the north side of both those lines before the Grand Prix came off the mountain. It would be a tight squeeze, but as long as the overhead gave ground crews permission to take action, he thought they could manage it.

By the time Bollier landed, Cagle had already scouted Snowdrop and developed a burn plan to create a buffer around the homes engulfed by brush. He told Bollier that all he needed now was permission to lay down fire. Bollier, however, told him to hold off. While in flight, he had received direct orders from his superiors that no firing operations were to take place. The overhead feared a burn operation would take off under the increasing winds, so until the fire came honking down the mountains, the hotshot crews out on the line were to keep their drip torches harnessed.

This came as a great disappointment to Cagle. He and his men had busted their asses running around Snowdrop Street, searching for the homes at greatest risk. The dozer line his fellow captain had put in was fine and dandy, but it wouldn't hold the fire. Judging by what he had seen over the last few days, the only thing that would hold it was a nice big patch of blackened earth. He felt that now was the prime opportunity to fire, before the winds really kicked up. But he had been given his trigger points, so he backed off.

With Cagle in a holding position for the time being, Bollier joined Linch to help him connect the dozer line that wound up and around Snowdrop with the dozer line down along the powerlines. It was slow going. Although much of the front country was referred to as "the flats," the area was anything but flat. Bumps and ridges and drainages ran from north to south, impeding their progress. Sometimes they had to cut line right through people's backyards. Many spots were just too treacherous for the dozers to move into, but luckily they had the Big Hill Helishots from the Eldorado National Forest helping them out.

Under normal circumstances, the Big Hill crew wouldn't have been in the area. They would have been flying over the fire in their helicopter, preparing to get dropped off on a remote fire front that hand crews traveling on foot couldn't reach. But the crew no longer had a helicopter. Two days prior their pilot had been conducting water drops on the Grand Prix when his bird had a mechanical problem. He set it down on a levee just west of Wardman Bullock Road in the eastern portion of town, thinking he would return the following day with mechanics to fix it. To ensure its safety, a couple of CDF inmate crews cut line around it, but the line hadn't been large enough. The fire came through so hot and heavy Friday morning that it scorched the tail boom and delaminated the rotors. Not wanting to miss the action, Big Hill had turned themselves into a hand crew.

Bollier appreciated the help. The division supervisors had graciously given him the ball, and now he ran with it. With a lot of walking and scrambling, they managed to push dozer line to the west above Haven structure group, Hermosa structure group, and Amethyst structure group. But when they reached Carnelian structure group, they got hung up. At the top of Carnelian Street sat King's Estates, a fenced community of million-dollar homes. It was a little farther north than the majority of homes along the interface, but what really concerned Bollier was the Upper King's Ranch, which sat on a knoll just north of King's Estates. It wouldn't have been such a big issue to cut around the lower estates, but that would have left the ranch house standing by itself. Once again, Bollier couldn't let homes burn without trying to save them.

None of the crews in the area had the slightest idea how they were going to extend the dozer line up and around the ranch house. It was rough country out there, filled with deep ravines and dense chaparral.

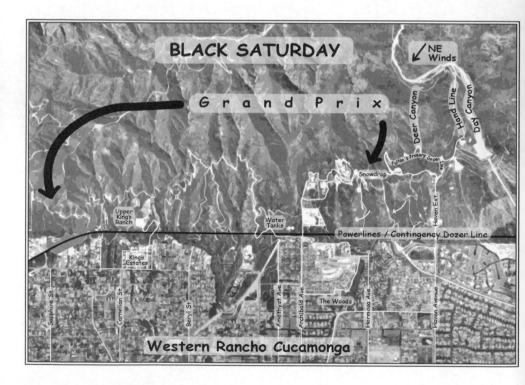

Bollier had realized this when he'd scouted the front country Friday morning, and during his helicopter flight he'd searched for a way around the ranch house. It would be tricky, but they weren't going to lose that residence.

After six hours of backbreaking work, Bollier and his crews had navigated the dozer line around the Upper King's Ranch and prepped the front country to the best of their ability given the time constraint. Now all they needed was to get permission from division to begin their firing operations. And there was a lot to burn. Bollier's plan was to start burning along the primary dozer line they had put in above Snowdrop and carry it around those homes and then down to the secondary dozer line along the powerlines. From there, they would carry fire straight out west. They would keep passing the firing operation on from one crew to the next, down the dozer line just north of the long row of houses.

They didn't get the chance to do that, however. The winds howled at this point, and there was a good chance that any fire that crews dropped to the ground would jump the dozer line and hit the homes. Before any firing took place, division wanted the Grand Prix close enough to suck in the flames. This made the Fulton crew nervous. Bollier knew that if they waited too long, they'd lose their window of opportunity. Judging by the fire behavior he'd seen on his helicopter flight, the Grand Prix would shoot down toward the row of homes faster than anyone could imagine. If it got past the wildland firefighters working for perimeter control, the municipal firefighters backed defensively against the houses would get hit with hundred-foot flame lengths. They were not accustomed to that kind of fight, but Bollier doubted if any of the strike teams would retreat. For almost everyone out on the line, the Grand Prix had become personal.

23

The Battle over Snowdrop

While the Fulton Hotshots waited for permission to begin their offensive firing operations, RCFD captain Dave Berry prepared to defend the homes in the Archibald structure group. The majority of homes at the top of the major north-south artery had been built with tile roofs and stucco walls, and Berry felt confident that some good old-fashioned firefighting could defend them as the fire came through. The tricky part would be saving the homes north of Archibald on Snowdrop Street, which also belonged to his structure group.

With more than a dozen high-dollar homes hidden out in the brush on Snowdrop, Berry had requested four strike teams of engines. There had been some hesitation to grant his request, because with almost fifteen miles of structures along the urban/wildland interface to protect, resources were stretched thin. But Berry held firm and pleaded his case. The rest of the structure groups would employ a tactic called "bump and run," in which once the main body of the Grand Prix moved past a structure group, the majority of engines in that group would immediately bump west to help the next structure group over. Most of the other structure groups only had three strike teams of engines assigned to them, but by the time the fire reached them, they could easily have six or seven. That wasn't the case with Snowdrop.

"Bump and run works very well with good visibility and good road conditions," said Berry. "But up at the top of Archibald we had a very narrow, winding road. Nobody up there was familiar with that area, so I didn't feel it was safe for them to be bumping and running in the fire and smoke conditions. . . . I didn't want to be responsible for one of those engines going off the side of that road."

The resources Berry assigned to Snowdrop would have to hold their positions until the entire body of the Grand Prix passed either around or overtop of them, which could take up to an hour. During that time, every engine up in the area would be stranded—no reinforcements, no way out. They were there for the long haul no matter what happened.

Berry got the engines he asked for, and he spent early Saturday morning strategically placing them in his structure group. He put five engines just north of Archibald where the road narrowed and the brush began. From there, he just worked his way along Snowdrop, assigning units as he went. There were seventeen homes in the area, and he put one unit on each house. If he felt a home would be extremely difficult to defend, he placed two units in the driveway. He made sure everyone had safety zones, and that everyone knew where those safety zones were. He also instructed every firefighter up on Snowdrop not to hesitate to climb into their structure protection gear for the blowover.

Once Berry had everyone in place, he went from home to home to see if there was anything he could do to better prepare his men for the assault. In places nothing separated the residences from the brush, and the Grand Prix would come barreling through there like a ton of bricks. The dense brush surrounding the homes had been a major concern, but then around noon Berry saw Fulton Hotshots captain Val Linch working with a group of dozers north of Snowdrop. Because everyone out on the line already had their hands full, communication between structure protection and perimeter control hadn't been the best. Berry had no idea that Fulton was working in the area, and he flagged Linch down.

"Nobody told me anything," Berry said. "What's the plan?"

"We're going to put in dozer line across all these homes, and then connect it with the secondary dozer line down below," Linch returned. "We're hoping to burn it all off, get enough black in there to stop the fire before it hits you."

Berry thought it was perfect. Over the past few hours, he had wondered if someone would do some burning above the homes. He would have come up with a plan himself, but Mayfield had told everyone that the only firefighters authorized to do any kind of burning were those assigned to perimeter control. Mayfield knew his men were more than capable of issuing burns, but as deputy branch director the decision wasn't up to him. He rode along with Mike Rohde, the branch director for the whole fire, and it had been Rohde's call.

At least it would get taken care of. And if it was done right, the four strike teams Berry had placed along Snowdrop might not even have to get into the fight. With Snowdrop being up in the foothills, once Fulton dropped fire north of the new dozer line, it would burn up and away from the structures. All the brush behind the homes would get consumed, forcing the Grand Prix around the whole area when it arrived. It was absolutely perfect—they might actually be able to save all the homes. And if the Grand Prix somehow jumped the new dozer line, tore past the engine crews, and burned through all the homes on Snowdrop, forces stationed below could still protect the long row of homes by burning off the secondary dozer line near the powerlines.

While Linch pushed the dozers farther west, Jim Topoleski arrived at the top of Haven Avenue. Topoleski's division reached from the very eastern portion of Rancho Cucamonga and ended on Haven Avenue, but his side of the fire, after burning over the Big Bear Hotshots and jumping the 210 freeway, had become surprisingly calm. With the eastern side of town pretty much out of the fire's reach for the time being, Topoleski had come over to help John Forester, who organized perimeter control efforts on the west side of town.

The moment Topoleski arrived at the top of Haven he saw what they were dealing with. After the initial strong gusts in the morning, the winds had calmed dramatically. The Grand Prix was no longer being driven by the Santa Ana winds, but it was anything but docile. Up on the mountain, it rose high into the sky in the shape of a massive mushroom, which meant that the fire was now under plume domination. "Under plume domination the fire can spread in all directions because it is pulling air in from all three sides, and the fire is generating vertically," said Topoleski. "As the mushroom goes up and caps off, things fall down out of the head. . . . The fire was just breathing immensely, throwing stuff everywhere."

The Grand Prix grew in size every minute, and as soon as the winds resurfaced, all that fire would come straight down the mountain. Topoleski had driven the entire front country two days prior, and he knew Snowdrop would be the first area to get steamrolled. Forester realized the same thing, and he wanted Topoleski's opinion on what to do. Should he have Fulton burn off the dozer line even though it might slop over into the homes? Should he keep Dave Berry's engine crews in there for the fight or pull them out because of the danger?

Both these decisions became a major debate. Up to this point, structure protection and perimeter control had worked side by side to achieve their goals, but now they were beginning to butt heads. Being wildland firefighters with wildland tactics, perimeter control wanted to start dropping fire, get the brush above Snowdrop burned off. Dave Berry wanted this as well, but he also wanted to remain in the area as it occurred. He didn't want to get pulled out, not under any circumstances.

With the debate as to what to do about Snowdrop just getting started, Topoleski ordered some of the engines mopping up on the east side of town to come over to Division B, which were then sent to reinforce Dave Berry. It gave Berry what he felt would be an adequate amount of resources to protect the homes up on Snowdrop, even if they decided against burning the dozer line up top. But then around four o'clock something strange happened. Just as the winds kicked back up, Berry received news that they were going to relieve the strike teams stationed along Snowdrop with a fresh batch.

At first Berry thought it was some kind of sick joke. Here they were in the heat of battle, and the overhead was worrying about getting the strike teams rest. The strike teams weren't tired—they had been waiting all day for the action. They had their lines deployed, they had scouted out the homes they were charged with protecting, familiarized themselves, prepped the property. "Firefighters, being the creatures that they are, went ballistic," said Berry. "They were not happy about that, but they followed orders. That is what they had to do. So the fire was bearing down on us and we had houses that were unprotected because of the shift change. We had spots that were starting a thousand feet ahead of the main front."

Getting the new strike teams assigned was not an easy task. They hailed from the Bay Area, L.A. city, and Orange County. None of them were familiar with the front country above Rancho Cucamonga, so Berry had to give them a safety briefing. By the time he got the engines deployed into the area, fire was already coming down off the hill, heading toward the easternmost houses on Snowdrop.

Berry didn't like how things were panning out, but matters shortly got worse. While he worked on situating the new engines, strike team leader Eric Moore, who had several units stationed at the homes and water tanks at the top of Archibald, contacted him over the radio and informed him that a hotshot crew was conducting a firing operation along the dozer line that followed the powerlines down below. Berry couldn't believe it. That was the craziest thing he had ever heard of— there was nothing stopping that fire from racing uphill at his men and him on Snowdrop.

Perhaps the hotshot crew had gotten confused. Communication hadn't been the best between structure protection and perimeter control, and perhaps the hotshots hadn't been told that there were homes north of the powerlines. If they had known that four strike teams of engines were hunkered out in the brush, there was no way they would have dropped fire down below. Whatever they were thinking, Berry and his men were in a good deal of trouble. They were on a midslope road, and now they had fire coming at them from the bottom, across from the east, and down from the north. They were faced with three fire fronts. It was the perfect storm.

If only they had burned off the dozer line above Snowdrop, none of this would be happening. The fire they dropped to the ground would have run uphill, right into the mouth of the Grand Prix. It would have left a huge chunk of blackened earth around all the homes, and the Grand Prix would've had no choice but to find a way around Snowdrop. But the firing operation just never materialized, and Berry didn't know why. Now they had fire coming at them from all sides.

Berry contacted Mayfield and informed him of the hotshots' actions down below.

"Are you guys going to be okay?" Mayfield asked.

"We'll be okay, but we need to get them to stop the firing."

The request went up the line, all the way to the command post. A few minutes later, the hotshot crew was ordered to reholster their drip torches and catch anything they'd already lit before it could gather steam uphill. The crew followed orders, eliminating one of Berry's problems. But now that everyone up the chain of command had their eyes on Snowdrop, the debate on what to do up there grew larger. The incident command team back at Glen Helen Park began to wonder if it was safe to have engines in the area.

Mayfield didn't want to pull Berry out; he wanted to keep the engines in there and fire the dozer line above. In addition to the homes, they also needed to protect the water tanks in the area so the city didn't lose its H_2O for the upcoming battle. He made the request to Mike Rohde, who was in charge of overall structure protection, but Rohde wanted to pull Berry out. While they argued back and forth, John Forester, in charge of perimeter control in the area, jumped into the mix. He agreed with Mayfield—they should keep Berry's men embedded and fire the dozer line. He was quite adamant about this.

As things started to get heated, Berry got involved. After all, it would be his ass on the line if something went wrong. He made it quite clear that he could defend the area even if they decided against burning the dozer line. Not under any circumstances did he want to pull his engines out.

With everyone's opinion having been heard, it was time to make a decision. Division sent a firing expert up to Dave Berry to see if they could pull off the firing operation and keep the engines in place. Berry greeted the CDF fireman up on Snowdrop a few minutes later.

"How familiar are you with this area?" Berry asked.

"I have never seen it before in my life."

"Come with me," Berry said, and then led the CDF firing expert up above Snowdrop to the highest point he could reach. When they stopped, they had a perfect view of the entire area. Berry pointed out Archibald and Haven, and then all the homes along Snowdrop between the two. To him, it seemed obvious that they had to save them.

"Some of those homes will be lost," the firing expert said.

Berry didn't agree. Even though they had fire coming at them from the north, east, and west, he still felt they could defend the homes. All he had wanted was for the hotshot crew to stop firing down below. He explained how he planned to handle everything several times, but then the firing expert turned to him and said, "I understand what you are saying, but it's moot."

"It's moot?"

"Yeah," he replied, and then walked away.

Berry couldn't believe what he had heard. How could saving homes be a moot point? Then, just a few minutes later, he got the official order to pull his strike teams out. This made his blood boil; the decision to pull him out had already been made prior to sending up the firing expert. He knew he could defend the homes, but now the arguing had come to an end and he had to follow orders. He headed back down to Snowdrop and informed all the strike teams that they were being ordered out.

"We're not going," said a battalion chief from Montebello.

"I know it's hard, but you have to," Berry reasoned. "Don't do this—you've got to go. Our orders are our orders, don't go insubordinate. This is not the time or the place to argue."

The battalion chief agreed, but Berry could tell that it broke his heart to abandon his post. It broke everyone's heart up on Snowdrop, including those who had made the decision to pull the strike teams out. They had basically written off all of the structures. "We didn't have the communications that we should have, and that is where you get into trouble," said Mayfield. "We had to pull our guys out of there because a hotshot crew fired around us and got us trapped in there. It was coming from one side, the other side, and then the top, and then it is too much to handle. If it comes from one side or the other it is fine, but when you get a triangulation, you get too much heat all at once. So we pulled them out."

As the strike teams slowly moved out of the area, Berry stopped by to see Ron Noreen, a retired Upland firefighter who had a home on Snowdrop. Throughout the course of the day, Berry had helped Noreen prep his home for the coming assault, but now he had to tell them that they were leaving.

"What!" Noreen shouted. "You've got to be kidding me."

"Ron," Berry said gently, "you need to leave too."

Noreen shook his head. "I'm not going."

"Well, I just had to tell you that."

"I understand, but that is a bunch of bull. I don't blame you guys, but the guys at the top . . . I just don't get it."

"I know," Berry said, patting him on the shoulder. "I know."

Fifteen minutes later, Safety Officer Dennis King found Noreen in his front yard. He was sitting on his quad, looking with tears in his eyes at the personal fire hoses he had laid out for the battle. The two headed off Snowdrop together.

24

A Last-Ditch Effort

Fifteen minutes before the overhead ordered Dave Berry to remove his strike teams, Fulton Hotshots captain Jake Cagle had begun firing off the north side of the dozer line above Snowdrop. He could have done this much earlier in the day, but it had been made very clear to him not to drop any fire until the Grand Prix came honking down the mountain. Well, the Grand Prix was now honking down the mountain.

For the first quarter of a mile everything went perfect. The fire Cagle and his men dropped raced uphill and met with the Grand Prix. The two came together, flared up, and then lay down. Cagle felt confident that he could get the entire dozer line burned off before the Grand Prix reached the homes, but then the fire behavior became erratic, just as it had for the past three days. A fire whirl filled with embers and ash lifted off up in the mountains, hovered for a few moments, and then headed south, straight over the dozer line and the homes along Snowdrop. It touched down just north of the powerlines and instantly the chaparral went up in flame.

This complicated matters. Cagle now had a spot fire directly below him, and it grew in size every second. In a matter of minutes, it would begin racing uphill toward Snowdrop, pinching Cagle and his men between the spot fire and the Grand Prix.

Cagle snatched up his radio and contacted Bollier, who was currently helping Linch steer the dozer line around the Upper King's Ranch to the west.

"We aren't going to be able to hold it," Cagle said. "We have spots down below us and we've lost it."

"Play it safe," Bollier returned. "Head back down to the top of Haven and get with division. Get down there and reassess; see what you can do."

Cagle pulled his men out. When they reached the top of Haven, the overhead from structure protection and perimeter control were debating whether to keep engines positioned along Snowdrop. It was getting heated, and eventually division made the call to pull them out. As the train of engines reluctantly abandoned their post, Cagle watched as the fire advanced on the structures up on Snowdrop. The longer he stood there, the more anxious he began to feel. He couldn't just watch those homes burn.

He waited and watched for twenty minutes, and then the wind began to die down again, just as he had predicted. It seemed like on every fire, no matter how calm it had been throughout the day, the moment they began a firing operation Mother Nature suddenly threw her worst at them. Then, the moment they pulled out, she would relax. Cagle waited a few more minutes to make sure it wasn't just a temporary lull, and when the winds remained calm, he made the decision to head back to Snowdrop. The fire activity in the area might have been too dangerous for a group of engines or even an entire hotshot crew, but he felt quite comfortable heading back in with just one other crew member to complete the firing operation around the homes.

He got his lookouts in place, positioning the most important one right there at the top of Haven Avenue. The lookouts would keep an eye on the mountain above, and if the fire really started cranking down the hill at the structures, they would notify Cagle and his helper to get out of Dodge. They would also keep an eye on the spot fire started by the fire whirl below Snowdrop. As long as he had those lookouts in place, he felt comfortable going back up there. After all, he had to do something.

A few minutes later, Cagle and his fellow crew member moved through the smoke and ash up on Snowdrop, searching for the best place to restart their firing operation. They found the location where their previous burn had ended, and they laid fire on the ground, hoping it would keep the advancing Grand Prix north of the structures. They managed to get another structure fortified, but then the winds picked back up again. Division down below got nervous, and they contacted Cagle by radio and ordered him out of the area.

Cagle followed orders, but he pulled only halfway out. Standing on the one-lane road extending off Haven, halfway between division down below and Snowdrop up above, he watched as the Grand Prix drew closer to the homes. Eventually, he made a judgment call. He decided to head back up there and fire another piece. He got on the radio and contacted Bollier, who had finished navigating the dozers around the Upper King's Ranch farther to the west, and told him what he planned to do. It was going to be a hairy operation, so Bollier rushed right over.

Once Bollier arrived, the three of them headed back into the mayhem. Despite the smoke and ash cutting their visibility to practically nothing, they managed to get the eastern portion of the dozer line above Snowdrop burned off, which would serve as a buffer for half a dozen homes. They were going to pull out, but Cagle didn't feel comfortable leaving the homes on the western portion of Snowdrop without doing something to prep them. He wanted to burn around those homes as well, so he left Bollier and his fellow crew member and hiked farther down Snowdrop. When he saw a patch of brush backed right up against a house, he swung his drip torch in an arc and burned it off. He worked at a feverish pace, trying to get everything before the Grand Prix arrived.

Bollier backed out to the extension off Haven so he could get a better view of what was going on. Keeping an eye on the Grand Prix up above, he clutched his radio, ready to pull his boy out at the first sign of danger. Danger, however, came from where he least expected it—down below. The game plan had been to burn the midslope dozer line above Snowdrop, which was just what Cagle was trying to do, but down below, just north of the long row of homes, another hotshot crew began burning off the secondary dozer line by the powerlines.

Bollier didn't know why this was being allowed to transpire—not yet, at least. All afternoon they'd had a plan to burn the dozer line by the powerlines. They would start the burn operation at Haven Avenue, and then pass it off from one crew to the next, taking it as far west as possible. But before any of that happened, the plan had been to do everything they could to save Snowdrop. Apparently, forces down below thought Snowdrop had already been lost.

With his eyes flicking from north to south, Bollier monitored the hotshots' operation to make sure it didn't endanger Cagle, who was still up along Snowdrop. Everything went all right at first, but then Bollier heard one of the crew members firing by the powerlines say over the radio, "We lost it." At first Bollier wondered how the hell they could have lost it—they were backed right up against the homes. But when he caught sight of their operation through all the smoke, he saw that they had lost it into the hedges in people's backyards.

"You just had to be really heads-up on how you fired a piece of ground," said Bollier. "If there was ever a way to fire a piece of ground, you'd better know some tactics. If not, you were going to put fire on the ground and it was going to go right over the top of your head. And I'm sure that is what happened—not to say it wouldn't have happened to us. It is going to happen. In those conditions all you can do is have a good offensive attack, and then you need to go into defense. It is kind of one of those catch-22s—you can't go right into defense. That is like saying, 'Let the fire come down and slam the structures without doing anything.' You can't do that—I can't do that. At least try."

The Grand Prix attacks the incident command post at Glen Helen Park.

With the hotshot crew having lost control of their firing operation, flames swept uphill toward Snowdrop. Bollier immediately contacted Cagle on the radio.

"In addition to the fire above you, you now have fire coming up from underneath you."

"I got it," Cagle responded.

"I want you to take a moment and look around. When I flew in the helicopter earlier in the day, I saw that there was a pool somewhere around there. Do you see it?"

"I see it."

"Well, if you get into any trouble, don't hesitate to jump in."

Cagle knew that when Bollier said such a thing, it was getting very close to the right time to leave. He looked around through the thick smoke, trying to find his escape routes. "Ron," he said over the radio, "could you turn on your lights? I want to see where you are at."

Bollier flipped on his overhead lights, and Cagle spotted them immediately. "I'm not jumping in any pool," he said back. "I'm done here."

Cagle took a few minutes to put the finishing touches on his burn, and then he navigated through the network of houses and found his way back to Bollier on Haven. The three of them looked up on the mountainside, at the fire shooting down onto the Snowdrop homes. They hoped their hard work would pay off, but there was no time to hang around and find out. In San Bernardino not twenty miles to the east, a fire that had started earlier in the day was getting out of hand. The minimal troops assigned to the blaze were getting their butts kicked. For an hour they had been screaming over the radio for reinforcements, so now Rancho Cucamonga was actually losing resources in its most critical hour. If they were going to stop the Grand Prix from wrecking the entire northern portion of the city, every firefighter had to suck it up and toe the line.

25

The Old Fire

After working on the Grand Prix all night and well into Saturday morning, the Del Rosa Hotshots hopped into their crew buggies a little past daybreak and headed down the 210 freeway toward their station, which was located in the foothills above the community of Del Rosa in San Bernardino. While en route, they heard over the radio that a fire had started in Area 36A. At first they thought there had been a mistake—Area 36A was right above their station. Every crew member looked toward the horizon, and sure enough, they saw a helitanker off in the distance dropping a load of retardant. Judging by the smoke column, the fire had most likely started somewhere on Old Waterman Canyon Road.

The cloud of smoke had grown considerably by the time they pulled into their Forest Service compound. In the old days, the crew would most likely have sharpened their tools and then headed right back out on the line. Jeff Koenig, the crew's superintendent, had fought fire since 1980, and back when he'd first started it wasn't uncommon for a hotshot crew to pull a twenty-hour shift, sleep one or two hours, and then leap right back into the action. But after a number of deaths, those ungodly workdays had been abolished. Koenig generally found the new work/rest guidelines appealing, especially now that he was responsible for twenty young lives, but at the current moment the rules stood in his

144

OLD FIRE — SATURDAY MORNING

Old Fire

Old Fire

Quail Canyon Road

Del Rosa Forest
Service Compound

David Way

Quail
Canyon
Road

E 40th St.

Del Rosa/San Bernardino

way. He wanted to attack this blaze before it got established and threatened his station.

Koenig called his superiors, but they told him to call it quits. There wasn't much else he could do, so he had all his men officially clock out at ten in the morning, approximately forty-five minutes after the new fire had started. Other than a few crew members who currently stayed in the station's barracks, everyone jumped into their personal vehicles and headed home. Koenig did the same, but along the drive he flipped on the radio and listened to the fire traffic. His stomach began to turn as he heard that the blaze, now labeled the Old Fire, was making a strong push toward the Del Rosa community. Having worked in the area for nearly two decades, he knew that a wind-driven fire pushing down into San Bernardino could quickly become a killer. When it came to fire in the foothills, history had a way of repeating itself.

In the San Bernardino Mountains, at 9:30 A.M. on November 24, 1980, an arsonist started a fire in Waterman Canyon a mile below Panorama Point. Jerry Newcome, fire chief of San Bernardino at the time, traveled up to the origin of the blaze shortly thereafter. The area hadn't received any rainfall in approximately six months, and there were strong Santa Ana winds blowing out of the northeast that day. Immediately Newcome knew where the fire was heading—straight down into his city.

The fire still burned in Forest Service jurisdiction, but the Forest Service already had its hands full. "We had a series of fires that took place," said Rocky Oplinger, who worked on a hotshot crew at the time. "We had a fire called the Thunder Fire that actually started before the Panorama, so that was where most of the hotshot crews ended up. We ended up in Ice Box Canyon up on the Angeles National Forest, so a lot of resources weren't available that morning when the Panorama Fire took off. And then a third fire took off on the Cleveland National Forest called the Indian Fire."

Under fierce Santa Ana winds, a Southern California fire siege had begun. Newcome returned to home base to prepare his city. He ordered engines from around the state and called in aircraft. Many of the engines, however, had to travel great distances to get there, and time was the last thing they had to spare. And aircraft didn't prove to be the clincher Newcome hoped it would be. The first pilot to take off struggled to keep his plane steady under the high winds, and he quickly canceled all of the airtankers. One sheriff's helicopter trying to work up into Waterman Canyon, in fact, reported that he was flying at an airspeed of ninety miles per hour, but when he looked down at the ground he saw he was actually creeping backwards.

The fire was coming, and there was nothing Newcome or the various fire agencies could do to stop it. By early afternoon, it had crawled out of the timber and chewed though dense thickets of chaparral along the foothills. "It burned down into the city under the wind, and spread very quickly and started destroying homes," said Newcome. "Between one o'clock and two o'clock, we lost 285 homes. Even though firefighters were familiar with the area, it was hard to know where you were with so many houses burning. You couldn't see street signs; you couldn't see anything. It would start on a block and just ignite, and then it was jumping ahead. The flying firebrands would go easily half a mile or more, and then catch other roofs on fire. We had a captain, a San Bernardino City captain, who came in and made the decision on his own house. He arrived, and it was so far gone that he passed it up and kept going down until he found one that he could save."

In all, four people died. Two of the victims were an elderly couple. They had packed up their vehicle and escaped the blaze, but then returned home to save their pets. Before they could reach their driveway, a hundred-foot wall of flame swept over them. Another was a middle-aged man who had been standing on the roof of his house near the periphery of the blaze. Upon seeing fire sweep over hundreds of homes, he had a heart attack, fell off his roof, and died. The last was an elderly woman in the neighboring city of Ontario who had been so concerned about fire reaching her home that she too had a heart attack. Investigators arrested a man who they believed set the blaze, but with four counts of murder now stacked on top of the arson charge, he refused to admit to any wrongdoing. They eventually released him from custody.

Jeff Koenig did not want a repeat of the Panorama Fire. He worried about the residents of San Bernardino, and he also worried about his compound. With the majority of his station's troops fighting the Grand Prix over in Rancho Cucamonga, the compound was defenseless.

Although Koenig didn't know it at the time, that wasn't correct. Inside the main building of the Del Rosa Forest Service station was a ten-man module from the Redding Hotshots, watching television. They weren't like most hotshot crews. Instead of being made up of a bunch of young men and women who'd proved themselves out on the line year after year to get on a hotshot crew, they had been pieced together from engine captains, helitack captains, and other firefighting veterans in search of more training. Because of this, the incident management team on the Grand Prix had been pressuring them to demobilize, return to their stations in Northern California, and then come back down leading their former crews. The Redding Hotshots were fine by this as long as they got to remain in the fight, but there was a problem. One of the crew's buggies had been red-tagged due to a brake problem. For the past several hours, a mechanic at the Del Rosa station had been working on it.

As they relaxed in the lounge area, watching television, two crew members got bored and walked outside. They came back less than a minute later with concerned looks on their faces. They approached the module's captain, Patrick Smith, and told him that it looked like there was another fire just north of the station.

Finding it hard to believe that yet another wildfire had broken, Smith shrugged his shoulders. "Probably just someone cooking on their barbecue."

The two crew members went back outside. This time they returned in just a few seconds. "No, you seriously have to check this out."

At that point, the entire module was interested. They all got up and headed out the door. Sure enough, just northwest of the station smoke billowed up into the blistering morning air. "Ah shit," Smith said. "This isn't going to be good."

As the crew went back into the lounge, the radio went crazy. From the sound of the transmissions, they still hadn't put any major resources on the fire. Smith sent his men to gear up, and while they pulled tools off their vehicle, Smith contacted his superintendent, Robert Holt, who'd spent the last hour with the crew's second ten-man module at Glen Helen Park, trying to get their release papers taken care of.

"I don't know if you guys want to come up to the Del Rosa station," Smith said. "There is another fire up here."

"I know," Holt responded. "We can see it from the highway and have been listening on the radio. We're about halfway there. We're going to meet you up there."

After he got off the radio with Holt, Smith contacted dispatch but got no answer. With practically every firefighting resource in the area currently positioned over in Rancho Cucamonga, dispatch was probably busy scrambling for people. Smith decided to leave a message. He said, "There is one module from the Redding Hotshots at the Del Rosa station. We are going to stay here and see what happens."

Before they could make a move, however, they first had to get their vehicle running. One crew member went into the shop, and the job that the mechanics had originally said would take an hour and a half quickly became a twenty-minute job. It became like a NASCAR scene in there, and once the mechanics had finished, they didn't even bother to wash their hands—they just hopped in their personal vehicles and sped away. A few minutes later, all the Forest Service logistics employees working at the station came out into the parking lot and said that they were evacuating.

Thirty minutes after the Redding crew first noticed the smoke in the near distance, the station had cleared out. If Smith's predictions were correct, the blaze would most likely sweep right across their current location in just a few hours. It was a beautiful station, but surprisingly vulnerable to fire. Located up on the mountainside, it had only one escape route: a narrow S-curve road that led down to the bulk of the city in the flats. Once the fire hit, that road would be cut off, and then the only other way to head would be up the S-curve road, but that only led to dozens of million-dollar homes higher in the mountains. Smith realized that if they were going to stay and fight there would most likely be no leaving until the fire had passed through, so he looked around the compound, which consisted of approximately a dozen buildings. Unlike the foothills over in Rancho, there were trees everywhere, massive eucalypti. Although there was good defensible space around the compound, if the Old Fire proved to be anything like the Grand Prix, then they would be dealing with hundred-foot flame lengths. And when it came to hundred-foot flame lengths, good defensible space meant little.

Smith was prepared to defend the compound, but he also thought that the Del Rosa Hotshots should know about the current situation. He had Koenig's cell phone number in his pocket, but he wasn't sure of the correct protocol. There had always been a little tension between hotshot crews from the north of the state and those from the south, and he didn't want to cross any kind of line. So instead of calling Koenig, he called Holt, who was still in transit.

"What should I do?" Smith asked.

"Give it a few more minutes, see what happens. If things start to go south, get him on the horn."

Just as Smith reholstered his radio, two of his crew members came running up. Apparently, several members of the Del Rosa Hotshots were asleep in the barracks, totally clueless to what was transpiring just north of their station. Smith's entire module rolled into the barracks and roused the sleeping crew members. The minute they learned what was going on, they got Koenig on the phone.

"I got a call from one of my crewmen telling me that they were evacuating the compound," Koenig later said. "I asked him how much time he thought we had, and he said thirty or forty minutes. I called the chief here on the forest, and he pretty much said, 'Do whatever it is you have to do. We are really limited on resources.' I told him that I was going to activate the crew again. That's when we all started to head back to defend our compound. I personally had a twenty-minute drive."

While the majority of the Del Rosa crew was en route to the station, Smith worked with his ten-man module to get the area prepped for the anticipated assault. They pushed all the vehicles that were parked along the perimeter of the compound out into the center of the parking lot— the last thing they wanted was for the cars to catch fire and explode. They found stacks of plywood underneath a couple of decks, so they removed that as well. Then they took all the patio furniture they found lying around and chucked it out into the woods. Two of their female crew members found a ladder, and they ran around to a few of the houses near the station and put sprinklers on top of them. Another of the crew's female members served as a lookout. The moment the fire got close, she would let everyone know so they could get aggressive.

The trigger point, they decided, would be when the fire came over the top of the ridge directly above the station. There was a small shack up there, and the minute they either saw that shack go up in flames or fire shoot over the lip of the ridge, they would throw fire of their own to the ground. They knew that once the fire got over the ridge, there would be heavy lift. When they lit their fire at the bottom of the hill, they hoped the convective heat would take their fire and send it straight up to the main body of fire rather than blowing it back on them. They figured the only way to be certain was to go for it.

As the module got everything set for their burning operation, Koenig and five other members of his crew arrived at the compound. Just below the station, in the community of Del Rosa, police went from door to door, evacuating everyone off the streets. A series of roadblocks had been set up, and not all of the Del Rosa crew had made it through. One of Koenig's captains, Frank Espendito, managed to maneuver past the roadblock and park at his parents' house, which happened to be directly below the station. When Koenig discovered his location, he jumped in a vehicle and went to pick him up. The rest of the crew, however, was stuck farther south behind police barricades.

Between the ten-man module from the Redding Hotshots and the seven crew members from Del Rosa that had made it up to the station, they had a full team. Before Koenig picked up where Redding had left off, he gave everyone a moment to calm down. The possibility of having to defend their own compound had rattled a few Del Rosa crew members, and Koenig needed everyone thinking sharp.

Once everyone had taken a breather and regained their composure, Koenig started talking safety. He told them that after the fire swept over-top of them, there was a high probability that it would cut off the road leading down to the city, which meant that they might be trapped up there for some time. But just because they didn't have an escape route didn't mean that they would be in danger. The station had a massive parking lot sitting in the middle of all the structures. If things got too hectic, they could always retreat to the middle of the parking lot and lie down. Things would probably get pretty smoky and warm, but they would be all right.

With everyone knowing what to do in case of an emergency, Koenig took the group on a tour around the compound. They had a radio shop, an automotive shop, a training center, barracks, Koenig's office, and half a dozen other outbuildings. As Koenig pointed out each building, he either labeled it "worth saving" or "not worth saving." With that said, he broke everyone up into two teams. The first team would be responsible

Firefighters try to save the Del Rosa Forest Service compound as the Old Fire comes through.

for fighting the fire itself, following through with Smith's plan by burning around the structures before the fire could reach them. The second
team would be responsible for protecting structures as the fire swept
through the compound. Koenig reminded everyone that the key was not
to drop fire too soon—they had to wait until they saw the flames right on
top of them. There were dozens of private homes located around the
compound, and the last thing they wanted was to be implicated in burning them to the ground.

Just as everyone fell into position, sixty-five-mile-per-hour winds
came shooting over the ridge and into their faces. Smoke poured into the
area, clouding their vision, but there was no mistaking the bright orange
glow above them. Team one immediately dropped fire on the ground
with their drip torches, and, just as they had expected, it took off up the
hill and was swallowed by the main fire. "It broke the back of the fire as
it came down," said Koenig. "It slowed down quite a bit, but it still went
over the top, fired over the compound, and kind of rolled through and
started burning structures in the neighborhood down below."

With numerous spot fires located throughout the ten-acre compound, as well as wildfire raging to their immediate east and west, the
seventeen crew members trapped at the Del Rosa compound began three
of the hardest, most heartbreaking hours of their lives.

Robert Holt, superintendent of the Redding Hotshots, decided not to
bring the crew's second ten-man module up to the Del Rosa compound.
Those were his boys up there, and they were in for the fight of their lives,
but he also had to think about the bigger picture. The wind howled, and
no matter how many firefighters they had up at the station, there was no
way they would be able to hold the fire up on the mountain. It would
jump right over them and come tearing down into the city.

Thousands of homes could be lost. Nearly every engine and firefighter, including those from San Bernardino, was currently stationed
over on the Grand Prix. San Bernardino was a sitting duck, and someone needed to protect the homes. Holt knew the main devastation would
not come from the main body of fire sweeping through the area, but
rather from small fires created by the millions upon millions of embers
that would waft through the streets once the fire had passed. In these
winds, it would only take a single ember to catch a roof or a porch on

fire. It wouldn't take much to put out those fires, but if left unattended, they would soon claim home after home.

He reached the S-curve road leading up to the Del Rosa station just past eleven o'clock, but instead of heading up, he turned right down a street that paralleled the base of the mountain. He drove through the smoke past fleeing citizens and police barricades, searching for a safe place to park his buggy while maneuvering through the traffic jam. Eventually he found a house that had a big front yard. Holt pulled into the driveway, parked, and then got out and looked around. Once he was certain that there was nothing in the immediate area that could catch the buggy on fire, he told the rest of the crew to join him.

Holt began breaking down the game plan, but a police officer interrupted his speech. "Hey, can you help this lady?" the officer said, pointing down the road. "She's going nuts."

"What's going on?" Holt returned.

"She says her baby is trapped in an apartment somewhere around here."

Holt told the crew to hang tight, and then he went down and talked to her. For the first few minutes she babbled incoherently, but Holt finally managed to calm her down.

"My baby is in my apartment complex, and I can't get to her," she cried. "I don't know if the father is there or not; no one is answering the phone."

Holt looked to the north. The fire would come tearing down at any minute and he needed to get his crew prepared. But saving lives always came first. "What's the address?"

The lady gave it to him and he ran back to his crew. They all hopped in the buggy, and a few minutes later they had found the apartment complex. Holt and a few of his men raced up the stairs. When they burst through the door, they found the father cradling his baby in his arms, huddled on the floor.

"What are you still doing here?" Holt wanted to know.

"I'm waiting for my wife. She hasn't come back yet."

"She's back at the police barricades. You need to get out of here right now."

The father agreed, and Holt gave him directions on how to reunite with his wife. The moment he stepped out of the apartment, however, an eerie feeling crept through him. The sun had been partially eclipsed by the smoke, and millions of embers swirled though the air. Other than his eight crew members in the buggy parked down below, there wasn't a soul on the street.

Time was running out, so Holt raced back to the buggy, hopped in, and then drove back to the house with the massive yard. Immediately he briefed his crew on what he wanted. "The big wave front is going to come through," he told them. "It's going to get real hot, real hairy. You need to duck down behind structures, behind cars, whatever you need to duck behind when that thing hits. Afterwards, the structure guys are going to try to keep up with the flames. They are just like moths going to the light. But what happens when they leave is all the little embers and stuff is going to burn the houses down. The embers will get into eaves and plants and burn down the houses. So that is going to be our job, to put everything out once it catches on fire. It doesn't look like anyone else is here, so that is going to be our job."

Holt broke the team down into five two-man modules. To ensure their safety, he pulled out a map and gave everyone their boundaries. Although the entire community would most likely need saving, he drew a box that went from 40th Street to David. He suspected that because the designated area was to the southwest of the Del Rosa station, it would get hit pretty bad. There were approximately a hundred and fifty houses in the area, and that was all he thought they could handle. No matter what the crew saw happening off in the distance, they were not to go beyond those boundaries. If shit hit the fan, he wanted everyone close enough to help each other.

Once everyone knew the game plan, they fell in behind a couple of structure engines parked at the top of North David. Moments later, the fire hit. The structure guys did an excellent job of dousing the blaze with their hoses and protecting structures from the main front, but once the head had passed by, shooting down into the residential area under sixty-mile-per-hour winds, all the engines pulled out. That's when Holt's ten-man module got to work.

Holt remained at the top of North David, moving through apartment complexes, extinguishing small spot fires on roofs and in yards with a garden hose. His crew boss trainee took the southern border of their designated box, and then another two-person squad worked through a neighborhood in the middle. As they pushed through the wind and smoke, searching for any sign of flame, powerlines came down around them and lawn furniture tumbled down the street. Because of the noise, they had not only lost communication with Smith's module up at the Del Rosa station, but also with one another. They resorted to hand signals and shouting over the wind.

As Holt worked through the neighborhood, he came across citizens who had not gotten out in time. They had stayed to gather up their valuables and then became trapped. By this point, houses were burning all around, and they needed all the help they could get. When Holt came across civilians, he tossed them a length of hose and gave a quick lesson on what to do. Pretty soon, he had a small force of residents helping him fight the blaze.

Things got hairier by the moment, and that worried Holt because anything that came their way had to first pass over the Del Rosa station. He could only imagine what the other half of his crew was up against.

After breaking the back of the main body of fire, the seventeen hotshots up at the Del Rosa station retreated from the hillside on the north side of the station. With sixty-mile-per-hour winds howling across the compound, several spot fires had started simultaneously. First they had to save the saw shop, and then Koenig's office. A little later on, they were forced to do another firing operation around the barracks, which was on the verge of getting overrun by flame.

The battle got intense, which shook several crew members from the Redding Hotshots. They were accustomed to fighting fire deep in the woods where there were clear escape routes and safety zones. Trapped in the middle of a very flammable compound didn't sit well in their stomachs, so they quickly grouped together and devised a game plan. They decided that if things got too hectic, they would all hop in their truck and bolt down the S-curve road into the city. Knowing how fast things could go south, they kept one of their crew members in the truck at all times with the engine running, and every half hour or so the driver would head a short ways down the road to ensure that powerlines hadn't fallen over and blocked their escape.

It made the ten Redding crew members feel a whole lot safer, which allowed them to get their heads back into the fight. Currently they possessed four hundred feet of hose. It wouldn't allow them to do much, so they scouted around the compound. A few minutes into their mission, they discovered three old fire engines tucked away, and when they checked the cargo holds, they hit a jackpot—another five hundred feet of hose. They quickly broke down into two-man teams and distributed the hose among them. Before going their separate ways, they made sure every team had a working radio so they could communicate.

Crew members scurried around the compound with an armload of hose, passing by the structures Koenig had labeled as "don't save" without a second glance. When they found an important structure burning, they hooked their length of hose up to the nearest nozzle, doused the flames before they really got going, and then moved on to the next building. While on this hunt, one of the teams noticed that a fire had started on a building with a canopy roof, and they rushed forward to save it. Along the way, however, they passed a flaming trailer that served as a storage shed. Inside there was paint and thinner stacked knee high, all of it burning. As two crew members rounded a corner, a toxic cloud of smoke hit them. It was so nasty and foul that it dropped them to their knees. Other crew members quickly hefted them up and stuck them into

The Del Rosa community devastated by the Old Fire.

the truck so they could get a breath of fresh air. By the time they recovered, two more hacking crew members replaced them. Because they didn't wear respirators like municipal firefighters, they inhaled all sorts of nasty fumes from the burning structures. In less than half an hour, each crew member had to spend a few minutes inside the crew buggy to recover.

With Redding circling the compound, several crew members from Del Rosa tried to save a private home just to the west of their station. They knew the owners of the home quite well, and they had all fallen in love with their dog, Conrad. But despite their best efforts, the house collapsed floor by floor. "The Del Rosa guys went to extraordinary efforts to try and not let that house go up," said Smith. "They were putting themselves at great risk. . . . But we only had eight guys with garden hoses."

No matter how tragic, watching homes burn to the ground was nothing new for the Del Rosa crew, which was responsible for fighting wildfire in one of the most densely populated urban/wildland interface areas in the United States. But for the Redding crew members, based out of Northern California, it was entirely new. Witnessing fellow hotshots bust their asses to save a home inspired them, so after defending the compound for more than an hour, the Redding Hotshots decided to see if they could save any of the homes along the S-curve road that wound farther up into the foothills.

Still teamed up in pairs, they exited the compound and dragged their hose down the street to the north. But moving forward proved difficult. Several times Smith looked down at his wind meter, and each time it was pegged out at sixty miles per hour. They kept their chin straps down so their helmets didn't blow off, and they squinted to shield their eyes against the pebbles, sparks, and other debris that whipped at them like bullets.

When they reached the first house, it was already engulfed in flame. One of the two-man crews broke off to see if they could save it while the other four teams forged ahead. They did this over and over for a quarter of a mile. In all, they tried to save more than a dozen houses by hooking their hoses up to spigots and then dousing the roof, the porch, anything that was on fire. "There was only one house that didn't go totally down," said Smith. "We tried the best we could, but we just had these little garden hoses. When the fire on a house got too hot, we pulled the guys out and tried to get to another house. We weren't in a position to enter homes, so we were a little bit out of our element. But we gave it our best shot."

After spending another couple of hours up on the S-curves, the crew members from Redding tied back in with Koenig and his group, which had been busy putting out spot fires in the compound. As bad as the Redding guys felt from breathing in smoke for the past four hours, they knew the Del Rosa guys were feeling much worse. "Any time you are protecting your own piece of land, there is a lot of emotions that go with that because you have a lot invested," said Koenig. "That is the place where you work. That is the place you call home when you are at work. There was just a lot of reasons to hang in there and do the very best we could protecting it. And that is our job; that is what we do. We had people on the crew who were worried about their homes, which were being threatened within the immediate fire area. One of my captains, Frank Espendito, wasn't able to get to the compound so he had to park his vehicle at his parents' house. We went down to pick him up so he could get through the roadblock, but by the time we were able to get back down there to see if everything was still okay, it wasn't. His parents had lost their house, his truck. It hit home. It became very personal then. . . . But they still hung in there, and nobody asked to go home. They had a job to do."

The crew members from Redding were willing to stay around, help Del Rosa out in any way they could, but Koenig told them that they could handle it from there. After mopping up a little more, Smith jumped on the radio and contacted Holt, who was still struggling with his module to extinguish fires a few hundred yards to the southwest. By this point, the entire northern portion of San Bernardino was burning.

"I got a call from B mod, from Patrick, after the main front had gone through town," said Holt. "He said that his guys were absolutely done, that they had sucked down enough smoke. I agreed. Personally, I couldn't think straight anymore. Everyone was just puking and could not function anymore. It finally got to the point where I told the guys 'This is it—let's head out to the 210 freeway and head north.'"

The two modules met back up fifteen minutes later at a gas station below Del Rosa, and as they drove toward their hotel all they could see was fire off in the distance, both in San Bernardino and Rancho Cucamonga. There was no doubt in their minds—it would be one hell of a night for every man and woman out on the line.

26

Hermosa

Back in Rancho Cucamonga, two of the homes up on Snowdrop were already totally involved with fire. Dave Berry hadn't given up on them. After pulling his troops down to Archibald, he had taken a strike team of engines over to the top of Haven hoping to get back onto Snowdrop from the west side once the fire had moved through, but the moment he got over there, he realized that it wasn't a possibility. With all the smoke and ash in the air, they couldn't see ten feet in front of them. In addition to that, a water line had broken up there and washed out a section of the road.

Kevin Woods, a Rancho fire investigator, eventually managed to get in there on his own, and he actually saved a house by extinguishing spot fires right on top of the structure with nothing but a shovel and some dirt. But Snowdrop soon got too hot and heavy. When Woods came back coughing and sputtering, he said that three homes had been lost for certain and another sustained serious damage. Berry realized that his troops could do nothing more in the area, and he returned to the top of Archibald to defend homes in the area. Before he got to see any of the action, however, the Grand Prix would first sweep across the Hermosa structure group between Haven and Archibald. With the major north-south artery ending out in the interface directly south of Snowdrop, it would be a fight.

Fire Marshal Mike Bell supervised the Hermosa structure group, and even though he hadn't seen a lick of fire all day, it had been stressful nonetheless. The main issue was that he didn't have a clue as to what was happening outside his designated area. He couldn't see more than fifty feet because of all the smoke, there were no field observers giving updates because of the amount of activity, and there was no air reconnaissance because of the high winds. Everyone who wasn't up on Snowdrop in the thick of battle was pretty much hanging in the dark. All they could do was wait.

Bell had used the time to prepare as best he could, spreading the three strike teams of engines assigned to him throughout his structure group, with the majority of them going to an area they called the Woods. It had garnered that name because a high-end residential development had been built among a large grove of eucalyptus trees. It had been a fear of the fire department for many years that a fire would crown

A firefighter amid the mayhem as the Grand Prix comes through Rancho Cucamonga on Black Saturday.

through those trees, spreading embers throughout the neighborhood. A fire in the Woods could easily carry a mile or more into the city.

As evening set in and he heard increased activity over the radio, Bell decided to head up to the top of Haven Avenue to get an idea of what he would face later on. He got to witness the whole debate over what to do up on Snowdrop, and then watched as the engines' crews were forced to pull out. "That was a killer decision. That is our community, we know people who live up there," said Bell. "You talk to Dave Berry; I know that really played on their morale because that was what they were there for. That was theirs—they were going to hold that ground. Nobody got hurt, so it is hard to second-guess that, even though in your heart of hearts you think you could have saved those homes. And you probably could have."

Now that Snowdrop had been overrun, Bell knew that things would happen fast. In no time at all, the Grand Prix would slam into Hermosa, so he headed back down and took his position.

The wind hit first. Although it blew more powerfully than he could have imagined, a smile crept across his face and he recalled the prayer they had made at the Rancho structure protection meeting the night before. Typically Santa Ana winds came out of the north on a slant, just as they had Friday morning. He had feared such a wind because it would shoot fire straight down into Hermosa. But the winds he now felt came more out of the east—almost directly out of the east. Instead of hitting the homes dead-on like a bag of hammers, fire would run parallel to them.

It was a great stroke of luck, but it didn't mean they wouldn't get hit hard. Bell watched as the fire drew closer and closer, and soon the winds gathered to gale force. He got on the radio with his strike teams and told them to hang on and get into position. A moment later, the Grand Prix hit like a freight train.

There was a big drainage at the top of Hermosa that cut right between all of the homes. The fire saw its opportunity for damage, and it worked down in there. In a matter of moments, it climbed up the sides of the drainage toward the homes located on both banks. Engines positioned out in front of the homes turned on their water. As hundred-foot flame lengths reached over the rooftops like massive orange hands, firefighters hit them with all they had. They knew there was no way to put the fire out, not with a thousand hoses, but that wasn't their intent. They just wanted to beat back the flames. Once the main body of fire had passed, that was when their real work began—putting out all the spot fires in the backyards, on the rooflines, on the eaves, the patio furniture, the woodpiles, anything that would spread the fire to the houses, across the neighborhood, down to the heart of Rancho Cucamonga. They had to stop it now before it gathered steam. Some of those in the Hermosa structure protection group could remember what had happened on the Panorama Fire over in San Bernardino two decades before. Home after home after home had been lost, a chain reaction so violent once it got started that all the troops could do was pull back and watch it go.

During the heat of battle, an engine crew stationed on Hermosa noticed a water tender sitting in someone's front yard. It wasn't a fire service tender, but rather a private one. A homeowner had rented it on his own accord and parked it in his driveway. The engine crew took the hint, so they tapped into the fresh water supply and went crazy.

After half an hour of intense battle, the main body of the Grand Prix moved farther to the west, heading toward the Archibald structure group. Bell kept several units in Hermosa to catch spot fires, but he bumped the rest of his units over. Everything was working according to Rancho's plan—they would bump and run all the way out to L.A. if they had to. Every time the Grand Prix tried to come south into the city, there would be dozens of engines at the ready. They would give it hell.

What Bell didn't know, however, was that the fire front sweeping across the front country was not the only fire front the Grand Prix had in store for them. Because no aircraft could get off the ground to scout the entire blaze, anything happening up on the mountain was still a mystery. Early in the morning, the Lassen Hotshots had checked the bottom part of the fire with their burn operation as it came down into the flats, pushing it back into the mouth of Deer Canyon. But instead of sitting there, the Grand Prix had stealthily pushed to the west behind the first ridge. Throughout the course of the day, unbeknownst to everyone down in the city, the fire had worked ten miles to the west, looking for another way out into the flats. Now, as the majority of forces chased the fire sweeping from Hermosa over to Archibald, the Grand Prix prepared to send another wall of fire out the mouth of Cucamonga Canyon in the very western portion of town. In the near future, both fronts of the fire would get drawn together. Their meeting point would be the Upper King's Ranch.

27

Structure Protection vs. Perimeter Control

Strike team leader Eric Moore had five engines stationed out in the interface at the top of Archibald Avenue. With the Grand Prix having just passed Hermosa Avenue, a wall of flame quickly headed his way. He felt ready for the challenge, especially after dealing with drama for the past twenty-four hours.

The night before, he had received orders to head over to the Archibald structure group, stage his five engines at the bottom of the street with the other strike teams, and wait for Dave Berry, the RCFD captain who had preplanned the entire area. Moore had followed orders and staged at the bottom of the street, but when several of the other strike teams arrived, they blew right past him and self-deployed at the very top of the structure group on Snowdrop Street. Although everyone had been informed not to freelance, Moore understood the reasoning behind their decision. They wanted to see the most action. At this point, it had become clear to everyone out on the line that Snowdrop would be one hell of a battle.

By the time Moore received his assignment from Dave Berry, the only location left was at the top of Archibald, just a few hundred feet north of the long row of homes. Moore knew they probably wouldn't see half as much action as the strike teams up above, but at least they had followed orders. He parked his rig at the top of Archibald where it turned into an unimproved road, and then hiked several hundred yards to the north to scout his area.

Two city water tanks sat on the west side of the Archibald extension. In order to ensure a healthy water supply for firefighters across the city, they would need protecting, so he stuck his Hermosa Beach engine right next to them. Just below the water tanks, also on the west side of the street, sat a beautiful home with a kennel in the front yard. It looked like it might take some serious heat when the fire came through, so he placed his El Segundo engine on it. On the east side of the street, he had two more homes to protect. He sent his Manhattan Beach engine to protect the southernmost home, which had a large stable out in front, and he sent his Torrance Beach engine to the home just to the north of it. He held his Redondo Beach engine back. Once the fire hit, he would send them to whichever house got hit the hardest.

Then they waited. Around noon, a Fulton Hotshot crew member directing a group of dozers came down into their area. They had cut a line around the top of Snowdrop with the intention of burning off the north side of it, and now they tried to connect the line with the existing dozer line under the powerlines, located just fifty yards south of Moore's position. When the dozer operators saw the water tanks, they decided to reinforce them. They tried to cut a circle around their perimeter, but in the process they snapped a water line. Within fifteen minutes, the contents of both tanks had run down to the top of Archibald. Moore's Hermosa Beach engine crew wasn't happy. Positioned right next to the tanks, they'd planned on using the water supply to fend off the fire. Now they were limited to the small tank on their engine.

They waited some more. Around five o'clock, Moore decided to hike up toward Snowdrop to see if he could catch a glimpse of the action. Before he made it a hundred yards, he got a call from the captain of the Hermosa Beach crew still stationed at the water tanks.

"They are firing right next to me," the captain said. "There is a crew down here by the tanks and they have drip torches in their hands. They are starting to do a backfire!"

That was impossible. Moore thought everyone out on the line knew that he had four engines just north of that location. If a backfire was begun now, their escape route would be cut off. Immediately he got on the horn with Dave Berry, and Berry contacted Mayfield. The topic went straight up the chain of command, and the crew doing the lighting was told to stomp out their fire. Shortly thereafter, the debate whether to pull the units off Snowdrop began. "The overall result of that discussion was the evacuation of those strike teams," said Moore. "That was the final decision that came from the top."

Moore thought that his strike team would also get pulled out, but that didn't occur. Berry understood that they might lose several, if not all, of the structures up along Snowdrop, but he refused to lose those homes just north of Archibald. He told Moore to hang tight and give the fire hell. Moore found this ironic. The strike teams that had done everything in their power to see the most action had been evacuated. Now Moore and his men would be the only ones to confront the Grand Prix head-on in the Archibald structure protection group. That was where they had decided to draw the line, at those four homes right there at the top of Archibald.

Darkness set in. Moore squinted through the smoke, trying to see what was happening around him, but it was hard to tell who was who and what was what. He heard over the radio that a crew had begun burning the dozer line above Snowdrop, but it didn't seem to work. Before too long, fire swept across the flats below Snowdrop, running straight into the Hermosa structure group. Moore didn't know if the wall of flame had jumped over Snowdrop or if a firing operation had gotten out of hand. Perimeter control had planned throughout the day to begin a firing operation along the dozer line near the powerlines, starting at Haven Avenue. Whether it had begun or not, he didn't know. All he knew for sure was that they had a wall of flame coming right at them.

It wasn't a familiar sight—not for Moore or any of the engine crews in his strike team. They fought fire in beach cities; Redondo Beach, Hermosa Beach, Manhattan Beach. They were experts when it came to fighting fire in structures, but none of the cities in which they worked the majority of the year had any urban/wildland interface. Their entire jurisdictions were covered with cement.

Positioned on the eastern side of the Archibald extension, the Torrance crew got hit first. As flames shot over their home, they let the water fly.

"Here it comes," Moore shouted over the radio. "Fast and hard."

While the rest of the engine crews waited for their turn, something strange happened. Currently all fire activity was occurring on the east side of Archibald, which suited Moore just fine. It meant that they only had one front of fire to contend with. But for some reason a hand crew from perimeter control had taken position on the west side of Archibald, right there along the dozer line beneath the powerlines. At first Moore hadn't thought much of it. After the incident earlier in the day, he had informed all the hand crews working in the area of the exact positioning of his engines. He had told them very clearly not to drop fire on the west side of the Archibald extension because it could endanger their lives.

Apparently he hadn't made himself clear, because just as they got struck with the force of the Grand Prix, the hand crew to the west of them began dropping fire along the dozer line. The hand crew knew that they were in there—one of the flares they shot off landed on top of Hermosa Beach's engine, for Christ's sake.

Moore was dumbfounded. If the crew had done their burning operation on the east side of the Archibald extension, the fire they created would have gotten sucked into the Grand Prix and taken some of the heat off their backs. Now the opposite happened. The two fires still drew together, but with the Archibald extension standing between them, they converged directly overtop of Moore and his men. They got pounded from both sides.

As Moore worked on a game plan, things got worse. The mixing of the two fires created a fire whirl. Moore couldn't take his eyes off it—he had only seen them on film. Still in its beginning stages, the funnel was no more than four or five inches around. It sounded like a dentist's drill, screaming so loud it hurt his ears. But as it grew in size, the high-pitched whirl transformed into a deep rumble. Soon it sounded like a freight train.

Completely mesmerized, Moore watched as the innocent fire whirl grew. All the men under his command did the same. It grew and grew, and eventually it became a mini-tornado. When it had a diameter of two hundred and fifty feet, everyone decided to run. "You had to run; there was no doubt in your mind," said Moore. "It was just an orange tornado. We ran down Archibald and got behind some of the bulldozers, hunkered down behind the blades. It ended up blowing over the top of my El Segundo unit at the kennel house and the Hermosa unit that was at the tanks. At one point, one of my firefighters had to get down behind a two-foot retaining wall in a driveway. He had his hose line turned on full blast, and the water was going out about a foot and then turning around. The winds were that strong."

By the time Moore and his men got back into position, the landscape had completely changed. "Everything was on fire," said Moore. "Telephone poles, the fences, anything on the ground, the trees, everything. Everything was on fire. So we just went to town trying to get the fire extinguished."

This proved difficult for the Torrance crew. When they returned to their house on the east side of the street, their engine was out of commission. An ember had gotten sucked up into the exhaust and started a fire in their air handling system. Their pump wouldn't work, so they had no water. Instead of retreating on foot, they pulled their hoses off their engine, connected them to a generator, and then began sucking water out of a plastic swimming pool in the backyard. This worked well for about twenty minutes, until the fire burned a hole in the side of the pool and all the water drained out. Still refusing to back out, they snatched up garden hoses, stuck their thumbs over the nozzles to get a good spray, and went back at it.

The other Archibald strike teams that had been pulled off Snowdrop waited impatiently below the powerlines, picking up what they could.

The apocalyptic setting of the various structure groups in Rancho Cucamonga as the Grand Prix pulls through on the night of Black Saturday.

As the main body of fire pushed over Moore and to the west, they went with it. Moore didn't budge. In order to save the four homes in the long run, they had to hang around for at least a couple of hours. If they pulled out now to stay at the front of the action, tiny embers landing on the roofs could reduce the houses to ash.

As Moore and his men mopped up, darkness settled in, giving them a clear view of Snowdrop up above. Moore could see homes burning, and it broke his heart. He felt grateful that the homes he was charged with protecting hadn't met a similar fate. There was a moment there, just after the hand crew had begun their firing operation to the west, in which he had honestly believed he and his men wouldn't make it out alive.

He felt the Rancho Cucamonga Fire Department had planned for this fire for many years. They had local knowledge and expertise of the area. They understood what they needed to do, and they had made sure all the strike team leaders were out in their structure groups hours ahead of time, planning everything down to the last detail. "So you have years of preplanning plus thirty-six hours of on-scene preplanning. And then when the fire started hitting, all of a sudden perimeter control comes marching in, and communication didn't occur, in my opinion," said Moore. "I think it probably should have occurred a lot earlier than it did instead of waiting until decisions were imminent. And what was right and what was wrong, I don't know. I can't make that judgment as far as which technique or method should have been used. All I knew was that communication didn't happen and it wasn't discussed much. It was interesting because perimeter control was saying that we were in their way, and we were saying, 'What the hell are you doing?'"

Little did he know, the conflict between structure protection and perimeter control had only just begun.

28

A Desperate Retreat

Only moments after the Grand Prix plowed over Eric Moore, Jim Dague saw a fistfight in the street near the top of Beryl Street. The neighborhood was completely abandoned except for these two men. One was in his early twenties, the other in his fifties or sixties. The sky glowed a dark red and millions of embers swirled through the air, yet these two beat on each other with punches and kicks, seemingly ignorant of what transpired around them. It was the oddest sight Dague had ever seen.

"What the hell are you two doing?" Dague shouted as he pulled his truck up to the pair.

The two stopped fighting and peered over at him with shocked looks on their faces. The older gentleman was too pissed off to speak, so the young man did the talking. He had come up to retrieve his father from his home, which was located near the top of Beryl. His father refused to leave, so things eventually got heated. The son was so intent on saving his father's life that he had actually dragged him two entire blocks.

"The fire is about to hit, and being out in the street is the worst place for you right now," Dague said, trying to talk some sense into them. "Take your dad back into the house, shut the door, and don't come out until I tell you it's safe."

After they both agreed, Dague dropped his truck into gear and proceeded to the top of Beryl. He'd spent all morning positioning the strike teams under his command at key locations on the top of Amethyst and Beryl, the two main north-south arteries in his group, and then he'd run himself ragged around the front country. He'd gone over to Haven Avenue to check on the location of the fire. He'd stopped by the staging area at Los Osos to grab his men sacks of food. He'd spent a considerable amount of time with a strike team of engines from an American Indian reservation that he had placed at the top of Beryl—they were a bunch of young kids, and from the looks of the fire behavior he'd seen over on Haven, they would be in for a fight. He'd even had talks about safety with the Rancho engine crews he'd placed at a grouping of homes stuck out in a brush field just above Amethyst, even though he knew they would be just fine. But now that the fire was about to strike the area he was charged with protecting, he needed to stop running around and take his position.

As he neared the urban/wildland interface, it looked like a scene from the movie *Apocalypse Now*. The sky glowed with embers, the wind blowing at over fifty miles per hour. The Rancho troops he had set up over on Amethyst were trying to beat back the flames rolling through the brush field, but there was no stopping them. The fire leapt over to the side streets east of Beryl, endangering dozens of homes. Dague had placed a lot of engines up in that area, but it wasn't enough. Luckily, Rancho had spent years practicing bump-and-run drills, and now it paid off. Just as the backyards of the homes started to catch fire, strike teams from both Hermosa and Archibald rolled up.

Dague ended up with eleven strike teams for the main assault. Trying to organize and maintain the safety of that many units was hard, but luckily the strike team leaders all had their act together. They got in there and did their job. The main problem Dague encountered had to do with all the Italian cypress and ornamental vegetation people had planted in their backyards. The ember production from the fire was incredible, and soon all the cypresses were going up like Roman candles. It was everywhere, through his whole structure protection group. He ran from one end of the group to the other, shouting at engine crews to leap on fires, trying to put fires out himself. He had been on a lot of fires during his career and thought he had seen some pretty rough things, but nothing compared to watching his city burn. Over the next couple of hours, he lost four structures in his group. "There was pandemonium on the radio. That was part of the problem," said Dague. "Nobody could get a word in edgewise because we had too many structure groups on the same frequency. At the time I didn't know how we were going to get through it without seriously hurting somebody."

As it turned out, injuries lay just around the corner.

The twenty-man Lassen Hotshot crew had taken position at the top of Beryl Street, in the very western corner of the Amethyst structure group. While Jim Dague's men had still been setting up to protect the homes in the area, the Lassen crew stood under the powerlines just to the north of them, eyes locked to the west. Perimeter control had been planning a firing operation all afternoon along the dozer line near the powerlines. Now that the Grand Prix had consumed homes up on Snowdrop, it would start any minute. The Big Hill Helishots would begin laying down fire along the dozer line over by Haven Avenue, they would pass it off to the Arroyo Grande crew at the top of the Hermosa structure group, and then Arroyo Grande would pass it off to Lassen at the top of Beryl. Once Lassen had it, they would light the brush with their drip torches and send it farther west to a module of the Fulton Hotshots, which would carry the firing operation past the Rancho Cucamonga boundary. The idea was to burn as much of the brush in front of the homes as possible to lessen the impact of the Grand Prix.

The Lassen crew hoped it would be as successful as the firing operation they had conducted that morning over on the east side of Haven Avenue. That block of brush they had burned off had actually stopped the Grand Prix from ripping into the city as the sun came up. They had been rewarded accordingly. As they finished their operation at noon, residents had flocked around them, offering them cookies and sandwiches and homemade lemonade. Having spent most of their time fighting fire in the forest miles away from the nearest resident, they soaked up the attention, accepting huge hugs from women who couldn't believe they had saved their homes.

They didn't have long to relish. Around two in the afternoon they had received a call from a captain of the Fulton Hotshots, who was trying to complete a dozer line out west but had run into some trouble at the top of Beryl Street. There was some rough terrain up there, a couple of spots where the dozers couldn't go, and he needed a hand crew to help connect the dots. Lassen had jumped in their crew buggies and headed over there. They spent all afternoon following the dozers and digging line. They needed to get the line put in as fast as possible, but as they helped push the line to the west, homeowners kept corralling them into their backyards. They wanted to know if their homes had any chance of surviving, and with many of them it didn't look good.

Seeing residents desperately trying to save their homes was hard for the crew members, especially for Brian Anderson. Although he had joined a hotshot crew based out of Northern California, he had grown up in Rancho Cucamonga. As a matter of fact, he had grown up on Beryl Street. Every time a resident asked him for his help, he gave it. On one occasion, a guy was standing in his backyard, so worried about his home burning up that he was almost in tears. Anderson quickly hopped the fence to begin clearing the brush out of his backyard. It wasn't until ten minutes into this project that he stopped and looked at what he was cutting—four-inch-thick-logs of poison oak.

Despite constantly getting roped into backyards, they completed the dozer line all the way down the powerlines and around the Upper King's Ranch house. With that taken care of, the Lassen Hotshots returned to the top of Beryl Street. That was their chunk of dirt, and their job was to fire it when the time was right and then stop any fire from slopping over the dozer line and down into the homes. But there was a problem. The long, straight row of homes was not that straight after all. Just above Beryl there was a winding road that led to a cul-de-sac out in the inter- face. On the right side of the cul-de-sac stood a multimillion-dollar home with a stable and a barn. The house had been built out of good material and had plenty of defensible space, but just like the Upper King's Ranch house a half mile to the west, it was surrounded by brush. If they carried the fire directly along the dozer line near the powerline, as were the plans, they would be putting fire directly below that home. That would call for a sacrifice, and Lassen was not willing to do that.

Lassen Hotshot captain Rob Moreno did a few minutes of scouting, and he saw how they could avoid losing that home. When the firing operation moved into their area, instead of carrying it straight down the existing dozer line, they would carry it up and around the home. Once the brush around the structure had been consumed, they would then bring the firing operation back down to the dozer line and continue pushing it west to the Fulton module. It wouldn't be an easy operation, but it was worth the effort. To make it work, however, they would need another hotshot crew. But with more than fifteen miles of front country to protect, along with the Old Fire burning to the east, extra hotshot crews weren't exactly in abundance.

To fill the spot, John Bristow, Lassen's superintendent, decided to split his crew in two, just as he had done earlier in the day. Captain Rob Moreno would take charge of module 91 and conduct the burn show down along the main row of homes. Squad boss Wade Salverson would take module 92 up to the horse barn, prep the area, and then hand the burn show back down to Moreno when the time came. Bristow would flip back and forth between the two, helping out wherever he could. They had a little pep talk before they split up, everyone pumped for action.

Lassen squad boss Wade Salverson had never seen anything like it. Standing in a dirt parking lot on the east side of the ranch house above Beryl, he watched the Grand Prix growing in the distance. The wall of fire that had torn across Snowdrop came right at them. To the north, the fire front that had been creeping west all afternoon behind the first ridge-line started to come out of the mouth of Cucamonga Canyon. Things were definitely going to hell.

Then Salverson saw the Big Hill Helishots start firing the dozer line over by Haven, but within a few minutes it had jumped their line and caught the backyards of half a dozen homes on fire. The Arroyo Grande crew, which was supposed to pick up the firing operation from Big Hill, tried to burn their chunk next, and it went just as badly. For as far as Salverson could see, there was fire. It was everywhere.

Standing next to him in the dirt parking lot were crew members Matt Radkey, Brian Anderson, Kyle Esparso, and two temporary replacements. They all had drip torches in their hands, ready to pick the firing operation up from Arroyo Grande, but Salverson knew it wouldn't come to that. After seeing what happened to the other crews the moment they put their drip torches into action, the firing operation had, without a doubt, been called off. Now Salverson was more concerned about the safety of his crew.

He had never before been in this type of leadership position. Usually Captain Chuck Lewis was in charge of module 92, but he hadn't been able to make it to SoCal because of prior engagements. It was nerve-racking. Salverson knew what he could expect out of Radkey, Anderson, and Esparso because he had worked with them all summer and knew that they made wise decisions in moments of stress, but he had no clue about the temporary replacements. They had been plucked off engine crews to fill the gaps in the team. They had certainly seen their share of fire, but being engine crew members, it had probably always been from a distance. They had probably never seen anything like this. Hell, Salverson had never seen anything like this, and he had spent the last four summers standing on the front lines of some of the biggest fires in the United States.

While prepping the ranch house earlier in the day, Salverson had felt that the home's dirt parking lot would be an adequate safety zone for his men when the fire burned around them. Now he wasn't so sure. Turning his back to the advancing flame, he scouted the area for another safety zone and spotted an aluminum barn back by the stables. He rushed down there to examine the roof and rap on the walls with his fist, and then he came running back to his crew.

"If I tell everyone to get in the barn," he shouted over the wind, "I want everyone to get into the barn."

They waited a few minutes to see what would happen, but it didn't take long for things to go bad. Arroyo Grande got the hell kicked out of them just to the east with the fire they had laid down. Salverson could hear the powerlines above his crew arcing and snapping under the heat and smoke, and every so often an electrical shiver ran down his spine. Then fire whirls began to lift off. The wind, which had been comparatively mild to this point, picked up to fifty miles per hour, and it carried fire whirls straight toward the dirt parking lot Salverson and his men had taken refuge in. One touched down in the brush that separated Salverson's module from the rest of the Lassen crew down along the main dozer line, starting yet another fire. Salverson radioed down to his superintendent, hoping he could get an engine on the spot so their escape route wouldn't get cut off, but everything happened too fast. Before he knew it, they had fire on all sides of them, closing in.

"Get in the barn!" Salverson shouted over the scream of flame.

No one hesitated. They made a straight line for the barn, sprinting with their drip torches in hand. As they ran, smoke poured into the area so thickly that they couldn't see ten feet in front of them. Then every-thing seemed to happen at once. The smoke came, the powerlines began arcing, spot fires started picking up all around them. Shit had just hit the fan. They could hear over the radio that the Arroyo Grande crew was booking tail farther to the west. A couple of guys on the crew started to panic as they ran. "You could feel the panic," said crew member Brian Anderson. "Eighty-mile-per-hour winds were hitting us. Leaves burn-ing. Shit blowing all around. All that was in front of us was smoke and brush and fire and trees. It got really dark, and there were red embers blowing everywhere; they were landing and burning."

Anderson was the last one to make it into the barn, and everyone screamed at him, "Close the door! Close the door!" Anderson shoved the door shut with a shoulder, and then he looked out through a crack. All he saw were red lines. Red lines everywhere. Bushes outside were shaking, and the fire hurt his ears. The sound, the sights, and the wind created an intense feeling he couldn't describe as anything other than "huge." He dropped his calmness and panicked. He lost himself in panic.

Although it was much calmer in the barn than outside, the smoke was so thick that they couldn't see the person standing in front of them. With everyone hacking and coughing, Anderson realized that they had another problem. The bottom of the barn was littered with strands of hay, and thousands of embers were blowing through the cracks and land-ing at their feet. The floor was beginning to catch on fire.

In a smoky darkness filled with panic it was hard to remember who did what, but someone dumped out a trash can resting in a corner, and another crew member found a hose and filled the can up with water. The four crew members trapped inside the barn doused the floor, putting out anything that looked like it was burning. As they did this, Anderson got a strange feeling in the pit of his stomach. All he could see was figures moving around him, little more than shadows, but something told him they were not all inside. He moved around, checking faces, and that's when he realized that Salverson was not with them. Now the panic gripped him with full force, and he shouted, "Where is Wade? He's not in here with us!"

The chorus became contagious; a moment later Esparso shouted the same thing. "Where is Wade? Where is Wade? I don't know where he is."

Radkey, the most experienced crew member in the barn, tried to calm everyone down. "You know, guys, everything is going to be all right," he said casually, almost as if they were conducting a routine fire drill. This was harder than it seemed, however, because inside he felt the same as them. He also wanted to know where Salverson had gone, only he knew that panicking wouldn't help them find him.

After taking a deep breath of smoke, Anderson grabbed his radio and called Salverson, but he couldn't hear anything but the roar of flame outside, consuming everything around them. When that didn't work, everyone went to the door and peeked out. All they could see was the whole world burning.

Crew member Kyle Esparso had never seen anything like that, and he too began to lose it. He started to panic like some of the others. It was the most intense situation he had ever been in, and he thought it was going to be close. Being inside the barn with all the hay and stalls, having the fire come at them like it was, he thought the barn would heat up to the point that their skin started to cook. Then they would all have to flee into the fiery world outside. "It really opened my eyes to how fast fire can move and what it can do," said Esparso. "How powerful it can be. One minute you think everything is totally fine, and then five minutes later you are fighting for your life. . . . I guess that is what hell would look like if you were down there."

Radkey calmed Esparso down. "It's all right," he said, talking as softly as he could and still be heard. "Wait for Wade to come in. Just wait for Wade to come in. We all need to calm down and think clearly. Act decisively."

Just as Esparso started to relax, some of the other stalls began to catch fire. While Radkey got the men organized to deal with the new development, Wade Salverson went through his own ordeal outside. He had chosen to remain out in the open to keep an eye on things, but shortly after the other crew members took refuge in the barn, he realized that it hadn't been the best idea. Powerlines arced and snapped over his head, and hundreds of glowing embers struck his sweating skin, stuck, and then fizzled out. In less than a minute, he decided to joint the rest of the crew. The door to the barn faced north, and the winds came out of the northeast. When he grabbed hold of the door and tried to open it, the winds and sparks and embers pushed him helplessly to the back side of the building. Putting his head down into the wind, he moved forward one foot at a time. By the time he reached the door, he realized that even if he could pry it open, the wind would blow sparks and embers inside. The last thing he wanted to do was endanger his crew, so he didn't try again, even though it meant putting his own safety on the line.

While contemplating what to do, Salverson noticed a massive haystack just to the right of the door. Embers had worked their way down inside, and it started to go up in flame. He tried to break it apart and scrape it out, but each time a piece fell off, it instantly caught fire. He knew it would be a problem because the haystack was right by the barn's entrance. If his crew members needed to deploy, they'd open the barn door and get a waft of flame right in the face.

Working his way past the haystack, he found a window and pried it open a few inches to talk to his crew, who at this point were more than excited to see that he was still with them.

"Find exits to the barn right now," Salverson said. "There is a haystack burning by the door and I want you all to have a way out."

With his crew briefed on the situation, Salverson went back out to see what the front of the fire was doing. He was concerned about making the right decisions. Although he didn't know it at the time, his crew had all the faith in the world in his ability to save their hides. Through a crack in the barn, Kyle Esparso watched him standing out in the rain of sparks, gazing off into the distance. When he saw that Salverson wasn't panicking, he began to relax. They were going to make it through this—they were going to save this home.

Just as it had with Eric Moore over on Archibald, the main front of the fire moved past them and continued to head west. Salverson hurried back to the horse barn and everyone came back out into the open. Palm trees whipped around them, reminding them of hurricane footage. The ranch house hadn't yet caught on fire, but there were several smaller outbuildings down below already engulfed in flame. They could see city firefighters wrapped up in their turnouts and shrouds trying to save them. Lacking that sort of fire-protective gear, Lassen felt overly exposed, but they quickly gathered their wits and got back into the fight.

Matt Radkey and Brian Anderson went to the west side of the building the municipal guys were working on, snatched up a garden hose, and went to town. The wind blew so hard it was difficult to walk or communicate with one another, and the smoke was so thick they couldn't see three feet in front of them, but they did what they could. The rest of the crew ran from one end of the ranch house to the other, extinguishing flaming haystacks that would have soon caught the ranch house on fire.

They spent the next half hour sucking down smoke. Eventually, after they had saved all the structures they set out to save, their superintendent, John Bristow, arrived to make sure they were all okay.

"You have a good time?" he asked, a concerned smile on his face.

It was nine o'clock at night. The crew had been on the clock since six o'clock that morning, having worked a total of thirty-six hours in the last two days. Although everyone in module 92 looked forward to a good night's sleep, they were even more eager to learn how the other half of their crew had made out along the powerlines below.

It had been a rough ride for Rob Moreno and module 91. After spending several hours prepping the homes in the area, cutting down anything that would impede their firing operation, they had parked their buggy at the top of Beryl and then hiked up past the powerlines to the dozer line. To the north a wall of fifteen-foot chaparral clung to the mountainside, a familiar sight that somehow calmed their nerves despite the energy stored in the age-old brush. Directly behind them, however, were multimillion-dollar homes, which made them all uncomfortable. Out in the woods it was just them and the fire, and if the fire managed to outwit or overpower their containment efforts, they simply dropped back and found a new plot of land on which to stand their ground. Now they were all beginning to realize that in Rancho Cucamonga they didn't have that luxury. Thousands of people's homes rode on the success of perimeter control.

They waited with drip torches in hand for module 92 to pick up the firing operation, steer it around the ranch house just to their northeast, and then pass it off to them so they could hand it off to Fulton. But the longer they waited, the more concerned Moreno became. He didn't like what he saw off to the east. The moment Arroyo Grande started lighting their section, it came back at them. The winds blew at forty or fifty miles per hour, and the fire hadn't even reached them yet. That meant the winds could pick up to sixty or seventy miles per hour when the fire came through the area. There was no question about it—they were out of their element.

With the firing operation obviously having been called off, there was no sense keeping the crew out in the interface, so they ran back to the buggy parked at the top of Beryl. Crew member Robert Rice jumped into the driver's seat, and once everyone had piled into the back, he hit the gas. Moreno wanted to reposition his crew several blocks into the city; that way, when the fire came through, they could take refuge behind the homes and pick up any spot fires that occurred. But getting two blocks into the city was not easy. Although the area had been under mandatory evacuation, hundreds of residents had decided to stay. Throughout the afternoon, homeowners had been standing on their front lawns, watering down their walls. One man, in fact, had been planting flowers in his backyard. But now that the sky glowed a bright red and embers tore down the streets at forty miles per hour, people started to panic. They jumped in their cars and sped down the street, running straight through red lights. And when they saw Lassen's buggy seemingly on the run, it only caused them to step heavier on the gas. Rice had to slam on his brakes several times to avoid smashing head-on into fleeing civilians.

A block down from the interface, Moreno told Rice to pull over. The winds had begun to kick up, and embers blew straight down the street, covering the houses. Several spot fires had already started in yards to both their left and right, so the crew piled out onto the blacktop, broke down into pairs, and then jumped fences to put them out. By the time they had put out the first few fires, others had already began. As the fight became more intense, several crew members returned to the buggy and pulled out their chainsaws. Mike Klemic, the team's lead sawyer, jumped a fence and then cut a notch into a burning palm tree so that it fell into a swimming pool. One crew member ran to and fro with his Pulaski, a hoe-like instrument used for tilling the earth, smashing locks off gates so crew members could reach the backyards. John Bristow, the crew's superintendent, went from yard to yard toting a garden hose, dousing flaming bushes and flowerbeds.

While crew members ran from one side of the street to the other, frantically trying to save homes, Rob Moreno stood farther south on Beryl, watching the horizon. The flashing lights of emergency vehicles reflected off all the carbon particles in the air, making it look like someone had dumped glitter from the sky. The wind howled, embers racing at fifty miles per hour down the street. Things were bad, but he knew that the Grand Prix had not yet hit them. Judging by what was already happening, it would be like nothing they had ever seen. "It was so smoky and red, it looked like Armageddon," said crew member Leeland Ratcliff. "It looked like the end of the world."

Moreno felt a sinking sensation in the pit of his stomach. Even though his boys were doing great work saving homes in the area, he needed to get them out of there. He tried to make the call over the radio, but it was impossible to hear anything over the fire and wind, so he began walking north, waving his hands to get his crew's attention. As he did this, he heard a voice to his left. He looked over, but he saw nothing more than a house with an open garage door. He started waving his hands again, working his way north, and then he heard the voice again. He took a better look this time, and his eyes slowly panned upward. That's when he saw a man standing on the roof of his home with a garden hose.

"How is it looking?" the man wanted to know.

"Not good," Moreno shouted. There was so much madness around him that seeing a resident standing on a roof only moments away from impact seemed almost natural. "By the way, embers are blowing into your garage."

"Would you mind closing it for me?"

Moreno obliged, and then headed back out into the street to snare his crew's attention. Their buggy was parked to the south of their current location, and they needed to get to it in a hurry.

Crew member Robert Rice was the first to see Moreno trying to gather them up. He passed the info on to the guys working around him, finished stomping out a small fire in a flowerbed, and then began heading down to his captain. That's when he came across the man standing on his roof. Rice was going to tell him to get down, that it wasn't safe, but he didn't have time. An eighty-mile-an-hour wind struck him in the back like a sack of bricks and knocked him face first to the ground. Not sure what had happened, he struggled to his feet. But the moment he found his balance, a clay tile from one of the roofs, which had been turned into an eighty-mile-an-hour projectile under the winds, struck him in the left arm, knocking him down once again. This time he did not rise. Clinging to his wounded arm, he rolled over onto his stomach and squinted to the north. He wanted to know what had just happened, where the rest of his crew had gone, but in just a matter of seconds the whole area had gone pitch black.

As Rice tried to tell who was who among the scrambling, falling, running silhouettes to the north, he heard a terrible noise, what sounded like a massive bone snapping in half. He looked to his left just in time to see the roof of the house the homeowner had been standing on tear away from the walls, lift fifteen feet into the air, hover for a moment, and then disappear up into the smoky darkness.

Rice felt terror rush through him—he had just watched a man die. After that, all he could think about was finding the rest of his crew, so he staggered to his feet. He took a few steps to the north, leaning into the wind, but dirt and embers kept pelting his face and eyes, blinding him. Then he saw a couple of his fellow crew members' hard hats go flying past him at what seemed to be a hundred miles per hour, and he started thinking about the documentaries he had seen on hurricanes. A sharp piece of tin flying through the air could slice his neck open. A big chunk of wood turned into a projectile could knock his head clean off. He hadn't been fighting fire for a long time, just three years, but this was the first time that he had ever been knee-shaking scared. The only thing he could think of at that point was RUN BACK TO THE BUGGY! He knew that the buggy weighed a couple of thousand pounds, and it seemed the best place to hide.

Rob Moreno, who was less than ten yards behind Rice, continued to shout for his men. When the fire first hit, he'd felt all the air in the neighborhood get sucked toward the flames in the north. He had grabbed a light post to keep from getting pulled to his knees, but then the wind blew back. It threw him to the ground, slamming his back on the pavement. He shouted at the man on the roof to get down, but when his vision cleared and he looked over, the roof was already gone. He stared at the empty space where the roof used to be, unbelieving. It wasn't until a couple of hard hats and a porta-potty came shooting down the street at him like bullets that he realized the lives of his men were still in danger. With one hand he reached out and grabbed hold of the light post, and with the other he held on to his helmet. He kept shouting for his men, but he couldn't even see Robert Rice, who was not thirty feet away. There was nothing he could do for them at this point.

Farther up the street, Leeland Ratcliff was picked up from a spot fire he had been working on in a backyard and tossed against a brick wall. Out in the street, a temporary replacement the crew had picked up less than a week before tried to dodge a porta-potty hurtling at him but took a direct hit to the back. Josh Smith, seeing tree ashes the size of basket-balls speeding through the air, thought it was the end of the world, threw down his tools, and staggered toward the buggy. Tyler Otterson tried to shield his face against a cloud of debris but ended up with a rock lodged in his eye. Bobby Willis, who had been trying to put out a fire in a flowerbed, felt his hard hat rip off his head. Less than a second later, he was struck in the stomach by another hard hat. He caught it, put it on, and then cinched down the strap.

While each crew member did what they could to save their own lives, they began to hear civilian men and women screaming for help. They didn't know if they were screaming because they were injured or if they were screaming for someone to save their homes. Either way, there wasn't much they could do. The winds fanned the spot fires in the backyards, and flames leapt over to the homes. The fire then jumped from one house to the next. In moments it seemed like the whole neigh-borhood was burning.

Despite the current chaos, everyone seemed to have the same game plan in mind—get back to the buggy. Rice was one of the first ones to make it, and he climbed into the driver's seat. A few seconds later, one of the back doors opened and a few more men climbed in, exhausted and out of breath. Within a couple of minutes, the buggy was full, and Moreno, one of the last to climb in, began counting heads. Surprisingly, everyone was accounted for, and no one looked severely injured. Rice had it the worst, gripping his left arm as blood poured out of a gash on his hand. Once they had all calmed down, Moreno heard powerlines nearby begin to arc and snap. That's when he started thinking about the guy on the roof.

A few minutes after module 91 took refuge in the buggy, the main body of fire and wind passed by and the crew climbed back out into the mad-ness. An ambulance arrived shortly thereafter. Robert Rice, who had been struck in the arm by a chunk of debris, and Tyler Otterson, who had a rock stuck in his eye, were both put into the back. As the ambulance sped off toward the hospital, Moreno ran north along the street, search-ing for any sign of the man who had been standing on his roof. He looked in bushes, in backyards, under cars. The only place he didn't think to look was on top of the roofless house. Eventually, he heard the man calling him. Moreno looked up and couldn't believe it. The guy was still up there. He was standing on a small patch of roof that hadn't been ripped away, clinging to the chimney.

After helping the man down, the crew got back into the fight. They ran up the street, snatched up their discarded tools, and then leapt from one backyard to the next. Each crew member worked to exhaustion, chopping down trees, jumping fences, digging into the earth, and wielding garden hoses. "That night we saved a lot of homes," said Ratcliff. "We put out fires that would have caught houses on fire, and we put out houses that were on fire with garden hoses. It was an intense few hours of firefighting."

Although there was still work to be done, there came a time when the overhead decided that their men had breathed enough smoke for the day and got them out of there. Several of the crew members were pretty banged up, but they didn't even know it because their adrenaline was so high.

Module 92 had come down from the horse barn, and the decision was made for everyone to meet at a gas station several miles from the urban/wildland interface. Their reunion was filled with hugs and slaps on the back, which was rare for this late in the season. After working side by side for four months, usually they were pretty much sick and tired of everyone on the crew.

After they had all embraced each other many times over, everyone piled into the buggies and headed a few miles east to bed down at Glen Helen Park. Meanwhile, Robert Rice and Tyler Otterson got to witness the full impact of the Grand Prix at the hospital. Hundreds of people were lined up out the door, suffering from smoke inhalation, minor burns, and lost homes. Rice, like most firefighters that day, felt somehow responsible. Everything was put into perspective, however, when a man was wheeled in on a stretcher. "I have seen some things in my life, but this was one of the saddest and worst things I have ever seen," said Rice. "A gentleman had actually got burnt up. I guess the wind blew his car out of control, and his car went into the fire. His body was probably 85 percent burned. He had no hair left on him, no clothes, there were chunks of skin hanging off of him. I'm sure the guy passed away because you can't take that much heat to your body. I felt so bad for the guy, and I was in there for a little arm injury. All the guy could say was, 'Please help me. Please help me.'"

Rice got the results of his X-ray. His arm wasn't broken, but it was severely bruised. Otterson got the piece of debris fished out of his eye. Both men were released back out into the night, but neither one could shake what they had seen. "I always knew that fire could burn you, but I never wanted to worry about that," said Rice. "I believed if you used your gear, did things right, you are not going to have problems. But this poor guy was helpless. He was trying to leave his house, trying to get out of there, and he got caught. It hit pretty hard. It showed me what fire could do to you."

Both Otterson and Rice knew that in many cases the tragedies could have been avoided. "You look back in time at the Oakland Hills Fire, it was the same deal," said Rice. "We tell people with homes out in the urban interface to brush out around their houses at least thirty feet. That way when a fire comes up it has nothing to burn. But there were houses in Rancho Cucamonga that had fifteen-foot-tall chaparral and poison oak hanging over their back fences. A lot of those people, if they had cleared out around their house, would have been fine. We tell them, but everyone thinks it won't happen to them. . . . A lot of those houses could have been saved if those people would have prepared."

The Grand Prix had made a lasting impression on Rice and Otterson, just as it would for the firefighters positioned at the Upper King's Ranch, located not half a mile northwest of where Lassen had made their stand. It was there, up on a high knoll out in the interface, that the three heads of the fire merged into one.

29

Showdown at the
Upper King's Ranch

After burning off the dozer line above Snowdrop earlier in the day, Fulton Hotshots crew members Ron Bollier and Jake Cagle hadn't hung around to see if their firing operation would save the dozen or so homes scattered throughout the midslope road. They hopped in their buggy, traveled down into the city, and then shot to the west. During the drive, Bollier could hear over the radio that the Arroyo Grande crew had started their portion of the firing operation near the powerlines, and from the sound of their voices, they were having just as hard a time as the Big Hill Helishots in keeping their operation from slopping over into the homes.

Bollier turned onto Carnelian Street, another major north-south artery a few miles west of Haven Avenue, and drove north. Before he made it up to the interface, he got a call from his captain, Val Linch, who informed him that another fire front was beginning to come out of the mouth of Cucamonga Canyon in the western portion of town. This didn't surprise Bollier. When he'd taken the helicopter flight at the beginning of the day to get a bird's-eye view of the Grand Prix, he had seen the upper portion of the blaze slowly working its way to the west behind the first set of ridges. He had predicted this outcome; it was the reason why he'd chosen to head up Carnelian Street rather than one of the other main north-south arteries. The fire coming out of the east

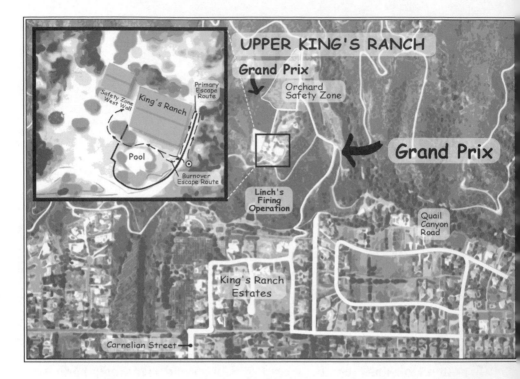

would suck in the fire coming out the mouth of Cucamonga Canyon. The two fronts would meet out in the interface above Carnelian.

When Bollier reached the end of the street, he pulled into King's Estates, a large tract of million-dollar homes. He wasn't too worried about them. A wall surrounded the housing development on all sides, and the homes had good defensible space. Just to the north of those homes, however, stood a ranch house on top of a knoll that overlooked the entire area. Bollier had spent a good portion of the afternoon maneuvering a dozer line around the home, but with both fronts of the fire going to hit the area in the near future, he needed to get back up there and reassess.

Once he found the back gate to King's Estates, he drove up the steep one-lane road to the top of the knoll. Stepping out of his buggy, he had a view of the entire valley, and he could see hundreds of firefighters battling the Grand Prix off to the east. He took a good look at the fire behavior, and then he examined the knoll on which he now stood. He went through an inner debate over whether or not they could save the ranch house, and he decided that they could. Once his crew had burned off some of the brush around the house and on the sides of the knoll, it might actually hold up quite well.

As Bollier worked out his game plan, a man in civilian clothes approached him. "How you doing?" the man said. "My name is Jeff King. I just wanted to let you know my wife and I are inside."

Bollier was shocked. "What are you still doing here?"

"We decided not to leave. We had a fire here back in 1969, and it only burned right across the top of us. We figured we would be okay."

"Well," Bollier said, "we've got a problem."

"What's that?"

"In 1969 the fire burned at you from above, but right now we've got fire coming from down below as well. You're right in the middle. The two fires are going to pinch us in between. You have to decide right now if you're going to stay or go."

"We're going to stay," the man said with determination.

"Okay. Just make sure you stay inside."

"We will."

After the man walked away, Bollier turned to his captain, Jake Cagle, who had nearly had to jump into a swimming pool up on Snowdrop to save his neck not ten minutes before, and told him to thoroughly

Mike Costello helping to organize the various structure protection groups to defend Rancho Cucamonga on the evening of Black Saturday.

scout each side of the knoll. Once he had a good idea of what needed to be done, he was to start prepping the home by laying down fire.

"Where are you going?" Cagle wanted to know.

Bollier explained that he would head down and help the crew's second captain, Val Linch, who planned to pick up the firing operation along the powerlines from the Lassen Hotshots and carry it as far west as he could. It would be a tricky operation. If Linch laid down fire too soon, the winds would push the flames over his head and into the homes behind him. But if he laid it down at exactly the right moment, just as the Grand Prix came at him, then the main body of fire would draw in his burn operation and protect the homes. It would be difficult, and Bollier wanted to make sure it went off without a hitch.

Cagle nodded, and then he got to work. Within ten minutes, he began dropping fire on the east side of the knoll, which would most likely take the first hit.

As Ron Bollier teamed up with Linch along the powerlines, RCFD battalion chief Mike Costello drove through King's Estates. His incident management team had been activated when the Grand Prix broke, but because the Grand Prix was already being run by such a team, he'd spent the first several days of the siege on the Roblar 2 Fire. It had been a battle near Camp Pendleton, but once he began hearing reports of Rancho's predicament, he had worked to get relieved from the Roblar 2 Fire so he could rejoin his brothers in Rancho. They had spent nearly a decade training and preparing for this fire, and he didn't want to miss it.

He had arrived this morning before first light. Mayfield had already assigned Rancho officers to the different structure protection groups, so Costello traversed the city several times throughout the course of the day, helping out wherever needed. In the early-morning hours, he had organized strike teams in the eastern part of the city to stop the Grand Prix from jumping the 210 freeway. Things had gotten rough over there, especially after the Big Bear Hotshot crew had their incident, but after calling in an additional two strike teams of engines, extinguishing more than a dozen fires burning in people's backyards, and coordinating his efforts with Topoleski, who had been in charge of perimeter control in the area, they had managed to push the fire back up onto the mountain without losing a single home.

Costello hadn't been fooled; he knew that once the winds resurfaced, the Grand Prix would come back down in the western portion of town and tear across all the homes out in the urban/wildland interface. In the late afternoon, the strike teams that had been sent to the Carnelian structure group called for help. Currently they didn't have a Rancho officer calling the shots over there. The area hadn't been overlooked—with the fire now affecting all of Rancho Cucamonga, Mayfield had simply run out of chief officers to head all the structure groups.

Mayfield eventually gave Costello the job. Costello positioned several strike teams of engines in King's Estates, but he didn't feel the housing development would get hit all that hard. A cement wall surrounded it on all sides, and everything inside had been built out of fire-retardant material. What would get hit hard, however, was the Upper King's Ranch that sat high above the main housing tract on a knoll. With fire coming down from the north and out of the east, the ranch house would get sandwiched right in between the two fronts.

With all of his strike teams already prepositioned at the top of Carnelian and in King's Estates, he would need to scrounge for additional engines if he planned on protecting the Upper King's Ranch. Taking engines away from the Hermosa or Archibald structure groups wouldn't work. They would get hit before Upper King's, and they needed every engine assigned to them and then some. It might be possible, however, to pull a few engines away from the Sapphire structure group to the west of Carnelian. By the time the fire got there, dozens of engines currently positioned on Hermosa and Archibald would have bumped into the area. Costello called Ray Ramirez, the Ontario battalion chief in charge of the Sapphire structure protection group, and asked him what he could spare.

As Glen Bales, a San Bernardino engine company captain, began preparing his crew for the anticipated assault on Sapphire, he was approached by Ray Ramirez. "I need a crew that is ready to take on an assignment that will probably get pretty hairy," Ramirez said. "Actually, I need a crew that is pretty much crazy. Do you feel up to the task?"

"You bet," Bales said. He'd woken up at the crack of dawn ready to fight fire, but his entire strike team had somehow been overlooked. They'd spent all day in staging at Los Osos. He was itching to see some action, as were his firefighter and engineer, the other two members of his crew.

"All right. You are going to head up to the top of Carnelian. There is a ranch house sitting out there in the middle of the brush up there. Your job will be to defend it."

"And who will I be reporting to?"

"Mike Costello."

Bales could hardly believe it. He had gone through the academy twenty-five years before with Costello, and they had been friends ever since. Not only was Costello a great guy, but he was also one of the best supervisors out there. As long as his old friend called the shots, Bales felt confident that they could deal with whatever the Grand Prix threw at them.

Five minutes later, Bales was on his way up the narrow, winding road leading to the Upper King's Ranch, and it became quite evident why Ramirez had wanted a crew that was part crazy for this assignment. Once fire swept into the area, everyone at the ranch house would get cut off. No matter what happened, there was no way out.

When Bales arrived to the top of the knoll, he took a few minutes to do some scouting, and he came to the conclusion that they weren't in such a tight spot after all. The house was actually quite defensible. There was approximately thirty to thirty-five feet of clearance between the home and the brush. With the recommended clearance being one and a half times the height of the fuel, they were looking pretty good. It addition to this, a large orchard of some sort that sat on the north side of the house could serve as a safety zone. If things got too hot, they could just head out into the field. They had talked at length about their options, what they would do in case of a catastrophic event. But, quite honestly, none of them felt it would come to that.

The fire front coming off the mountains in the north would probably reach them first. And it was a pretty pissed-off fire front; it threw brands of flame hundreds of feet out in front of the main body. The brands would land, start a spot fire, and then its mother would suck the small fires back uphill into her embrace. Despite the eerie behavior, Bales didn't feel it would hit them with that much force. A crew member from the Fulton Hotshots was currently burning around the edges of the knoll, which would take a lot of heat off their heads when the Grand Prix arrived.

After parking his engine on the west side of the ranch house and extending a hose lay to the front of the house to tackle the fire coming from the north, Bales went over and had a reunion with Costello. He even had a quick conversation with Jake Cagle of the Fulton Hotshots, just to make sure they were all operating on the same page. He wanted to maintain contact with the perimeter control forces, keep each other informed of what would happen when, but after half an hour or so he lost track of the hotshots' movements.

Jake Cagle's entire ten-man module had come up to help with the firing operation around the Upper King's Ranch, but he had kept them in the buggy. At this point, the firing operation had become a one-man job, and he saw no sense in having anyone out in the open who didn't need to be.

As Cagle walked around the perimeter of the knoll, searching for patches of brush to burn, a man dressed in jeans and a T-shirt stepped out of the ranch house and approached him. At first Cage thought he was a firefighter who had stripped off all his gear—there was no way a civilian was still up there with him.

"I'm inside with the homeowner and his wife," the man said, nervously shuffling back and forth. "They're planning on staying, but is there any way you could take me down the hill?"

Cagle walked to the south side of the knoll to get a look at what was going on below. For the past several hours, the wind had blown primarily out of the north, but it had switched in the past few minutes. Now it blew more out of the east, pushing fire rapidly across the interface. In no time at all, the road leading up to Upper King's would get cut off.

"It's not safe for anyone to leave now," Cagle said. "If we are going to save this house, I'm going to have to continue burning. Just stay inside."

Cagle walked away without saying another word. He didn't want to be rude, but he had a job to do. It became clear to him at this point that things would get pretty hot and heavy up here, so he went to the apple orchard just to the north of the ranch house. Knowing that they could use the orchard as a safety zone when things got hot and heavy, he burned the brush around the edges. Once that was completed, he instructed his fellow crew members to park the buggy in the middle of the orchard and stay inside. They might have to drive around a little to avoid the heat, but it was better than having them out in the open.

With his crew situated, Cagle headed back to the ranch house with the intention of burning off the remaining brush. In his mind, the more they burned, the safer they would be when the fire came through.

Rancho's Mike Costello, who had been watching the Grand Prix's progress, stopped Cagle before he had a chance to lay down any more fire. He understood what Cagle wanted to achieve. Costello had actually started his firefighting career in the U.S. Forest Service, and unlike many municipal firefighters, he understood how valuable a tool a drip torch could be. What worried him were all the strike teams of engines scattered through the structure groups down below, primarily on Sapphire. Some of the best municipal crews in the state had taken position down there, but they were not used to fighting wildfire. Right now, they expected to get hit with the front coming from the east. If Cagle put fire on the south side of the knoll, it would help put a buffer around Upper King's, but the winds might also carry the fire down on top of the unsuspecting engine crews. It was a trade-off Costello didn't feel comfortable taking.

"But I just caught up with it," Cagle reasoned. "Let me finish getting the buffer around the house and we will be good to go."

It was a hard call to make, but Costello went with his gut instinct. He just knew that a few of the engine crews down on Sapphire would get thrown by the two fronts coming at them at once, and he would never forgive himself if a firing operation in his structure group caused a crew to get burned over.

Unsure what to do, Cagle contacted Bollier, who was still down with his captain Val Linch, waiting for the Grand Prix to get close enough so they could begin firing along the dozer line near the powerlines. Five minutes later, Bollier once again arrived at the Upper King's Ranch. He took a look at the firing operation Cagle wanted to conduct and agreed that it was the best way to protect the ranch house.

"We have fire coming at us from all sides," he said to Costello. "We need to get this structure prepped."

"I understand what you are saying, but I know the guys in those structure groups down there, and they are not expecting it. You have a good plan, but I'm worried about how they are going to react."

Bollier understood Costello's concerns. The last thing he wanted to do was blindside an unsuspecting engine crew, especially one that didn't understand wildland tactics, so he decided that his next best option was to pull his crew out of the area. But just as Cagle began loading up the truck, the winds suddenly surged out of the east. The fire made a big push directly below them, ripping through the four hundred yards of brush that separated King's Estates from the Upper King's Ranch. In the blink of an eye, they had all been cut off.

"Jake, light!" Bollier shouted.

Now that fire had just reached the engine crews positioned down below, sending fire down on top of them from the north was no longer a major concern. Costello and Bollier, the best of the best in their individual fields, were on the same page, not only working together to save the Upper King's Ranch, but also their firefighters and the three civilians taking refuge in the ranch house.

Everyone got moving. Cagle worked around the knoll, burning as much brush as he could. His ten-man module climbed out of the buggy and cut down any remaining ornamental vegetation around the house. Costello went to check on Glen Bales to make sure his crew was ready. Bollier, looking ahead, snatched up his radio and contacted Linch, who was still waiting down by the powerlines to pick up the firing operation from Lassen.

"You are going to need to get around to the bottom of us," Bollier told Linch. "I want you to come underneath us, position yourself at the bottom of the knoll. When I tell you to fire the bottom, you fire the bottom. Get fire coming up at us so that it will pull the main heat of the Grand Prix away from the structure. Then I want you to continue on west and chase this thing as it goes by us. We are going to be in here for a little bit, and it's going to have to cool down before I can come out and start moving again. So just keep chasing it."

"Okay," Linch responded, well aware of the plan. He got moving, abandoning his current project. The firing operation they had been planning all afternoon along the powerlines had not worked out as planned anyhow. With sixty-mile-per-hour winds now ripping out of the east, the crews to the west had touched fire to the ground only to have it jump their line and threaten the houses behind them.

Linch maneuvered his crew through King's Estates, out the back gate, and then took position at the bottom of the knoll. He could see Arroyo Grande and Lassen getting the hell kicked out of them to the west, so he tried contacting them over the radio but got no reply. Then he waited, drip torch in hand, for Bollier to give him the word to lay down fire.

Up at the top of the knoll, Cagle continued to burn under Bollier's orders. "The fire was making its way, and we knew we were going to get hit hard, so we were burning as much as we could," said Bollier. "We secured it pretty good with fire, and then here comes the big front, the main front. It came from the east. The first thing the municipal guys do is run over to the hose lays to do a frontal assault. You're looking at a frontal assault on 250- or 300-foot flame lengths. I grabbed my guys and we hid behind the house. I told them to stay there, let the heat wave hit, subside, and then go check for fire on the house."

Once Bollier had his men secure behind the structure, he called Linch on the radio and told him to start lighting at the bottom of the knoll. Linch immediately did as he was instructed, and it worked perfectly. The fire he dropped raced uphill and met with the fire Cagle had started up above. After flaring up for a brief moment, both fires lay down at the halfway point between the bottom and top of the knoll, creating a fuel break that would hopefully lessen the impact of the Grand Prix when it arrived. It looked to Linch, standing down at the bottom, as if there would be no negative by-product. Then the wind caught a few of the embers from his fire and threw them approximately two hundred feet to the west. In no time, three spot fires had started. They grew quickly, and in a matter of minutes they headed down toward the homes.

While Linch chased the main front out west, burning in people's backyards to lessen the impact of the Grand Prix, Bollier prepared for the main assault at Upper King's Ranch. They would get hit hard from the east, and the safest place to be when that happened was on the western side of the house. That wouldn't have been true if the house had been on flat ground. The fire would have hit the eastern wall, wrapped over the house, and then burned them all alive on the western side. What would save them, Bollier understood, was the fact that the house had been built on a knoll with steep sides. The fire would tear across the foothills and hit the eastern side of the knoll like a ramp. At the top of the ramp, the flames would shoot up and over the house. They would most likely have a blanket of fire directly above them, but as long as they stayed away from the edges of the knoll they should be all right.

Cagle and Victor Harris, another Fulton crew member, were already on the west side of the house, taking cover. Bollier had stuck the rest of the crew in the buggy, which was parked in the middle of the orchard. With his men all taken care of, Bollier then went around to everyone still out in the open, which included Glen Bales, Bales's three firefighters, and Mike Costello. Bollier suggested that they all get behind the west side of the house as well.

With that said, Bollier went to take cover himself. Just before he stepped behind the house, however, he noticed that Glen Bales and his two firefighters were still out in the open, manning their hose lay and running the pump on their engine. They were determined to save the house, but Bollier knew this wasn't the right time.

"We have to go," Bollier shouted over the wind. "Get your guys behind the house."

Bollier slipped behind the western wall. By his side were Jake Cagle, Victor Harris, and Mike Costello. A few seconds later, the fire front coming out of the east struck the bottom of the knoll and then shot up and over the ranch house, just as Bollier expected. Bollier looked up, and he saw a solid blanket of fire forty feet above. The entire knoll was now trapped under a burning orange dome so thick the sky couldn't be seen. While marveling at this, Bollier realized something wasn't right. Costello did as well. Glen Bales and his firefighters were still not with them.

Glen Bales and his crew, which consisted of his engineer, his firefighter, and a battalion chief they had brought along, had prepared for the fire front coming out of the north. Bales had parked his engine on the west side of the house and deployed his hose line in such a way that he could attack the fire coming down from the mountain. Everything had been set up, they were ready to rock and roll, and then the wind shifted. Whether it was a by-product of the firing operation going on down along the powerline or just an act of Mother Nature, Bales didn't know. Either way, a front of fire now came at them directly out of the east.

The shift caught them by surprise, but Bales, who had scouted the entire knoll, felt confident that they'd have enough time to reposition their hose lay to the east side of the ranch house. Before they could do that, however, they first had to sort out an escape route in case things got hairy.

A six-foot wrought-iron fence ran down the east side of the house and then wrapped around a swimming pool in the backyard. It would have been nice if the house had been built close enough to the edge of the knoll so that they could stand on the inside of the fence and fight the fire as it came at them from the east. If that had been the case, all they would have had to do in case of an emergency was drop their hose, run around the swimming pool, and then take refuge behind the western wall. That, however, wasn't the case. In order to catch the fire coming up over the lip, they would have to man their hose lay on the outside of the fence, which meant a much more difficult escape route. If things turned bad, they would have to skirt along the fenceline twenty feet to the north, step through a gate into the side yard, skirt back down the fence-line to reach the backyard, and then over to the western wall.

The only thing that worried Bales about their escape route was the journey they had to make down the side-yard walkway. Several orna-mental bushes had been planted right up against the fenceline, and they had grown to the size of trees. Bales gave them a good looking over; they were quite green, and with a good twenty-five feet of defensible space around the entire home, he figured the chance of those bushes catching fire and blocking their path was next to none. "We had all dis-cussed it," said Bales, "and all of us felt very comfortable with that escape route."

With everyone knowing where to head in case of trouble, they repo-sitioned their hose lay on the eastern side of the house. While the rest of the firefighters up on the knoll took refuge on the west side of the struc-ture, Bales and his men held fast. They felt that they would probably take some heat, but they also felt that they could escape if need be. They were determined to save the home.

Bales squinted to the east, monitoring the fire behavior. Soon fifty-foot flame lengths swept up the east side of the knoll, and his men charged the hose and began doing what they did best—fighting fire. They wore standard brush gear—gloves, hoods, shrouds, helmets, and pants and shirts made from Nomex, a fire-resistant material. They took some heat as the wall of flame rose up in front of them, but all in all, Bales felt everything was fine. "We knew that we were in a precarious situation, but we also knew our escape route," he said. "We were protect-ing the home and felt very comfortable with it. It was a touch-and-go situation, but we all felt it was manageable."

When the massive flame lengths began to subside, Bales and his men assumed that the full force of the Grand Prix had already hit them. Then Bales felt a small shift in the wind. The fire had been coming directly from the east, but the gusts he now felt blew almost out of the southeast. Just as this shift registered in his mind, the main body of the Grand Prix hit the slope of the knoll and blew up to three times its former size, engulfing Bales and the three other firefighters standing on the outside of the fence. In less than a second, they had gone from fighting fire to being completely submerged in it.

Bales could see nothing more than a red glow around him. All he could hear was the sound of a jet engine, which appeared to be coming from inside his head. Firebrands two inches in diameter hit him in the chest and face, and it felt as if someone was pelting him with scalding rocks. Although Bales had never been in this situation before, he knew what had just happened—they had gotten burned over. Instantly, images of his wife and family flashed in his mind. He was dead. Without a doubt, these were the last moments of his life.

In less than a second, reason kicked in. He had to save his men. His engineer, firefighter, and the battalion chief stood only a few feet away, but he could barely make them out. Bales reached forward and grabbed his firefighter's shoulder.

"Get out! Get out! Get out!" he screamed.

They all turned and got moving. Bales saw his engineer and the battalion chief scramble toward the fence, and he followed after them. Their former escape route was no longer an option. Fire had swept up the knoll with such force that all the defensible space in the world meant nothing. The bushes along the narrow walkway leading to the backyard were already ablaze. They were cut off on all sides, getting burned alive. The only way to safety was over the six-foot fence.

Bales pumped forward with four strides and then leapt up onto the iron. His body caught at the top for a moment, and the fire crept up the back of his shirt and melted his face shield. He landed on the other side already in a full sprint. When he got behind the west side of the house, his men were already collapsed on the ground.

Safety Officer Dennis King was standing at the top of Carnelian Street in the King's Estates housing development when the eastern front of the Grand Prix slammed into the tall knoll just to his north. King did not know that a ranch house stood on top of the knoll, nor did he know that there was a group of firefighters up there making a courageous stand.

Because he had no idea that lives were in jeopardy, he simply watched the fire activity. Earlier in the day he had spotted a hundred-foot communications tower standing just east of the knoll. Now he couldn't even see the tower—the flames moving through the area had totally engulfed it. Amazed by the fire behavior, he pulled out his camera and started taking pictures.

A few minutes later, he heard shouting over the radio. "We got burned over! We've got firefighters burned! They're taking refuge in the house."

King had no idea where these communications came from; it could have been from any one of a thousand locations along the front country. He approached a strike team leader, who was also gazing up at the knoll.

"Do you hear this?" King asked, pointing to his radio.

"I hear it."

"Where is it coming from?"

The strike team leader pointed to the knoll, which at this point was completely covered by a dome of fire. King found it impossible to believe that anyone up there was still alive. The initial transmissions sounded bad, news of a burnover and firefighters taking shelter in a house. He felt that there was a high probability that they were looking at several dead, but with the winding driveway leading up to the Upper King's Ranch currently cut off by fire, there was no way to get any help up there. For the time being, all they could do was hope for the best.

Mike Costello had attempted to reach Bales and his men after the first wave of fire hit the knoll, but the moment he came out from behind the house, the entire east side of the knoll blew up. He watched his friend, Glen Bales, as well as the three firefighters he had with him, vanish behind a wall of flame. He thought they were dead; there was no doubt in his mind. "I just saw them disappear," said Costello.

Then, less than a minute later, the four firefighters emerged one by one from the flames and came running to the back side of the house. Immediately Costello assessed their injuries. The battalion chief had second-degree burns to his cheeks and nose. Bales's firefighter had second-degree burns to the right side of his neck and cheek, and Bales's engineer had a second-degree burn to his nose, though he didn't admit to it. Bales also appeared to be injured, grimacing as he gripped at his arm, but he claimed to be just fine. All four of them were hopped up on adrenaline and fear, and they wanted to get back into the fight. There was no telling, however, what damage had been done to their lungs from sucking in the hot fire gases.

Bollier and Costello had a quick conversation on what to do. Getting the engineer and the firefighter down the hill was out of the question; they wouldn't have made it more than ten feet down the winding road before getting overrun with flame. Shielding them in the backyard was a possibility. It was surprisingly calm on top of the knoll, even though they still had a dome of fire sitting overtop of them. But keeping them outside would be a risk. Embers flew everywhere, and if the winds picked up and began pressing the blanket of fire closer to the ground, everyone had to be mobile. It was decided that the wounded men should be moved inside the house.

Bollier got on the radio with the rest of his crew, which had been driving in circles out in the orchard to dodge the massive flame lengths coming at them. Once Bollier knew they were all right, he told them to send up one of the crew's emergency medical technicians. The technician arrived on the west side of the house a few minutes later, and they all brought the injured firemen to the front door.

Jeff King and his wife answered, both on the verge of panic. They had been watching everything out a back window, and after seeing Bales and his men come running out of a wall of fire, they had nearly lost it.

The wounded men were brought into the living room and laid out on the floor, where Fulton's EMT examined them. As the wounded men's adrenaline began to fade, the pain kicked in.

Every firefighter in the room wanted to stay by their side and support them, but the battle to save the Upper King's ranch house, as well as the seven people now taking refuge inside, was not yet over. They had just been hit with the front coming out of the east, but momentarily they would get hit with the fire front coming out of the mouth of Cucamonga Canyon in the north. The two would come together right on top of them. "We like to call it the magnetic effect," said Bollier. "When we get two fires near each other they suck together."

With Bollier and Costello tending to the wounded men, Bales, his engineer, and Cagle from the Fulton Hotshots regrouped to head back out. After having the eastern front blanket over the entire house, they figured the same would happen with the next fire front to hit them. As

The Upper King's Ranch, saved by a brave group of municipal and wildland firefighters.

long as they stayed away from the edges of the knoll, they should be all right. What they had to worry about was the embers blowing through the area—they would start small fires on the roof, on the eaves, and in the ornamental vegetation backed up to the home. With the wind howling over the knoll, they had to catch the little fires the moment they started or the whole house would go up.

When the trio got back outside, small fires had started all over the yard, the east side of the home had taken some direct flame impingement, and a barn on the south side of the property had caught fire. The hose Bales had used on the west side of the home was no longer of use (his firefighter had dropped it to hop the fence, and it was burned to a crisp), so Bales headed to the engine and pulled off his secondary line. Then a problem occurred to him; with his firefighter lying inside, he had no one to man the hose lay.

Cagle, who had been trained to fight fire with fire and hand tools, quickly came to the rescue. He had been in the service long enough to know how to use a hose, so he snatched it up and began taking direction from Bales. They took the hose around to the back side of the building, into the same area where most of them had taken refuge from the blowup, and beat back the flames charging up on the knoll. After that side of the house seemed secure and thoroughly wetted down, Bales took control of the nozzle and brought it around to the south side of the home, where he managed to save the barn from getting consumed. Once that was complete, Bales handed the hose back to Cagle so he could go extinguish a few of the eaves that now burned on the east side of the house.

Then things began to calm down. The dome of fire passed, and although they still had fifty-foot flame lengths licking up at them, the most pressing issue was putting out the eaves. Eventually Bales decided to go inside to check on his firefighter, but the moment he stepped through the door, he began to notice that his arms hurt worse than he had previously thought. He had the EMT from Fulton take a look, and was informed that he had second-degree burns. Somehow, probably when he'd gotten stuck on top of the fence, the fire had found a way underneath his sleeve. Either that or the fire was so hot it burned right through two layers of protective gear.

As Bales sat down next to the battalion chief and his firefighter, Cagle and the municipal engineer continued to protect the home. Fifteen minutes into their battle, they discovered smoke rising from the roof, so

Members of the Rancho Cucamonga Fire Department.

Cagle climbed up there with an ax, busted the roof open, and found a small fire in the attic. He got some hose up there, put the fire out, and wetted down the rest of the roof. By the time he came back down, the fire had passed through the area and an ambulance had arrived.

As Bales and his men climbed into the back, it dawned on them what this meant. They were getting pulled off the Grand Prix. Each of them would admit later on that when the fire blew over them, they had never before felt that kind of fear. They thought they were dead, plain and simple. Yet none of them wanted to leave. At the bottom of the hill, the ambulance picked up a safety officer to get the details on what had happened. Bales knew him well, and he kept shouting, "Sign the papers because I'm going back out. Just put a bandage on my arm!" In the back of Bales's mind, he could see homes burning off in the distance, and he just knew that he had to get back out there to save them.

30

The Miracle

Rancho Cucamonga fire chief Dennis Michael couldn't take it anymore. Ever since he'd gone into unified command with Mike Dietrich's incident command team on Wednesday afternoon, he'd spent the majority of his time cooped up in a trailer in Glen Helen Park, working on financial issues and logistics. Friday morning had been tough, listening over the radio as the fire bumped against the 210 freeway, but it was nothing compared to what he went through tonight. Over the radio he could hear firefighters shouting about fire whirls and hundred-foot flame lengths ripping toward the structure protection groups in the western portion of town. Those were his men out there on the line.

"You don't need me here for the next few hours," he told the incident commander just before dark. "I'm going into my city to see what's going on."

Fifteen minutes later, Michael drove up Haven Avenue through the smoke and ash with tears in his eyes. Up ahead, all he could see was fire. They were going to lose everything. The blaze would jump from one home to the next until the entire city burned to the ground. He said a prayer for every man and woman out on the line; he prayed that they would somehow find a way to make it through this.

Over the next few hours, he witnessed one of the bravest firefights in his life. He also witnessed a miracle. Everyone had expected the Santa

Ana winds to blow out of the north as they had the previous morning, pushing the Grand Prix due south into the homes and those standing their ground to save them. But after pushing the fire across Snowdrop Street, the winds shifted. They began blowing more out of the east. Fire hit the structure groups at an angle, and through an incredible job of firefighting, local, state, and federal troops managed to steer the flames around the majority of the homes.

It had been a knock-down, drag-out fight. Men had been completely engulfed in flame and homes had been lost, but as the head of the Grand Prix moved beyond Rancho's western border, not a single fireman called it quits. Those pulled off the fire line due to injury went kicking and screaming. The rest jumped into their engines and crew buggies and chased the Grand Prix with vengeance in their eyes.

As the fire made an unbelievable sixteen-mile push along the foothills during the night, firefighters chasing the head of the blaze hoped it would lie down when it reached the Williams Fire, which had burned a wide section of the chaparral along the front county in eastern L.A. County the year before, but the Grand Prix managed to squeeze through a sliver of brush that hadn't burned. For some reason, in the

A home saved by Rancho Cucamonga firefighters.

L.A. County city of Claremont there was no extraordinary staffing or planning, and it got hit hard. Without a solid structure protection plan, troops scrambled as the fire jumped from home to home. A debate ensued about whose fault it had been. Claremont felt the incident command team assigned to the Grand Prix hadn't given them proper notification. The command team, which at the time was transferring from Mike's Dietrich's Type II team to Don Studebaker's Type I unit, had told the Claremont fire representative at Glen Helen to "take appropriate actions, it has potential." Whether someone was to blame or not, it became obvious that a structure protection plan such as the one Mayfield had devised could have benefited everyone.

For Michael, it had been the perfect success story to end his twenty-five years of service to Rancho Cucamonga. "I remember telling my wife that I hoped I would be able to get to the end of my career without a serious incident that caused a great deal of controversy and problems for the community," he said. "It was almost as if the Lord said, 'You know what, Dennis, you are not getting out of there until you have one major incident, one last opportunity to be a part of something you will always be proud of.' And I am very proud of all our people, proud of all the relationships we have built and the training we have done. Sometimes as a fire chief, the best thing you can do is step back and let your people do what they were trained to do."

THE SIEGE

31

An Early Warning

Three days before the Old Fire started, on the morning of October 22, earth scientist Richard Minnich sat in his office at the University of California–Riverside, staring intently at the current National Weather Service maps he had pulled off the Internet. He could see a high pressure system forming over the Pacific Northwest while a low pressure system formed over Mexico. In a matter of days, the north-south pressure gradient would bring Southern California's infamous Santa Ana winds.

Immediately Minnich thought about the resort community of Lake Arrowhead nestled among the twenty million dead trees up on the mountaintop. He strongly suspected that the Forest Service had seen the weather models and knew what was headed their way, but he wanted to be certain. He picked up the telephone and called Doug Pumphrey, director of lands, resources, and minerals for the San Bernardino National Forest.

"Doug, even without a fire I would evacuate Lake Arrowhead," Minnich said to his longtime acquaintance. "If a fire starts from the north, blowing with the wind into Arrowhead, the town will be toast. You have the potential for not only a crown fire in an overly dense forest, but also a flash crown fire in what is largely a dead forest. Everyone leaving all

The Old Fire climbing toward the mountaintop.

at once is going to jam the roads up, and then they won't be able to get out. We don't want people to be caught in the middle of that. This is the safety of Lake Arrowhead—get those people out of there!"

Pumphrey respected Minnich's opinion, and he understood his concern. But the Forest Service was unable to pull the trigger point at that time. "We just really need an incident to set things in motion," Pumphrey said.

Minnich found this frustrating, but he realized that in many ways the Forest Service's hands were tied. If they started crying wolf at the first sign of danger, then people might not pay attention in the future. But the current situation they faced was so dangerous, Minnich felt it was highly deserving of evacuating residents whether or not there was a fire. Lake Arrowhead being an end-holding town within a national forest, there was no road grid to use, just a few highways. They had to understand through an exercise in evacuation just how dangerous the mountaintop had become. They had at least a two-day leap—Minnich called on Wednesday, and he said by Friday night or Saturday they'd be in big trouble. Minnich made his opinion very clear, that he thought a lot of lives could be lost, but the Forest Service did not agree with him that they should evacuate Lake Arrowhead without a fire.

Having done all he could, Minnich could just sit back and hope for the best. The fire service, on the other hand, had spent the last two years preparing for the worst.

32

Twenty-four Hours

Four days after Minnich tried to convince the Forest Service to evacuate Lake Arrowhead, the Old Fire turned to the north after destroying hundreds of homes in the city of San Bernardino. Soon hundreds of firefighters lined out along Highway 18, which ran parallel to the ridgeline just below Lake Arrowhead and Crestline. As the fire charged upward, troops began a massive firing operation on the south side of the road, pushing flames down toward the advancing Old Fire. The idea was to fight fire with fire. If their aggressive tactic failed and the Old Fire jumped Highway 18, the consequences would be severe.

Having to assume the worst-case scenario would occur, Chief John Hernandez of the San Bernardino Sheriff's Department worked on evacuating fifty thousand residents in Lake Arrowhead, Crestline, Running Springs, and half a dozen smaller communities in between. Judging by the size and speed of the fire front racing upward, he had less than twenty-four hours to accomplish his mission.

When Hernandez had first assumed command of the mountain rim communities in 2000, such a feat would not have been possible. Despite the region's being the most populated urban mountain community in the United States, there had been no preexisting evacuation plan. Those in charge of protecting the communities just hadn't seen the need. In over a hundred years, the area hadn't been the victim of a single catastrophic fire. But after meeting with fire experts, Hernandez quickly realized that they no longer had the luxury of simply hoping for the best. Due to a hundred years of fire suppression, along with the recent drought and bark beetle infestation, the entire forest had become a tinderbox.

Shortly after realizing the volatility of the mountaintop, Hernandez made calls to the Red Cross, Southern California Edison, the California Highway Patrol, Cal Trans, the U.S. Forest Service, and the California Department of Forestry—everyone he would need to help with evacuations. Each agency had its own idea of what needed to get done and when, and it dawned on Hernandez that although they were all experts at managing a crisis, no one was operating on the same page. Communication was there, but it wasn't the best, and with a potential disaster of magnificent proportions looming before them, they all had to be working off the exact same sheet of music or they would all fail.

Key players from each agency began getting together in 2002, hoping to break down the barriers that had stood between them for decades. The first few meetings didn't go well. Working as a team would require sacrifices on everyone's part, and none of the organizations were keen on sacrifice. Those who had taken a chance by coming together were told by their superiors to back away and keep things how they always were—totally separate. But this was not something men like Hernandez or Mike Dietrich could do. Having now seen all sides of the equation, they realized just how serious the problem had become; at any moment they could have a devastating, catastrophic wildfire tear across the mountaintop, and none of them were prepared.

The meetings continued, and the Mountain Area Safety Task Force (MAST) was born. They had their hearts set on hashing out a foolproof evacuation plan, but they soon realized that such a goal was next to impossible. There were just too many variables to factor in. There was no way to tell where the fire would break, how fast it would travel, or how it would behave once it got established. To get an idea of the potential, they brought a chalkboard into the meetings and wrote "Worst-Case Scenarios" at the top. Everyone put their minds to work, and ideas began to flow. They asked questions such as, "If two of the three roads leading off the mountain are blocked by fire, how are we going to get the residents to safety?" At one meeting, someone even brought up the topic of a terrorist planting incendiary devices around the forest and then having them go off at the same time. Nothing was too ridiculous to consider.

Once the chalkboard was full of disaster possibilities, they spent several months trying to figure out how to deal with the different scenarios they had laid out. The result was the first version of their evacuation plan. It was far from complete, but, understanding that fire could behave in ways they couldn't even imagine, their intent was no longer to draw up a foolproof plan. They simply wanted to develop a process, one that they were all a part of. They tried to revolve around what they called the "Three C's"—communication, coordination, and cooperation. As long as they stuck together, they could deal with issues as they arose.

Words soon turned to action. To keep the roads leading off the mountain from getting blocked by dead trees fallen under Santa Ana winds, Cal Trans and CDF joined forces in tree removal. CDF hand crews knocked down the trees with their chainsaws, and Cal Trans workers toted them away. The U.S. Forest Service and CDF put their heads together and preplanned how they would fight fire in the forest, much as a local fire department preplanned each building in their community. Things began to come together, but all the planning in the world couldn't save lives. If they were going to succeed, they would need the communities behind them.

Attempting to keep the Old Fire off the mountaintop.

In January 2003, the MAST group began a series of town hall meetings where they could talk with the residents about pending forest fire problems and disaster preparedness. At the first meeting, they had nothing but a bunch of empty seats. No one wanted to listen. Instead of giving up, the MAST group found other ways to force residents to recognize the danger that surrounded them. They started issuing newsletters and writing newspaper articles. In a few months, they had fifteen residents at their meeting. MAST kept the broken record spinning, and as summer approached, people started to get the idea that the problem wasn't going away. "The bottom line is we put fear into them," said Hernandez.

By August, their meetings had standing room only. They talked to a thousand residents in Lake Arrowhead and six hundred residents in Crestline. Hernandez implored them to leave the moment they saw smoke, and he promised that his men and he would remain in the area and guard their homes from looters. He handed out evacuation maps and a list of tips they could pin to their refrigerators. The MAST members did everything they could think of to prepare the residents for a fire on the horizon.

Then the Bridge Fire broke out three miles north of Lake Arrowhead on September 5, 2003. The Mountain Area Safety Task Force jumped into action, evacuating more than a thousand residents in just a few hours without a single hitch. It was a huge success, but the Bridge Fire hadn't occurred under Santa Ana conditions. They all knew that seventy-mile-per-hour winds fanning a fire could disintegrate even the most rock-solid plan in a matter of hours. They worked fourteen-hour days to sort out the details as to who would do what in a number of worst-case scenarios.

Critics of their organization were hushed on October 21 when the Grand Prix broke. Over the next five days, the tactics and procedures they'd developed for the mountaintop were employed to evacuate Lytle Creek, Fontana, and Rancho Cucamonga. It looked as if they had evacuated all threatened areas by Friday, but then the Old Fire broke the following morning. "The winds were blowing, and everything went to hell in a handbasket," said Hernandez. "We were caught off guard because the fire started in the lower foothills of the city of San Bernardino. You just never know what an incident will do until it does it. You can plan for something, but you just don't know what it's going to be—big, small, somewhere in between. Well, the wind got a hold of it and houses started to burn. The Grand Prix was already full blown. You could imagine the chaos that we had. But we had good radio communication, we had good discipline, and we had good talking. We were prepared. So all that helped us stabilize and keep on the heel in administering resources to the emergencies that we had."

Saturday morning had been rough, but things were certain to get even rougher when the Old Fire reached the mountaintop.

Hernandez took position behind the firefighters lined along Highway 18 in the early afternoon of October 25, watching the upward progress of the fire. At nine o'clock that night, when the fire hit the four-thousand-foot elevation mark, he issued a mandatory evacuation for the western portion of the mountaintop, which included Cedarpines Park, Valley of Enchantment, Crestline, and Twin Peaks. Several hundred of his personnel fanned out into the communities, and within a matter of hours thousands of cars packed with people and belongings headed toward Big Bear on Highway 18, the only road open due to the spread of fire. The highway patrol went to key intersections where they had blockades and cones stashed by the side of the road and began directing traffic. Cal Trans workers climbed into trucks that had been parked for months alongside the highway. Massive push bars were mounted on the fronts of the trucks, and everyone in the community had been informed as to their purpose. If a car stalled or broke down while heading out of town, the passengers would be removed and placed into another vehicle, and then the truck would shove the broken vehicle off the side of the road. The goal was to keep traffic from backing up, which had occurred in the Oakland Hills Fire back in 1991. The last thing they had wanted was for residents to be forced to abandon their vehicles and head out of the area on foot.

While the majority of residents moved out of town, a special team went around the communities with a list of all addresses of homebound or elderly residents who were unable to leave on their own. Because the list had been developed months earlier, the team knew every area they had to hit. They went from door to door, followed by an ambulance, a fire truck, and a transportation bus. Next came all the boys' and girls' camps. At the majority of the camps, parents had dropped their children off and then headed home. That left the camps with fifty or a hundred kids that they didn't have the means to transport. Hernandez had foreseen this, and

Hook Creek homes destroyed by fire.

working with the various organizations he had arranged it so that charter buses had been standing by all summer to take the children down off the mountain. He had also anticipated the power outages, which would inevitably cut off the water supply. Generators had been brought in to take over, but the one thing that had been overlooked was that the generators would eventually run out of gas. When this happened, panic did not ensue. Because they had already designed the process of working together, the MAST group quickly found people to work the pumps and keep the water flowing.

Once the streets were abandoned, Hernandez lived up to his promise and had his law enforcement officers patrol the neighborhoods. They caught seven looters red-handed. One of them had actually been following firefighters all afternoon, stealing the nozzles off the hoses being laid out for the firing operation on the south side of Highway 18.

With more than fifty thousand people evacuated off the mountaintop in less than twenty-four hours, there was no doubt in anyone's mind that the progress the MAST organization had made over the past two years was worth the sacrifices each agency had been forced to make. The only question now was whether they could keep the miracles coming.

As the Old Fire approached the top of the ridge, firefighters beat back hundred-foot flame lengths. It was more fire than most of the men and women out on the line had ever seen, but they toed the line just as they had in Rancho Cucamonga, drawing off one another for support. "It was beyond what any of us had ever and will ever expect in our careers," said Mike Dietrich, who had returned to the forest to help the incident management team in charge of the Old Fire. "We needed to maintain composure and leadership, because if we lost it, all the people working for us would lose it."

For hours firefights kept the fire at bay on the south side of Highway 18, protecting the communities and $7.5 billion in infrastructure, but just as it looked as if they might be able to hold it for the long haul, the Old Fire flared up and jumped the eastern portion of the highway by Cedar Glen. Hernandez sent in a rescue team to make sure everyone had evacuated. They went from door to door and found no one, so they headed out of the area. But one worker had a strange feeling about a house he had visited, a premonition, so he turned back and broke inside. He found an elderly lady in a wheelchair who hadn't been able to make it to the door. They rushed her to safety, and twenty minutes later the Old Fire tore through Cedar Glen.

"Everything in there got burned," said Hernandez. "Three hundred and fifty homes completely devastated, just melted. You have to see that to believe just how intensely hot fire can get. It just melted everything in sight. It's a storm you can't stop. Firefighters will say there is only so much they can do, that sometimes they have to run themselves. And that is what happened in that area. That's the worst-case scenario fire that we pictured in the community."

Once the fire had pushed through Cedar Glen, Hernandez sent the search-and-rescue teams in with dogs to search for the bodies of home-owners who had refused to leave. He had been certain they would find human remains, but they didn't recover a single body. Apparently, the points they had made at the town hall meetings had sunk in. It was then that he realized just how much ground they had broken with the MAST organization. In the course of just twenty-four hours, they had evacuated fifty thousand residents off the mountaintop, and they hadn't had a single injury or accident. "It was quite a feat," said Hernandez. "I never want to go through that again, but we accomplished it because of our planning, our operations with one another, our communication, and the community working with us. Without that, it wouldn't have happened."

It gave Hernandez hope that they could keep the successes coming. Firefighters had stopped the majority of the blaze from leaping over Highway 18, but while they were occupied with this, the Old Fire hooked around to either side and pushed farther up into the high country. It was only a matter of time before it closed in on Lake Arrowhead and the other communities on the mountaintop from all sides. Finding the resources to keep that from happening would not be easy. In addition to the Grand Prix just to the west, there were now ten other major wildfires burning in Southern California.

33

Chaos Unleashed

When three major wildfires broke out in Southern California within a four-hour window on Tuesday, October 21, firefighting resources were stretched thin. The Roblar 2 Fire, the number one priority due to threatened structures, wreaked havoc at Camp Pendleton, threatening military communications and a training facility. The Grand Prix worked up the slopes of the San Bernardino Mountains, and the Pass Fire, just north of Moreno Valley in Riverside County, gave firefighters hell as it shifted directions under the wind, climbed into inaccessible terrain, and burned down three residences and two outbuildings. As thousands of firefighters struggled to bring the blazes under control before the arrival of the Santa Ana winds, they got more bad news on Friday. The Verdale Fire was reported at shortly after 1 P.M. four miles west of Santa Clarita, and then two hours later the Happy Fire started ten miles east of Santa Ynez on Highway 154. By Friday evening, more than twenty thousand acres of wilderness were burning in Southern California, seven serious injures had been reported to date, a high-voltage powerline supplying the L.A. basin had burned down, and almost five thousand firefighting personnel were out in the field. Even firefighters who had battled flame for thirty years had never seen anything like it, and everyone was sure they had seen the worst.

Unfortunately, Saturday, October 25, proved them wrong. Firefighters assigned to the Grand Prix were in the battle of their lives out in the front country above Rancho Cucamonga. A few miles to the east, the city of San Bernardino took a direct hit from the Old Fire, which by evening had grown into a ten-thousand-acre beast and become the number one priority. Engines and hand crews on the Old Fire scrambled beneath firebrands that carried a half mile or more over their heads,

The aftermath of the Old Fire.

trying to extinguish hundreds of homes that burned simultaneously. To add insult to injury, the Playground Fire started at 7:20 P.M. near Crestline, eventually merging with the already out-of-control Old Fire. With firefighting aircraft having been grounded due to the severe winds, ground forces threw themselves into the face of danger, fighting to save their communities.

While this occurred, more than four hundred firefighters farther south responded to the Cedar Fire, which had been started by an arsonist in the area of Cedar Creek and Boulder Creek roads in San Diego County. When the troops arrived fifty structures were threatened, but the blaze was small, no more than ten acres. Everyone got to work, thinking they could contain the fire by morning. What worked against them, however, was that there were no firefighting aircraft circling above, dropping water and retardant. With dozens of aircraft having crashed in the past flying over fires at night, a cutoff time had been implemented for safety. As it turned out, the Cedar Fire had started just a few hours too late.

On an equally grim note, the Verdale Fire in Santa Clarita found new life with the Santa Ana winds, forcing firefighters to back away from its aggressive wall of flame. Firebrands leapt through the air, creating numerous spot fires sometimes a mile out in front of its main face. One such spot fire managed to get established on the opposite side of Highway 126, and in less than a day it had grown to nearly a hundred thousand acres. In order to deal with the different fronts, the incident was split in two. The section of fire threatening the Moorpark and Simi Valley areas became the Simi Fire.

By the end of the twenty-fifth, the damage suffered was unlike anything Southern California had experienced from fire sieges in the past. The Old Fire had claimed two civilian lives, and there had been thirty serious injuries to date. More than a hundred thousand acres had burned, a hundred structures destroyed, and the fire suppression costs were over twelve million dollars. There were evacuated hospitals, power outages on a massive scale, threatened universities, and thousands of evacuees scrambling to find loved ones. On every city block near the fires there were residents crying, and out of every plume of smoke emerged firemen with blackened faces and singed necks.

Once again firefighters thought they had seen the worst of it, and once again the following day proved them wrong. After sweeping past Rancho Cucamonga, the Grand Prix consumed another forty-five homes as it expanded to fifty-two thousand acres, four times its size, on the twenty-fourth. With sixteen miles now separating the incident command post and the west flank of the Grand Prix, it took troops up to an hour to reach the front line, and communications were failing. It was decided that the incident should be split into two, and the portion of the fire threatening L.A. County became the Padua Fire.

The Old Fire in San Bernardino behaved just as badly, crawling upslope toward the mountain communities. Before nightfall, the western portion of the Old Fire joined with the eastern flank of the Grand Prix, turning it into a massive wall of flame that stretched from one side of the San Bernardino Mountains to the other. An Old Fire damage assessment had come in from the previous day—three hundred homes had been lost. It was a startling figure for everyone, especially the city's municipal firefighters, but there was no time to grieve. Nestled among the dead timber in the north stood thousands of homes.

In Santa Clarita, firefighters had gallantly defended more than seven hundred homes and managed to keep the Verdale Fire under ten thousand acres. By nightfall she was 85 percent contained, a tamed beast, but her daughter was making up for lost ground in the near south. Shortly after jumping Highway 126, the Simi Fire exploded across the landscape, chewing toward seven thousand homes and destroying six. She was moving too fast and hot, much like the Verdale Fire had done on the previous day, for firefighters to attack directly, so they backed off and did what they could, which primarily came in the form of structure protection.

Both Ventura and San Bernardino counties were getting pounded hard, but the largest firefights occurred farther south. Between 1 P.M. and 1:30 P.M., three new fires were reported. First it was the Otay/Mine Fire in San Diego County. The blaze had started in Mine Canyon near the community of Otay, and despite firefighters managing to halt a portion of it though aggressive line construction, by evening it had grown to ten thousand acres. Five minutes after the Otay/Mine Fire was reported, firefighters stationed in Riverside County began heading to the Wellman Fire close to the community of Anza. There were immediate complications. Power outages hindered refueling, and the drivers of wildland water tenders couldn't find any H_2O close to the blaze. These setbacks hurt their efforts to contain the fire, but they made up for it through aggressive tactics out on the line. As they worked to keep the blaze from expanding beyond a hundred acres, they could hear reports of the

Paradise Fire, which had begun only twenty-five minutes after the Well-man Fire in the Valley Center area of San Diego County.

The gut-turning losses suffered on these fires, however, were considered minor compared to what went on closer to the heart of San Diego. The Cedar Fire, having escaped initial attack efforts the previous afternoon, pushed out into rugged, dangerous terrain during the night, forcing firefighters to back off. It was a difficult decision to make for the incident commanders, backing away from a fire that could easily become a killer, but the safety of their troops was always their number one priority. But just because they had backed out during darkness didn't mean they planned to retreat. They ordered up resources, which included a fleet of aircraft, with plans of pouncing aggressively on the blaze at first light.

But the Cedar Fire had its own plans, and it put them into effect around midnight when the Santa Ana winds kicked up. The blaze took off at unbelievable speeds, chewing across the Cleveland National Forest and then through surrounding communities, including Country Estates, Barona Mesa, Mussey, Lakeside, Crest, Ramona, Alpine, Grade, Peutz Valley, and San Diego. Residents fled for their lives, but many did not make it out in time. A few hours after the Santa Anas arrived, thirteen civilians lost their lives, overrun by a wall of flame.

Firefighters flooding to the area were blind due to the smoke and ash billowing from the blaze, which had grown to nearly two hundred thousand acres in size. All night the Cedar Fire had burned to the southwest, but as day progressed the Santa Anas were replaced by an onshore wind, giving the fire a new direction in which to head. It grew at an astonishing rate, twelve thousand acres an hour, now pushing toward Cuyamaca and Julian.

The streets of the threatened and overrun communities looked like a war zone, with panic everywhere. Firefighters swerved and dodged down roads packed with fleeing vehicles, trying to reach the communities to saves lives and structures, but the Cedar Fire moved too fast for them to keep up. Everywhere homes burned, and firefighters began to feel helpless. Waves of panic and grief and guilt swept over them as they came across vehicles containing the burnt bodies of men and women. The natural instinct when faced with such suffering and horror is to turn the other way and flee, but that did not happen on the morning of the twenty-sixth. Firemen, clinging to their training and loyalty to perform their duty at all costs, headed into the smoke and flame not knowing what they would find on the other side. The shift lengths and safety regulations they had been trained to live by were abandoned. They knew that if they didn't confront the blaze, it could claim thousands of lives in the hours to come. They forged ahead despite the danger, the sights they encountered, and the negative media attention from the Cedar that already flooded over the airwaves.

"You couldn't have written a much better horror story," said Mike Dietrich, who had been fighting fire for thirty years. "First you get the Grand Prix, then you get the next one, then you get the next one, then you get all these arson fires. Then you get the east wind."

There seemed to be no end. Fifteen civilians had been confirmed dead, and there were dozens of other possible fatalities lingering on the horizon. Nearly five hundred homes had burned, several small planes had crashed due to poor visibility, three hundred and fifty thousand acres had been consumed, and fire suppression costs were just under twenty million dollars. More than five thousand residents wandered through evacuation centers, looking for loved ones. Stifling smoke and large power outages had cast hundreds of thousands into panic. Freeways, railroads, supermarkets, schools, and airports had been shut down. The impact of the fire siege had become so severe that the outgoing governor, Gray Davis, declared a state of emergency in the counties of Los Angeles and San Diego. By this point, much of the world had their eyes locked to their television screens, watching Southern California burn and praying that the firefighters in the thick of battle would be able to bring the horror to an end.

Such an overwhelming goal consumed every man and woman out on the line both physically and mentally. CDF public information officer Bill Peters, who transferred from the Grand Prix to the Simi Fire incident command team on October 25, saw this firsthand. "We had to tell our firefighters after a day and a half of firefighting that they had to go back out because we had no relief for them," he said. "We had no relief for us, for anyone. We told them, 'We shouldn't be asking you to work seventy-two straight hours, you shouldn't have to, but there is nothing we can do, the fire is still burning.' And God bless them, no one complained. Everyone had to do that because there just wasn't enough of what you needed. And it took a while to catch up, and the potential for injuries because of the fatigue was just phenomenal."

Injuries did roll in; everything from minor scrapes and bruises to severe burns. One injury report from the Old Fire read: "Employee was active in wildland fire suppression when protection line burst. Crew overrun by fire. Employee escaped fire by jumping over a six-foot cyclone fence, landing in cactus garden." These types of injuries were too numerous to count, and many of them went unreported. Reporting wounds meant getting pulled from the fire line, and that was something the communities the firefighters protected couldn't afford. But the determination came at a price. When firefighters returned to base camp, physically and mentally exhausted, many of them found themselves overwhelmed by the things they had seen and experienced. These men and women who felt they could withstand just about anything found themselves confused and lost. In many cases, they needed someone to talk to, and in the incident command posts of most fires, that someone wasn't far away.

34

A Meltdown of Morale

Eight months prior to the siege, CDF assistant chief Jay Donnelly developed a new program called Employee Support Services in anticipation of a wind-driven fire kicking off in the San Bernardino Mountains. If such a fire should occur, there was a high probability that lives and homes would be lost, which would cause firefighters' stress levels to shoot through the roof. Donnelly felt that local, state, and federal firefighters coming off the line should have a place to go and people to talk to when they were feeling confused about the suffering and loss occurring around them, so he began coordinating with the mental health professionals the Forest Service had under contract. If a fire broke out on or near the San Bernardino National Forest, Donnelly would set up a peer support tent at the command post, and the mental health professionals would man it.

Due to the rugged nature of firefighting, there had been skeptics of his program, but the majority of them fell silent four days after the Grand Prix took off. As Donnelly had predicted, many of the men and women battling on the front line had homes in the path of the blaze, leading to confusion as to what their first priority should be—stay and fulfill their duty, or return to protect their homes, their loved ones, and their neighborhoods? In many cases, firefighters' families had been evacuated, and due to the fire burning down a number of cell sites, they had lost communication with their loved ones. All the crews worked long hours without decent work/rest cycles, and during the first three days the ability to feed the troops had been compromised on more than one occasion. Several hand crews had been overrun, and other crews had near misses. Everything was touch and go, putting people on the edge.

Perhaps the greatest concern among the troops during the first days was the feeling that the fire had gotten the jump on them, that their efforts weren't making a difference. By nature, firefighters thrive on production. They develop a plan, and then use their communications to deploy their forces and implement that plan. For a while, the fire moved so fast and in so many directions that the ability to produce a plan and keep up with the rate of spread became impossible, and chaos was the result. Firefighters assigned to one division ended up on another. Firefighters assigned to the Old Fire ended up on the Grand Prix. And many firefighters found themselves stuck at the incident command post as the overhead tried to decide where they should go and when. By the time firefighters found a chunk of the blaze and dug in, they weren't coming off the fire line. They just weren't coming down off the mountain. At one point, cooks at the command post prepared huge buckets of food, expecting hundreds of hungry firefighters to arrive shortly. An hour later, they still had a couple of hundred empty seats. It got so bad that eventually the Red Cross started feeding the troops out on the fire line just to ensure they didn't keel over from hunger.

This went on for days and days, but eventually the fatigue and pressure became too much. By the morning of the twenty-fifth, firefighters with a "thousand-yard stare" filled Donnelly's peer support tent on the Grand Prix. Counselors talked to firefighters who'd spent four days out on the fire line without coming in once. They had been determined to beat the fire before it had a chance to tear into homes, but they now realized that wouldn't happen.

"Mostly we listen to them," said Donnelly, "validate the emotions they are feeling, that they are very normal for a very abnormal situation. We tried to encourage them to recognize that they can't take ownership for this—it's far bigger than any of us. Firefighters tend to be control freaks, and they think they can get everything under control. We try to educate, relating to the fact that this is far beyond anybody's ability to corral within three or four days."

When the Old Fire broke, destroying hundreds of homes in the city of San Bernardino in a matter of hours, stress levels got another boost. Instead of fighting fire deep in the woods, wildland engine crews found themselves in the heart of the city, trying to extinguish blazing homes. But with a limited amount of water in their tanks, they were forced to pick and choose which homes to save. "The fire blows by, and you've got three houses on fire. Two of them you know you can knock down, one of them you just have to let go," said Donnelly. "So you are always making those value judgments. Some residents didn't leave right away, and they were actually yelling at engine companies, 'Put my house out!' But their whole roof was already on fire. You could tell firefighters were stressed because they applied water to houses that were just totally involved, which is a no-no. You have five hundred gallons in your booster tank, what are you going to do with a totally involved structure with five hundred gallons? Nothing. You shouldn't even open the bail of your nozzle. . . . They were forced to do those kind of things. Decision after decision, house after house after house, for twenty-four, forty-eight, seventy-two hours. It was nothing for people to work seventy-two or eighty-four hours without any sleep. And they'd see whole blocks of homes go up. It was a critical incident, something that overwhelms any person. It was beyond what a normal person could cope with."

The crews that came from outside California to help out had their own worries. Many of them had never fought a wind-driven fire as violent as the Grand Prix, and they quickly found themselves in over their heads. Donnelly had run Southern California crews for three years, and during that time it wasn't uncommon to fight five fires in a single week. Firefighters that came from some of the other states, however, often didn't fight five fires a *year*.

"We have a lot of chaparral. The fuel loading, topography, and weather are dramatically different than in other portions of the United States," said Donnelly. "Once a fire gets established, it really runs. So you get pretty confident, and also your ability to deal with stressors is enhanced by the experience level. I had crews show up from North Carolina, and the largest flame length they had ever seen was three feet. Now they were looking at hundred-and-fifty-foot flame lengths. They had never been on a 'hotline,' and they were supposed to support a burning operation? They were scared out of their minds. They were learning, trying to do what they could do, but that was a stressor. So you get a whole bunch of people who are tired, inexperienced, and totally out of their element, and you throw them into the element that they were in, and it became a pretty heavy weight."

With thousands of firefighters out on the line, each dealing with anxiety and suffering in a different way, the personnel of the peer support tents saw everything from sleep deprivation to nightmares to loss of the ability to make rational decisions. Some firefighters could no longer eat, and others just sat there, staring off into nothing. Some lost their ability to keep their cool, shouting and ranting when the slightest thing went wrong.

Between the Grand Prix and the Old Fires, Donnelly's support services had their hands full. Then fires in San Diego began breaking, one after another, each becoming an incident just as tense as those in the San Bernardino National Forest. Donnelly kept a team to deal with the

A resident returns to her home destroyed in the Old Fire.

Grand Prix and the Old incidents, and then he took some of his personnel down to the Cedar and Paradise fires. As it turned out, their services
came in handy. On the Paradise Fire, a fire crew witnessed perhaps one
of the most tragic events of the siege.

"There was a family trying to evacuate, and the fire blew across the
road," said Donnelly. "The older brother swerved and ended up hitting a
tree, blocked the driveway out. The two sisters were in the vehicle
behind him, and they got overrun by fire. One of them jumped out and
tried to run, got hit by the wall of fire. The other one stayed in the vehicle. One died at the scene, and the other one was burned over 85 percent
of her body. The brother, the mother, and the father were at the gate
watching it all. The engine companies were right at the gate trying to get
in, but the road was blocked by the other kid's car and they couldn't get
in. It was ugly. We did some critical stress for that, obviously."

Every firefighter felt the world close in, even the incident commanders. With each passing hour, the fires grew larger and their tasks more
immense. The command teams collected mountains of data, processed
that data, and then came up with a plan. But the fires moved so fast
that when they went to implement that plan, the fire was already five
miles down the road. Then they had the media on their back, which in
San Diego was primarily negative. Entire command teams began melting down.

Everyone's stress and fatigue and pain got put into perspective on
October 26. The Santa Ana winds had died down, and the Cedar Fire
headed east toward Cuyamaca and Julian. Hundreds of engine and hand
crews worked around the clock to save the communities from devastating loss, putting their own lives at great risk. During the fight, a Novato
engine company got cut off from their escape route and were overrun by
flame. Thirty-eight-year-old Steven Rucker, an eleven-year firefighting
veteran, lost his life in the line of duty.

"When Rucker was killed, even though he wasn't killed on the
Grand Prix or the Old, it affected everybody," said Donnelly. "All the
local government resources, all the Forest Service, all the CDF—it hit
everybody right in the gut. For a twenty-four-hour period, the morale
definitely took a dump."

As thousands of firefighters lined up for morning briefing the day after
the incident, you could have heard a pin drop. The incident commanders

did a stellar job of getting the troops' heads back in the game, sharing with them the fact that yes, they had lost a comrade, but the best way to honor that comrade was to get back out on the line and make sure no one else got hurt or killed. Despite their losses and personal pain, both municipal and wildland firefighters pressed on. They were not accustomed to backing away from a fight once it had begun. After the siege claimed their communities, their homes, and one of their own, the fight had become personal.

35

Down the Road

The heroic stand firefighters made on Highway 18 kept the Old Fire at bay long enough to evacuate the homes scattered around the San Bernardino National Forest, but things began to look grim in the coming days. Fire had moved higher up into the mountains to both the east and west of the mountain rim communities, and it was only a matter of time before it closed in on them. As newly elected Governor Schwarzenegger toured the incident command posts, firefighters tried to keep their spirits high, but many began to feel that there was little hope for the thousands of homes on the mountaintop. Then, beginning on October 31, they got an unbelievable stroke of good luck. A cold front set in, bringing snow to the higher elevations.

"I would love to tell you it was brilliant firefighting, that we had this great, grandiose plan," said CDF public information officer Bill Peters, "but what happened is Mother Nature said, 'That's enough.' The cold weather hit, and that's what really stalled it and allowed us to go in there."

As firefighters got a handle on the Old Fire, the majority of other fires raging in Southern California were well on their way to being contained. The damage caused by the siege was of extraordinary proportions. Twenty-two lives had been lost, 3,657 residences destroyed, nearly eight hundred thousand acres burned, and fire suppression costs were estimated at $123 million. As people slowly returned home to piece their lives back together, questions began to form. They wanted to know why Southern California had gone up in flames.

Shortly after the Bear Fire of 1970, which claimed fifty-three thousand acres and fifty-four structures in less than two days up in the San Bernardino Mountains, Richard Minnich of the University of California–Riverside asked himself a similar question. He had spent considerable time as a child exploring the forest surrounding his family's cabin in Big Bear, and he had found it hard to believe that such intense wildfires were a natural process. Determined to figure out what had transpired, Minnich contacted one of his old professors who received money from NASA to take aerial photographs.

"If you fly the fire and take pictures," Minnich told him, "I will give you a map that explains how and why the fire burned as it did."

A few months later, at the beginning of 1971, Minnich sat down before a pile of aerial photographs. While constructing his maps, he realized that contrary to popular belief, wildfire was not a chaotic beast. "I realized that there are absolutely predictable patterns in the way fire burns," he said. "Most people associate fire with utter chaos, but it is just not that way at all. I learned that fire is highly predictable and correlates to the vegetation. The problem in the Bear Fire was that the forest was overly dense and could carry a fire long distances."

This led Minnich to ask one very important question—had the forest always been so dense, allowing fire to burn with overwhelming intensity, or had humans drastically changed the fire regime after a hundred years of impact on the natural terrain?

In an attempt to answer his question, he began researching historical documents. He read the accounts of government surveyors who traversed the San Bernardino Mountains when they were removed from the public domain and placed into the timber reserves in 1892, and their words painted a different picture from what currently existed. The forest was often described as open and parklike, consisting of large stands of trees spaced great distances apart. Even the chaparral, the dense thicket of shrubs that now entirely covered the lower slopes of the mountains, had been described as patchy. Old newspaper articles followed fires that had burned for two or three months, but instead of destroying everything in their path as did the Bear Fire, those fires were less intense, cleaning out the understory while leaving the larger trees intact. The burn zone of a fire one year would serve as a firebreak for a blaze twenty or thirty years down the road. It was a natural cycle, one that had kept the forest healthy since the conclusion of the last ice age.

What then had led to such a drastic change in the vegetation and fire regime of the San Bernardino Mountains over the last hundred years? Through his research, Minnich discovered that the excessive logging of large trees had allowed a dense growth of younger trees to take their place, but perhaps the most crucial component had been fire suppression, which began at the turn of the century to prevent erosion and protect watersheds and property.

The various agencies responsible for fire suppression in the early 1900s had great success in the beginning, primarily because they had inherited a fine-grained mosaic. But once they had largely eliminated fire from the mountains, dead and dying fuel quickly piled up. In addition to forests growing thick and unhealthy up on the mountaintop, the chaparral along the foothills crawled in all directions. Formerly, each bush sprouting from the foothills had belonged to a specific stand of vegetation. There had been thousands of such stands, all of different ages. Young chaparral tends not to burn, and although the exact age is subject to controversy, many believe it takes as long as thirty years before it will ignite under normal weather conditions. So when a fire broke in an old stand of vegetation, it would quickly lie down when it reached a young stand along its border.

Fire suppression destroyed that self-propagating pattern. After two decades of fire having been successfully kept off the slopes, the young stands reached an age where they could burn. Now when a fire got away, instead of burning a few thousand acres and then being stopped by a young chaparral stand, it traveled for miles. The next stand of chaparral to arise had no age boundaries. It was now one homogenous tract of brush. Suppression had done away with the little fires spaced out over time, but it had basically guaranteed a massive fire every thirty or forty years.

That cataclysmic cycle began in the early 1920s when Southern California had its first great fire outbreak. Although thousands of acres were turned into a moonscape both in the forests and along the foothills, the general public had forgotten that just twenty years prior large-scale wildfires were practically unheard of, so they naively continued to support fire suppression efforts.

In Minnich's opinion, the fire service had been shooting itself in the foot for the past century. It's goal was to protect life, property, and the environment, but by extinguishing the majority of small fires, which were completely natural, it was only prepping the forest in the future for catastrophes like the Bear Fire, which were very unnatural. Once he made his opinion known, skeptics came out of the woodwork, claiming that large crown fires were quite common, that they had been occurring for thousands of years.

To add to his research, which had been based primarily on historical records, Minnich went across the U.S.-Mexico border to the mountains of Baja California, which had never been influenced by fire suppression. There he found a forest that much resembled the descriptions early explorers had offered for the San Bernardino Mountains—large trees and open stands, a result of small, cleansing wildfires.

"A hundred years ago, the forest in the San Bernardino Mountains was not nearly as thick as it is today," said Minnich. "In 1929, trees that were four inches in diameter existed in open stands, about forty trees per acre. Right now, there are about double to triple that in those diameter classes. Plus, there are all kinds of other trees that are less than four inches in diameter. It is just explosively flammable, and when this stuff catches fire, it crowns. That is not normal. What is normal is an under-story fire. They are rather intense, but it leaves the big trees and kills the young and middle-sized trees. That is what happens in Mexico. As soon as you cross the border, the fires are smaller. That is how you get open stands. After a fire, you get an open stand, and young trees come in. When the next fire curve arrives roughly fifty years later, it rips through and kills the young trees again."

Minnich wrote a book on the subject, as well as dozens of research papers, and argued until he was blue in the face, but it did no good. He was forced to sit back and watch fire suppression continue in the San Bernardino Mountains for the next thirty years.

Of course, there were reminders of the danger building in everyone's backyard, such as the Panorama Fire of 1980, which was started by an arsonist in Waterman Canyon and then tore down into the city of San Bernardino, claiming 285 homes and four lives. Minnich had hoped that such incidents would force the public to realize that fire management in the San Bernardino Mountains needed to be drastically reconsidered, but any lessons learned quickly faded.

It wasn't until a severe drought hit Southern California in 2002, leading to overwhelmingly high tree mortality in the San Bernardino

Mountains, that residents in the various mountaintop communities truly opened their eyes to the struggling forest around them. For years they had fought to hold on to every tree, every branch, every leaf, and now they couldn't get rid of the dead timber fast enough. "The main problem was that they had no infrastructure; there were no sawmills, there was no anything," said Minnich. "Most people living in the mountains of Lake Arrowhead, Gregory, and Big Bear are tree huggers, and they wanted to protect everything. . . . They were just clueless as to what they were sitting in." It had gotten to the point that it was no longer a matter of *if* the forest would go up in flame, but *when*.

The U.S. Forest Service, responsible for managing much of the lands in the San Bernardino Mountains, was not unaware of the problem. One way they attempted to minimize the fuel buildup caused by fire suppression was to section off particularly hazardous areas and issue prescribed burns. Unfortunately, in many of these hazard areas burns were not allowed to take place. Thousands of families had moved into communities like Lake Arrowhead to escape the bustling city. Few residents were in favor of the Forest Service setting fires that blackened the earth, polluted the air, and jeopardized their million-dollar homes. If CDF or the Forest Service wanted to burn off a portion of the forest near residences, they had to get the property owners to approve it. Sometimes that took four years. Sometime it never happened at all.

"Forest systems burn, and we try to live in them," said San Bernardino county commissioner Dennis Hansberger. "We try to modify that burning process to accommodate us on the forest. We talk about saving the forest, but most of the time we are really trying to save ourselves. We don't have an alternate program to help the forest be healthy and so we stop fire. We also let the forest grow in an unnatural way. Clearly many of us have been aware of it for a long time, but it is very difficult for us to address."

In addition to dealing with homeowners when trying to issue prescribed burns, the Forest Service also had to hurdle roadblocks put up by the U.S. Fish and Wildlife Service, which was often more concerned about how a small prescribed fire might disrupt an endangered species than how a major crown fire might obliterate them. Such was the case in Waterman Canyon. After the Panorama Fire came tearing down the canyon into San Bernardino, the fire service wanted to treat the area to keep history from repeating itself. For years they had searched for a way to fund the prescribed burns, and in 1995 they got their chance. President Clinton tasked FEMA with issuing grants for prescribed burns to cities that had areas of extreme fire potential. San Bernardino quickly jumped at the opportunity to treat Lower Waterman Canyon, right along the edge of the city where the Panorama Fire had done the most damage. In order to get the funding, all the city needed to do was get Fish and Wildlife's approval, but that never happened.

Every one of the areas the fire service had identified has now burned, and every one has had a loss of structures.

Like many people in the fire service, CDF public information officer Bill Peters found this frustrating, to say the least. In an attempt to understand where Fish and Wildlife was coming from, he decided to attend their meetings. At one such gathering, Fish and Wildlife accused CDF of wanting to issue burns so that developers could get permission to build in the vegetation-free areas. As absurd as it sounded, Peters realized they had a point. History had proved that prescribed burns on private lands were usually the first step to development. It had occurred in San Diego, Riverside, and Orange counties, as well as other parts of the state. The Fish and Wildlife Service lost land every year, and they would never get it back.

In this particular case, however, Peters knew it was a scapegoat.

"Let me understand this, because I want to be clear," he said to Fish and Wildlife representatives at the meeting. "You don't want us to issue a controlled fire that will burn off the overstory, clean it up, and then bring in new plant growth which will bring animals back to the area, which will be an improvement to the environment. You would rather wait for a catastrophic fire that will destroy the animals, destroy the plant and root structures, and then you will have denuded land. Is that what I understand?"

"No, that is not what we meant," they came back.

Unfortunately Peters never found out what they were really trying to say because he was never invited back to another meeting. The cooperation between the fire service and Fish and Wildlife remained as poor as ever, and the process of getting everyone to sign off on a prescribed burn just as cumbersome. When a Southern California representative of Fish and Wildlife was asked if they had a conflict of interest with the Forest Service, she answered, "Our responsibilities are to implement the Endangered Species Act and work with local, state, and federal entities in which their projects are in compliance with the Endangered Species Act. . . . Our mission is to work with others to preserve native plants and animals. It's not a question of being at odds or conflicting missions. It is working to ensure that the variety of missions the Forest Service has can take place and they can meet those missions, at the same time also ensuring that threatened and endangered species are also preserved. . . . The U.S. Forest Service generally prepares an assessment of a project and looks at what species may be in the area that the project is going to occur in, and what types of impacts there could be. And then we look at their information and sometimes we need some additional information. . . . We have not prevented any prescribed burn projects for the U.S. Forest Service."

Peters, as well as a handful of others who were trying to implement more aggressive fuel management in the San Bernardino Mountains, disagreed. In addition to Fish and Wildlife throwing a monkey wrench into their plans to burn off areas with extreme fire potential, they also had to leap over hurdles laid out by air quality control, water management, and a number of other government agencies that viewed fire, even controlled fires set by the Forest Service, as something utterly disruptive. Each organization had to have their say, and they all had their own rules. It got to the point where many employees in the fire service wanted to shout, "Look, guys, if we don't put fire on the ground here to reduce this fire threat, a catastrophic fire is going to come tearing through here. Then we are going to have hundreds of thousands of tons of particulate matter in the air, entire species are going to get destroyed, and you are not going to have a nice, fresh habitat come back because the ground is going to be destroyed."

Unfortunately, that was often the case. Don Studebaker, a battalion chief on the Cleveland National Forest, ran into this problem on his home turf down in San Diego. While out surveying, his team discovered two drainages that had extreme fire potential, and they set out to treat the fuels with a prescribed burn. Fish and Wildlife came back and said that a pair of spotted owls had been sighted in the area, and with the drainages being classic spotted owl habitat, the burn could not take place, even though the spotted owls had not been sighted in either of the drainages. Studebaker's group understood their concern, so they suggested burning off the understory one drainage at the time. That way, any spotted owl in the area would still have somewhere to go while the burn took place. Worried about the fire service destroying the drainages, Fish and Wildlife still didn't let the burns commence.

Not long after, the La Jolla Fire tore through the area, not only nuking both drainages, but any spotted owls in the general vicinity. "You have to realize that these plants and animals have evolved in a fire-adaptive ecosystem," said Studebaker. "[Fish and Wildlife] lose sight of the ecology of it all, that has been my impression. And they are forced to look at it in black-and-white rules and regulations. So my impression is in many cases they present a situation where they are accelerating species decline rather than helping them recover."

The environmental movement is like any other political movement in that it was built on victimhood, with nature in this case being the victim, but the politics that now governs the Fish and Wildlife Service no longer matches the scientific truths of ecology. Fish and Wildlife receives a vast sum of money to protect endangered species, and in order to continue receiving that funding, it must continue to protect those species, even if that protection will not be beneficial to the species in the long run. Along the border of Bureau of Land Management land in San Diego, Studebaker's team conducted a series of prescribed burns that resulted in the restoration of an endangered butterfly. Everywhere they burned, the butterfly flourished. They wanted to keep burning in the area, but Fish and Wildlife told them they could not. When they asked why, Fish and Wildlife gave a simple answer—because that land is now home to an endangered butterfly.

In order to solve such recurring dilemmas, Studebaker feels it is important for the fire service to have biologists monitor and post-inventory sites of prescribed burns. After they have collected all the data, they can attack the politics governing Fish and Wildlife and hopefully be granted an allowable take from the regulatory side of their program.

Minnich has a more drastic opinion. In order to avoid another cataclysmic event in the future, he feels that the Endangered Species Act, which forces micromanagement instead of macromanagement for public safety, needs to undergo some serious revisions before it is too late.

"You don't need that much burning to keep up with productivity," said Minnich. "If a forest burns every forty years, then only 2.5 percent of the land needs to get burned off each year. That is not much. All that amounts to is about ten thousand acres of burning per summer for the

Forest Service. Three burns, three canyons, that's all you need to do. But use the current mosaic, we have moonscapes now created by these massive fires. . . . Putting these people in the face of danger is completely unnecessary. These fires are not fightable. . . . They just lucked out with some backfires in Lake Arrowhead, that's it. If it had been an ignition from the north, that would have been total failure. They would have actually walked away from Lake Arrowhead, and we would have had twenty to thirty thousand structures burned. It would have been far worse than the Oakland Fire. Easy twenty or thirty thousand structures lost. It could happen this year, not a problem."

If only the media, the general public, and the government agencies that need to sign off on controlled burns had learned from the Texas Fire, the Myers Fire, and the Panorama Fire, had learned that when it came to fire in Southern California history had a way of repeating itself, they would have seen a glimpse of the tragedy that struck their communities in October 2003. And if the media, the general public, and the various government agencies that need to sign off on controlled burns would take a step back and truly look at the 2003 fire siege, they would get a glimpse of the tragedy that will strike their communities ten or twenty or thirty years down the road.

Instead, the media and politicians have gone into fault-finding mode. There was criticism that the fire service should have turned to the military, but those in the fire service knew it wasn't that easy. Studebaker related it to the military walking into a shopping mall, rounding up eight thousand people, putting them on a plane to Iraq, and then giving them M-16s with the intention of having them pacify the country. Without any formal military training, without any idea of what an infantry soldier should do, how well would their mission go? It would be the same thing as taking the military and sticking them on the fire line. Putting a request in for the military was certainly an option, but it takes at least two weeks to get them trained. And time was not a luxury they had in the 2003 fire siege.

The fire service certainly made mistakes, especially on the Cedar Fire. Evacuations could have been better, communication could have been better, the straight-up firefighting could have been better. "But all in all, in an entirely perfect world, we still only have so many firefighters, so many fire engines, etcetera," said Bill Peters. "And so if you are burning up three-quarters of a million acres of land—when you are burning up the state of Rhode Island only in six different places—it makes it a little harder."

With past fires having run similar paths as the Cedar Fire, the agencies responsible for fighting fire in San Diego could have benefited greatly from dropping jurisdictional boundaries and forming a single alliance like those in the San Bernardino National Forest. They could have brought in the sheriff's department, the California Highway Patrol, Cal Trans, politicians, the media, and, most importantly, the residents. With many of the homes destroyed in the Cedar Fire having burned down three times in the past thirty years, they could have worked on improving building codes and having residents put defensible space around their homes. They could have even brought insurance companies aboard to help assist with developing appropriate standards and codes. If such measures are to be taken by the fire service in the future, it will require a fight—a fight with residents who can't afford to rebuild their homes up to fire standards; a fight with Fish and Wildlife to allow residents living in the urban/wildland interface to clear a hundred feet around their homes, which would result in habitat loss; a fight with each other to make sacrifices so they can execute their goal of saving lives and property.

If the fire service takes on this challenge and is not supported at all levels, from federal, state, and local government down to the residents living in the urban/wildland interface, the cycle will go on and on. Studebaker calls it the "social-economic fire-dependent housing cycle of Southern California." It puts everyone in business, from insurance adjusters on the front end, to the construction and timber industry with rebuilding homes, all the way down to the final event where firefighters get involved trying to put the fires out. Then it starts all over again.

Index

Page numbers in *italics* refer to illustrations.